InfoPath 2010 Cookbook 2

101 Codeless Recipes for SharePoint 2010

S.Y.M. Wong-A-Ton

InfoPath 2010 Cookbook 2 – 101 Codeless Recipes for SharePoint 2010
Copyright © 2011 by S.Y.M. Wong-A-Ton

All rights reserved. No part of this book may be reproduced or transmitted in any form or by any means, electronic or mechanical, including photocopying, recording, or by any information storage or retrieval system, without the prior written permission of the copyright holder.

Trademark names may appear in this book. Rather than use a trademark symbol with every occurrence of a trademarked name, we use the names only in an editorial fashion and to the benefit of the trademark owner, with no intention of infringement of the trademark.

The information in this book is distributed on an "as is" basis, without warranty. Although every precaution has been taken in the preparation of this book, neither the author or publisher shall have any liability to any person or entity with respect to any loss or damage caused or alleged to be caused, directly or indirectly, by the information contained in this book. The publisher and the author disclaim all warranties, including without limitation warranties of fitness for a particular purpose. The advice and strategies contained in this book may not be suitable for every situation. If professional assistance is required, the services of a competent professional person should be sought.

Cover photo © by S.Y.M. Wong-A-Ton: Snow-capped mountains seen through lifting fog and low hanging clouds, South Island, New Zealand

To Dona

Thanks for being there

Table of Contents

Introduction v

Who should read this book? vi

How to use this book vii

About the author vii

Support viii

Chapter 1: SharePoint List Forms 1

SharePoint list form basics 1

   1   Customize a SharePoint list form from within SharePoint 1

   2   Customize a SharePoint list form from within InfoPath 8

   3   Create a SharePoint list form to manage multiple list items with one form 13

   4   Add a new field to a SharePoint list through InfoPath 16

   5   Delete a field from a SharePoint list through InfoPath 19

   6   Restore the default ASP.NET form of a SharePoint list 20

Query data through SharePoint list forms 22

   7   Add query functionality to a SharePoint list form 22

   8   Query for multiple items in a SharePoint list form 24

   9   Perform wildcard searches with a SharePoint list form 29

   10   Add new record functionality to a SharePoint list form 31

   11   Refresh secondary data sources in a SharePoint list form 32

Display SharePoint list forms 34

   12   Embed a SharePoint list form on a SharePoint page 35

   13   Use an InfoPath form for a master/detail view on two linked SharePoint lists 38

   14   Use an InfoPath form as the detail view for items in a master SharePoint list 43

Chapter 2: SharePoint Form Library Forms 47

Design SharePoint form library form templates 47

   15   Create a SharePoint form library form template 48

   16   Create a form library and edit its form template 52

Configure forms for submit to a form library 58

   17   Hide or show toolbar buttons for a form 60

   18   Submit a form to a form library and then close it 62

   19   Submit a form to a folder in a form library based on a condition 67

   20   Submit a form and switch to a 'Thank You' view 70

Publish a form template to a form library 72
   21   Publish a form template to a form library 72
   22   Republish a form template 81
   23   Promote form fields to columns of a form library 82
   24   Promote form fields to existing site columns 87
   25   Delete a column linked to a promoted field 89

Publish a form template as a site content type 90
   26   Publish a form template as a site content type 90
   27   Enable different types of forms to be created in one form library 94
   28   Change the default form template of a form library 99
   29   Rename a form template listed on the New Document menu 100
   30   Delete a form template from a form library 102

Display SharePoint form library forms 104
   31   Add a link to open a form from a SharePoint page 104
   32   Add a link to open a form from the Quick Launch 108
   33   Embed an InfoPath form on a SharePoint page 110
   34   Master/detail across two forms linked through one field 112
   35   Pass data from a selected row in a repeating table to another form 119
   36   Create an InfoPath form as part of a document set 125

Merge InfoPath forms in SharePoint 130
   37   Create an InfoPath survey form suitable for merging 131
   38   Design an InfoPath form to summarize merged data 136
   39   Merge InfoPath forms from a SharePoint form library 138

Move InfoPath forms between form libraries 141
   40   Move a form to another form library on the same site 141
   41   Move a form library to another site 146
   42   Relink InfoPath forms in a form library 149

Chapter 3: Retrieve SharePoint List Data 153

Retrieve and display SharePoint list data 153
   43   3 Ways to retrieve data from a SharePoint list 154
   44   Display SharePoint list data in a repeating table 166
   45   3 Ways to copy SharePoint list data to form fields 168
   46   Map rows of a repeating table to SharePoint list items 175

Sort and filter SharePoint list data 177
   47   Statically sort SharePoint list data on one field 178
   48   Statically sort SharePoint list data on multiple fields 179
   49   Dynamically sort SharePoint list data on one or more fields 183
   50   Filter SharePoint list data using an exact match 185
   51   Filter SharePoint list data using a BETWEEN match 188
   52   Filter SharePoint list data using a LIKE match 191

53	Display master/detail data from linked lists	195
54	Display a list of people from the current user's department	196
55	Retrieve the top X items from a SharePoint list	200
56	Paginate and navigate through a SharePoint list using previous and next buttons	202

Retrieve and display forms from a form library 207

57	Retrieve a list of forms from a form library	207
58	Retrieve a list of forms created by the current user from a form library	209
59	Open a form in the browser from another form	211
60	Use SharePoint Search in InfoPath to search for documents – method 1	216
61	Use SharePoint Search in InfoPath to search for documents – method 2	225

Chapter 4: Use InfoPath Controls with Data from SharePoint 233

Drop-Down List Box 233

62	Cascading drop-down list boxes using one SharePoint list	233
63	Cascading drop-down list boxes using linked SharePoint lists	239

Combo Box 244

64	Dynamically add an item to a combo box populated by a SharePoint list	244

Picture 250

65	3 Ways to get an image from a picture library	251
66	Browse through images in a SharePoint picture library	261

Person/Group Picker 263

67	Get email addresses from a person/group picker	265
68	Get the details of the manager of a selected person in a person/group picker	268

Multiple-Selection List Box 275

69	Fill a multi-select list box on a SharePoint list form with SharePoint list data	275
70	Get a list of email addresses from selected users in a multi-select list box	279
71	Fill a multi-select list box with email addresses from a person/group picker	284

Chapter 5: Use SharePoint Designer Workflows with InfoPath Forms 289

72	Create a workflow that runs on new forms in a specific form library	289
73	Manually start a workflow to run on a form	298
74	Start a workflow from a custom action in a library	300
75	Create a workflow that runs on a specific type of form	304
76	Add a workflow to a specific type of form in a form library	308
77	Pass data to a workflow at startup	312
78	Pass data to a workflow when attaching it to a library	321
79	Get the value of an InfoPath form field in a workflow	325
80	Set the value of an InfoPath form field through a workflow	327
81	Send an email to the manager of a selected person	333
82	Set a task form field value from an initiation form in an approval workflow	336

83	Add an event to a SharePoint calendar with a check for overlapping events........	346
84	Start a SharePoint workflow by clicking on a button on an InfoPath form	352
85	Create a new InfoPath form through a workflow	356
86	Create a new form and link it to an existing form through a workflow	365
87	Move a form from one form library to another using a workflow	372
88	Make a specific type of form read-only to a user when added to a form library ..	375

Chapter 6: Use Word, Excel, and Access with InfoPath via SharePoint............................... 381

Use a document information panel in Word 381

89	Use a Word document as a template for documents in a document library	381
90	Link Word document fields to document panel fields	386
91	Create a document information panel from within SharePoint	389
92	Create a document information panel from within InfoPath	392
93	Change settings for a document information panel	394

Use InfoPath data in Word through SharePoint 396

94	Automatically generate simple Word documents from InfoPath forms	397

Use Excel data in InfoPath through SharePoint 400

95	Display Excel data in a browser form – method 1	401
96	Display Excel data in a browser form – method 2	404
97	Calculate work days between two dates using Excel Services – method 1	410
98	Calculate work days between two dates using Excel Services – method 2	420
99	Send InfoPath form data to an Excel workbook	426

Use Access data in InfoPath through SharePoint 430

100	Display Access data in a browser form	431
101	Edit and update Access data through a browser form	433

Appendix 437

Index 447

Introduction

In *InfoPath 2010 Cookbook: 101 Codeless Recipes for Beginners*, you learned the basics of designing InfoPath 2010 forms and working with controls. *InfoPath 2010 Cookbook 2: 101 Codeless Recipes for SharePoint 2010* is all about taking those basics skills you acquired from *InfoPath 2010 Cookbook* and extending them to working with InfoPath 2010 forms in SharePoint 2010.

InfoPath 2010 has several integration points with SharePoint 2010, but there are four main types of InfoPath forms you can use with SharePoint:

1. SharePoint list forms
2. SharePoint form library forms
3. Workflow forms
4. Document Information Panels

SharePoint list forms are probably the quickest and easiest types of forms to design, but they do have their limitations. Because a SharePoint list form is tightly bound to a SharePoint list, the controls you can place on SharePoint list forms are limited by the data types that are available in SharePoint. For example, because SharePoint has no data structures to accommodate repeating structures such as repeating tables or repeating sections, you cannot use these controls on SharePoint list forms. In addition, InfoPath 2010 does not allow you to write code for SharePoint list forms.

Therefore, if you require any of the aforementioned functionality or functionality that may degrade usability (such as for example, more than 50 fields on a SharePoint list form), you must use a SharePoint form library form instead. SharePoint form library forms allow for greater flexibility when designing and publishing InfoPath forms and they also allow you to write code. You will learn more about SharePoint list forms in Chapter 1 and about SharePoint form library forms in Chapter 2.

Because one of the core elements of SharePoint are SharePoint lists, you may often want to retrieve data from lists or libraries in SharePoint from within any one of the types of InfoPath forms. Chapter 3 offers several solutions for retrieving data from SharePoint lists and then using this data in InfoPath forms.

Controls are an integral part of InfoPath forms. While you have already learned to work with several types of controls in *InfoPath 2010 Cookbook: 101 Codeless Recipes for Beginners*, Chapter 4 takes a deeper look into how you can integrate a couple of specific controls (in particular, the person/group picker control) with SharePoint data.

From the four types of forms, a workflow form is the only type of form that cannot be created from scratch from within InfoPath Designer 2010. Workflow forms are generated by SharePoint Designer 2010 when you publish a workflow to SharePoint. And once generated, you can use InfoPath Designer 2010 to customize them. You will learn how to create workflow initiation, association, and task forms in Chapter 5. Chapter 5 also shows you how you can go beyond workflow forms to create SharePoint Designer workflows that run on, create, and interact with InfoPath forms stored in a form library.

While document information panel forms are not actually displayed in the browser through SharePoint like the other three form types are, their form templates are stored in SharePoint and their fields are related to columns defined on content types. You will learn more about document information panels in Chapter 6. Furthermore, Chapter 6 shows you several ways to integrate Word, Excel, and Access with InfoPath forms through SharePoint.

InfoPath Forms Services is available in SharePoint Server 2010 and is required for InfoPath forms to be displayed in a browser through SharePoint. If you are reading this book, I assume you have already installed InfoPath 2010, Word 2010, Excel 2010, Access 2010, SharePoint Designer 2010, and that you have a SharePoint Server with InfoPath Forms Services at your disposal. This book does not explain the administrative tasks you need to perform to install and configure SharePoint with InfoPath Form Services.

Who should read this book?

This book was written for Microsoft Office users who already have basic knowledge of InfoPath 2010 and SharePoint 2010 as separate products, but who are yet to start integrating the two with each other. This book was also written specifically for beginner to intermediate users who are not necessarily programmers. While this book may also be beneficial to programmers, it does not contain any code instructions. And apart from setting permissions and creating search scopes at the administration level, this book does not contain any information on how to administer SharePoint 2010 or InfoPath Forms Services, so is not geared towards SharePoint administrators.

While this book assumes that you already have basic knowledge of SharePoint 2010, you do not need to know anything about the SharePoint components that are related to InfoPath, since that information is covered within the book. For example, you do not need to know how to work with SharePoint form libraries, site content types, or know anything about workflows in SharePoint Designer 2010, because the basics of those topics are explained in the book.

This book follows a practical approach. Almost each chapter presents you first with a small amount of theory explaining a few key concepts and then slowly builds your InfoPath with SharePoint integration skills with step-by-step recipes (tutorials) that follow a logical sequence and increase in complexity as you progress through the book. Almost every recipe has a discussion section that expands on the steps outlined in the recipe and offers additional information on what you have learned.

You will not find everything you can do with InfoPath and SharePoint explained in this book, because this book is not meant to be used as reference material. The goal of this book is to expand the knowledge you have already acquired from *InfoPath 2010 Cookbook: 101 Codeless Recipes for Beginners* into the SharePoint 2010 realm, and provide you with ideas on how you can integrate InfoPath with SharePoint by using one of four types of InfoPath forms in SharePoint, including the use of SharePoint Designer, Word, Excel, and Access with InfoPath through SharePoint.

How to use this book

This book has been set up in a cookbook style with 101 recipes. Each recipe consists of 3 parts: A description of the problem, a step-by-step outline of the solution, and further discussion highlighting important parts of the recipe, expanding on what you have learned, or providing you with background information on a specific topic.

Chapters 1 and 2 are meant to teach you the basics of creating and working with two of the most common types of InfoPath forms in SharePoint, so I recommend you do these chapters in full before moving onto any other chapter.

Recipes 43 through 46 in Chapter 3 teach you the basics of connecting to and using data from SharePoint lists, so I recommend you do these first before moving onto the recipes in other chapters. While the recipes in Chapter 4 stand on their own, they make use of techniques discussed in Chapter 3.

For Chapter 5, I recommend you start with recipes 72 through 80 in sequence to learn the basics of SharePoint Designer 2010 workflows. After this, you can randomly choose recipes from Chapter 5.

Recipes 89 through 93 in Chapter 6 should be done in sequence. And before you do recipe 94, ensure you have gone through the recipes in Chapter 5. All other recipes in Chapter 6 are pretty independent and can be done in any order you like.

While all of the recipes in this book are ordered in a way to build on each other, any recipe that requires knowledge you should have acquired from previous recipes will reference those recipes so that you can go back and do those recipes if you skipped them.

About the author

My name is S.Y.M. Wong-A-Ton and I have been a software developer since the start of my IT career back in 1997. The first Microsoft products I used as a developer were Visual Basic 4 and SQL Server 6.5. During my IT career I have developed as well as maintained and supported all types of applications ranging from desktop applications to web sites and web services. I have been a Microsoft Certified Professional since 1998 and have held the title of Microsoft Certified Solution Developer for almost as long as I have been in IT.

I was originally trained as a Geophysicist and co-wrote (as the main author) a scientific article while I was still a scientist. This article was published in 1997 in the Geophysical Research Letters of the American Geophysical Union.

I started exploring the first version of InfoPath in 2005 in my spare time and was hooked on it from day one. What I liked most about InfoPath was the simplicity with which I was able to quickly create electronic forms that were in reality small applications on their own; all this without writing a single line of code!

While exploring InfoPath, I started actively helping other InfoPath users, who were asking questions on the Internet, to come up with innovative solutions. And because the same questions were being asked frequently, I decided to start writing tutorials and articles about InfoPath on my web site "Enterprise Solutions", which evolved into what is known today as "Biz Support Online" and can be visited at http://www.bizsupportonline.net.

Shortly after starting to share my knowledge about InfoPath with others, I received recognition from Microsoft in the form of the Microsoft Most Valuable Professional (MVP) award, and have received this award every year after then, which as of writing has been 6 years in a row.

I have worked with SharePoint since its first version was released and while continuing to explore SharePoint throughout the years, I have found many InfoPath with SharePoint solutions, which I have shared with the InfoPath community through free articles, blog posts, and videos.

This book is a continuation of my sharing of knowledge, tips, tricks, and techniques with you, but most importantly, of providing you with codeless solutions for working with InfoPath and SharePoint. So I sincerely hope that you not only enjoy reading this book, but that it also inspires you to extend the solutions it contains to find more integration points between InfoPath and SharePoint without having to write a single line of code.

Support

Every effort has been made to ensure the accuracy of this book. Corrections for this book are provided at http://www.bizsupportonline.com.

If you have comments, suggestions, improvements, or ideas about this book, please send them to bizsupportonline@gmail.com with "InfoPath 2010 Cookbook 2" in the subject line.

Chapter 1: SharePoint List Forms

Every SharePoint list has a set of forms you can use to add, view, or edit list items. These forms are by default SharePoint ASP.NET list forms that display the columns of a list as fields on a form. You can use InfoPath Designer 2010 to create SharePoint list forms that replace the default SharePoint ASP.NET list forms and are based on what's called a SharePoint list form template in InfoPath.

In this chapter you will learn how to create and work with SharePoint list form templates.

SharePoint list form basics

A customized SharePoint list form is an InfoPath form that is tightly bound to one particular SharePoint list. There are two types of SharePoint list forms:

1. SharePoint list forms with which you can manage one list item at a time.
2. SharePoint list forms with which you can manage multiple list items at a time.

You can use InfoPath Designer 2010, SharePoint 2010, or SharePoint Designer 2010 to start the process of customizing a SharePoint list form in InfoPath Designer 2010 as you will learn from the recipes below.

1   Customize a SharePoint list form from within SharePoint

Problem

You want to create an InfoPath form that can be used to view, add, or edit SharePoint list items.

Solution

You can use one of two methods to customize a SharePoint list form depending on the content type associated with the list. If you want to customize the default content type of an existing SharePoint list, you can use the **Customize Form** option that is available on a SharePoint list to open a new or an existing form template in InfoPath Designer 2010. And if you want to customize a specific content type that is associated with an existing SharePoint list, you can go through the list settings to access the form settings page to open a new or an existing form template in InfoPath Designer 2010.

If you require background information about content types and how to add multiple content types to a SharePoint list, see *Add existing content types to a SharePoint list* in the Appendix.

InfoPath 2010 Cookbook 2

To customize the SharePoint list form for the default content type of a SharePoint list from within SharePoint:

1. In SharePoint, navigate to an existing SharePoint list or create a new one.
2. Click **List Tools** ➤ **List** ➤ **Customize List** ➤ **Customize Form**. This should open InfoPath Designer 2010 with a new form template that is based on the columns of the default content type of the SharePoint list. If the SharePoint list form has already been previously customized, so a list form template already exists for the SharePoint list, the existing form template should open in InfoPath Designer 2010.

Figure 1. Customize List group on the List tab in SharePoint 2010.

3. In InfoPath, customize the form template to suit your needs, and then click **File** ➤ **Info** ➤ **Quick Publish**, click **File** ➤ **Publish** ➤ **SharePoint List**, or click the **Quick Publish** button on the **Quick Access Toolbar** to publish the form template back to SharePoint.

To customize a SharePoint list form for a specific content type that is associated with a SharePoint list from within SharePoint:

1. In SharePoint, navigate to an existing SharePoint list or create a new one.
2. Click **List Tools** ➤ **List** ➤ **Settings** ➤ **List Settings** to navigate to the **List Settings** page.
3. On the **List Settings** page under **General Settings**, click **Form settings**.
4. On the **Form Settings** page, select the content type for which you want to customize its SharePoint list form from the **Content Type** drop-down list box, and click **OK**. This should open InfoPath Designer 2010.

Figure 2. Selecting a specific content type for which to customize its SharePoint list form.

5. In InfoPath, customize the form template to suit your needs, and then click **File** ➤ **Info** ➤ **Quick Publish**, click **File** ➤ **Publish** ➤ **SharePoint List**, or click the

Quick Publish button on the **Quick Access Toolbar** to publish the form template back to SharePoint.

In SharePoint, navigate to the SharePoint list for which you customized its form, and add an item. The customized InfoPath form should appear.

Discussion

The methods in this recipe can be used to create a new InfoPath form for a SharePoint list as well as update or modify an existing InfoPath form for a SharePoint list. While it may seem like you used a SharePoint list as the basis for a SharePoint list form, in reality, you used a content type that is associated with that SharePoint list as the basis for a SharePoint list form.

A SharePoint list may or may not have multiple content types associated with it depending on whether management of content types has been enabled or not (also see *Add existing content types to a SharePoint list* in the Appendix), so there are two situations that can take place:

1. If management of content types is not enabled on a SharePoint list, the default content type of that SharePoint list is used as the basis for the SharePoint list form.
2. If management of content types is enabled on a SharePoint list and there are multiple content types associated with the SharePoint list, you can use any one of those content types to base the SharePoint list form on.

In the solution described above, you used the **Customize Form** button on the Ribbon in SharePoint to customize the InfoPath form that is linked to the default content type of the SharePoint list, and you used the **Form Settings** page, which you accessed via the **List Settings** page, to customize the SharePoint list form for a specific content type that was associated with the SharePoint list. Note that you could have also used the **Form Settings** page to start the customization of an InfoPath form linked to the default content type, and that you could have also assigned a different content type to be the default content type and then used the **Customize Form** button to edit the SharePoint list form linked to that content type. So you can use either method for customizing a SharePoint list form for a particular content type. However, you cannot customize the SharePoint list form for all types of lists in SharePoint. For example, the SharePoint list form for a **Calendar** list cannot be customized, because the **Customize Form** button is not present on the Ribbon, neither are the options on the **Form Settings** page.

When you create a SharePoint list form template, the columns of the content type associated with the SharePoint list you use as the basis for the form template along with standard list columns such as **ID**, **Created By**, etc. become fields of the Main data source of the form.

Figure 3. The Fields task pane in InfoPath showing the Main data source and content type fields.

And when you fill out a SharePoint list form, the data you enter into the fields on the form are stored as an item in the SharePoint list. So unlike SharePoint form library forms, which you will learn more about in Chapter 2, SharePoint list forms are not stored as separate XML files within SharePoint, but are used rather as front-end forms that channel data through to a SharePoint list that functions as the data store.

This also immediately highlights one disadvantage of SharePoint list forms: The types of fields you are allowed to place on a SharePoint list form depend on the types of columns you can add to a content type associated with a SharePoint list. And because complex data structures such as repeating or nested data cannot be defined as data types of columns in SharePoint, they are not supported by SharePoint list forms. So if you want to add repeating structures (for example, repeating tables or repeating sections) to a form, you must use a SharePoint form library form instead of a SharePoint list form.

In addition, because a SharePoint list form is tightly bound to its data store, you cannot publish or republish the form template to another location. If you go to the **Publish** tab in InfoPath Designer 2010, you will see that there are no other publishing options available other than the option to publish the form template to the SharePoint list it was originally bound to. So once you have created a SharePoint list form template, you cannot change its (quick) publish location in InfoPath Designer 2010.

To be able to create a SharePoint list form template for an existing SharePoint list, you must have **Design** permission on the site where the SharePoint list is located, **Design** permission on the SharePoint list, and the type of SharePoint list must be customizable. If you want to use finer-grained permissions, you can create a custom permission level (also see *Add a custom permission level* in the Appendix) that includes the following permissions:

Chapter 1: SharePoint List Forms

- Manage Lists (list permission)
- Edit Items (list permission)
- View Items (list permission)
- Open Items (list permission)
- View Application Pages (list permission)
- Add and Customize Pages (site permission)
- Browse Directories (site permission)
- View Pages (site permission)
- Open (site permission)

And then grant the permission level to a user or group on both the site and list.

If you want to prevent a user from customizing a SharePoint list form, but still allow her to change settings on the list, you must assign the **Limited Access** permission level to the user on the SharePoint site and the **Design** permission level (or the custom permission level mentioned earlier) on the SharePoint list. These permission levels should disable the **Customize Form** button in SharePoint.

Figure 4. User can edit list settings, but not customize the list form.

While the user would still be able to open the form template via InfoPath Designer 2010 or SharePoint Designer 2010, she would not be able to make changes and publish those changes back to SharePoint, because the **Limited Access** permission level on the site would not allow her to do so.

Before you customize a SharePoint list form, the SharePoint list uses default ASPX pages as list forms and only the following three items are displayed in the **Modify Form Web Parts** drop-down menu, which you can access via the **List Tools ▶ List ▶ Customize List ▶ Modify Form Web Parts** command on the Ribbon:

1. Default New Form
2. Default Display Form
3. Default Edit Form

InfoPath 2010 Cookbook 2

After you customize and publish an InfoPath form template to a SharePoint list, you will see the following three items appear on the **Modify Form Web Parts** drop-down menu under a **Content Type Forms** section:

1. (Item) New Form
2. (Item) Display Form
3. (Item) Edit Form

The content type name is listed between brackets in front of each one of the forms. If there are multiple content types associated with the SharePoint list, each content type, for which you customized its list form, would have its own set of forms listed under the **Content Type Forms** section of the drop-down menu as shown in the following figure.

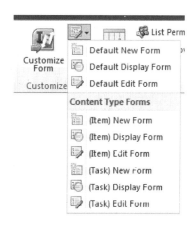

Figure 5. Both the Item and Task content types have customized list forms on this SharePoint list.

The content type forms are web part pages that host the customized SharePoint list form template you modified in InfoPath. If you click on any one of these three items, a web part page containing an InfoPath form for the corresponding type of form should open in the browser. The InfoPath form on the web part page is embedded in an InfoPath Form Web Part, which you will learn more about in recipe *12 Embed a SharePoint list form on a SharePoint page*. For now, just remember that you can customize this web part page to suit your needs and that the one form template you customized for the content type on the SharePoint list in InfoPath is used for all three types of forms (new, display, and edit).

And finally, you can also use SharePoint Designer 2010 to perform the steps outlined in this recipe as follows:

1. In SharePoint Designer 2010, open the SharePoint site where the SharePoint list for which you want to customize its form is located.
2. In the left **Navigation** pane, click **Lists and Libraries**.
3. On the **Lists and Libraries** page, click the list for which you want to customize a form.

Chapter 1: SharePoint List Forms

4. When the details page for the list opens, click **List Settings ➤ Actions ➤ Design Forms in InfoPath** and then select the content type for which you want to customize its form. This should open the SharePoint list form for customization in InfoPath Designer 2010.

Figure 6. Design Forms in InfoPath command in SharePoint Designer 2010.

5. In InfoPath, customize the form template to suit your needs, and then click **File ➤ Info ➤ Quick Publish**, click **File ➤ Publish ➤ SharePoint List**, or click the **Quick Publish** button on the **Quick Access Toolbar** to publish the form template back to SharePoint.

While you are still in SharePoint Designer 2010, now is also the time to learn where SharePoint stores the customized InfoPath form templates:

1. In the left **Navigation** pane, click **All Files**.
2. On the **All Files** page, click the **Lists** folder.
3. On the **Lists** page, click the SharePoint list for which you want to locate the customized InfoPath form template.
4. On the page for the SharePoint list, click the folder that has the name of the content type for which you want to locate the form template. If the SharePoint list only has a default **Item** content type associated with it, the folder would be called **Item**. Otherwise, the folder should have the same name as the content type.

Once you are in the folder for the content type (for example, the **Item** folder), you should see an InfoPath form template named **template.xsn** and also three ASPX pages (displayifs.aspx, editifs.aspx, and newifs.aspx) that are used as the web part pages to embed the SharePoint list form. Note that from here you could click on the **template.xsn** file to open and modify it in InfoPath Designer 2010.

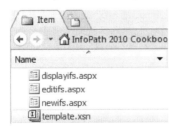

Figure 7. SharePoint list form template and form web part pages in SharePoint Designer 2010.

7

2 Customize a SharePoint list form from within InfoPath

Create a SharePoint list form for a new SharePoint list

Problem

You want to create an InfoPath form template that is based on a SharePoint list, but do not yet have a list in SharePoint, so would like to create the SharePoint list through InfoPath when you create the new form template.

Solution

You can create a SharePoint list form template in InfoPath Designer 2010 and specify that you would like to create a new SharePoint list for the form template.

To create a new SharePoint list and SharePoint list form template from within InfoPath:

1. In InfoPath, click **File** ➤ **New** ➤ **SharePoint List** ➤ **Design Form** to create a new **SharePoint List** form template.

2. On the **Data Connection Wizard**, enter the URL of the SharePoint site where you want to create the new SharePoint list, and click **Next**.

3. On the **Data Connection Wizard**, leave the **Create a new SharePoint list** option selected, type a name for the list in the **List Name** text box, and click **Next**.

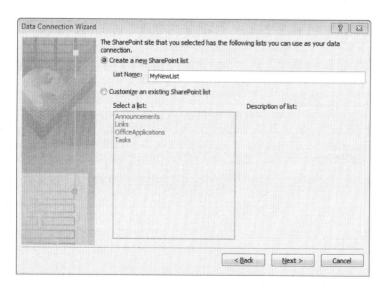

Figure 8. Creating a new SharePoint list in InfoPath Designer 2010.

4. On the **Data Connection Wizard**, leave the **Manage multiple list items with this form** check box deselected, and click **Finish**.

InfoPath should create a new list in SharePoint for the form template and place controls for the **Title** and **Attachments** fields on an **Edit item (default)** view of the form template in InfoPath Designer 2010.

Discussion

To be able to design a SharePoint list form template for a new SharePoint list, you must have **Design** permission on the SharePoint site where you want to create the SharePoint list. If you want to use finer-grained permissions, you can create a custom permission level that includes the same permissions as those mentioned for the custom permission level in the discussion section of recipe *1 Customize a SharePoint list form from within SharePoint*, and then grant the permission level to a user or group on the site.

Once you have created a form template that is bound to a new SharePoint list, you can add controls to the view of the form template or fields to the Main data source of the form (see recipe *4 Add a new field to a SharePoint list through InfoPath*). And once you publish the form template to SharePoint, the fields that you added in InfoPath Designer 2010 should become columns of the content type associated with the underlying SharePoint list.

Create a SharePoint list form for an existing SharePoint list

Problem

You want to use InfoPath Designer 2010 to design a form template and create a form with which users can view, add, or edit SharePoint list items.

Solution

You can use the **SharePoint List** form template in InfoPath Designer 2010 to design a form template and create a form with which you can view, add, or edit SharePoint list items.

Suppose you have a SharePoint list named **OfficeApplications** that contains the following data:

Title	Color
Word	Blue
Excel	Green
Access	Red
PowerPoint	Orange

InfoPath 2010 Cookbook 2

Title	Color
OneNote	Purple
InfoPath	Purple
Publisher	Blue

Note:

> You can use the **OfficeApplicationsList.stp** file (which you can download from www.bizsupportonline.com) to load the **OfficeApplications** SharePoint list into a SharePoint test environment (also see *Upload a list template to a List Template Gallery* in the Appendix).

To customize a SharePoint list form for an existing SharePoint list from within InfoPath:

1. In InfoPath, click **File ➤ New ➤ SharePoint List ➤ Design Form** to create a new **SharePoint List** form template.

2. On the **Data Connection Wizard**, enter the URL of the SharePoint site where the **OfficeApplications** SharePoint list is located, and click **Next**.

3. On the **Data Connection Wizard**, select the **Customize an existing SharePoint list** option, select the **OfficeApplications** SharePoint list, and click **Next**.

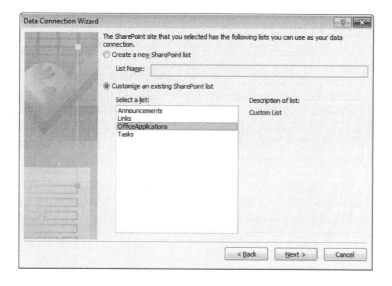

Figure 9. Customizing the list form for an existing SharePoint list in InfoPath Designer 2010.

4. The **OfficeApplications** SharePoint list does not have multiple content types associated with it, so after step 3 you would go directly to step 5. But had you selected a SharePoint list that has multiple content types associated with it, InfoPath would have presented you with an extra screen where you would have been able to select the content type for which you wanted to customize its SharePoint list form.

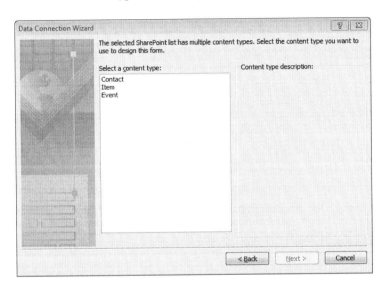

Figure 10. Selecting a content type to customize a SharePoint list form.

5. On the **Data Connection Wizard**, leave the **Manage multiple list items with this form** check box deselected, and click **Finish**.

InfoPath should create the form template and place controls on an **Edit item (default)** view. If the InfoPath form for the SharePoint list has already been customized previously, InfoPath should open the existing, already customized InfoPath form template, instead of creating a new one.

Discussion

SharePoint lists that are not customizable using InfoPath are not listed in the **Select a list** list box on the **Data Connection Wizard** where you can choose a SharePoint list to customize.

When you create a SharePoint list form template, InfoPath displays the fields of the Main data source of the form by default in **basic view** mode on the **Fields** task pane. **Basic view** mode does not show you the structure of the form template and only displays fields with which you can add, edit, or display (not query) data.

InfoPath 2010 Cookbook 2

Figure 11. Fields task pane in InfoPath Designer 2010 showing the basic view for form fields.

To see the structure of the form template, on the **Fields** task pane, click **Show advanced view** at the bottom of the **Fields** task pane.

Figure 12. Fields task pane in InfoPath Designer 2010 showing the advanced view for form fields.

From the **advanced view** you can see that the Main data source of the form consists of two main group nodes:

1. queryFields
2. dataFields

The **queryFields** group node contains the fields that can be used to query (search for or filter) data in the SharePoint list, while the **dataFields** group node contains fields that can be used to display data from the SharePoint list. The fields under the **dataFields** group node are also used to submit data to the SharePoint list through the main data connection of the form. The main data connection of a SharePoint list form submits data to the SharePoint list the form is connected to, and it cannot be changed to submit data to another SharePoint list or to multiple SharePoint lists.

The controls that InfoPath placed on the view of the form template when you created it are bound to fields that are located under the **dataFields** group node. Because those controls are used to edit a list item, they are placed on a view named **Edit item (default)** (see **Page Design** ➤ **Views** ➤ **View**). To verify that the fields bound to those controls are indeed located under the **dataFields** group node, click on any of the fields on the view and then look which field is highlighted on the **Fields** task pane.

You can add new controls to the view of the form template or new fields to the Main data source of the form (see recipe *4 Add a new field to a SharePoint list through InfoPath*), and once you publish the form template, those fields should become columns of the content type associated with the underlying SharePoint list.

3   Create a SharePoint list form to manage multiple list items with one form

Problem

You want to create an InfoPath form with which users can add, edit, or delete one or more SharePoint list items through the one form.

Solution

You can use the **SharePoint List** form template in InfoPath Designer 2010 to design a form template and create a form with which you can manage multiple list items.

Suppose you have a SharePoint list named **OfficeApplications** as described in *Create a SharePoint list form for an existing SharePoint list* of recipe *2 Customize a SharePoint list form from within InfoPath*.

To create a SharePoint list form with which you can manage multiple list items:

1. In InfoPath, click **File** ➤ **New** ➤ **SharePoint List** ➤ **Design Form** to create a new **SharePoint List** form template.

InfoPath 2010 Cookbook 2

2. On the **Data Connection Wizard**, enter the URL of the SharePoint site where the **OfficeApplications** SharePoint list is located, and click **Next**.

3. On the **Data Connection Wizard**, select the **Customize an existing SharePoint list** option, select the **OfficeApplications** SharePoint list, and click **Next**.

4. On the **Data Connection Wizard**, select the **Manage multiple list items with this form** check box, and click **Finish**.

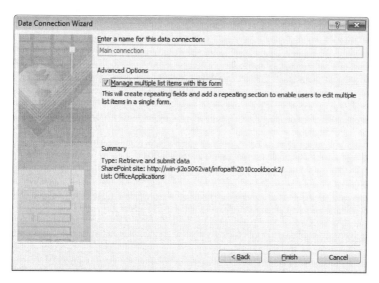

Figure 13. Selecting the Manage multiple list items with this form check box in InfoPath 2010.

InfoPath should create the form template and place controls in a repeating section on the **Edit item (default)** view.

Discussion

In the solution described above you saw that enabling a SharePoint list form to manage multiple items is a matter of selecting the **Manage multiple list items with this form** check box on the last screen of the **Data Connection Wizard**. While you customized the form for an existing SharePoint list in this recipe, the check box should also be available when you create a new SharePoint list (also see step 4 in *Create a SharePoint list form for a new SharePoint list* of recipe *2 Customize a SharePoint list form from within InfoPath*). If the check box is missing when you connect to an existing SharePoint list from within InfoPath, it means that the SharePoint list form has already been previously customized to allow for single item viewing and editing. Once you have customized a SharePoint list form, you cannot change it from managing multiple items to managing one item or vice versa, unless you first delete the list form as described in recipe *6 Restore the default ASP.NET form of a SharePoint list* and then customize the form again to manage either one or multiple items.

Chapter 1: SharePoint List Forms

Adding or editing multiple SharePoint list items instead of one works just like adding or editing one SharePoint list item, which means that you can apply the same techniques to both where querying and refreshing data are concerned. The only difference is that when you enable management of multiple list items, the form fields are stored under a **my:SharePointListItem_RW** repeating group node

Figure 14. SharePointListItem_RW is a repeating group for a form that manages multiple items.

instead of a non-repeating group node as is the case for a SharePoint list form that manages a single item.

Figure 15. SharePointListItem_RW is a non-repeating group for a form that manages a single item.

This also means that any fields you drag-and-drop onto the view, should be placed within a repeating table or a repeating section control. By default, InfoPath places controls within a repeating section control when you enable management of multiple items, but you could as easily place the controls in a repeating table control as follows:

1. Delete the repeating section control along with all of the controls it contains from the view of the form template.
2. On the **Fields** task pane, if **basic view** is being shown, click **Show advanced view**.
3. On the **Fields** task pane, expand the **dataFields** group node, drag-and-drop the **my:SharePointListItem_RW** repeating group node onto the view, and when you drop it, select **Repeating Table** from the context menu that appears.
4. Delete any fields from the view by selecting their respective columns within the repeating table and pressing **Backspace** on your keyboard or by selecting **Table Tools ➤ Layout ➤ Rows & Columns ➤ Delete ➤ Columns** on the Ribbon.

You can add new controls to the repeating section or repeating table on the view of the form template or new fields under the **my:SharePointListItem_RW** repeating group node in the Main data source of the form (see recipe *4 Add a new field to a SharePoint list through InfoPath*), and once you publish the form template, those fields should become part of the content type associated with the underlying SharePoint list.

4 Add a new field to a SharePoint list through InfoPath

Problem

You have a SharePoint list form template open in InfoPath Designer 2010 and want to add a new field to the underlying SharePoint list of the form from within InfoPath.

Solution

When designing a SharePoint list form template in InfoPath, you can add fields or controls to the form template, which will then automatically be added to the content type of the underlying SharePoint list when you publish the form template.

To add a new field to a SharePoint list through InfoPath by adding a control to the form template:

1. In InfoPath, create a new SharePoint list form template or open an existing one as described in recipe *1 Customize a SharePoint list form from within SharePoint* or recipe *2 Customize a SharePoint list form from within InfoPath*.

2. Click on the view of the form template to place the cursor where you want to insert a new control, and then from the **Controls** group on the **Home** tab, select the control you want to add.

3. With the control still selected, change the **Name** of the field on the **Properties** tab under the **Properties** group to a name that is suitable to be used as a SharePoint list column.

In InfoPath, on the **Fields** task pane, click **Show advanced view**. The **queryFields** and **dataFields** group nodes in the Main data source should appear. Verify that a new field has been added under the **my:SharePointListItem_RW** group node under the **dataFields** group node.

You can also add a new field to a SharePoint list by adding it directly to the Main data source and not binding it to any control on the view.

To add a new field to a SharePoint list through InfoPath by adding a field to the Main data source of the form:

1. In InfoPath, create a new SharePoint list form template or open an existing one as described in recipe *1 Customize a SharePoint list form from within SharePoint* or recipe *2 Customize a SharePoint list form from within InfoPath*.

2. On the **Fields** task pane, if **basic view** is being shown, click **Show advanced view**.

3. On the **Fields** task pane, expand the **dataFields** group node, right-click the **my:SharePointListItem_RW** group node, and select **Add** from the drop-down menu that appears.

4. On the **Add Field or Group** dialog box, enter a **Display Name** and a **Name** for the field (InfoPath automatically generates a **Name** based on the **Display Name**

Chapter 1: SharePoint List Forms

you enter, but you can change the generated **Name** if you wish), select the data type from the **Data type** drop-down list box, and click **OK**. The new field should appear under the **my:SharePointListItem_RW** group node under the **dataFields** group node in the Main data source of the form.

When you publish the form template to SharePoint, the new field should be added as a new column to the content type the form is linked to as well as to the SharePoint list.

Discussion

SharePoint list forms do not support the full range of controls that is available in InfoPath, because they are limited by the types of fields you can add to a SharePoint list. If you open the **Controls** section in InfoPath, you will notice that some controls such as repeating tables and sections are not available when you are designing a SharePoint list form template, and that the amount of controls that is available is less than for example when you create a **Blank Form** or **SharePoint Form Library** template.

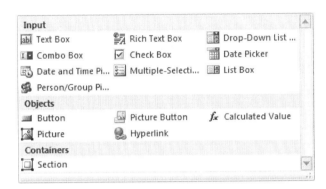

Figure 16. InfoPath controls you can place on a SharePoint list form.

So if you know that you may need to use controls that are not available for SharePoint list form templates, you may want to consider creating a SharePoint form library form template (see Chapter 2) instead of a SharePoint list form template.

While the first method for adding controls to a form template described in the solution above is quick and easy, it does not give you much flexibility where selecting the data type of the field that is bound to the control is concerned. InfoPath offers many more options for selecting the data type of a field when you first add that field to the Main data source of the form and then bind it to a control on the view, than when you first add a control to the view and then change its data type or the data type of the field it is bound to.

For example, when you add a text box control to the view of the form template, it is automatically bound to a single line of text field. But what if you wanted to bind it to a lookup field? That option would not be available to you after you add the text box to the view. If on the other hand you first add a lookup field to the Main data source, you have the choice of binding it to several types of controls on the view.

InfoPath 2010 Cookbook 2

Perform the steps from the second method described in the solution above again, and when you are on the **Add Field or Group** dialog box, go through the list of data types. As you select a data type, you may see other data entry options being enabled or disabled on the dialog box. For example, if you choose any of the **Choice** data types, an **Edit Choices** button with which you can enter a list of choices, is enabled.

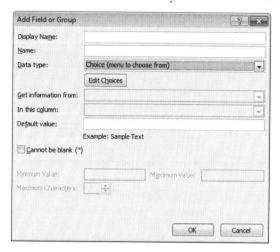

Figure 17. Selecting a Choice data type on the Add Field or Group dialog box in InfoPath 2010.

If you choose **Currency** as the data type, the **Minimum Value** and **Maximum Value** text boxes are enabled. If you choose **Single line of text** as the data type, you can specify the maximum amount of characters that the field should support. You can also select **Lookup** as the data type and select where the information should come from.

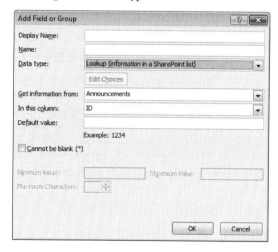

Figure 18. Selecting a Lookup data type on the Add Field or Group dialog box in InfoPath 2010.

Once you publish the form template to SharePoint, the new fields you added to the form template will be locked and their data types cannot be changed anymore. You can see

Chapter 1: SharePoint List Forms

whether a field is locked by the small padlock that appears in the upper right-hand corner of the field's icon on the **Fields** task pane.

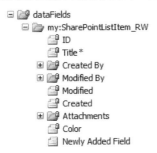

Figure 19. Newly Added Field has not yet been added to the SharePoint list.

In the figure above, all fields except for **Newly Added Field** have a padlock icon on them, which means that **Newly Added Field** does not yet exist on the SharePoint list in SharePoint. Once you publish the form template, **Newly Added Field** should appear as a column in the SharePoint list and then also get a padlock icon in InfoPath Designer 2010.

The solution described above adds a field to a SharePoint list from within InfoPath, so the direction is from InfoPath to SharePoint. But you could also go in the opposite direction by first adding a column to the SharePoint list (or content type) and then updating the Main data source in InfoPath to contain a new field that corresponds to the new SharePoint column. To update the Main data source in InfoPath after you have added a new column to a SharePoint list (or content type) while you had the form template open in InfoPath Designer 2010, click **Data ➤ SharePoint Form Data ➤ Refresh Fields**.

5 Delete a field from a SharePoint list through InfoPath

Problem

You have a SharePoint list form template open in InfoPath and want to delete fields from the underlying SharePoint list from within InfoPath.

Solution

You must delete the field from the Main data source of the SharePoint list form template and publish the form template in order for that field to be deleted from the content type associated with the underlying SharePoint list.

To delete a field from a SharePoint list through InfoPath:

1. In InfoPath, create a new SharePoint list form template or open an existing one as described in recipe *1 Customize a SharePoint list form from within SharePoint* or recipe *2 Customize a SharePoint list form from within InfoPath*.

2. On the **Fields** task pane, if the **basic view** for the Main data source is being shown, click **Show advanced view**. The **queryFields** and **dataFields** groups in the Main data source should appear.

3. On the **Fields** task pane, expand the **dataFields** group node, expand the **my:SharePointListItem_RW** group node, right-click the field you want to delete, and select **Delete** from the drop-down menu that appears. Note: You can also click the field and then click on the drop-down arrow that appears on the right-hand side to expand the drop-down menu and select **Delete** from the menu.

4. On the **Microsoft InfoPath** message box, click **Yes**.

5. If a control was previously bound to the field you deleted, it will remain unbound on the view of the form template unless you delete it. So select that control on the view and press **Delete** on your keyboard to delete the control from the view.

6. Publish the form template to SharePoint.

In SharePoint, navigate to the SharePoint list for which you customized its list form and verify that the column does not exist anymore on the list.

Discussion

In the solution described above you used the **Fields** task pane to delete a field and consequently also a column from a SharePoint list once the form template was published to SharePoint. It is important to remember that when you delete a control from a view of a form template, you do not automatically also delete the field that that control is bound to from the Main data source of the form, so neither from the content type or underlying SharePoint list. So you must use the **Fields** task pane to delete fields.

You can also delete a field from the content type or from the SharePoint list in SharePoint via the **List Settings** page of the SharePoint list instead of from within InfoPath. If you delete a field via SharePoint, you can click **Data ▶ SharePoint Form Data ▶ Refresh Fields** in InfoPath Designer 2010 afterwards to remove the deleted field from the list of fields in the Main data source of the form.

6 Restore the default ASP.NET form of a SharePoint list

Problem

You customized the list form for a content type associated with a SharePoint list, but now you want to revert back to the original default ASP.NET forms that SharePoint creates for SharePoint lists.

Solution

You can change the type of form used by a SharePoint list through the **List Settings** page.

Chapter 1: SharePoint List Forms

To restore the default ASP.NET form of a SharePoint list:

1. In SharePoint, navigate to the SharePoint list for which you want to restore its list form, and click **List Tools** ➤ **List** ➤ **Settings** ➤ **List Settings**.

2. On the **List Settings** page under **General Settings**, click **Form settings**.

3. On the **Form Settings** page, select the **Use the default SharePoint form** option button, select the **Delete the InfoPath Form from the server** check box, and click **OK**. If you do not select the **Delete the InfoPath Form from the server** check box, the customized SharePoint list form will remain on the server and will be used as the starter form template if you ever decide to customize the form again in the future.

In SharePoint, add a new item to the list or edit an existing item from the list to verify that the InfoPath form is not being used anymore as the SharePoint list form. The InfoPath-related options under the **Modify Form Web Parts** command on the Ribbon (**List Tools** ➤ **List** ➤ **Customize List**) should also be gone, and you should only see **Default New Form**, **Default Display Form**, and **Default Edit Form** listed as options.

Discussion

In the solution described above, you learned that you can select the **Delete the InfoPath Form from the server** check box on the form settings page when restoring the forms back to the default ASP.NET forms. By doing this, you would delete all of the files (ASPX and XSN files) that are located in the content type's folder (see the discussion section of recipe *1 Customize a SharePoint list form from within SharePoint*). If you do not choose to delete the InfoPath form from the server, the next time you customize the list form, the old InfoPath form template would be retrieved and used for customization.

You can verify that the files have been deleted by opening the site in SharePoint Designer 2010, navigating to the list using the **All Files** option in the **Navigation** pane, and then checking the contents of the content type folders for that list (for example the **Item** folder if you deleted the SharePoint list form for an **Item** content type associated with the list). Note that if a SharePoint list has multiple content types associated with it, SharePoint will display a drop-down list box on the **Form Settings** page from which you can choose the content type for which you want to revert back to its default ASP.NET forms.

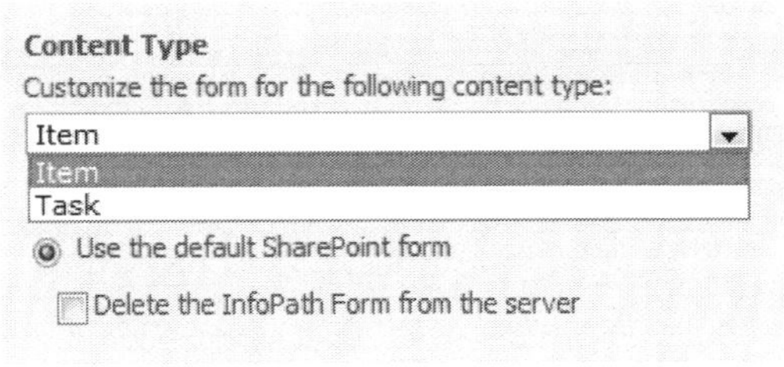

Figure 20. Drop-down list box with two content types on the Form Settings page in SharePoint 2010.

Query data through SharePoint list forms

The main data connection of a SharePoint list form not only submits data to the SharePoint list the form is connected to, but it also supports retrieving data from the SharePoint list through querying. The recipes in this section will show you how to run queries on SharePoint list forms to retrieve specific data from a SharePoint list.

7 Add query functionality to a SharePoint list form

Problem

You have a SharePoint list form with which you can view, add, or edit one SharePoint list item at a time. You want to be able to type the name of a specific list item in a text box, and then retrieve data for that particular item, so that you can edit it.

Solution

You can use the fields that are located under the **queryFields** group node in the Main data source of the form to search for an existing SharePoint list item and populate the form with its data.

To add query functionality to a SharePoint list form:

1. In InfoPath, create a new SharePoint list form template or open an existing one as described in recipe *1 Customize a SharePoint list form from within SharePoint* or recipe *2 Customize a SharePoint list form from within InfoPath*.

2. On the **Fields** task pane, if the **basic view** for the Main data source is being shown, click **Show advanced view**. This should display the **queryFields** and **dataFields** group nodes in the Main data source.

3. On the **Fields** task pane, expand the **q:SharePointListItem_RW** group node under the **queryFields** group node, and then drag-and-drop the **Title** field onto the view to automatically bind it to a text box control.

4. Add a **Button** control to the form template, and change its **Action** property from **Rules** to **Run Query**.

Figure 21. Selecting the Run Query action for a button in InfoPath Designer 2010.

Chapter 1: SharePoint List Forms

5. Preview the form.

When the form opens, click the **Run Query** button. The data for the first item in the list should be retrieved and displayed on the form. Note that if you created a SharePoint list form that manages multiple list items (also see recipe *3 Create a SharePoint list form to manage multiple list items with one form*), all of the SharePoint list items would be retrieved and displayed on the form. Type the title for an existing item in the **Title** field, and click the button. The form should be populated with data for that specific item in the SharePoint list.

Figure 22. The InfoPath form displaying the query results for a search on 'infopath'.

Discussion

In general, when you are editing SharePoint list items directly in a SharePoint list, you can open a specific item without performing a query to find the right item to edit. Therefore, the solution described above is better suited for scenarios where you do not want to have users access a SharePoint list directly, but rather place an InfoPath form on a web page, so that they can search and edit items through a web page (also see recipe *12 Embed a SharePoint list form on a SharePoint page*).

When you add a button control to a SharePoint list form, you can set the button to perform one of the following actions:

- Run Query – Runs a query on the main data connection.
- Submit – Submits data to the SharePoint list.
- New Record – Clears all of the fields on the form for entering new data.
- Rules – Allows you to add custom rules to a button.
- Update Form – Updates form data in an incremental manner.

When you set the **Action** property of a button to anything other than **Rules**, you are only allowed to add additional formatting rules to the button, but no other custom action rules. If you want to add custom action rules to a button, you must set the **Action** property of the button to **Rules**.

There is an additional button action named **Refresh** with which you can refresh one or all of the secondary data sources in an InfoPath form using the corresponding data connections. This action only appears in the list of button actions when you add one or more secondary data sources to a form template.

If you want to retrieve all of the data contained in a SharePoint list without filtering it, you can add a button to the view of the form template and set its **Action** property to **Run Query**. This is the quickest way to create a "query and return all" button. A second way is to add a button to the form template and set its **Action** property to **Rules**, and then add an **Action** rule to the button that has a **Run Query** action that queries the main data connection of the form. The first option requires fewer steps to implement.

The **Run Query** button action has a built-in check on data changes in a form. This causes the form to display the message "This action will delete all information in the current form" every time you retrieve a list item, change some of its data, and decide to retrieve fresh data again by clicking on the **Run Query** button. If you want to ignore data changes and not alert a user that she will lose any data changes she has made prior to clicking the button, you could create a button that has a **Rules** action instead of a **Run Query** action, and then add an action that queries the main data connection of the form.

8   Query for multiple items in a SharePoint list form

Problem

You created a SharePoint list form with which you can manage multiple list items. Because the list is fairly long, you want to be able to query for specific items in the list, so that you can quickly retrieve and edit them.

Solution

You can add query functionality to a multi-itemed SharePoint list form by using the fields that are located under the **queryFields** group node in the Main data source of the form.

Suppose you have a SharePoint list named **OfficeApplications** as described in *Create a SharePoint list form for an existing SharePoint list* of recipe *2 Customize a SharePoint list form from within InfoPath* and you want to be able to search on either the **Title** or the **Color** field. You can add a drop-down list box to the form template that switches between searching on **Title** or **Color**, and then use the selected item in the drop-down list box to set the value of the **Title** or **Color** field that is located under the **q:SharePointListItem_RW** group node under the **queryFields** group node in the Main data source of the form before running the query.

Because you must bind a drop-down list box to a field and there is no field in the Main data source that provides the names of fields, you can use a secondary data source that contains the field names as a helper data source. Note that if you add a field to the Main data source to bind the drop-down list box to, it would create an unnecessary column (a column that does not really have anything to do with describing a property of a list item) in the SharePoint list. To avoid this, you can make use of a secondary data source, because data from secondary data sources is not stored permanently in the form itself

Chapter 1: SharePoint List Forms

unless you opt to store a copy of the data in the form template when you create the data connection. Either way, a secondary data source does not affect the structure of the Main data source of the form, so also does not add unnecessary columns to the SharePoint list.

To create a drop-down list box that contains the names of fields you want to query on, you can create an XML file named **FilterColumns.xml** (or you can download the **FilterColumns.xml** file from www.bizsupportonline.com) that has the following contents:

```
<?xml version="1.0" encoding="UTF-8" ?>
<filtercolumns>
  <selectedvalue/>
  <columns>
    <column>Title</column>
    <column>Color</column>
  </columns>
</filtercolumns>
```

To query for multiple items in a SharePoint list form:

1. In InfoPath, create a new SharePoint list form that manages multiple items as described in recipe *3 Create a SharePoint list form to manage multiple list items with one form*.

2. Select **Data ▶ From Other Sources ▶ From XML File** and add an XML data connection to the **FilterColumns.xml** file to the form template, name the data connection **FilterColumns**, and ensure you leave the **Automatically retrieve data when form is opened** check box selected.

3. Click **Insert ▶ Custom Table**, and add a custom table with one row and two columns above the repeating section on the view of the form template.

4. On the **Fields** task pane, if the **basic view** for the Main data source is being shown, click **Show advanced view**, and then select **FilterColumns (Secondary)** from the **Fields** drop-down list box.

5. Right-click the **selectedvalue** field, drag it to the view of the form template, drop it in the first column of the custom table, and select **Drop-Down List Box** from the context menu that appears.

6. Open the **Drop-Down List Box Properties** dialog box, and configure the list box choices to come from the **FilterColumns** data source, with the value of the **Entries** property set to the **column** repeating field under the **columns** group node, and both the **Value** and **Display name** properties set to . . Click **OK** to close the dialog box when you are done.

25

InfoPath 2010 Cookbook 2

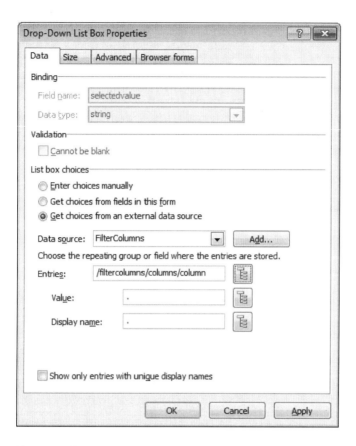

Figure 23. Configuration settings for the drop-down list box.

7. On the **Fields** task pane, select **Main** from the **Fields** drop-down list box.

8. On the **Fields** task pane, expand the **queryFields** group node, expand the **q:SharePointListItem_RW** group node, drag-and-drop the **Title** field in the second column of the custom table, and then drag-and-drop the **Color** field and place it below the text box for the **Title** field in the second column of the custom table.

9. Add a **Button** control below the custom table on the view of the form template and set its **Action** property to **Run Query**.

10. Add an **Action** rule to the **selectedvalue** drop-down list box with the following two actions that say:

    ```
    Set a field's value: Title = ""
    Set a field's value: Color = ""
    ```

    where **Title** and **Color** are the fields located under the **q:SharePointListItem_RW**

26

Chapter 1: SharePoint List Forms

group node under the **queryFields** group node in the Main data source. This rule clears any text you previously entered in either the **Title** or **Color** query text boxes.

11. Add a **Formatting** rule to the **Title** query text box that has a **Condition** that says:

    ```
    selectedvalue ≠ "Title"
    or
    selectedvalue is blank
    ```

    with a formatting of **Hide this control**. Here, **selectedValue** is the **selectedValue** field in the **FilterColumns** secondary data source and **Title** is a static piece of text. This rule hides the **Title** query text box if no item has been selected from the drop-down list box or if **Title** has not been selected from the drop-down list box.

12. Add a **Formatting** rule to the **Color** query text box that has a **Condition** that says:

    ```
    selectedvalue ≠ "Color"
    or
    selectedvalue is blank
    ```

    with a formatting of **Hide this control**. Here, **selectedValue** is the **selectedValue** field in the **FilterColumns** secondary data source and **Color** is a static piece of text. This rule hides the **Color** query text box if no item has been selected from the drop-down list box or if **Color** has not been selected from the drop-down list box.

13. Preview the form.

When the form opens, select a field to search on from the drop-down list box, for example, **Title**. The query text box for **Title** should appear. Type a piece of text into the text box, for example, **Word**, and click the **Run Query** button. The SharePoint list item containing **Word** in its **Title** field should appear. Repeat these steps and search for items that have the same color (if your SharePoint list does not have any such items, add a few items). Multiple items that have the same color should appear in the repeating section.

Figure 24. The InfoPath form displaying Office applications that have a 'Blue' color.

Discussion

The solution described above made use of an XML file that provided data for a drop-down list box. This XML file contained a field (**selectedvalue**) which you used to bind the drop-down list box to, as well as the items (**column** repeating field) to fill the drop-down list box. Adding this XML file to the form template and then binding the drop-down list box to a field in the secondary data source for the XML file helped you avoid having to add unnecessary fields to the underlying SharePoint list of the form for the sole purpose of adding query functionality.

As you know, drop-down list boxes can also be populated with static values. But in the case of SharePoint list forms, as soon as you try to add a drop-down list box via the **Controls** task pane or the **Controls** group on the **Home** tab, you are prompted to enter choices manually or look up the choices in a SharePoint list. Selecting either option would create a field in the Main data source and in the underlying SharePoint list of the form.

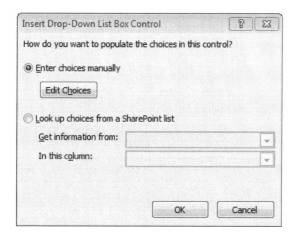

Figure 25. Dialog box to select choices for a drop-down list box on a SharePoint list form.

Tip:

> If you ever need fields to provide supporting functionality in a SharePoint list form, but do not want to add those fields as columns to the SharePoint list, you can create an XML file that contains the supporting fields and then add that XML file as a secondary data source to the form.

9 Perform wildcard searches with a SharePoint list form

Problem

You created a SharePoint list form with which you can manage multiple list items. You want to be able to type a piece of text into a text box, and then have the SharePoint list items that match part of, or the entire search term, appear on the form.

Solution

You can use conditional formatting on the repeating section or repeating table that displays the SharePoint list items in combination with the **contains** and **translate** functions to be able to perform filtering on items in a SharePoint list.

Suppose you have a SharePoint list named **OfficeApplications** as described in *Create a SharePoint list form for an existing SharePoint list* of recipe *2 Customize a SharePoint list form from within InfoPath* and you want to be able to perform a wildcard search on the **Title** field.

Because you require a separate field in which a user can type a search term and because any fields you add to the Main data source of the form will also be added to the underlying SharePoint list, you can make use of a secondary data source in order not to add unnecessary columns to the SharePoint list. For the latter you can use the **FilterColumns.xml** file you used in the previous recipe.

To perform wildcard searches with a SharePoint list form:

1. In InfoPath, create a new SharePoint list form that manages multiple items as described in recipe *3 Create a SharePoint list form to manage multiple list items with one form*.

2. Select **Data** ➤ **From Other Sources** ➤ **From XML File** and add an XML data connection to the **FilterColumns.xml** file, name the data connection **FilterColumns**, and ensure you leave the **Automatically retrieve data when form is opened** check box selected.

3. On the **Fields** task pane, if the **basic view** for the Main data source is being shown, click **Show advanced view**, and then select **FilterColumns (Secondary)** from the **Fields** drop-down list box.

4. Drag-and-drop the **selectedvalue** field onto the view of the form template just above the repeating section. It should automatically get bound to a text box control.

5. Click **Data** ➤ **Rules** ➤ **Form Load** and add an **Action** rule with an action that says:

   ```
   Query using a data connection: Main Data Connection
   ```

   This rule retrieves all of the data from the SharePoint list every time the form opens.

InfoPath 2010 Cookbook 2

6. Add a **Formatting** rule to the repeating section control (the **my:SharePointListItem_RW** repeating group node) that has a **The expression** condition that says:

   ```
   not(contains(translate(my:Title, "ABCDEFGHIJKLMNOPQRSTUVWXYZ",
   "abcdefghijklmnopqrstuvwxyz"),
   translate(xdXDocument:GetDOM("FilterColumns")/filtercolumns/selectedvalue,
   "ABCDEFGHIJKLMNOPQRSTUVWXYZ", "abcdefghijklmnopqrstuvwxyz")))
   ```

   and a second condition that says:

   ```
   or
   selectedvalue is blank
   ```

   with a formatting of **Hide this control**. Here, **selectedValue** is the **selectedValue** field in the **FilterColumns** secondary data source and **Title** is the **Title** field that is located under the **my:SharePointListItem_RW** group node under the **dataFields** group node in the Main data source. This rule hides any section in the repeating section if the **Title** does not contain the piece of text entered into the **selectedvalue** text box.

7. Preview the form.

When the form opens, type a piece of text in the **selectedvalue** text box, and then click away or press **Tab** on your keyboard. A section should appear for each SharePoint list item in which the piece of text you searched for forms part of the **Title** field of the SharePoint list item.

Figure 26. SharePoint list form to perform a wildcard search on items in a SharePoint list.

Discussion

The solution described above made use of an XML file so that you could bind a field to a text box control on the form without having to add this field to the underlying SharePoint list for the sole purpose of adding search and filter functionality to the form (also see the discussion section of recipe *8 Query for multiple items in a SharePoint list form*).

In addition, you made use of the **translate** function in a condition of a formatting rule to be able to perform non-case-sensitive filtering on the data in the repeating section.

30

10 Add new record functionality to a SharePoint list form

Problem

You have a SharePoint list form, which you would like to use to add new items to a SharePoint list.

Solution

You can add a button that has its action set to **New Record** to the view of the form template to clear the form in preparation for entering new data for a new SharePoint list item.

To add new record functionality to a SharePoint list form:

1. In InfoPath, create a new SharePoint list form template or open an existing one as described in recipe *1 Customize a SharePoint list form from within SharePoint* or recipe *2 Customize a SharePoint list form from within InfoPath*.

2. Add a **Button** control to the view of the form template and set its **Action** property to **New Record**. The **Label** for the button should automatically change to the text **New Record**.

3. Click **Data** ➤ **Rules** ➤ **Form Load** and add an **Action** rule with an action that says:

   ```
   Query using a data connection: Main Data Connection
   ```

   This action rule ensures that the SharePoint list items are retrieved and that the first item in the list is displayed. If you opened an existing SharePoint list form that already has a mechanism for retrieving data, you can skip this step. This step is only to demonstrate the functionality of clearing the form when the button is clicked.

4. Preview the form.

When the form opens, it should get populated with data (if it is not, populate it with some data by either retrieving data or manually filling out the fields). When you click the **New Record** button, the form should be cleared. Now you can enter fresh data and then click **Submit** to submit the data as a new item to the SharePoint list.

Figure 27. The InfoPath form displaying the first item in the list at startup.

InfoPath 2010 Cookbook 2

Figure 28. The InfoPath form with cleared fields after clicking the New Record button.

Discussion

The **New Record** button action clears a form in preparation for entering data for a new record or list item as in the solution described above. Note that you can only add formatting rules to a **New Record** button, and that you cannot add any validation or action rules to it.

11 Refresh secondary data sources in a SharePoint list form

Problem

You have a SharePoint list form that contains several secondary data sources for which you want to retrieve updated data.

Solution

You can add a button that has its action set to **Refresh** to the view of the form template to refresh data in secondary data sources of the form.

To refresh data in secondary data sources in a SharePoint list form:

1. In InfoPath, create a new SharePoint list form template or open an existing one as described in recipe *1 Customize a SharePoint list form from within SharePoint* or recipe *2 Customize a SharePoint list form from within InfoPath*.

2. Add a SharePoint list data connection to the form template as described in *Use a SharePoint list data connection* of recipe *43 3 Ways to retrieve data from a SharePoint list*, click **Show advanced view** on the **Fields** task pane if the **basic view** for the Main data source is being shown, select the secondary data source from the **Fields** drop-down list box, and then bind the data source to a repeating table as described in recipe *44 Display SharePoint list data in a repeating table*. Important: You must have one or more secondary data sources in the form for the **Refresh** action to appear in the list of actions for button controls.

3. Add a **Button** control to the view of the form template.

Chapter 1: SharePoint List Forms

4. Open the **Button Properties** dialog box, and then on the **General** tab, select **Refresh** from the **Action** drop-down list box, and then click **Settings**. The **Label** of the button should automatically change to **Refresh**.

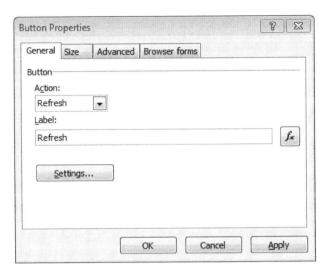

Figure 29. Refresh action selected on the Button Properties dialog box.

5. On the **Refresh** dialog box, leave the **All secondary data sources** option selected, and click **OK**. Alternatively, if you want to refresh only one specific data source, you could select the **One secondary data source** option and then choose the data source you want to refresh from the drop-down list box.

Figure 30. The Refresh dialog box in InfoPath Designer 2010.

6. On the **Button Properties** dialog box, click **OK**.
7. Preview the form.

33

When the form opens, make changes to the data at the source of the secondary data source (for example, if a secondary data source is getting its data from a SharePoint list, change data in the SharePoint list via SharePoint), and then click the **Refresh** button. The data in all of the secondary data sources should be updated to display the latest changes.

Figure 31. The InfoPath form displaying updated data for 'Publisher' after clicking Refresh.

Discussion

Typically, a SharePoint list form contains one main data source and optionally one or more secondary data sources. To refresh data in the Main data source, you can add a button control with an **Action** rule on it to **Query for data** using the main data connection. To refresh data in secondary data sources of the form, you could use one of two methods:

1. Add a button control with an **Action** rule on it to **Query for data** using the data connection for each secondary data source you want to refresh.
2. Add a button that has its action set to **Refresh**, and then specify whether one specific secondary data source or all of the secondary data sources of the form should be refreshed.

The **Refresh** button is particularly useful if you want to refresh all of the secondary data sources in a form all at once. Had you used a normal button with a rule, you would have had to add a **Query for data** action for each secondary data source you wanted to refresh.

Display SharePoint list forms

SharePoint list forms are by default displayed embedded in an InfoPath Form Web Part on three web part pages that are used for viewing, adding, or editing SharePoint list data (also see the discussion section of recipe *1 Customize a SharePoint list form from within*

Chapter 1: SharePoint List Forms

SharePoint). While you can customize these web part pages to further suit your needs, you can also use the InfoPath Form Web Part on other pages within a SharePoint site to display a SharePoint list form. The recipes in this section show you how to do the latter.

12 Embed a SharePoint list form on a SharePoint page

Problem

You want to place the InfoPath form for a SharePoint list on a page in a SharePoint site so that users can easily fill out the form without having to navigate to the SharePoint list.

Solution

You can use an **InfoPath Form Web Part** to embed an InfoPath form on a web page (wiki page or web part page) in SharePoint.

To embed a SharePoint list form in an InfoPath Form Web Part on a SharePoint page:

1. In InfoPath, create a new SharePoint list form template or open an existing one as described in recipe *1 Customize a SharePoint list form from within SharePoint* or recipe *2 Customize a SharePoint list form from within InfoPath*, and publish it to SharePoint.

2. In SharePoint, navigate to the wiki page or web part page on which you want to embed the SharePoint list form, and click **Site Actions** ➤ **Edit Page**. Note: You can create a wiki page or a web part page just like any other object in SharePoint via **Site Actions** ➤ **More Options** or via **Site Actions** ➤ **View All Site Content** ➤ **Create**.

3. If you are adding the list form to a wiki page, click anywhere on the page where you want to embed the InfoPath form, and then click **Editing Tools** ➤ **Insert** ➤ **Web Parts** ➤ **Web Part**.

Figure 32. Inserting a web part on a SharePoint wiki page.

If you are adding the list form to a web part page, click **Add a Web Part** in any zone of the web part page.

35

Figure 33. Add a Web Part link in the Right Column zone of a SharePoint web part page.

4. At the top of the page, select **Forms** in the **Categories** list, select **InfoPath Form Web Part** in the **Web Parts** list, and click **Add**.

Figure 34. Selecting the InfoPath Form Web Part in SharePoint 2010.

5. Once the web part has been added to the page, you must configure it to display the SharePoint list form. On the web part, click on the text that says **Click here to open the tool pane**.

Figure 35. InfoPath Form Web Part on a SharePoint page.

6. On the web part tool pane on the right-hand side of the page, select the SharePoint list that is connected to the SharePoint list form you want to embed from the **List or Library** drop-down list box.

Chapter 1: SharePoint List Forms

7. On the web part tool pane, select the content type for which you want to display its SharePoint list form from the **Content Type** drop-down list box. The content types that have InfoPath forms associated with them, so for which you have customized their SharePoint list forms, are listed in the **Content Type** drop-down list box. So if a SharePoint list is associated with more than one content type that has a customized SharePoint list form, multiple content types should be listed in the drop-down list box.

8. If you want to display a read-only form for a list item when the form initially opens, you can select the **Display a read-only form (lists only)** check box on the web part tool pane. Users would then have to click the **Edit Item** button on the Ribbon before they can edit and save a list item. Leave this check box deselected for now; this should display an editable form for a list item as soon as the form opens.

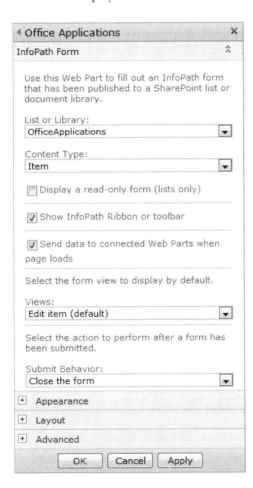

Figure 36. The options selected on the web part tool pane.

Note that you can choose what to do with the form once the list item has been saved by selecting either the **Close the form**, **Open a new form**, or **Leave the form open**

InfoPath 2010 Cookbook 2

option from the **Submit Behavior** drop-down list box on the web part tool pane. Also note that these options are not linked to the **After submit** options that you can select on the **Submit Options** dialog box in InfoPath Designer 2010, and that the embedded SharePoint list form behaves according to the web part settings.

9. On the web part tool pane, expand **Appearance** and change the **Title** for the web part to a suitable title (for example **Office Applications**).

10. On the web part tool pane, configure any other options you would like to configure, and then click **OK**.

11. If you are editing a wiki page, click **Page ➤ Edit ➤ Save & Close** on the Ribbon. If you are editing a web part page, click **Page ➤ Edit ➤ Stop Editing** on the Ribbon.

The InfoPath form should now be embedded in the web part on the page and you should be able to fill it out and save it.

Figure 37. The InfoPath form embedded on a SharePoint wiki page.

Discussion

In the solution described above you placed the InfoPath Form Web Part on a wiki page or web part page to be able to embed a SharePoint list form on a SharePoint web page. In general, wiki pages offer more flexibility where formatting is concerned than web part pages do, while web part pages have an array of fixed layout templates you can choose from to arrange web parts on a page.

13 Use an InfoPath form for a master/detail view on two linked SharePoint lists

Problem

You have two related SharePoint lists and you want to use the display form of the base SharePoint list to edit an item, but also display its related items from the related SharePoint list and access any of those items for editing.

Solution

You can add a filtered list for the related list to the **Display Form** web part page of the base SharePoint list to create master/detail functionality.

Suppose you have a base SharePoint list named **ShoeBrands** with the following contents:

Title
Saucony
Brooks
ASICS
Mizuno
New Balance

And a second SharePoint list named **RunningShoes** that is related to the **ShoeBrands** list through the **ShoeBrand** lookup column (linked to the **Title** column in the **ShoeBrands** list) and that has the following contents:

Title	ShoeBrand (Lookup in Title in ShoeBrands)
Wave Alchemy	Mizuno
Wave Renegade	Mizuno
GEL-Evolution	ASICS
GT-2150	ASICS
Ariel	Brooks
ProGrid Stabil CS	Saucony
New Balance 1012	New Balance

InfoPath 2010 Cookbook 2

Note:

> You can use the **ShoeBrandsList.stp** and **RunningShoesList.stp** files (which you can download from www.bizsupportonline.com) to load the data for the SharePoint lists into a SharePoint test environment (also see *Upload a list template to a List Template Gallery* in the Appendix). You will have to manually add the **ShoeBrand** lookup column to the **RunningShoes** list and then link the items from the two lists with each other.

To modify the **Display Form** web part page for the **ShoeBrands** SharePoint list to be able to create master/detail functionality between two linked SharePoint lists:

1. Customize the SharePoint list form for the **ShoeBrands** list as described in recipe *1 Customize a SharePoint list form from within SharePoint*.

2. In SharePoint, navigate to the **ShoeBrands** list, and select **List Tools** ➤ **List** ➤ **Customize List** ➤ **Form Web Parts** ➤ **(Item) Display Form**.

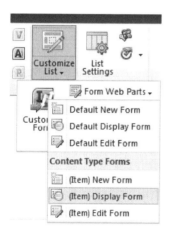

Figure 38. Selecting to edit the Display Form of a content type of a SharePoint list.

This should open the web part page for the **Display Form** in edit mode. Note that the text **(Item)** may vary in your case depending on the content types you have associated with the list. Also note that the SharePoint list form is embedded within an InfoPath Form Web Part on the web part page.

3. On the **Display Form** web part page, click **Add a Web Part**.

4. At the top of the page, select **Lists and Libraries** in the **Categories** list, select **RunningShoes** in the **Web Parts** list, and click **Add**. This should add the web part above the InfoPath Form Web Part for the **ShoeBrands** list that was already present on the page.

Chapter 1: SharePoint List Forms

5. Rearrange the web parts by dragging-and-dropping the **RunningShoes** web part to a location below the InfoPath Form Web Part for the **ShoeBrands** list.

6. Click the down arrow in the upper right-hand corner of the **RunningShoes** list web part, and select **Connections ▶ Get Filter Values From ▶ InfoPath Form Web Part**.

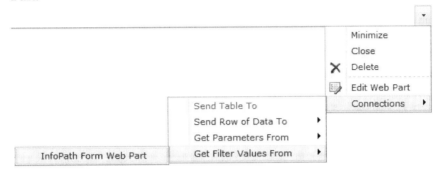

Figure 39. Initiating the configuration of the web part connection.

7. On the **Configure Connection** webpage dialog, leave **ID** selected in the **Provider Field Name** drop-down list box, select **ShoeBrand** from the **Consumer Field Name** drop-down list box, and click **Finish**.

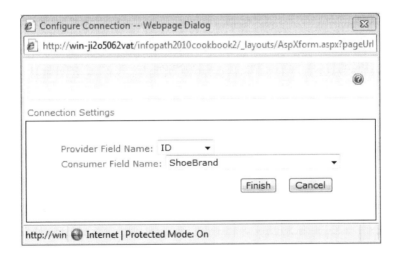

Figure 40. Configuring the web part filter connection in SharePoint 2010.

With this you have configured the **RunningShoes** list web part to be filtered on the **ID** of the item displayed in the **ShoeBrands** InfoPath Form Web Part.

8. Click **Page ▶ Edit ▶ Stop Editing** on the Ribbon to close the web part page.

In SharePoint, navigate to the **ShoeBrands** SharePoint list and click on an item in the list. When the display page opens, the running shoes corresponding to the brand you selected

InfoPath 2010 Cookbook 2

should be displayed below the form with which you can edit the information for the shoe brand.

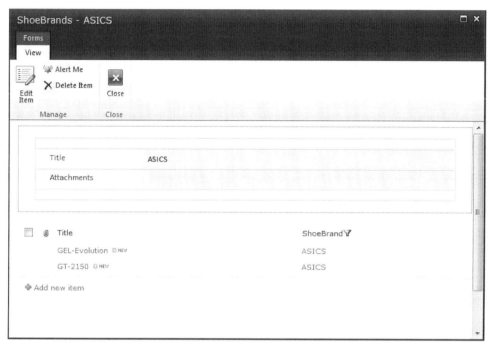

Figure 41. The Display Form for a SharePoint list item showing related items below the master view.

Click **Add new item** to add another running shoe for the brand. Enter the details for the new running shoe, ensure you relate the new running shoe to the running shoe brand you currently have open, and then save the item. The new running shoe should appear in the running shoes list below the form for the shoe brand. If you want to edit any details for the shoe brand itself, you can click **Edit Item** on the Ribbon. If you want to edit the details for an existing running shoe, you can click on the running shoe you want to edit to open its display page.

Discussion

Once you have customized a form for a SharePoint list, that form is embedded in an InfoPath Form Web Part on web part pages for the new, edit, and display pages of a SharePoint list item. You can open and edit these web part pages via the **Modify Form Web Parts** drop-down list box under the **Customize List** group on the **List** tab on the Ribbon. And once you are in edit mode for the web part page, you can treat this page like any other web part page by adding and removing web parts, customizing the web parts to suit your needs, and setting up web part connections.

In the solution described above, you modified the **Display Form** web part page to include an extra SharePoint list web part that used a filter to only display those items that were linked to the item displayed by the InfoPath form. A caveat of this solution is that when you click to add a new detail item, the drop-down list box that contains the names of the shoe brands on the **New Item** page for the detail item does not automatically select the correct shoe brand pertaining to the master item.

14 Use an InfoPath form as the detail view for items in a master SharePoint list

Problem

You customized the form of a SharePoint list. Because the SharePoint list contains many columns, you want to only display the **Title** column of the list in a web part on the left-hand side of a page and then when you select an item from this list, display the selected item's details in an InfoPath form on the right-hand side of the page.

Solution

You can create a SharePoint view for the SharePoint list to reduce the amount of columns being displayed, embed the SharePoint list in a SharePoint list web part, and then use web part connections to connect the SharePoint list web part to an InfoPath Form Web Part that displays the details for a list item.

Suppose you have a SharePoint list named **RunningShoesDetails** with the following contents:

Title	Brand	Model	Price
GEL-Foundation 9	ASICS	GEL-Foundation	$90.00
Adrenaline GTS 11	Brooks	Adrenaline GTS	$100.00
GEL-Foundation 8	ASICS	GEL-Foundation	$80.00
ProGrid Stabil CS 2	Saucony	ProGrid Stabil CS	$130.00
Wave Alchemy 10	Mizuno	Wave Alchemy	$110.00

Note:

> You can use the **RunningShoesDetailsList.stp** file (which you can download from www.bizsupportonline.com) to load the data for the SharePoint list into a SharePoint test environment (also see *Upload a list template to a List Template Gallery* in the Appendix).

InfoPath 2010 Cookbook 2

To use an InfoPath form as the detail view for items in a master SharePoint list on a page:

1. Customize the SharePoint list form for the **RunningShoesDetails** list as described in recipe *1 Customize a SharePoint list form from within SharePoint*.

2. In SharePoint, navigate to the **RunningShoesDetails** list, and click **List Tools ➤ List ➤ Manage Views ➤ Create View**.

3. On the **Create View** page, click **Standard View**.

4. Because you want to display only the titles of running shoes in a list on the left-hand side of a page, you must create a separate view for the **RunningShoesDetails** list that only contains the **Title** column and which can be selected to be used as the view for a list embedded in a web part. So on the **Create View** page, enter a **View Name** (for example **TitleOnlyView**), deselect all of the check boxes under the **Display** column except for the check box for the **Title** column, and click **OK**.

5. Click **Site Actions ➤ More Options**.

6. On the **Create** page, select **Page** under **Filter By**, select **Web Part Page**, and click **Create**.

7. On the **New Web Part Page** page, enter a name for the web part page (for example **RunningShoesDetails**), select the **Header, Left Column, Body** layout template, select the **Site Pages** document library to save the web part page in, and click **Create**.

8. When the new web part page opens, click **Add a Web Part** in the **Left Column** web part zone.

9. At the top of the page, select **Lists and Libraries** in the **Categories** list, select **RunningShoesDetails** in the **Web Parts** list, and click **Add**.

10. Click the down arrow in the upper right-hand corner of the **RunningShoesDetails** list web part, and select **Edit Web Part** from the drop-down menu that appears.

11. On the web part tool pane, select **TitleOnlyView** from the **Selected View** drop-down list box, click **OK** on the warning message box that appears, and then click **OK** to close the web part tool pane.

Chapter 1: SharePoint List Forms

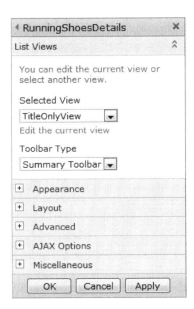

Figure 42. Selecting the view to use on the web part tool pane.

12. On the web part page, click **Add a Web Part** in the **Body** web part zone.

13. At the top of the page, select **Forms** in the **Categories** list, select **InfoPath Form Web Part** in the **Web Parts** list, and click **Add**.

14. Click the down arrow in the upper right-hand corner of the InfoPath Form Web Part you just added, and select **Connections ▶ Get Form From ▶ RunningShoesDetails** from the drop-down menu that appears.

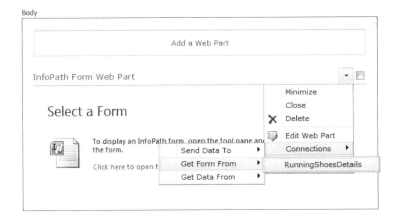

Figure 43. Configuring the InfoPath Form Web Part to use the customized list form.

45

With this you have set the InfoPath Form Web Part to use and display the **Edit Form** SharePoint list form of the **RunningShoesDetails** list.

15. Click **Page ➤ Edit ➤ Stop Editing** on the Ribbon to close the web part page.

In SharePoint, navigate to the **RunningShoesDetails** web part page. Click on an arrow in the **Select** column of any item in the SharePoint list web part. The details corresponding to the item you selected on the left should appear in the InfoPath Form Web Part on the right.

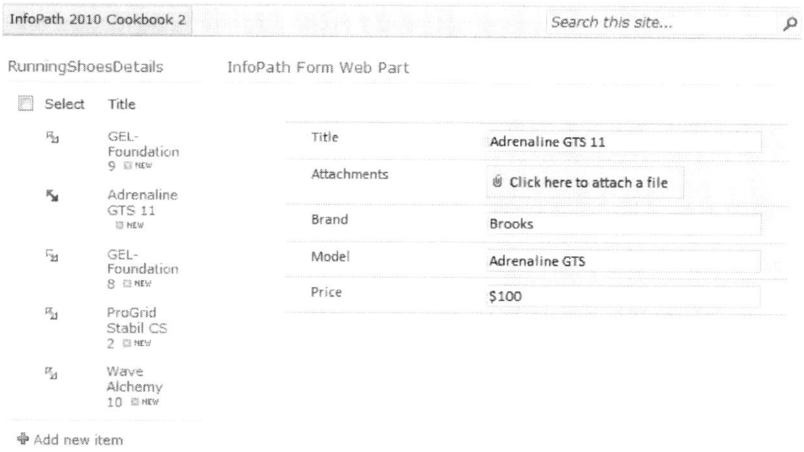

Figure 44. InfoPath Form Web Part connected to a SharePoint list web part through a list form.

Discussion

In the solution described above, you learned how to connect an InfoPath Form Web Part to a SharePoint list web part, so that the InfoPath Form Web Part could use the customized list form of the SharePoint list. Note that when you connect an InfoPath Form Web Part to use the form that has been defined on a SharePoint list, you will be unable to change the web part to use a different list or library through the web part tool pane unless you first disconnect the InfoPath Form Web Part from the current list through its web part connections by clicking on an existing selected connection (one that has a check mark in front of it) and confirming that you want to delete the connection.

An item is by default displayed as editable whenever you embed a SharePoint list form in an InfoPath Form Web Part. If you want an item to be displayed as read-only, you must select the **Display a read-only form (lists only)** check box on the web part tool pane of the InfoPath Form Web Part, or customize the SharePoint list form to include a read-only view, which you can then select from the **Views** drop-down list box on the web part tool pane when you configure the InfoPath Form Web Part. Note that if you choose to create and use a read-only view for a SharePoint list form to completely prevent users from editing data, you should not select the **Display a read-only form (lists only)** check box, since the latter would still allow users to click the **Edit Item** command on the Ribbon to initiate editing data.

Chapter 2: SharePoint Form Library Forms

Unlike SharePoint list forms, SharePoint form library forms are forms that are physically stored as XML files in a SharePoint form library. And while the process for designing and publishing SharePoint form library form templates is slightly more involved than that for desiging and publishing SharePoint list form templates, SharePoint form library form templates offer more flexibility where the availability of controls, the data structure of a form, and form deployment options are concerned.

Designing and publishing SharePoint form library form templates is a 3-step process:

1. You must design a browser-compatible form template in InfoPath Designer 2010.
2. Optionally, you must configure a submit data connection on the form template if you want to have forms submitted instead of saved.
3. You must publish the form template to a form library or as a site content type, and browser-enable the form template when you publish it.

The recipes in this chapter are intended to guide you through each one of these steps.

Design SharePoint form library form templates

While you can create SharePoint form library form templates that are not browser-compatible, this book provides instructions for forms that should be filled out through a browser via SharePoint. InfoPath offers two starter form templates you can use to create browser-compatible form templates that can be used for creating forms that are stored in SharePoint form libraries:

1. Blank Form
2. SharePoint Form Library

The main difference between these two form templates is that a **SharePoint Form Library** form template starts with a built-in layout on its default view, while a **Blank Form** template starts with a standard blank page layout on its default view. You can use the same types of controls on both form templates, both form templates have their compatibility set to **Web Browser Form**, and both form templates require InfoPath Forms Services, which is part of SharePoint Server (not SharePoint Foundation), to be able to fill out forms through a browser. If InfoPath Forms Services is not installed and/or has not been configured on SharePoint, InfoPath Filler 2010 must be installed locally on users' computers to be able to fill out web forms.

InfoPath also offers a non-browser-compatible form template named **Blank Form (InfoPath Filler)** you can use to create forms that can be stored in SharePoint form libraries, but which can only be filled out through InfoPath Filler 2010. Unlike the other two types of form templates, if you design a **Blank Form (InfoPath Filler)** template, you have the full range of controls that is available in InfoPath at your disposal. The only limitation with regards to SharePoint is that while users can navigate to a SharePoint form library in their browser to open a form, the form will always open in InfoPath Filler 2010 instead of the browser. This also means that all users who fill out forms based on this type of form template must have InfoPath Filler 2010 installed locally on their computers.

The following table lists the functionality offered by the three aforementioned types of form templates.

	SharePoint Form Library	Blank Form	Blank Form (InfoPath Filler)
Start with a built-in layout	✓		
Publish to SharePoint	✓	✓	✓
Fill out forms through a browser	✓	✓	
Users must install InfoPath locally			✓

While InfoPath Filler 2010 may or may not be required to fill out InfoPath forms depending on the form type, you must always install InfoPath Designer 2010 if you want to design and publish InfoPath form templates.

15 Create a SharePoint form library form template

Problem

You want to design an InfoPath form template that can be published to SharePoint and used to create forms that can be filled out through a browser and stored in a SharePoint form library.

Solution

You can use either the **SharePoint Form Library** template or the **Blank Form** template in InfoPath Designer 2010 to design and create forms that can be stored in a SharePoint form library.

To create a SharePoint form library form template in InfoPath Designer 2010:

1. Open InfoPath Designer 2010.

Chapter 2: SharePoint Form Library Forms

2. Click **File ▶ New** and then under the **Popular Form Templates** section, select either **SharePoint Form Library** or **Blank Form**, and click **Design Form**.

3. Design the form template to suit your needs by adding views, controls, and rules to the form template as described in the recipes in *InfoPath 2010 Cookbook: 101 Codeless Recipes for Beginners*.

Discussion

Form templates that are based on the **Blank Form** or **SharePoint Form Library** starter form templates are browser-compatible form templates that when saved in SharePoint, are saved as physical XML files in a SharePoint form library; not as SharePoint list items as is the case when you save a SharePoint list form.

The main difference between SharePoint list forms and SharePoint form library forms is that the schema (or Main data source) of a SharePoint list form depends on the columns of the content type associated with the underlying SharePoint list, while the schema of a SharePoint form library form is independent of the columns defined on a SharePoint form library. Therefore, while you cannot use nested or repeating data structures in a SharePoint list form, you have no such limitation with SharePoint form library forms. So SharePoint form library forms offer far more flexibility where defining the structure of your forms and the use of controls are concerned.

You can verify that the **Blank Form** and the **SharePoint Form Library** form templates are browser-compatible form templates by checking the **Form type** that is located under the **Compatibility** category on the **Form Options** dialog box (**File ▶ Info ▶ Form Options**) and which should be set to **Web Browser Form** or **Web Browser Form (InfoPath 2007)**. Note that the **Workflow Form** form type, which you will learn more about in Chapter 5, also creates browser-compatible form templates.

Browser-compatible form templates come with a couple of limitations when you compare them to InfoPath Filler forms. In addition to having fewer controls available in the **Controls** section on the Ribbon and task pane, you are also not able to display message boxes from browser forms. For example, when you use a **Close the form** action in a rule on a button, you cannot prompt a user to save a form when closing it.

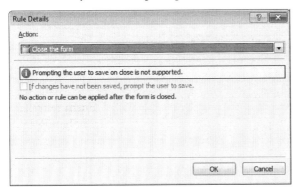

Figure 45. Prompting the user to save the form before closing it is not supported in browser forms.

User roles (**Data ➤ Roles ➤ User Roles**) are also not available in browser-compatible form templates, so if you want to simulate the use of user roles in web browser forms, you must make use of the User Profile Service to retrieve group membership and other profile information for a user, and then use this information in a form to provide user role functionality.

Because browser-compatible form templates are generally hosted and displayed through InfoPath Forms Services in SharePoint, you must ensure that whatever controls or business logic you add to a form template are supported by InfoPath Forms Services in SharePoint, because any incompatibilities at design time may result in the form template producing errors or the form template not being able to be browser-enabled on the server when you publish it.

There are a few things you can do to ensure that any browser-compatible form templates you design will work in InfoPath Forms Services and a web browser. The first thing is to use the **Design Checker** task pane to find any incompatibilities. You can open the **Design Checker** task pane via **File ➤ Info ➤ Design Checker**. Click **Refresh** on the **Design Checker** task pane to find incompatibilities, and if there are any issues, you should resolve them before publishing the form template.

Figure 46. The Design Checker task pane in InfoPath Designer 2010.

The second thing you can do is verify that the form template will work correctly on the server where you are going to publish it. For this you can select the **Verify on server** check box on the **Design Checker** task pane, and click **Refresh** to resolve any browser optimization issues you find. Note that for the **Verify on server** option of the **Design Checker** to work, you must specify the URL of the server to use on the **Form Options** dialog box. You can click **Change settings** on the **Design Checker** task pane to set the server URL.

Chapter 2: SharePoint Form Library Forms

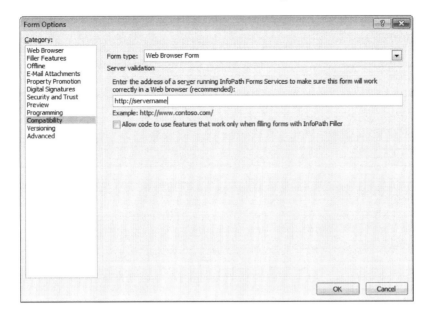

Figure 47. Setting the URL to validate the form on the server through the Form Options dialog box.

The final thing to note is that InfoPath offers some browser-specific features such as the **Browser forms** tab on the **Properties** dialog box of controls. This tab allows you to select when data should be sent back to the server.

Figure 48. Browser forms tab on the Properties dialog box of a control in InfoPath 2010.

The **Postback settings** are set by default on **Only when necessary for correct rendering of the form (recommended)**, but you could also choose **Never** or **Always**. If you choose **Always**, be aware that this could degrade the performance of forms.

In addition, InfoPath Forms Services allows a maximum of 75 postbacks per session by default, so a user could hit that target very quickly if you chose the **Always** postback setting. After the maximum amount of postbacks allowed is hit, the user will see the following message appear:

This session has exceeded the amount of allowable resources

If a user gets this error, you must either modify your form template in such a way to reduce the amount of unnecessary postbacks, or increase the maximum amount of postbacks for InfoPath Forms Services in SharePoint. Your administrator can change the maximum amount of postbacks in SharePoint Central Administration via **General Application Settings ➤ InfoPath Forms Services ➤ Configure InfoPath Forms Services ➤ Thresholds**.

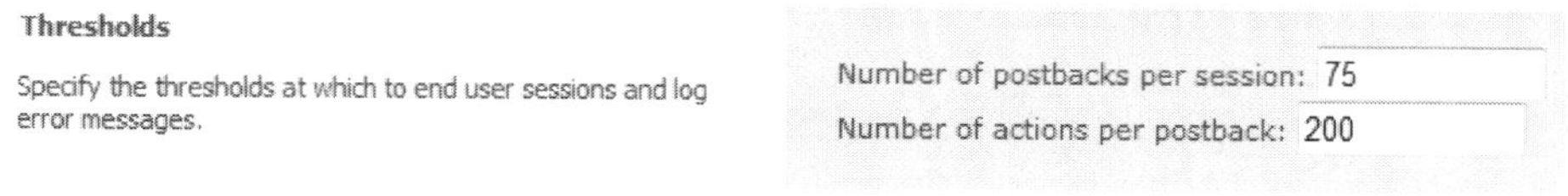

Thresholds
Specify the thresholds at which to end user sessions and log error messages.

Number of postbacks per session: 75
Number of actions per postback: 200

Figure 49. Configuring Thresholds for InfoPath Forms Services in SharePoint.

Another browser-specific feature is a button action called **Update Form**, which you can select from the **Action** drop-down list box on the **General** tab of the **Button Properties** dialog box or on the **Properties** tab of the Ribbon. When you select this action, the button is only shown on web browser forms (so not in InfoPath Filler 2010 or in preview mode in InfoPath Designer 2010).

You can use the **Update Form** button action to refresh data and send data to the server on demand. This helps improve performance of forms. For example, instead of selecting the **Always** postback setting as discussed earlier, you could place an **Update Form** button on a form, so that users can manually perform postbacks whenever they require form data to be refreshed or if form data fails to refresh despite having set the postback setting to **Always**. The **Update Form** action lines up user actions in a batch waiting to be processed, and then when the user clicks the button, these actions are sent to the server all at once, processed, and the data in the form refreshed. The **Update Form** button action works similar to the **Update** button that is located on a form's toolbar. This button is disabled by default, but you can enable it to appear on the toolbar through the **Form Options** dialog box (also see recipe *17 Hide or show toolbar buttons for a form*).

16 Create a form library and edit its form template

Problem

You want to edit an InfoPath form template that belongs to an existing SharePoint form library.

Chapter 2: SharePoint Form Library Forms

Solution

You can edit the template that is linked to the **Form** content type of the SharePoint form library. This will open the form template in InfoPath Designer 2010, so that you can modify it.

Before you can modify the form template of a form library, you must have a form library at your disposal. You can use an existing form library or create a new form library as the instructions in this recipe demonstrate. Before you create a form library, you must ensure you have the proper rights on the SharePoint site where you want to create the form library.

To manually create a SharePoint form library:

1. In SharePoint, navigate to the site on which you want to create a form library, and click **Site Actions** ➤ **More Options**.

Figure 50. More Options menu item on the Site Actions menu in SharePoint 2010.

2. On the **Create** page in the left menu under **Filter By**, click **Library**, and then in the right pane select **Form Library**.

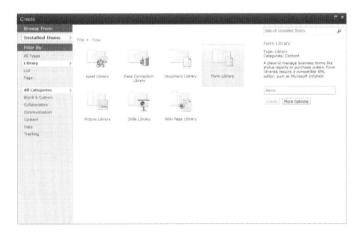

Figure 51. Page to create a Form Library in SharePoint 2010.

53

3. Enter a name for the form library in the **Name** text box, and then click **Create**.

SharePoint should create the form library and redirect you to the newly created form library.

To edit the form template of a form library:

1. In SharePoint, navigate to the form library for which you want to edit its form template, and click **Library Tools** ➤ **Library** ➤ **Settings** ➤ **Library Settings**.
2. On the **Form Library Settings** page under **General Settings**, click **Advanced settings**.
3. On the **Advanced Settings** page, under the **Document Template** section, you should see a **Template URL** listed, and beneath that an **Edit Template** link.

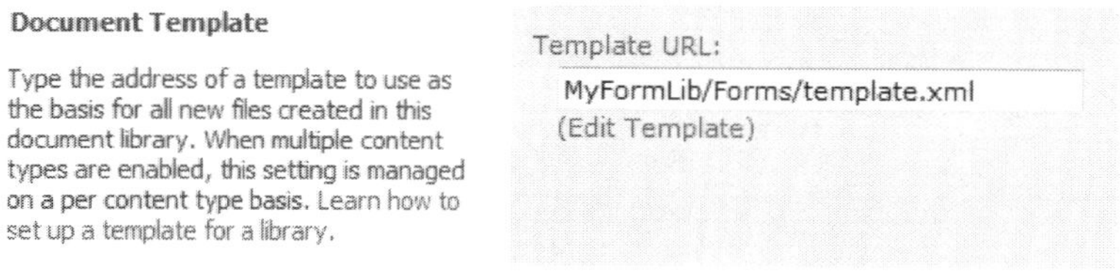

Document Template

Type the address of a template to use as the basis for all new files created in this document library. When multiple content types are enabled, this setting is managed on a per content type basis. Learn how to set up a template for a library.

Template URL:
MyFormLib/Forms/template.xml
(Edit Template)

Figure 52. Document Template section on the Form Library Settings page in SharePoint 2010.

Note: The **Edit Template** link is not present when management of content types is enabled.

4. Click **Edit Template** to open the form template in InfoPath Designer 2010 for editing.

You should now be able to edit the form template in InfoPath Designer 2010.

Discussion

A SharePoint form library, just like a document library, is a specialized type of list in SharePoint. One of the main differences between a form library and other types of lists is that a form library is designed to store InfoPath forms, i.e. XML files that contain processing instructions for InfoPath. And just like other lists and libraries in SharePoint, a form library can be associated with one or more content types, and is typically associated with content types that inherit from the **Form** content type. If you need background information about content types, refer to *Content types and site columns* in the Appendix.

While you can create a new form library from within InfoPath Designer 2010 when you publish a form template (see recipe *21 Publish a form template to a form library*), there may be instances when you may have to manually create a form library, for example if security restrictions have been put in place and you need to pre-create form libraries for other users who do not have the necessary permissions to create form libraries on a particular SharePoint site.

If you go back to the **Advanced Settings** page in SharePoint, you should see an URL such as the following listed in the **Template URL** text box:

Chapter 2: SharePoint Form Library Forms

```
FormLibraryName/Forms/template.xml
```

By default, when you create a new form library, SharePoint creates an XML file and places it in the **Forms** folder under the form library. You can download this file to view its contents by entering the template URL in the browser's address bar (ensure you prepend

```
http://servername/sitename/
```

to the URL when you enter it in the browser's address bar). The XML file you download should have contents similar to the following:

```
<?xml version="1.0" encoding="utf-8"?>
<!-- _lcid="1033" _version="14.0.4762" _dal="1" -->
<!-- _LocalBinding -->

<comment>Replace this file with a template file type supported by your Microsoft SharePoint Foundation-compatible forms editor</comment>
```

When you publish a form template from within InfoPath Designer 2010 to a SharePoint form library, the **template.xml** file is replaced by the form template and gets the name **template.xsn**. With this you now also know that if you see **template.xml** listed as the template URL, it is highly likely that a valid form template has yet to be published to the form library.

Click on **Edit Template** again to open the file in InfoPath Designer 2010. If you look at the **Quick Publish** button on the **Quick Access Toolbar** at the top of the screen, you should see that it is enabled, which also means that the form template you currently have open in InfoPath is already linked to a form library. You can verify this by going to the **File ➤ Info** tab and looking for the URL of the form library listed under **Publish your form**. So now you also know that you can click **Quick Publish** to quickly publish the form template back to the new form library you created. Typically, before you publish any form template to SharePoint, InfoPath will prompt you to save it locally on disk.

Tip:

> If you ever misplace a form template or have inherited a project from someone else who forgot to supply you with a form template, but you still have access to the form library the form template was published to, you can always try to recover a copy of the form template by using the **Edit Template** link in SharePoint to open the form template in InfoPath and then save it locally on disk again.

Another thing worth mentioning is the form type. If you click **File ➤ Info ➤ Form Options**, and then check the **Compatibility** section, you will see that the form template created is by default a **Web Browser Form** template, and thus suitable for filling out forms in the browser. So the form template that is created when you click **Edit Template** in SharePoint is equivalent to a **Blank Form** template in InfoPath.

When you created the form library in SharePoint, you only had to enter the name of the form library to be able to create it. But there are more options you could have selected and chosen to fill out when creating a form library. Had you clicked the **More Options** button on the **Create** page, the **Create** page would have displayed fields where you could have entered additional information such as a description for the form library, and where you could have selected settings such as whether to display the form library on the **Quick Launch** navigation or enabled versioning for the form library.

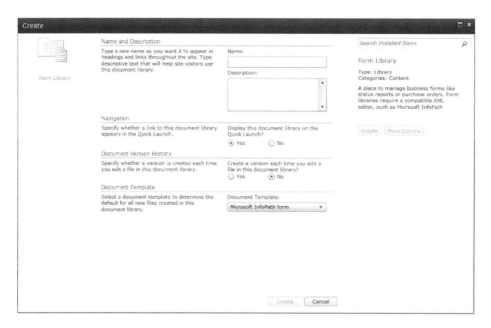

Figure 53. The page to create a form library in SharePoint 2010 after clicking More Options.

You are not required to select these options when creating a form library, because you can always change or set them afterwards via the **Form Library Settings** page.

In SharePoint, go back to the **Form Library Settings** page. The **Form Library Settings** page is an important page where you can manage all of the properties and settings for a form library, in addition to performing management tasks and setting permissions on the form library. Take a moment to familiarize yourself with all of the links on this page; the links are pretty self-explanatory. The most important links you will be working with throughout this book are:

- **General Settings ▶ Advanced settings** – Allows you to edit the form template for the form library if management of content types is disabled, enable management of content types on the form library (see recipe *27 Enable different types of forms to be created in one form library*), and set the opening behavior of forms.

- **Permissions and Management ▶ Delete this form library** – Allows you to delete a form library.

Chapter 2: SharePoint Form Library Forms

- **Permissions and Management ▶ Save form library as template** – Allows you to save a form library as a list template so that you can for example copy or move a form library or forms between sites (see recipe *41 Move a form library to another site*).

- **Permissions and Management ▶ Relink documents to this library** – Allows you to relink forms to form templates if the links have been broken for example if they were copied or moved (see recipe *42 Relink InfoPath forms in a form library*).

- **Columns ▶ Add from existing site columns** – Allows you to add site columns to the form library.

To go back to the form library, click on the form library name in the breadcrumb trail at the top of the page.

Figure 54. Using the breadcrumb trail to navigate back to the form library in SharePoint 2010.

Or if there is a link in the **Quick Launch** navigation on the left-hand side of the page, you can access the form library from there too. Once you are on the form library page, you will see a link that says **Add document**.

Figure 55. Add document link in a SharePoint form library.

If you click the **Add document** link, InfoPath Filler 2010 will open and prompt you to select a form template through the **Open With Form Template** dialog box.

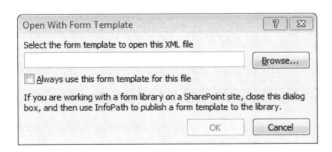

Figure 56. The Open With Form Template dialog box in InfoPath Filler 2010.

This is because while you have manually created a form library, the form library does not yet have a valid InfoPath form template it can use to create forms. Remember that it is currently still using an XML file as a document template; not an XSN file. So for the **Add** document link to work properly, you must first publish a form template to the form library from within InfoPath (also see recipe *21 Publish a form template to a form library*) or associate the form library with a content type that has an InfoPath form template as its document template (also see recipe *26 Publish a form template as a site content type* and recipe *27 Enable different types of forms to be created in one form library*) and make this content type the default content type for the form library (also see recipe *28 Change the default form template of a form library*). Do not worry if all this sounds foreign to you right now, because you will learn more about document templates of content types later in this chapter.

When you click **Add document** in a form library, SharePoint uses what is called the default content type that is set on the form library to create a document (see the discussion section of recipe *28 Change the default form template of a form library*). SharePoint allows you to configure more than one content type on lists and libraries. This is what enables you to use one form library to create more than one type of form (see recipe *27 Enable different types of forms to be created in one form library*). So if you have only configured one form template on a form library and have not enabled management of content types on the form library, you can click **Add document** to create a form that is based on that form template. But if you have configured a form library to use more than one form template through the use of multiple content types, you must click **Library Tools** ➤ **Documents** ➤ **New** ➤ **New Document** and then select the form template you want to use from the drop-down menu that appears. If you look at the **New Document** drop-down menu for a newly and manually created form library, you should only see one item listed.

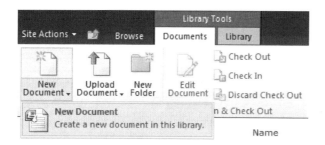

Figure 57. New Document button under the New group on the Documents tab in SharePoint 2010.

Configure forms for submit to a form library

Where browser forms in SharePoint are concerned, you can either save a form in a form library or submit it to a form library. When you save an InfoPath form in SharePoint, you are presented with a **Save As** page.

Chapter 2: SharePoint Form Library Forms

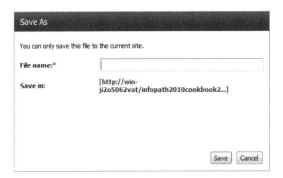

Figure 58. Save As page in SharePoint 2010.

You can then enter a name and click **Save** to save the form back to the form library; not to your local disk drive. If you want to save a copy locally, you must use the **Download a Copy** command on the Ribbon or on the context menu of a form when you select a form.

At this stage, you as a user are in control of the name you assign to the form. If a form with the same name already exists in the form library, you will be prompted with a message asking whether you want to replace the existing file or not; no error takes place.

Figure 59. Save As page prompting to replace an existing form in a form library.

One final thing to note is that once you save the form you must manually close it by clicking the **Close** button on the toolbar.

When you submit a form in SharePoint, the form can be submitted to a form library, but does not have to be. You could configure the form to be submitted to another destination such as for example an e-mail address or a web service. You could even configure the form to be submitted to multiple destinations at the same time, for example to a form library and a web service. The latter is not possible when saving a form.

Where the assigning of file names to forms is concerned, when submitting a form, users are not able to enter a name for the form (unless you provide them with an InfoPath form field in which they can enter a file name and then use this field in the submit data connection for the form library), so the form template designer is pretty much in control of configuring the form template to generate a unique file name when submitting a form

59

to a form library. Therefore, if you do not want users to enter their own names for forms saved in form libraries, you must configure those forms to be submitted instead of saved.

In addition, you must also ensure that form names you generate are unique or that you configure forms to be overwritten if their names already exist in a form library, otherwise users will be presented with a warning message that the form cannot be submitted because of an error. The exact message would say:

The form cannot be submitted to the specified SharePoint document library. The document library already contains a file with the same name. A value in the form may be used to specify the file name. If you know what that value is, modify it and try submitting the form again.

When a user receives this message, she is genuinely stuck and cannot proceed with submitting or saving the form, especially if you have disabled the save functionality by removing the button from the toolbar as described in recipe *17 Hide or show toolbar buttons for a form*.

And finally, where having to manually close a form after saving it is concerned, when you configure a form to be submitted, you can also configure it to be automatically closed, to remain open, or to have a new form be opened after the form has been submitted. These options are not available when you manually save a form.

So while there may be genuine scenarios in which you would want to give users total flexibility when saving forms, there may be times when you may want to take control of saving the forms or want to perform actions that are just not available when saving forms. In the latter cases, you may want to submit a form instead of save it.

17 Hide or show toolbar buttons for a form

Problem

You want to hide a few or all of the buttons that appear on the toolbar for forms or on the Ribbon when you have a form open in SharePoint.

Solution

You can hide toolbar buttons for a form by deselecting them through the **Form Options** dialog box in InfoPath.

To remove buttons from the toolbar or the context Ribbon for a form:

1. In InfoPath, open the form template for which you want to remove buttons from the toolbar, and click **File ➤ Info ➤ Form Options**.
2. On the **Form Options** dialog box, ensure **Web Browser** is selected in the **Category** list, and then deselect the check boxes for the commands corresponding to the buttons you want to remove (**Submit**, **Save**, **Save As**, **Close**, **Views**, **Print Preview**, or **Update**).

Chapter 2: SharePoint Form Library Forms

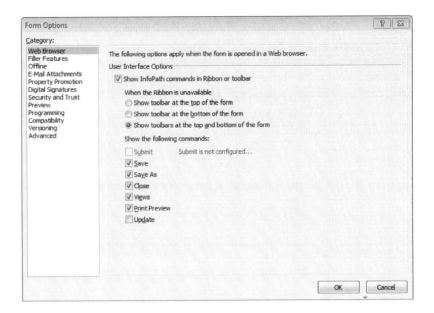

Figure 60. Form Options dialog box screen to hide or show toolbar buttons.

You could also hide the entire toolbar by deselecting the **Show InfoPath commands in Ribbon or toolbar** check box.

3. On the **Form Options** dialog box, click **OK**.

4. Publish the form template to a SharePoint form library as described in recipe *21 Publish a form template to a form library*.

In SharePoint, navigate to the form library where you published the form template and add a new form. When the form opens, verify that the buttons you deselected in InfoPath Designer 2010 are not present on the toolbar.

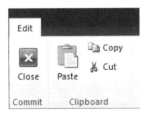

Figure 61. The Ribbon commands for a browser form with only the Close button enabled.

Discussion

When filling out a browser form in SharePoint, a toolbar with commands can be displayed at the top or bottom of the form if the Ribbon is not present. If the Ribbon is present, such commands are displayed on the Ribbon. Commands on the toolbar include:

61

Submit, **Save**, **Save As**, **Close**, **Views**, **Print Preview**, and **Update**. You can hide one or all of these commands through the **Form Options** dialog box in InfoPath.

Figure 62. The full array of toolbar buttons available for a browser form.

If you have configured a submit data connection for a form template, it makes sense not to allow users to manually save forms that are based on that form template. Therefore, you should consider removing the **Save** and **Save As** buttons from the toolbar if you are displaying the **Submit** button. Note that the check box for showing the **Submit** button is disabled by default and that you can only show or hide the **Submit** button after you have configured a submit data connection for the form template.

When submitting forms, you have the option to use either the **Submit** button on the toolbar or use a custom submit button on the form with a **Submit data** action rule set on it. While the **Submit** button on the toolbar is quick and easy to configure and show, you may want to use a custom submit button on a form for example if you want to conditionally show the submit button. You do not have much control over the **Submit** button in the toolbar other than either showing or hiding it by configuring this statically when you design the form template, and not dynamically when a form is being filled out. The latter is only possible when you use a custom submit button.

The **Current View** drop-down menu becomes available only if you have enabled the **Views** options on the **Form Options** dialog box and if the form template has more than one view.

The **Update** button is not enabled by default, but you can enable it to allow users to force sending data to the server and thereby refresh data in the form. You may want to use this button for example if you have disabled automatic postbacks on controls to minimize the amount of postbacks and therefore need a way to allow users to refresh form data on demand as was discussed in recipe *15 Create a SharePoint form library form template*.

18 Submit a form to a form library and then close it

Problem

You want to be able to submit a form to a form library and then close the form immediately afterwards.

Chapter 2: SharePoint Form Library Forms

Solution

You can add a form library submit connection to the form template, which by default has an action to close the form after it has been submitted.

To submit a form to a form library and then close it:

1. In InfoPath, create a new SharePoint form library form template or use an existing one.

2. Click **Data** ➤ **Submit Form** ➤ **Submit Options**.

3. On the **Submit Options** dialog box, select the **Allow users to submit this form** check box. This should enable the rest of the options on the dialog box.

4. On the **Submit Options** dialog box, leave the **Send form data to a single destination** option selected, and then select **SharePoint document library** from the drop-down list box below it. Note: If you want to submit the form to multiple destinations as you will do in recipe *19 Submit a form to a folder in a form library based on a condition* you must select to submit the form using either rules or code.

5. Because you have not yet configured a submit data connection for the form template, the drop-down list box below the label that says **Choose a data connection for submit** is disabled, so you must first configure a submit data connection. On the **Submit Options** dialog box, click **Add**.

6. On the **Data Connection Wizard**, enter the URL of the form library to which you want to submit the form. The URL should have the following format:

   ```
   http://servername/sitename/libraryname
   ```

   where **servername** is the name of the SharePoint server and **sitename** is the name of the site where a form library named **libraryname** is located. Ensure you do not append **/Forms** behind **libraryname**, so do not use an URL such as

   ```
   http://servername/sitename/libraryname/Forms
   ```

   because this would make the form submit to the **Forms** folder of the form library. The **Forms** folder is used to store ASP.NET pages for the form library as well as an InfoPath form template (if you published a form template directly to the form library). The **Forms** folder is invisible when you are looking at the contents of a form library in SharePoint, so any forms you submit to this folder will also remain invisible to users.

7. On the **Data Connection Wizard**, click the formula button behind the **File name** text field.

8. On the **Insert Formula** dialog box, construct a formula that generates a unique form name, such as for example:

   ```
   concat("Form - ", userName())
   ```

or

```
concat("Form - ", now())
```

and click **OK**. Note that the first formula uses the user's logon name and the second formula uses the current date and time to generate a file name for the form using the **concat** function. Also note that this would mean that when a form that uses the first formula is resubmitted, the form would have to be overwritten (unless another user resubmits the form), while a new name would automatically be generated for a form that uses the second formula every time the form is resubmitted.

The formula you choose to use depends largely on how you want to deal with the resubmission of existing forms. If you want a new file name to be generated for a form every time a form is submitted to the form library, you can construct a formula that is similar to the second formula using a date and time. If you want an existing form to be overwritten every time that form is resubmitted, you can use a formula that is similar to the first formula (the user name does not change every second, but it is unique to each user), but then you must also select the **Allow overwrite if file exists** check box on the **Data Connection Wizard**, so that the user is not shown an error message when the form is resubmitted and a form that has the same name already exists in the form library.

Note: If you want to allow a user to specify a file name upon submitting the form and not automatically generate a file name based on a date or a user name, you could add a text box control to the view of the form template and then use the **Insert Field or Group** button on the **Insert Formula** dialog box to select the field that is bound to the text box control in the formula that generates the file name for the submitted form. And if you do not want a user to be able to change the file name anymore after a form has already been submitted once before, you can add conditional formatting to the text box to disable the field (in which the file name is stored) if the value of the field is not blank, and then also select the **Allow overwrite if file exists** check box on the **Data Connection Wizard** to avoid getting an error message if the form already exists when it is resubmitted to the form library.

9. On the **Data Connection Wizard**, select the **Allow overwrite if file exists** check box depending on your scenario (see the discussion in the previous step), and click **Next**.

10. On the **Data Connection Wizard**, name the data connection **SubmitToFormLibrary**, and click **Finish**.

11. On the **Submit Options** dialog box, click **Advanced**, and ensure that **Close the form** is selected in the **After submit** drop-down list box. This is the default selection, so if you are setting up the form submit for the first time you do not have to check it.

12. On the **Submit Options** dialog box, click **OK**.

13. Preview the form.

When the form opens in InfoPath Filler 2010, fill out the form and then submit it. The form should close after you submit it. In SharePoint, navigate to the form library that you used for the submit data connection and verify that the form has indeed been submitted to the form library with the file name from the formula you used in step 8.

Discussion

There are two ways to submit a form to a form library:

1. Submit a form and generate a new name every time the form is submitted or resubmitted.
2. Submit a form with a specific name and use this name every time the form is resubmitted.

Depending on how you want to handle resubmitting of a form, you may have to select the **Allow overwrite if file exists** check box as described in step 8 of the solution described above.

You can extend the solution described above by removing the **Save**, **Save As**, and **Close** buttons from the toolbar as described in recipe *17 Hide or show toolbar buttons for a form*, because you do not really need to display them when you configure a form to be submitted and closed.

Users must be granted permissions to a site and to the form library on the site to be able to save or submit forms. You can use either the default permission levels in SharePoint or create custom permission levels to grant users permissions for saving or submitting forms. See *Add a custom permission level* in the Appendix for information on how to create a custom permission level.

The table below lists the permissions that are required to perform a particular action (view, add, edit, or delete) on a form in a form library.

	View	Add	Edit	Delete	Submit & Resubmit	Save
Site Permission						
Open	×	×	×	×	×	×
View Pages	×	×	×	×	×	×
List Permission						
View Items	×	×	×	×	×	×

	View	Add	Edit	Delete	Submit & Resubmit	Save
Open Items						×
Add Items		×			×	×
Edit Items			×		×	×
Delete Items				×		
Default Permission Level						
Limited Access (on site)	×	×	×	×	×	×
Read (on library)	×					
Contribute (on library)		×	×	×	×	×

Table 1. Permissions required for performing actions on forms in a form library.

By combining permissions listed above in custom permission levels, you can grant users only those permissions they really need to do their work. But if you do not want to give users the least amount of privileges required to save or submit forms, you can also use default SharePoint permission levels to grant users access as indicated in the table above.

For example, if a group of users only need to be able to submit or resubmit forms (add new or edit existing forms), but not delete forms, you can create a custom permission level that includes the **Open**, **View Pages**, **View Items**, **Add Items**, and **Edit Items** permissions, but excludes the **Delete Items** permission. You can then place the users in a group and use the custom permission level you created to grant the group permission on the form library. If you want users to only be able to submit a new form and not be able to edit and resubmit it afterwards, you must remove the **Edit Items** permission from the permission level.

Permissions not only affect the enabling and disabling of the **Add document** link and Ribbon commands of a form library, but they also affect the buttons that may become available on the toolbar for a form. For example, if a permission level does not contain the **Open Items** permission, the **Save** and **Save As** buttons will not be present on the Ribbon or toolbar of forms in a form library even if you selected the buttons to be shown from within InfoPath Designer 2010 (see recipe *17 Hide or show toolbar buttons for a form*). So if the buttons to save a form are missing and you are sure it is not because of the settings in the form template, double-check the permissions that have been granted to the user who cannot see the buttons.

19 Submit a form to a folder in a form library based on a condition

Problem

You have a form which you want to submit either to the root folder of a form library or to another folder in a form library based on whether a check box on the form has been selected.

Solution

You can add two submit connections to the form template and then use action rules to submit the form based on conditions.

To submit a form to a folder in a form library based on a condition:

1. In SharePoint, manually create a new form library as described in recipe *16 Create a form library and edit its form template* or navigate to an existing one.

2. If the form library does not contain any folders, click **Library Tools** ➤ **Documents** ➤ **New** ➤ **New Folder** to create a new folder.

3. On the **New Folder** page, enter a name for the new folder (for example **MyFolder**), and click **Save**.

4. In InfoPath, create a new SharePoint form library form template or use an existing one.

5. Add a **Check Box** control named **submitToSubfolder** to the view of the form template.

6. Click **Data** ➤ **Submit Form** ➤ **To SharePoint Library**.

7. On the **Data Connection Wizard**, enter the URL of the form library from step 1 in the **Document Library** text box. Tip: You can copy the URL from the browser's address bar and strip everything from the URL starting from **/Forms** until the end of the URL. A sample URL would look like the following:

   ```
   http://servername/sitename/formlibraryname
   ```

   where **servername** is the name of the SharePoint server and **sitename** is the name of the site where a form library named **formlibraryname** is located. Because the URL is pointing to the form library itself, this **Submit** data connection will be used to submit a form to the root folder of the form library.

8. On the **Data Connection Wizard**, click the formula button behind the **File name** text box.

9. On the **Insert Formula** dialog box, enter a formula that generates a unique name for the form submitted based on the current date and time. For example:

```
concat("Form - ", now())
```

and click **OK**. Refer to the short discussion in step 8 of recipe *18 Submit a form to a form library and then close it* to decide what kind of formula to use to generate the file name.

10. On the **Data Connection Wizard**, select the **Allow overwrite if file exists** check box, and click **Next**. This will allow users to resubmit and overwrite any forms they have previously submitted.

11. On the **Data Connection Wizard**, name the data connection **RootFolderSubmit**, leave the **Set as the default submit connection** check box selected, and click **Finish**.

12. Click **Data** ▶ **Submit Form** ▶ **To SharePoint Library**.

13. On the **Data Connection Wizard**, enter the URL of the **MyFolder** folder in the form library from step 3 in the **Document Library** text box. Tip: You can copy the URL from the browser's address bar and strip off everything in the URL from **/Forms** till the end of the URL and then append the name of the folder. For example:

```
http://servername/sitename/formlibraryname/MyFolder
```

where **servername** is the name of the SharePoint server, **sitename** is the name of the site where the form library is located, **formlibraryname** is the name of the form library, and **MyFolder** is the name of the folder in the form library. Because the URL is pointing to a folder, this **Submit** data connection will be used to submit a form to the **MyFolder** folder in the form library.

14. On the **Data Connection Wizard**, click the formula button behind the **File name** text box.

15. On the **Insert Formula** dialog box, enter a formula that generates a unique name for the form submitted based on the current date and time. For example:

```
concat("Form - ", now())
```

16. On the **Insert Formula** dialog box, click **OK**.

17. On the **Data Connection Wizard**, select the **Allow overwrite if file exists** check box, and click **Next**.

18. On the **Data Connection Wizard**, name the data connection **MyFolderSubmit**, leave the **Set as the default submit connection** check box deselected, and click **Finish**.

19. Click **Data** ▶ **Submit Form** ▶ **Submit Options**.

20. On the **Submit Options** dialog box, you should see the default submit connection already configured as the submit connection for the form. Because you want to

submit to either the root folder or another folder, and not only to the root folder of the form library, you must configure the form to be submitted to two destinations based on a condition. Therefore you must use rules, so select the **Perform custom action using Rules** option and click **OK**. This should open the **Rules** task pane for the **Form Submit** event.

21. On the **Rules** task pane, you should see an **Action** rule already added for the default submit connection. The action should say:

```
Submit using a data connection: RootFolderSubmit
```

You must now add a condition to this rule so that the action only runs if the **submitToSubfolder** check box is deselected. So on the **Rules** task pane, select **Rule 1**, click the text under **Condition**, and add a condition that says:

```
submitToSubfolder = FALSE
```

where **submitToSubfolder** is the field that is bound to the check box control.

22. On the **Rules** task pane, add a second **Action** rule with a **Condition** that says:

```
submitToSubfolder = TRUE
```

and an action that says:

```
Submit using a data connection: MyFolderSubmit
```

This action rule submits the form to the **MyFolder** folder in the form library if the **submitToSubfolder** check box has been selected.

23. Preview the form.

When the form opens in InfoPath Filler 2010, select the **submitToSubfolder** check box, and click **Submit**. In SharePoint, navigate to the form library where the form should have been submitted and click on the **MyFolder** folder in the form library. The folder should contain the form you just submitted. In InfoPath, preview the form again, leave the **submitToSubfolder** check box deselected, and click **Submit**. In SharePoint, navigate to the root folder of the form library. It should contain the form you just submitted.

Note: If you get a security notice when you try to submit the form from within InfoPath Filler 2010, temporarily give the form template full trust through **File ➤ Info ➤ Form Options ➤ Security and Trust ➤ Full Trust**. Remember to set the security level of the form back to **Domain** or **Automatically determine security level (recommended)** before you publish the form template, so that you are not forced to perform an administrator-approved deployment. The **Domain** security level should be enough for the form template to work properly in SharePoint. The fact that it requires **Full Trust** on your computer most likely has to do with the security settings on your computer.

Discussion

In the solution described above, you learned how to submit a form to one of multiple destinations based on a condition. To make this possible, you had to:

1. Create two submit data connections to submit the form to your destinations of choice.
2. Enable submitting the form to multiple destinations using rules.
3. Add action rules to submit the form to each destination based on a condition.

This technique of using rules to submit a form is not limited to form library submit connections, but can be used with any type and number of submit data connections. And whenever a scenario calls for submitting a form based on one or more conditions, you must use rules (or code) to submit that form.

20 Submit a form and switch to a 'Thank You' view

Problem

You want to be able to submit a form to a form library and then switch to a 'Thank You' view after the form is submitted.

Solution

You can submit the form using a rule with two actions that will first submit the form to a form library and then switch views.

To submit a form to a form library and then switch views to display a 'Thank You' view:

1. In InfoPath, create a new SharePoint form library form template or use an existing one.
2. Click **Page Design** ➤ **Views** ➤ **New View** to add a new view to the form template. Name the view **ThankYouView**.
3. Open the **View Properties** dialog box, and then on the **General** tab, deselect the **Show on the View menu when filling out this form** check box, and click **OK**.
4. Type a piece of text on the view, for example "Thank you for filling out this form".
5. Add a **Button** control to the **ThankYouView** view and label it **Close Form**.
6. Add an **Action** rule to the button with an action that says:

   ```
   Close this form: No Prompt
   ```

   This action rule closes the form without prompting the user to save any changes.

7. Click **Data** ➤ **Submit Form** ➤ **To SharePoint Library**.

Chapter 2: SharePoint Form Library Forms

8. On the **Data Connection Wizard**, enter the URL of the form library to which you want to submit the form. Tip: You can copy the URL from the browser's address bar and strip everything from the URL starting from **/Forms** until the end of the URL. A sample URL would look like the following:

   ```
   http://servername/sitename/formlibraryname
   ```

   where **servername** is the name of the SharePoint server and **sitename** is the name of the site where a form library named **formlibraryname** is located.

9. On the **Data Connection Wizard**, click the formula button behind the **File name** text field.

10. On the **Insert Formula** dialog box, construct a formula that would generate a unique form name, such as for example:

    ```
    concat("Form - ", userName())
    ```

    or

    ```
    concat("Form - ", now())
    ```

    and click **OK**. Refer to the short discussion in step 8 of recipe *18 Submit a form to a form library and then close it* to decide what kind of formula to use to generate the file name.

11. On the **Data Connection Wizard**, select the **Allow overwrite if file exists** check box depending on your scenario, and click **Next**.

12. On the **Data Connection Wizard**, name the data connection **SubmitToFormLibrary**, leave the **Set as the default submit connection** check box selected, and click **Finish**.

13. Now that you have created a submit connection, you must configure the submit options, so click **Data ▶ Submit Form ▶ Submit Options**.

14. On the **Submit Options** dialog box, the **Allow users to submit this form** check box should already be selected and **SharePoint document library** should be the selected item in the drop-down list box, because when you created the submit connection you indicated that it should be set as the default submit connection.

15. On the **Submit Options** dialog box, click **Advanced**, and then select **Leave the form open** from the **After submit** drop-down list box. Because you want to switch to the **ThankYouView** view after you submit the form and not close the form, you must change the submit options so that the form is left open after it has been submitted.

16. Because you want to submit the form and then switch to display the **ThankYouView** view, you must execute two actions upon submitting the form, so you must run an **Action** rule instead of just running one submit action by sending the form to the form library. So on the **Submit Options** dialog box, select the

Perform custom action using Rules option, and click **OK**. This should open the **Rules** task pane for the **Form Submit** event.

17. On the **Rules** task pane, there should already be one rule present with an action that submits the form to the form library. Add a second action to this rule to switch to the **ThankYouView** view. So the two actions on the rule should now say:

```
Submit using a data connection: SubmitToFormLibrary
Switch to view: ThankYouView
```

The first action submits the form to the form library, while the second action switches to display the **ThankYouView** view.

18. Preview the form.

When the form opens in InfoPath Filler 2010, fill out the form and then submit it. The form should remain open and switch to display the **ThankYouView** view. Click the **Close Form** button. The form should close.

Discussion

You can extend the solution described above by removing the **Save**, **Save As**, and **Close** buttons from the toolbar as described in recipe *17 Hide or show toolbar buttons for a form*, since users would be submitting the form by clicking on the **Submit** button on the toolbar and then closing the form using the **Close Form** button on the **ThankYouView** view.

Publish a form template to a form library

Once you are done designing a browser-compatible form template, you can publish it to SharePoint to make it available to users for creating forms from it. From within InfoPath Designer 2010, you can either publish user form templates to SharePoint or prepare form templates for publishing by an administrator. User form templates are form templates that can be published directly by users to either a SharePoint form library on a site or as a site content type. User form templates do not require Full Trust to run.

Throughout this book you will be creating user form templates, so will not go through the administrator-approved publishing process for InfoPath form templates.

21 Publish a form template to a form library

Problem

You designed a form template and want to publish it to a form library on a SharePoint site.

Chapter 2: SharePoint Form Library Forms

Solution

You can use the **Publishing Wizard** in InfoPath to publish a form template to a SharePoint form library.

To publish a form template to a SharePoint form library:

1. In InfoPath, create a new SharePoint form library form template or use an existing one.

2. Click **File** ➤ **Publish** ➤ **SharePoint Server** to start publishing the form template. InfoPath may prompt you to save the form template.

3. On the **Publishing Wizard**, enter the URL of the SharePoint site to which you want to publish the form template, and click **Next**.

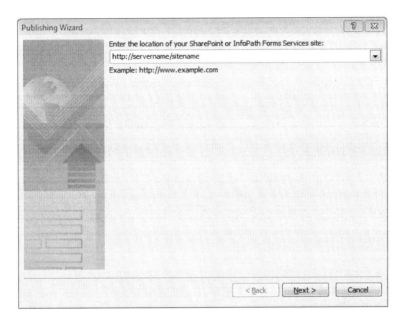

Figure 63. Entering a SharePoint site URL on the Publishing Wizard in InfoPath 2010.

4. On the **Publishing Wizard**, ensure **Form Library** is selected, ensure the **Enable this form to be filled out using a browser** check box is selected, and click **Next**.

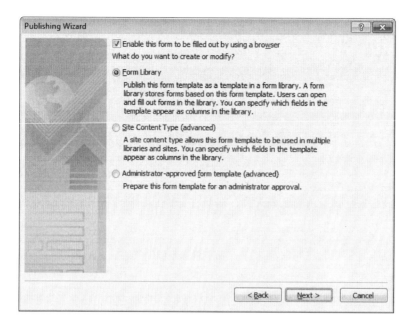

Figure 64. Selecting Form Library on the Publishing Wizard in InfoPath 2010.

5. On the **Publishing Wizard**, ensure the **Create a new form library** option is selected, and click **Next**.

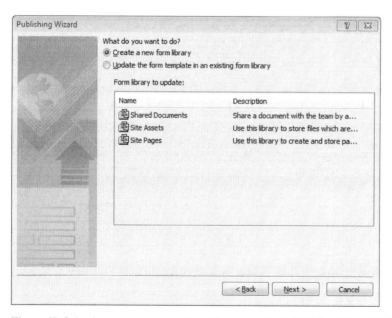

Figure 65. Selecting to create a new form library on the Publishing Wizard in InfoPath 2010.

Chapter 2: SharePoint Form Library Forms

Note: If you want to update an existing form library instead of create a new form library, you would have to select the **Update the form template in an existing form library** option instead, and then select an existing form library to update.

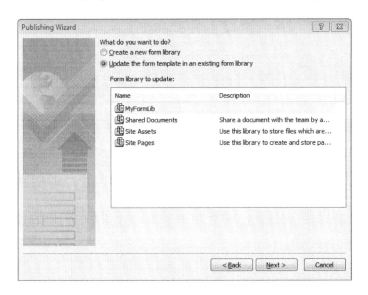

Figure 66. Selecting an existing form library to update on the Publishing Wizard.

6. Only if you are publishing a form template to a new form library: On the **Publishing Wizard**, enter a name for the new form library, and click **Next**.

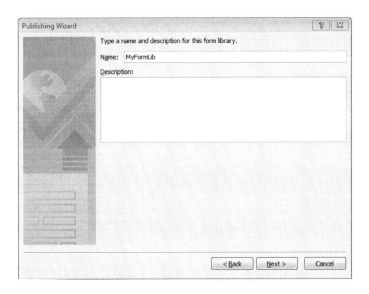

Figure 67. Entering a name for the new form library on the Publishing Wizard in InfoPath 2010.

75

7. The following screen is for adding fields you want to promote to SharePoint or Outlook as columns (see for example recipe *23 Promote form fields to columns of a form library*) and for adding fields you want to use as parameters in web part connections (see for example recipe *34 Master/detail across two forms linked through one field*).

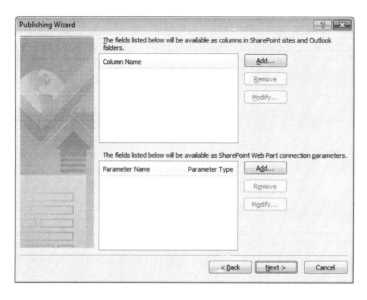

Figure 68. Publishing Wizard screen to promote fields and add parameters.

On the **Publishing Wizard**, click **Next**.

8. On the **Publishing Wizard**, click **Finish**.

In SharePoint, navigate to the SharePoint form library where you published the form template, and then click **Add document** to create and add an InfoPath form to the form library. An InfoPath form should open in the browser.

Tip:

> Always pay close attention to any warnings InfoPath displays on the very last screen of the **Publishing Wizard** after you click **Finish** and after the form template has been published, since this screen may contain additional information that could indicate that the form template was not successfully published or for example that the form cannot be filled out through a browser for one reason or another.

Chapter 2: SharePoint Form Library Forms

Discussion

When you publish a form template directly to a form library as described in the solution above, a **Form** list content type is automatically associated with the form library and the InfoPath form template you published becomes the document template of that content type. Publishing a form template directly to a form library always updates the default content type (the first content type listed) for the form library (also see recipe *28 Change the default form template of a form library*).

The following two steps are an absolute must when you want to publish an InfoPath form template that creates forms that can be filled out through a browser and stored in a form library:

1. You must have used one of the browser-compatible form templates (**SharePoint Form Library** or **Blank Form**) when creating the form template.
2. You must browser-enable the form template when publishing the form template to SharePoint through the **Publishing Wizard**.

If you skip one or both of these two steps, your InfoPath forms will fail to open in the browser. The terms browser-compatible and browser-enabled tend to confuse form template designers who are new to InfoPath, so let us first look at what they mean.

A form template that is browser-compatible is a form template that is suitable to create forms that can be displayed and filled out through a browser as well as through InfoPath Filler 2010. The way such form templates are identified is with an attribute called **runtimeCompatibility**, which is set to a value of **client server** in the manifest of the form template, where **client** refers to InfoPath Filler 2010 and **server** refers to SharePoint. When the **runtimeCompatibility** attribute has a value of **client**, the forms based on the form template can only be opened with InfoPath Filler 2010; not a browser. The value of the **runtimeCompatibility** attribute is set when you create a form template and when you change the form type through the **Form Options** dialog box.

A form template that is browser-enabled is a form template in which a 'switch' has been turned on that says that the form template has been enabled to create browser forms on a particular server. The way such form templates are identified is with an attribute called **browserEnable**, which is set to a value of **yes** in the manifest of the form template. The **browserEnable** attribute is created and the value of the attribute is set during the form template publishing process.

While you take care of making a form template browser-compatible in InfoPath Designer 2010, the SharePoint server you publish the form template to dictates whether the form template can or cannot be browser-enabled. Always remember that designing and publishing browser-compatible form templates to SharePoint is not something you only do in InfoPath Designer 2010. The publishing process requires teamwork between InfoPath and SharePoint. For example, if you are failing to successfully browser-enable or publish a form template to SharePoint, or if you are getting any other types of errors, you must ensure that everything is working and is configured properly both in InfoPath as well as in SharePoint. This includes ensuring that you have the required permissions on SharePoint to publish form templates.

On the second screen of the **Publishing Wizard**, there is a check box with the label **Enable this form to be filled out by using a browser**. You must select this check box to browser-enable a form template. If you do not see the check box, but instead see a message that says

This form template is browser-compatible, but it cannot be browser-enabled on the selected site

InfoPath Forms Services in SharePoint may not be configured to allow form templates to be browser-enabled.

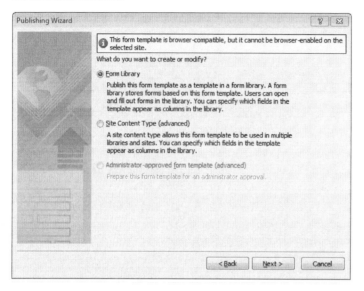

Figure 69. Browser-enable check box is missing from the Publishing Wizard in InfoPath Designer.

Before you can browser-enable a form template from within InfoPath Designer 2010, an administrator must configure the following setting for InfoPath Forms Services in SharePoint Central Administration under **General Application Settings ➤ InfoPath Forms Services ➤ Configure InfoPath Forms Services ➤ User Browser-enabled Form Templates**:

- **Allow users to browser-enable form templates** – This option is selected by default, but if an administrator deselects it, you will only be able to publish form templates that are not browser-enabled, so the forms will open in InfoPath Filler 2010 instead of the browser.

The **Allow users to browser-enable form templates** setting only gives form template designers the ability to publish browser-compatible form templates to SharePoint and browser-enable them during the publishing process. An administrator must also enable the following setting for InfoPath Forms Services in SharePoint Central Administration under **General Application Settings ➤ InfoPath Forms Services ➤ Configure InfoPath Forms Services ➤ User Browser-enabled Form Templates** for forms to open in a browser:

Chapter 2: SharePoint Form Library Forms

- **Render form templates that are browser-enabled by users** – This option is selected by default, but if an administrator deselects it, users will not be able to use a browser to fill out browser-enabled forms, so will be forced to use InfoPath Filler 2010 to open and fill out forms.

And finally, when you create a SharePoint form library, it is automatically set to open forms in the browser, but it can also be set to force forms to open in InfoPath Filler 2010. If a SharePoint form library has been set to open InfoPath forms in InfoPath Filler 2010, you can change it to open InfoPath forms in the browser by selecting either the **Open in the browser** option or the **Use the server default (Open in the browser)** option on the **Advanced Settings** page of the form library, which you can access through the library settings page.

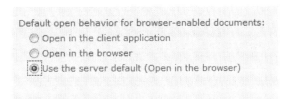

Figure 70. Opening Documents in the Browser setting on a SharePoint form library.

The following three publishing options are shown on the second screen of the **Publishing Wizard**:

1. **Form Library** – Select this option to publish the form template as the default content type of a SharePoint form library.

2. **Site Content Type (advanced)** – Select this option to publish the form template as a content type on the SharePoint site. You will have to perform extra steps afterwards to add the content type to one or more form libraries (also see recipe *26 Publish a form template as a site content type*), which is why the text **advanced** has been placed in brackets behind this option.

3. **Administrator-approved form template (advanced)** – Select this option to prepare the form template to be published by an administrator. You must use this option if the form template contains code and cannot be published as a sandbox solution, if the form template needs Full Trust to run, if the form template contains data connections that go across domains, or if the form template contains links to centrally managed data connections. Because this book teaches you how to create codeless form templates that do not access data across domains, access centrally managed data connections, or require Full Trust to run, you can ignore this option for now and choose one of the other two options.

The difference between the first and second publishing options is that publishing a form template to a form library creates or updates the default content type of that form library, while publishing a form template as a site content type creates a site content type that you must manually associate afterwards in SharePoint with one or more form libraries. So whether you publish a form template to a form library (as in the solution described above)

79

or as a site content type, in both cases a content type is updated or created in SharePoint, and both content types will have the form template you published set as their document template.

To be able to publish a form template to a SharePoint site, you must have the necessary permissions on the site if you are creating a new form library and on the form library as well if you are updating an existing form library. In SharePoint, you can assign a default permission level or create your own custom permission level for publishing InfoPath form templates and add only those permissions to it that are really required. The table below lists the permissions that must be granted to be able to publish a form template to a new form library, to an existing form library, or as a site content type.

	Publish to new form library	Publish to existing form library	Publish as site content type
Site Permission			
Open	×	×	×
View Pages	×	×	×
Browse Directories	×	×	×
Add and Customize Pages	×	×	×
List Permission			
Manage Lists	×	×	×
View Items	×	×	×
Open Items		×	×
Edit Items	×	×	×
Delete Items	×		
Default Permission Level			
Design (on site)	×		×
Contribute (on site)		×	
Design (on library)		×	

Table 2. Permissions required for publishing a form template.

22 Republish a form template

Problem

You previously published a form template to a form library and now want to republish it to a different form library.

Solution

You must use the **SharePoint Server** command on the **File ➤ Publish** tab and not the **Quick Publish** button if you want to republish a form template to a different location.

To republish a form template to the same location:

1. In InfoPath, open a previously published form template.
2. Click the small **Quick Publish** button on the **Quick Access Toolbar**, click **File ➤ Info ➤ Quick Publish**, or click **File ➤ Publish ➤ Quick Publish**.

Figure 71. Quick Publish button on the Quick Access Toolbar in InfoPath Designer 2010.

To republish a form template to a different location:

1. In InfoPath, open a previously published form template.
2. Click **File ➤ Publish ➤ SharePoint Server** and follow the instructions on the **Publishing Wizard** as described in recipe *21 Publish a form template to a form library*.

Discussion

When you successfully publish a form template for the first time, InfoPath stores the publish location and uses it as the default publish location the next time you republish the form template. This allows you to use the **Quick Publish** functionality in InfoPath to quickly publish a previously published form template to the same location. The **Quick Publish** command is meant to save you time, because you only have to click one button to republish the form template.

However, if you want to republish a form template to a different location (another form library or site content type), you must go through all of the steps of the **Publishing Wizard** again to republish the form template. After you have done this, InfoPath will once again use the new publish location for all subsequent publishing attempts when you click the **Quick Publish** button.

InfoPath 2010 Cookbook 2

Note:

> InfoPath does not allow you to change the publish location for certain types of form templates; not even through the **Publishing Wizard**. For example, the publish location of a SharePoint list form (see Chapter 1) or workflow form (see Chapter 5) are tightly bound to the list or workflow they belong to, so their form templates cannot be republished to a different list or workflow.

23 Promote form fields to columns of a form library

Problem

You want to be able to fill out a couple of fields in a form that is stored in a SharePoint form library through the datasheet or properties page in SharePoint, so without having to open the InfoPath form itself.

Solution

You can promote form fields to columns of a form library to enable data to be entered through a form library item's properties page.

To promote form fields to columns of a form library:

1. In InfoPath, create a new SharePoint form library form template or use an existing one.

2. Add a **Text Box** control named **fullName** to the view of the form template.

3. Start publishing the form template to a SharePoint form library as described in recipe *21 Publish a form template to a form library*, and when you reach the columns and parameters configuration screen of the **Publishing Wizard** as shown in the figure below, click **Add** on the right-hand side of the list box at the top of the screen.

Figure 72. Property promotion screen of the Publishing Wizard in InfoPath Designer 2010.

82

Chapter 2: SharePoint Form Library Forms

4. On the **Select a Field or Group** dialog box, select the field you want to promote (**fullName** in this case) from the **Field to display as column** tree view.

5. On the **Select a Field or Group** dialog box, select one of the following items from the **Site column group** drop-down list box:

    a. **(None: Create a new column in this library)**, if you want to create a new column in the form library, and then type the name of the column in the **Column name** text box.

    b. **(This form library)**, if you want to use an existing column in the form library, and then select the existing column from the **Column name** drop-down list box.

6. On the **Select a Field or Group** dialog box, select the **Allow users to edit data in this field by using a datasheet or properties page** check box, and click **OK**.

Figure 73. Dialog box to promote a form field to a column in SharePoint.

7. On the **Publishing Wizard**, click **Add** to add another field and go through steps 4 through 6 again, click **Modify** to change the settings for an existing promoted field and go through steps 4 through 6 again, click **Remove** to delete an existing promoted field, or click **Next** to continue publishing the form template.

In SharePoint, navigate to the form library where you published the form template. You should see the fields you promoted displayed as columns of the form library. Add a form to the form library if the library is empty. Open the properties page of the form by selecting the check box in front of the form and then clicking **Library Tools ➤ Documents ➤ Manage ➤ Edit Properties**; or hover over the form, click the drop-down arrow that appears on the right-hand side of the form's name, and select **Edit Properties** from the drop-down menu that appears.

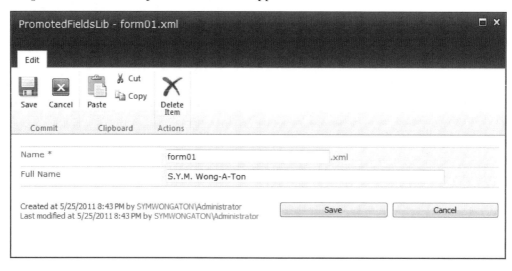

Figure 74. The properties page of an InfoPath form in SharePoint 2010.

You should be able to change the values of the fields you promoted on the properties page of the form. Change the value of a field you promoted and click **Save**. Then open the InfoPath form in the browser by clicking on its name in the form library and verify that the changes you made on the properties page have been written to the form itself.

Discussion

In the solution described above you learned how to promote an InfoPath field to a column of a form library in SharePoint. Promoting fields to columns of a SharePoint form library is a two-step process:

1. You must map the field you want to promote either to a new or an existing column.
2. You must select whether the field should be editable through the datasheet or properties page.

Note that when you publish a form template as a site content type (see recipe *26 Publish a form template as a site content type*), the options to promote a field are slightly different than the ones you get when you publish a form template to a form library. However, the process for property promotion remains the same, because promoting a field to a form library is equivalent to updating a column on the default content type of that form library. So in both cases you would be updating a content type.

When you publish a form template to a form library, you can promote a field to:

1. A new column of the form library.
2. An existing column of the form library.

3. An existing site column on the site.

When you publish a form template as a site content type, you can promote a field to:

1. An existing column of the content type.
2. A new site column on the site.
3. An existing site column on the site.

You can preconfigure the column names for fields you want to promote via the **Form Options** dialog box (**File ➤ Info ➤ Form Options ➤ Property Promotion**).

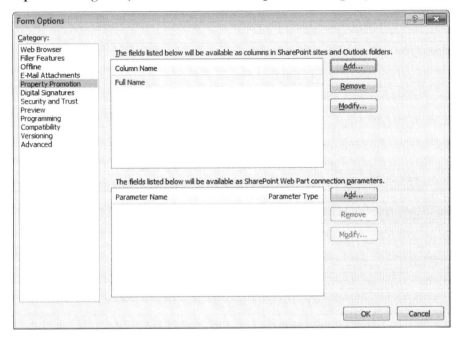

Figure 75. Property Promotion via the Form Options dialog box in InfoPath Designer 2010.

Any column names you enter through the **Form Options** dialog box will automatically be used to create new columns on the form library when you publish the form template to a form library, or to create new site columns on the site and content type when you publish the form template as a site content type. If you want to promote fields to existing columns in a form library, on a content type, or on a site, you must configure the property promotion through the **Publishing Wizard** when you publish the form template instead of through the **Form Options** dialog box.

Note that not all types of fields can be promoted. For example, fields bound to file attachment and picture controls that have the data type **Picture or File Attachment (base64)** cannot be promoted. However, you can promote a picture that has been included in the form template as a link, so which has the **Hyperlink (anyURI)** data type. The following table lists the matching of data types in InfoPath 2010 with data types in SharePoint 2010 when you promote a field.

Data Types in InfoPath 2010	Data Types in SharePoint 2010
Text (string)	Single line of text
Rich Text (XHTML)	Multiple lines of text (plain text)
Whole Number (integer)	Integer
Decimal (double)	Number
True/False (Boolean)	Yes/No
Hyperlink (anyURI)	Hyperlink or Picture
Date (date)	Date and Time
Time (time)	Date and Time
Date and Time (dateTime)	Date and Time
Picture or File Attachment (base64)	Not supported

Table 3. Property promotion data type matching between InfoPath 2010 and SharePoint 2010.

In addition, repeating groups and repeating fields are aggregated to display only one value when you promote them to columns in SharePoint. Repeating fields are single fields that are child nodes of a repeating group node, such as for example the fields in a repeating table; or repeating nodes that are child nodes of a single group node, such as for example the repeating fields of a multiple-selection list box.

InfoPath provides an extra **Function** drop-down list box containing the following functions you can choose from when promoting repeating fields:

- first
- last
- count
- merge
- sum
- average
- min
- max

From the list above, the **sum**, **average**, **min**, and **max** functions are displayed in the **Function** drop-down list box, only if the data type of a repeating field is a number (**Whole Number** or **Decimal**).

When you promote a repeating group (instead of a repeating field), you can select only the **count** function; all other functions become unavailable. The **count** function promotes the field as the total number of nodes in a group. When promoted to SharePoint, the data type assigned is **Integer**.

The **first** and **last** functions promote only the first or last nodes in a group of nodes. When promoted to SharePoint, the data type assigned depends on the data type of the node.

The **merge** function promotes a repeating field as a concatenation of all of the fields that have the same name and that repeat. When promoted to SharePoint, the data type assigned is **Multiple lines of text** and each field is displayed on a separate line in a concatenated string.

If you change the data type of a field in InfoPath after you publish the form template and after already having promoted that field once before, and then republish the form template, the data type will not change in SharePoint. To update the column in SharePoint, you must perform the following two actions in succession:

1. Remove the promoted field as described in recipe *25 Delete a column linked to a promoted field*. This will delete the column from the form library (or site content type) in SharePoint.

2. Republish the form template in InfoPath and add the promoted field with the modified data type back to the list of promoted fields either before or while publishing the form template. This will create a column with the new data type in SharePoint.

And finally, in the solution described above, you selected the **Allow users to edit data in this field by using a datasheet or properties page** check box, because you wanted to be able to edit data through the datasheet or properties page in SharePoint. If you only want to display data from forms in columns of a form library and not edit the data through the datasheet or properties page, you can leave this check box deselected when promoting fields.

24 Promote form fields to existing site columns

Problem

You want to promote fields on an InfoPath form to site columns, so that you are able to fill out a couple of fields on a form that is stored in the form library to which those same site columns have been added without having to open the form itself.

InfoPath 2010 Cookbook 2

Solution

You can promote form fields to site columns instead of list columns when you publish the form template.

To promote form fields to existing site columns:

1. In SharePoint, create new site columns as described in *Create a new site column* in the Appendix or select existing ones to use.

2. In InfoPath, create a new SharePoint form library form template or use an existing one.

3. Add a **Text Box** control named **fullName** to the view of the form template.

4. Start publishing the form template to a SharePoint form library (see recipe *21 Publish a form template to a form library*) or as a site content type (see recipe *26 Publish a form template as a site content type*), and when you reach the columns and parameters configuration screen of the **Publishing Wizard**, click **Add** on the right-hand side of the list box at the top of the screen.

5. On the **Select a Field or Group** dialog box, select a field you want to promote (**fullName** in this case) from the **Field to display as column** tree view.

6. On the **Select a Field or Group** dialog box, select the site column group that contains the site column you want to use from the **Site column group** drop-down list box. Typically if you created a site column as described in *Create a new site column* in the Appendix, the site column group to select would be **Custom Columns**.

7. On the **Select a Field or Group** dialog box, select the site column you want to promote the field to from the **Column name** drop-down list box. When selecting a site column you must ensure that the data type of the field you want to promote matches that of the site column you select. For example, you cannot promote a date field to a column that only accepts Boolean values (see the data type matching table in the discussion section of recipe *23 Promote form fields to columns of a form library* for more details). If you try to promote fields to columns that do not have matching data types, InfoPath will display the following warning message:

   The data type of the selected site column does not match the data type of the field to promote.

8. On the **Select a Field or Group** dialog box, select the **Allow users to edit data in this field by using a datasheet or properties page** check box, and click **OK**.

9. On the **Publishing Wizard**, click **Add** to add another field and go through steps 5 through 8 again, click **Modify** to change the settings for an existing promoted field and go through steps 5 through 8 again, click **Remove** to delete an existing promoted field, or click **Next** to continue publishing the form template.

In SharePoint, navigate to the form library associated with the content type for the form template you published. You should see the fields you promoted displayed as columns of

Chapter 2: SharePoint Form Library Forms

the form library. Add a form to the form library if the library is empty. Open the properties page of the form by selecting the check box in front of the form and then clicking **Library Tools** ➤ **Documents** ➤ **Manage** ➤ **Edit Properties**; or hover over the form, click the drop-down arrow that appears on the right-hand side of the form's name, and select **Edit Properties** from the drop-down menu that appears. You should be able to change the values of the fields you promoted on the properties page of the form. Change the value of a field you promoted and click **Save**. Then open the InfoPath form in the browser by clicking on its name and verify that the changes you made on the properties page have been written to the form itself.

Discussion

In the solution described above you learned how to promote an InfoPath field to an existing site column in SharePoint. Because you cannot preconfigure property promotion of fields to existing site columns through the **Form Options** dialog box, you must use the **Publishing Wizard** when promoting form fields to existing site columns. And once you select a site column to promote a field to, you cannot reselect that same site column to promote another field to it, because InfoPath removes it from the list of site columns you can select. In addition, if you promote a field to a site column that does not already exist on a form library (if you are publishing the form template to a form library) or a content type (if you are publishing the form template as a site content type), that site column will be added to the form library or content type when you publish the form template.

25   Delete a column linked to a promoted field

Problem

You promoted an InfoPath form field to a column in SharePoint, and now you want to delete this column from the form library or content type in SharePoint.

Solution

You must remove the field from the list of promoted fields in InfoPath and republish the form template to delete the column from the form library or content type in SharePoint.

To delete a column linked to a promoted field:

1. In InfoPath, open the form template you published to the form library or as a site content type, and used to promote the field to a column in SharePoint.
2. Click **File** ➤ **Info** ➤ **Form Options**.
3. On the **Form Options** dialog box under **Category**, select **Property Promotion**.
4. Select the promoted field you want to delete in the list box at the top of the dialog box, click **Remove**, and then click **OK**.

5. Click **Quick Publish** on the **Quick Access Toolbar** at the top of InfoPath Designer 2010 to republish the form template.

In SharePoint, navigate to the form library that had the column for the promoted field assigned to it and check whether the column has been deleted. If you published the form template as a site content type, navigate to the **Site Content Types** page, click on the content type, and verify that the column has been removed.

Discussion

In the solution described above you deleted a column for a promoted field from within InfoPath Designer 2010. This action not only deletes the column from the form library or site content type in SharePoint, but also correctly updates the InfoPath form template linked to the form library or content type. And while you used the **Form Options** dialog box and **Quick Publish** option to delete a column, you could have also gone through the steps of the **Publishing Wizard** again to remove the promoted field and then republish the form template.

Note:

> Removing promoted fields from a form library or content type does not affect the actual data stored within existing InfoPath forms in the form library or forms that are based on the content type. This action only removes public access to InfoPath form fields. However, you should still be able to edit the values of form fields by opening the InfoPath form, unless you deleted the fields from the form template itself.

Publish a form template as a site content type

26 Publish a form template as a site content type

Problem

You have an InfoPath form template which you want to use to create InfoPath forms that are stored in multiple SharePoint form libraries on sites in a site collection.

Solution

You can publish the InfoPath form template as a site content type to SharePoint so that you can use it across multiple form libraries.

To publish an InfoPath form template as a site content type:

Chapter 2: SharePoint Form Library Forms

1. In InfoPath, create a new SharePoint form library form template or use an existing one.

2. Click **File ➤ Publish ➤ SharePoint Server** to start publishing the form template. InfoPath may prompt you to save the form template.

3. On the **Publishing Wizard**, enter the URL of the SharePoint site to which you want to publish the form template, and click **Next**. Remember to take the scope of content types (also see the discussion section of *Create a new site content type* in the Appendix) into consideration when choosing the SharePoint site on which the content type should reside.

4. On the **Publishing Wizard**, select **Site Content Type (advanced)**, and click **Next**.

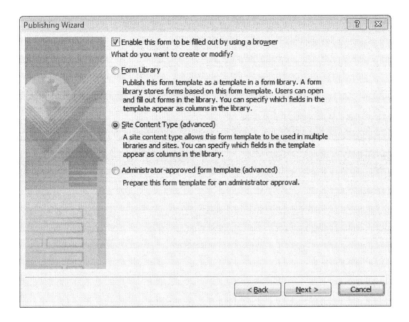

Figure 76. Selecting to publish a form template as a site content type in InfoPath 2010.

5. On the **Publishing Wizard**, leave the **Create a new content type** option selected, leave **Form** selected as the content type to base the new content type on, and click **Next**. Note that if you were republishing the form template or wanted to update the document template of an existing content type, you would have to select the **Update an existing site content type** option instead of the **Create a new content type** option.

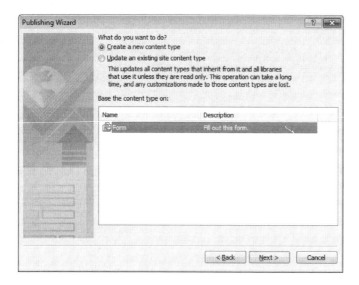

Figure 77. Creating a new content type based on the Form parent content type.

6. On the **Publishing Wizard**, enter a name for the content type, and click **Next**.

7. On the **Publishing Wizard**, click **Browse**.

8. On the **Browse** dialog box, browse to and select a SharePoint document library (on the site to which the form template is being published) in which you want to store the form template, enter a **File name** for the form template, and then click **Save**.

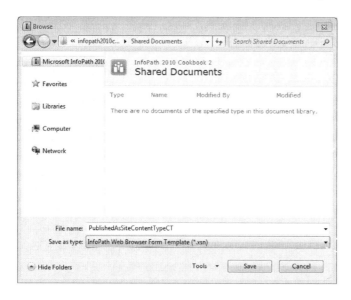

Figure 78. Saving the content type in a SharePoint document library.

Chapter 2: SharePoint Form Library Forms

Note that the location you choose for the form template or the form template itself (if you are using item-level permissions) must be accessible (**View Only** permission should be enough) to users who need to fill out forms that are based on that form template otherwise they will see the error

There has been an error while loading the form.

when they try to fill out a form.

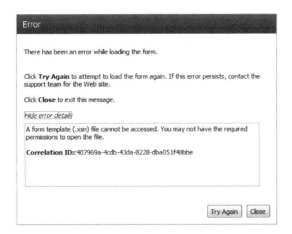

Figure 79. Form template file cannot be accessed error.

9. On the **Publishing Wizard**, click **Next**.

10. On the **Publishing Wizard**, promote any fields you want to promote as described in recipe *23 Promote form fields to columns of a form library* or recipe *24 Promote form fields to existing site columns*, and click **Next**.

11. On the **Publishing Wizard**, click **Publish**.

12. On the **Publishing Wizard**, click **Close**.

The form template should have been published as a site content type on the SharePoint site you specified through the **Publishing Wizard**. In SharePoint, navigate to the site where you published the form template. Click **Site Actions** ➤ **Site Settings**, and then on the **Site Settings** page under **Galleries**, click **Site content types**. On the **Site Content Types** page, verify that the new site content type is listed under the **Microsoft InfoPath** group. Now the form template is ready to be added as a content type to form libraries (see recipe *27 Enable different types of forms to be created in one form library*).

Discussion

In the solution described above, you published a form template as a site content type. When you publish a form template as a site content type, a site content type is created on the site you specified through the **Publishing Wizard** and the InfoPath form template you published becomes the document template of that content type. You can publish an

InfoPath 2010 Cookbook 2

InfoPath form template as a site content type whenever you want to reuse a form template across several SharePoint form libraries that reside on the same site or on a child site of the site to which you publish the form template. After you publish a form template as a site content type, it is not ready for use yet. The next step would be to add the content type to a SharePoint form library as described in recipe *27 Enable different types of forms to be created in one form library*.

When you publish a form template as a site content type, you do not need permissions to create or access a form library, but you do need permissions to:

1. Access the SharePoint site on which you want to publish the form template.
2. Query the content types on the site and create or update a content type.

In terms of SharePoint permissions required to do the aforementioned, you must have either the **Design** permission on the site or you can create a custom permission level that includes the permissions listed in Table 2 in the discussion section of recipe *21 Publish a form template to a form library*.

27 Enable different types of forms to be created in one form library

Problem

You want users to be able to select from one of several form templates that can used to create different types of InfoPath forms in one form library.

Solution

You can enable management of content types on a form library and then add all of the content types for the form templates, which you want users to use to create different types of InfoPath forms in the form library, to the form library.

To enable different types of InfoPath forms to be created in one SharePoint form library:

1. In InfoPath, create a SharePoint form library form template or use an existing one, and publish it as a site content type (see recipe *26 Publish a form template as a site content type*).
2. In SharePoint, navigate to the form library for which you want to enable one or more form templates to be used, and click **Library Tools** ➤ **Library** ➤ **Settings** ➤ **Library Settings**.
3. On the **Form Library Settings** page, you must enable management of content types to be able to add content types to the form library. So under **General Settings**, click **Advanced settings**.
4. On the **Advanced Settings** page, select the **Yes** option for **Allow management of content types**, and click **OK**.

Chapter 2: SharePoint Form Library Forms

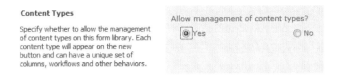

Figure 80. Content Types section on the Form Library Settings page in SharePoint 2010.

5. Back on the **Form Library Settings** page, you should now see a **Content Types** section present on the page.

Figure 81. Content Types section on the Form Library Settings page.

Click the **Add from existing site content types** link under the **Content Types** section to add an existing site content type to the form library.

6. On the **Add Content Types** page, select **Microsoft InfoPath** from the **Select site content types from** drop-down list box, select the content type you want to add to the form library (this would be the content type pertaining to the form template you published as a site content type) from the **Available Site Content Types** list box, click **Add** to add it to the **Content types to add** list box, and click **OK**. Note that when you publish a form template as a site content type from within InfoPath Designer 2010, that content type is placed under the **Microsoft InfoPath** content types group in SharePoint.

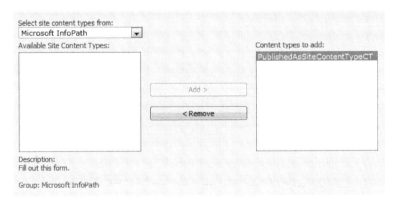

Figure 82. Selecting a content type to add to a form library in SharePoint 2010.

95

InfoPath 2010 Cookbook 2

The content type for the InfoPath form template should now appear under the **Content Types** section on the **Form Library Settings** page.

Content Type	Visible on New Button	Default Content Type
Form	✓	✓
PublishedAsSiteContentTypeCT	✓	

Figure 83. Content Types section after the content type has been added to the form library.

And when you go to the form library and select **Library Tools ▶ Documents ▶ New ▶ New Document**, the content type should be listed as a menu item on the **New Document** button drop-down menu.

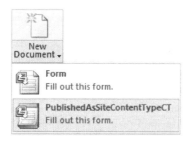

Figure 84. Content type listed under the New Document button of the form library.

Discussion

In the solution described above, you learned how to add one site content type to a form library. That site content type was linked to a particular form template you published as a site content type to SharePoint. If you want a form library to allow users to choose from several InfoPath form templates with which they can create different types of forms, you must repeat step 5 to add the site content types that are linked to the form templates you want to add to the form library. Note that in step 6 you can select multiple content types at once by holding the **Ctrl** key pressed down on your keyboard while you click to select the content types you want to add.

Go back to the **Advanced Settings** page of the form library. There you may have noticed that when you enabled management of content types, the **Edit Template** link disappeared and the **Template URL** text box was disabled. This means that you cannot edit the form template anymore from this location as you did in recipe *16 Create a form library and edit its form template* and that you need to go elsewhere if you want to access it.

Chapter 2: SharePoint Form Library Forms

Go back to the **Form Library Settings** page. Under the **Content Types** section, you should see a content type called **Form** listed with two check marks: One for **Visible on New Button** and another one for **Default Content Type**. If a content type has a check mark in the **Default Content Type** column, that content type is the content type that is used to create forms when you click the **Add document** link in the form library as well as the content type that is listed as first on the **New Document** button drop-down menu on the Ribbon. So when you have more than one content type listed under the **Content Types** section, you can set another content type to be the default content type (also see recipe *28 Change the default form template of a form library*), and therefore also set which form template is used to create forms whenever a user clicks **Add document** in the form library.

So the default content type can be defined as the first content type in the list of content types on a list or library and as the content type that SharePoint uses to create a document in a document library when you click **Add document**. The default content type is also the content type that SharePoint uses if you do not explicitly choose a specific content type to use when creating documents in a document or form library that supports multiple content types.

The **Visible on New Button** refers to the **New Document** button on the Ribbon. You can choose which content types to and not to show on the drop-down menu of the **New Document** button by either enabling or disabling their visibility. You can enable or disable visibility of a content type on the menu by clicking the **Change new button order and default content type** link under the **Content Types** section, and then selecting or deselecting the **Visible** check box for the content types which you want to show or hide on the **New Document** button drop-down menu.

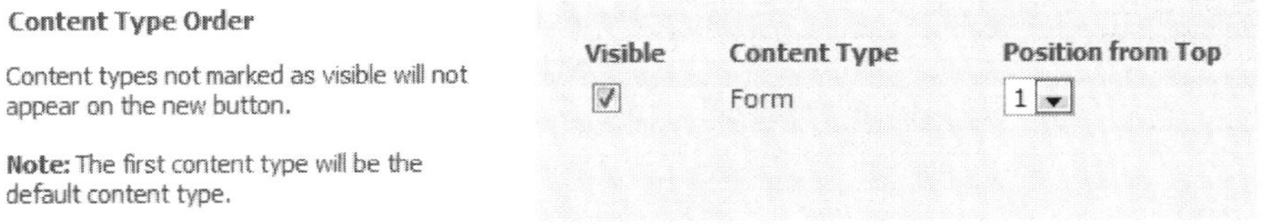

Figure 85. Setting the visibility and order of content types in SharePoint 2010.

If you click on **Form** under **Content Types**, you should be taken to the details page of the **Form** content type. At the top of the page, you should see a title that says: **List Content Type Information**.

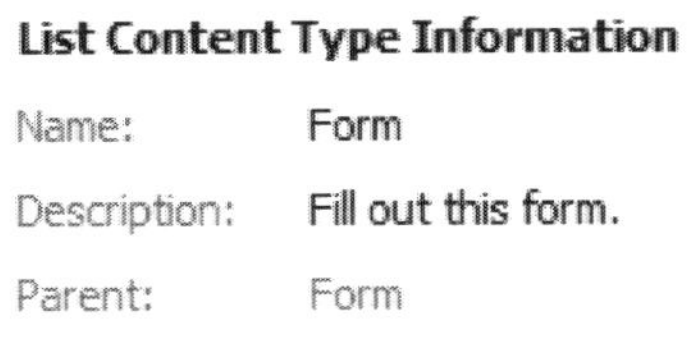

Figure 86. List Content Type Information section for a Form list content type in SharePoint.

Under **List Content Type Information**, you should also see that **Form** inherits from a parent content type named **Form**. If you click on **Form**, you should be taken to the details page of the parent content type. If you now look at the title, it should say **Site Content Type Information** instead of **List Content Type Information**.

Site Content Type Information

Name:	Form
Description:	Fill out this form.
Parent:	Document
Group:	Document Content Types

Figure 87. Site Content Type Information section for a Form site content type in SharePoint.

So this **Form** content type is a site content type (you can read more about the difference between list and site content types in *Content types and site columns* in the Appendix) and one of the default content types that comes with SharePoint. This **Form** content type inherits from the **Document** parent content type. You can keep clicking on parent content types until you reach the root parent content type, which is the **System** content type. So as you can see, content types follow an inheritance hierarchy.

Go back to the details page of the **Form** list content type, and under **Settings**, click **Advanced settings**. You should see the **Edit Template** link that was previously available on the **Advanced settings** page of the form library. From this location you could edit the form template as you did in recipe *16 Create a form library and edit its form template*. So while you cannot access the form template anymore from the **Advanced Settings** page of the form library, you can still edit it from within SharePoint by clicking on the **Edit Template** link on the **Advanced Settings** page of the **Form** list content type. This method of starting the editing process of form templates does not only apply to the **Form** content type, but to any content type you have added to the form library.

In summary: When you publish a form template as described in recipe *21 Publish a form template to a form library*, a **Form** list content type is automatically created on the form library and the InfoPath form template you published becomes the document template of this content type. The **Form** list content type is not visible on the settings page of the form library unless you enable management of content types on the form library. Once management of content types has been enabled, you can edit the form template linked to the **Form** list content type from the **Advanced settings** page of the content type instead of from the **Advanced settings** page of the form library. This technique of starting the editing process for form templates linked to content types can be applied to any content type that has been added to the form library, so also for form templates that were published as site content types as described in recipe *26 Publish a form template as a site content type* and then manually added to the form library as described in this recipe.

28 Change the default form template of a form library

Problem

You have added the content types for one or more form templates to a SharePoint form library and want to make one of those content types the default content type of the form library.

Solution

You can set a form template to be the default template that is used by a form library after you have added one or more content types to the form library, and then use the **Form Library Settings** page to make any of those content types that are linked to the form template you want to make the default form template for the form library, the default content type of the form library.

To make a form template the default form template of a SharePoint form library:

1. In InfoPath, create a SharePoint form library form template or use an existing one, and publish it as a site content type (see recipe *26 Publish a form template as a site content type*)

2. In SharePoint, add the site content type for the form template to a new or an existing form library as described in recipe *27 Enable different types of forms to be created in one form library*.

3. On the **Form Library Settings** page under the **Content Types** section, click **Change new button order and default content type**.

4. On the **Change New Button Order and Default Content Type** page, select **1** from the **Position from Top** drop-down list box for the content type you want to make the default content type, and click **OK**. Note that the position for all other content types associated with the form library should automatically rearrange themselves.

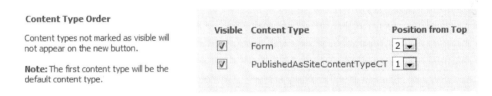

Figure 88. Setting the content type order in SharePoint 2010.

In SharePoint, navigate to the form library, and verify that the changes were successful by clicking the **Add document** link of the SharePoint form library and checking the order of form templates listed under the **New Document** button on the Ribbon.

Discussion

The default content type of a form library is the first content type that is listed under the **New Document** button menu and also the content type that SharePoint uses by default when a user clicks the **Add document** link of a form library. In the solution described above, you learned how to use the **Change New Button Order and Default Content Type** page to change the order of content types on a form library. If you have more than two content types associated with a SharePoint form library, you can use the **Position from Top** setting to rearrange the order in which the form templates belonging to those content types should appear on the **New Document** button menu of the form library. Once you have made a content type the default content type of a form library, users can click the **Add document** link of the form library to quickly add forms to the form library instead of having to use the **New Document** button menu on the Ribbon.

You can also use the **Change New Button Order and Default Content Type** page to make any content types invisible (by deselecting the **Visible** check box in front of a content type), that is, remove them from the **New Document** button menu, but not from the form library itself.

29 Rename a form template listed on the New Document menu

Problem

You published an InfoPath form template as a site content type and added it to a form library, but the newly added form template appears on the **New Document** button menu with the same name you gave the site content type. You want to rename the form template that appears on the **New Document** button drop-down menu, so that it displays a name that is meaningful to users.

Solution

To rename a form template that is listed on the **New Document** button drop-down menu on the Ribbon, you must first enable management of content types on the form library, and then rename the content type linked to the form template via the details page of the content type.

To rename a form template that is listed on the **New Document** button drop-down menu on the Ribbon:

1. In SharePoint, navigate to the form library where you want to change the name of the form template listed on the **New Document** drop-down menu on the Ribbon, and click **Library Tools ➤ Library ➤ Settings ➤ Library Settings**.
2. On the **Form Library Settings** page under the **Content Types** section, click on the name of the content type you want to rename. If the **Content Types** section is missing, because you either manually created the form library as described in recipe

16 Create a form library and edit its form template or you published the form template directly to a form library as described in recipe *21 Publish a form template to a form library*, refer to the discussion section for information on how to rename the **New Document** menu item that is listed on the **New Document** button drop-down menu.

3. On the details page of the content type under **Settings**, click **Name and description**.

4. On the **Settings** page for the content type, enter a new name in the **Name** text box, change the **Description** if you wish (the text you enter here will appear below the menu item name on the **New Document** button drop-down menu on the Ribbon), and click **OK**.

In SharePoint, navigate to the form library that is linked to the content type for which you changed its name (and description). Click **Library Tools** ➤ **Documents** ➤ **New** ➤ **New Document** and verify that the new name and (optionally) description you entered appear in the drop-down menu.

Figure 89. Form template with a user-friendly name on the New Document button drop-down menu.

Discussion

The solution described above assumed that you published a form template as a site content type (see recipe *26 Publish a form template as a site content type*) and then added that content type to the form library as described in recipe *27 Enable different types of forms to be created in one form library*. In doing so, the **Content Types** section would be present on the **Form Library Settings** page. If you did not take this route to publish a form template, but rather published a form template directly to the form library as described in recipe *21 Publish a form template to a form library*, the **Content Types** section would be missing from the **Form Library Settings** page. In such a case, you would first have to enable management of content types as described in steps 3 and 4 of recipe *27 Enable different types of forms to be created in one form library* to have the **Content Types** section appear on the **Form Library Settings** page. Once you have enabled management of content types, you can click on the **Form** content type listed under the **Content Types** section and follow steps 3 and 4 of the solution described above to rename the menu item. Note that before you enable management of content types on the form library, the menu item has the name **New Document**. This menu item name should change to **Form** after you enable management of content types on the form library.

30 Delete a form template from a form library

Problem

You want to remove a form template that is currently associated with a form library from that form library.

Solution

You can delete the content type that is linked to the form template you want to delete from a form library through the details page of the content type. Proceed with caution.

Warning:

> Never delete any site content types that are part of a default SharePoint installation.

To delete a form template from a SharePoint form library:

1. In SharePoint, navigate to the form library from which you want to delete a form template, click **Library Tools** ➤ **Library** ➤ **Settings** ➤ **Library Settings**, and enable management of content types as described in steps 3 and 4 of recipe *27 Enable different types of forms to be created in one form library* if it is not already enabled.

2. On the **Form Library Settings** page under the **Content Types** section, click on the name of the content type of the form template you want to delete.

3. On the details page of the content type under **Settings**, click **Delete this content type**.

List Content Type Information

Name: PublishedAsSiteContentTypeCT
Description: Fill out this form.
Parent: PublishedAsSiteContentTypeCT

Settings

- Name and description
- Advanced settings
- Workflow settings
- Delete this content type
- Document Information Panel settings
- Information management policy settings

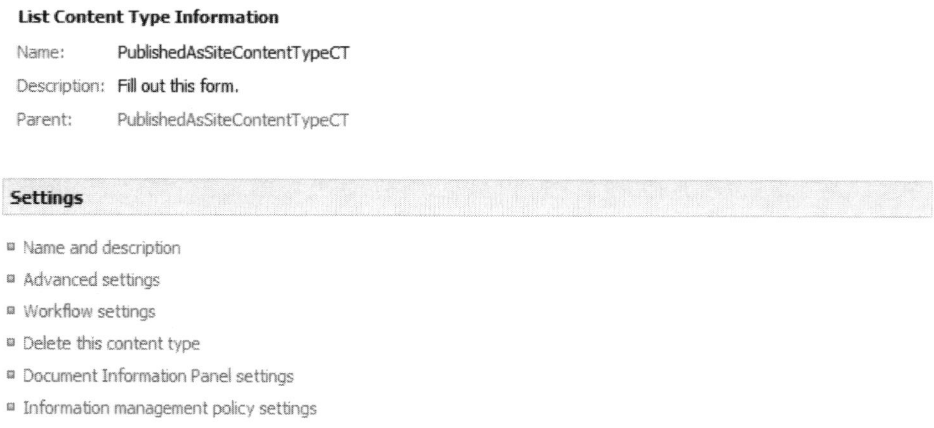

Figure 90. Content type settings on the details page of the content type in SharePoint 2010.

4. Click **OK** on the message box that asks you whether you are sure you want to delete the content type.

The content type should not be listed anymore under the **Content Types** section on the **Form Library Settings** page.

Discussion

A form template, when published to SharePoint, becomes the document template of a content type. So if you want to delete a form template from a form library, you must delete the content type for that form template from the form library. But you can only delete or disassociate a content type from a form library if there are no forms that are linked to the form template of that content type. If there are forms that are still linked to the form template of the content type you are trying to delete from the form library, you should get an error that says:

Content Type is still in use

If you see an error message or page appear immediately after trying to delete a content type, it probably means that that content type is still being used.

In addition, when you disassociate a content type from a form library, you only delete the content type that has been copied onto the form library, i.e. the list content type. The original site content type from which the list content type was initially created when you associated the site content type with the form library remains intact, so theoretically speaking you could re-add the content type to the form library at a later stage. You can verify that the site content type has not been deleted by going to the **Site Content Types** page, which is accessible through **Site Actions** ➤ **Site Settings** ➤ **Galleries** ➤ **Site content types**, and verify that the content type is still listed under the **Microsoft InfoPath** group.

You could also delete the **Form** list content type that is automatically updated when you publish a form template directly to a form library, in which case you would not have an original site content type to restore the list content type from; you would have to republish the form template to have that content type restored. Also note that you would have to manually add a **Form** content type back to the form library (click **Add from existing site content types** and then select the **Form** site content type from under the **Document Content Types** category), make the newly added **Form** list content type the default content type of the form library, and then republish the form template from within InfoPath Designer 2010. These steps are necessary, because when you publish a form template directly to a form library, the document template of the default content type of the form library is updated. So if you have another content type listed as the default content type, that content type would be updated instead of the **Form** list content type.

If you want to perform a total cleanup of a form template that you have previously published to SharePoint as a site content type, you can perform the following steps:

1. In SharePoint, navigate to any form library that is making use of the content type and delete all of the forms that are based on the content type from those form libraries.
2. Navigate to the settings page for each form library that is associated with the content type and delete the content type as described in the solution described above. This action deletes the list content type from each form library.
3. Navigate to the **Site Content Types** page, locate the site content type you want to delete, click on it to go to its details page, and then under **Settings**, click **Delete this site content type** to delete the site content type. This action deletes the original site content type that was published to SharePoint. Important: Never delete the original **Form** site content type that is installed by default when a SharePoint site collection is created.
4. Navigate to the document library where you stored the form template for the site content type, and delete the form template.
5. Navigate to the **Recycle Bin** of the site, and delete the form template.

Display SharePoint form library forms

SharePoint form library forms can be displayed through the standard **FormServer.aspx** page, embedded in InfoPath Form Web Parts, or shown as links on SharePoint pages, in SharePoint navigation menus, or in a Content Query Web part.

The recipes in this section will guide you through a couple of scenarios for displaying SharePoint form library forms in the browser. In addition, the last recipe in this section will show you how you can set up an InfoPath form to be automatically created as a document in a document set when the document set is created.

31 Add a link to open a form from a SharePoint page

Problem

You want to add a link on a web page on a SharePoint site to be able to click it to open and fill out a new InfoPath form. When the form is closed, saved, or submitted, you want the user to be redirected back to the page where the link is located.

Solution

You can add a hyperlink on a SharePoint wiki page to open a new InfoPath form.

To add a link to open a form from a SharePoint wiki page:

1. In InfoPath, create a new SharePoint form library form template or use an existing one, and publish it to a SharePoint form library.

2. In SharePoint, navigate to the form library where you published the form template and add a new form. When the form opens, copy the URL from the browser's address bar, paste it in Notepad, and modify it by removing the **Source** query string parameter (delete all of the text starting from

   ```
   &Source=
   ```

   until before the next ampersand

   ```
   &
   ```

   in the URL). For example, you should change an URL that looks like the following:

   ```
   http://servername/sitename/_layouts/FormServer.aspx?XsnLocation=http://servername/sitename/formlibraryname/Forms/template.xsn&SaveLocation=http%3A%2F%2Fservername%2Fsitename%2Fformlibraryname&Source=http%3A%2F%2Fservername%2Fsitename%2Fformlibraryname%2FForms%2FAllItems%2Easpx&DefaultItemOpen=1
   ```

   into an URL that looks like the following:

   ```
   http://servername/sitename/_layouts/FormServer.aspx?XsnLocation=http://servername/sitename/formlibraryname/Forms/template.xsn&SaveLocation=http%3A%2F%2Fservername%2Fsitename%2Fformlibraryname&DefaultItemOpen=1
   ```

   Close the form without saving or submitting it. Note: If you want a user to be redirected back to the form library and not to the page where the form's link is located, you must leave the entire URL intact and not delete the **Source** parameter.

3. Navigate to the SharePoint wiki page on which you want to place a link, and click **Site Actions ➤ Edit Page** or click the small **Edit** button on the Ribbon.

4. Once the page is in edit mode, click anywhere on the page where you want to place the link, and then select **Editing Tools ➤ Insert ➤ Links ➤ Link ➤ From Address** on the Ribbon.

5. On the **Insert Hyperlink** page, enter the text that should be displayed for the link in the **Text to display** text box, copy the URL from Notepad and paste it into the **Address** text box, and then click **OK**.

6. Click the small **Save & Close** button or click **Page ➤ Edit ➤ Save & Close** on the Ribbon.

You should now be able to click on the link and have a new form open. After you fill out and save or submit the form, you should be redirected back to the page where the link is located, and not to the form library. Navigate to the form library and verify that the new form was added to it.

Discussion

In the solution described above you used the URL of a new form to add a link to a SharePoint wiki page. You also removed the **Source** query string parameter from the URL, so that users would be redirected back to the location where the link is located when the form is closed. There are more query string parameters in the URL of a browser form you can modify to manipulate the behavior of a form. A few of these query string parameters worth mentioning are:

- **SaveLocation** – Specifies the URL of a folder in a form library on a site in the site collection where the form should be saved. The folder can be the root folder or a subfolder of a form library.

- **Source** – Specifies a location to which the user should be redirected when the form is closed. This location must be in the same site collection as where the form or form template is opened. When a form is opened from a form library, if **Source** is not specified, the message "The form has been closed" will be displayed. When a form is opened from a link, if **Source** is not specified, the user will be redirected back to the page where the link is located.

- **XmlLocation** – Specifies the URL of an existing form that should be opened. **XmlLocation** and **XsnLocation** are mutually exclusive, which means you should not specify both in the URL.

- **XsnLocation** – Used to open a new form that is based on a form template. For the **XsnLocation** query string parameter to work properly in a link on a page:
    - A **SaveLocation** should also be specified if you want to display the **Save** and **Save As** buttons on the toolbar for the form when displaying it in the browser.
    - If you omit the **Source** parameter for a link as you did in the solution described above, the form template will be downloaded instead of a new form opened in InfoPath Filler 2010. If you want a new form to open in the browser without specifying the **Source** parameter, you must explicitly specify the **OpenIn** parameter with a value of **Browser** or the **DefaultItemOpen** parameter with a value of **1**. Example:

    ```
    http://servername/sitename/_layouts/FormServer.aspx?XsnLocation=h
    ttp://servername/sitename/formlibraryname/Forms/template.xsn&Save
    Location=http%3A%2F%2Fservername%2Fsitename%2Fformlibraryname&Ope
    nIn=Browser
    ```

- **DefaultItemOpen** – This parameter is overridden by the **OpenIn** parameter, so you should use the **OpenIn** parameter instead.

    ```
    DefaultItemOpen = 0
    ```

    is equivalent to

    ```
    OpenIn = PreferClient
    ```

    and

    ```
    DefaultItemOpen = 1
    ```

Chapter 2: SharePoint Form Library Forms

is equivalent to

```
OpenIn = Browser
```

- **OpenIn** – Specifies whether a form should be opened in the browser, in InfoPath Filler 2010, or in the web page used for rendering on mobile devices. You can set it to one of 4 values: **Browser**, **Client**, **PreferClient**, **Mobile**. If you do not specify the **OpenIn** or the **DefaultItemOpen** parameter in the URL of a link to a form or form template:
    - **PreferClient** will be the default value for the **OpenIn** parameter, if you specify both the **XsnLocation** and **Source** parameters in the URL. To force a new form to open in the browser, set **OpenIn** to **Browser**.
    - The form template will be downloaded instead of a new form opened in InfoPath Filler 2010, if you only specify the **XsnLocation** parameter in the URL.
    - **PreferClient** will be the default value for the **OpenIn** parameter, if you specify both the **XmlLocation** and **Source** parameters in the URL. To force a form to open in the browser, set **OpenIn** to **Browser**.
    - The form will be downloaded instead of opened in InfoPath Filler 2010, if you only specify the **XmlLocation** parameter in the URL.

- **NoRedirect** – If set to **true** and **XmlLocation** is specified, the actual XML file for the form will be downloaded instead of the form being displayed in the browser. Its default value is **false**. This parameter does not have any effect when used in the URL of a link. The following applies to links:
    - If you want to open a form in the browser, you must specify the **XmlLocation** and **OpenIn** parameters in the URL, and set the value of the **OpenIn** parameter to **Browser**. For example:

        ```
        http://servername/sitename/_layouts/FormServer.aspx?XmlLocation=/sitename/formlibraryname/XMLFileName.xml&OpenIn=Browser
        ```

    - If you want to download the actual XML file for a form, you must specify only the **XmlLocation** parameter in the URL and/or set the **OpenIn** parameter to **PreferClient**. For example:

        ```
        http://servername/sitename/_layouts/FormServer.aspx?XmlLocation=/sitename/formlibraryname/XMLFileName.xml
        ```

        or

        ```
        http://servername/sitename/_layouts/FormServer.aspx?XmlLocation=/sitename/formlibraryname/XMLFileName.xml&OpenIn=PreferClient
        ```

InfoPath 2010 Cookbook 2

You can find the full list of parameters and descriptions for their behavior when used in combination with form libraries in an article entitled *How to: Use Query Parameters to Invoke Browser-Enabled InfoPath Forms* on MSDN.

Once you have added a link to a wiki page, you can go back to modify that link or delete it if you want to.

To modify the link you added:

1. In SharePoint, navigate to the wiki page where the link is located, and click the small **Edit** button on the Ribbon or click **Site Actions** ➤ **Edit Page**.
2. Once the page is in edit mode, click on the text for the link you want to modify. This will make the **Link Tools** tab appear on the Ribbon.
3. Click **Link Tools** ➤ **Format** to bring the tab forward.
4. Modify the link as you see fit by changing its URL, description, or its behavior, and then click the small **Save & Close** button or click **Page** ➤ **Edit** ➤ **Save & Close** on the Ribbon.

To remove the link you added:

1. In SharePoint, navigate to the wiki page where the link is located, and click the small **Edit** button on the Ribbon or click **Site Actions** ➤ **Edit Page**.
2. Once the page is in edit mode, select the entire text for the link you want to remove, and press **Delete** on your keyboard. Note that you can undo the deletion by pressing **Ctrl+Z** or by clicking **Undo** under the **Clipboard** group on the **Format Text** tab on the Ribbon.
3. Click the small **Save & Close** button or click **Page** ➤ **Edit** ➤ **Save & Close** on the Ribbon.

32 Add a link to open a form from the Quick Launch

Problem

You want to add a link for an InfoPath browser form to the Quick Launch navigation of a SharePoint site.

Solution

You can edit the look and feel of a site to add a link with which you can open a form to the Quick Launch navigation of a site.

To add a link to open a form from the Quick Launch navigation:

1. In InfoPath, create a new SharePoint form library form template or use an existing one, and publish it to a SharePoint form library.

Chapter 2: SharePoint Form Library Forms

2. In SharePoint, navigate to the form library that contains the InfoPath form you want to use, and click on the form to open it in the browser. If you want to add a link to a new InfoPath form, open a new form in the browser by either clicking on **Add document** or selecting a form template (content type) to use via the **Library Tools ➤ Documents ➤ New ➤ New Document** button drop-down menu.

3. Copy the URL of the form from the browser's address bar, and then close the form. Paste the URL in Notepad, replace all references to the server with relative URLs, and replace all of the **%2F** characters with a slash (**/**). For example, you should change an URL that looks like the following

   ```
   http://servername/sitename/_layouts/FormServer.aspx?XsnLocation=http://servername/sitename/Shared%20Documents/formtemplateCT.xsn&SaveLocation=http%3A%2F%2Fservername%2Fsitename%2Fformlibname&Source=http%3A%2F%2Fservername%2Fsitename%2Fformlibname%2FForms%2FAllItems%2Easpx&DefaultItemOpen=1
   ```

   into an URL that looks like the following

   ```
   /sitename/_layouts/FormServer.aspx?XsnLocation=
   /sitename/Shared%20Documents/formtemplateCT.xsn&SaveLocation=/sitename/formlibname&Source=/sitename/formlibname/Forms/AllItems%2Easpx&DefaultItemOpen=
   1
   ```

   where **servername** is the name of the SharePoint server and **sitename** is the name of the site where the form or form library is located. Note that the URL for a new form was used in the example given above. When you are done modifying the URL, copy the modified URL to the Windows clipboard.

4. Navigate to the SharePoint site on which you want to add a link to the Quick Launch navigation, and click **Site Actions ➤ Site Settings**.

5. On the **Site Settings** page under **Look and Feel**, click **Navigation**.

6. On the **Navigation Settings** page under **Navigation Editing and Sorting**, select **Current Navigation**, and click **Add Heading**.

7. On the **Navigation Heading** webpage dialog, enter a **Title** for the new heading (for example **Custom Links**), and click **OK**.

8. On the **Navigation Settings** page under **Navigation Editing and Sorting**, select the folder for the heading you just added (**Custom Links**), and click **Add Link**.

9. On the **Navigation Link** webpage dialog, enter a **Title** for the new link, paste the URL of the InfoPath form in the **URL** text box, select the **Open link in new window** check box if you want the form to open in a new browser window, and click **OK**.

InfoPath 2010 Cookbook 2

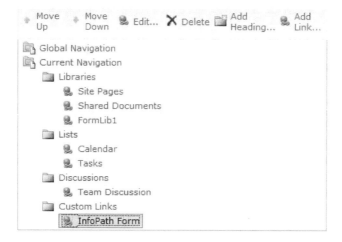

Figure 91. Link added to the Quick Launch on the Navigation Settings page in SharePoint.

10. On the **Navigation Settings** page, click **OK**.

In SharePoint, navigate to the site where you added the link to the Quick Launch navigation. You should see both the heading and the link listed in the Quick Launch navigation. Click on the link to verify that the InfoPath form can be opened.

Discussion

In the solution described above, you copied the full URL of an InfoPath form and added it as a link to the Quick Launch navigation. Therefore, when you close the form, you should be redirected to the location that was specified in the **Source** parameter of the URL. See the discussion section of recipe *31 Add a link to open a form from a SharePoint page* for a list of parameters you can use in the URL of a form.

If you want to edit a previously added link, you must go back to the **Navigation Settings** page, select the link you want to edit, and then click **Edit** at the top of the **Navigation Editing and Sorting** section. And if you want to delete a previously added link or heading, you must select the link or heading, and then click **Delete** at the top of the **Navigation Editing and Sorting** section. Note that deleting a heading will not automatically delete the links under that heading; you must delete them separately.

33 Embed an InfoPath form on a SharePoint page

Problem

You want to place an InfoPath form on a SharePoint page so that users can easily access and fill out the form.

Chapter 2: SharePoint Form Library Forms

Solution

You can use the **InfoPath Form Web Part** that comes with SharePoint Server 2010 to embed an InfoPath form on a SharePoint page.

To embed an InfoPath form in an InfoPath Form Web Part on a SharePoint wiki page:

1. In InfoPath, create a new SharePoint form library form template or use an existing one, and publish it to a form library.

2. In SharePoint, navigate to the wiki page on which you want to embed the InfoPath form, and click **Site Actions** ➤ **Edit Page** or click the small **Edit** button on the Ribbon.

3. Click anywhere on the page where you want to embed the InfoPath form, and then click **Editing Tools** ➤ **Insert** ➤ **Web Parts** ➤ **Web Part** on the Ribbon.

4. At the top of the page, select **Forms** in the **Categories** list, select **InfoPath Form Web Part** in the **Web Parts** list, and click **Add**.

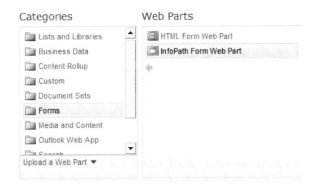

Figure 92. Selecting the InfoPath Form Web Part in SharePoint 2010.

5. Once the web part has been added to the page, you must configure it to display a specific InfoPath form. On the web part, click on the text that says **Click here to open the tool pane**.

Figure 93. InfoPath Form Web Part on a SharePoint page.

111

6. On the web part tool pane on the right-hand side of the page, select the form library you published the InfoPath form template to from the **List or Library** drop-down list box.

7. On the web part tool pane, select the content type that should be used to create the form from the **Content Type** drop-down list box. Typically, if you associated multiple content types with a form library as described in recipe *27 Enable different types of forms to be created in one form library*, this drop-down list box should contain those content types. However, if you published the form template to the form library without adding any additional content types, only a **Form** content type should be listed in the drop-down list box.

8. On the web part tool pane, select the view to use when the form is opened from the **Views** drop-down list box. If the form has multiple views, all of those views would be listed in this drop-down list box.

9. On the web part tool pane, expand the **Appearance** section, change the **Title** of the web part to a suitable title, configure any other options you would like to configure, and then click **OK**.

10. Click the small **Save & Close** button or click **Page ➤ Edit ➤ Save & Close** on the Ribbon.

The InfoPath form should now be embedded in the web part on the page and you should be able to fill it out and save or submit it.

Discussion

You can use an InfoPath Form Web Part to not only embed an InfoPath form on a SharePoint page, but also set up web part connections between two InfoPath forms as you will see in the next two recipes. In the solution described above you placed an InfoPath Form Web Part on a SharePoint wiki page, but you could have also placed the web part on a SharePoint web part page instead of a wiki page. In general, wiki pages offer more flexibility than web part pages where formatting is concerned.

34 Master/detail across two forms linked through one field

Problem

You have a SharePoint list containing information about project managers. You want to create an InfoPath form to enter project information. The form should contain a repeating table that has one column in which a drop-down list box is located. The drop-down list box should be populated with the names of the project managers from the SharePoint list. You want to give users the ability to not only select and add managers to a project, but also modify the SharePoint list data for a selected manager if required.

Chapter 2: SharePoint Form Library Forms

Solution

You can create a SharePoint list form for the project managers list, create a SharePoint form library form to enter project information, and then use InfoPath Form Web Parts and web part connections to set up passing parameters between the two forms.

To create master/detail functionality across a SharePoint form library form and a SharePoint list form and link the two forms through one field:

1. In SharePoint, create a SharePoint list named **ProjectManagers**. Ensure the list contains a column named **ManagerName** and any other relevant columns you require. Populate the list with data. Note: You can use the **ProjectManagersList.stp** file (which you can download from www.bizsupportonline.com) to load the **ProjectManagers** SharePoint list into a SharePoint test environment (also see *Upload a list template to a List Template Gallery* in the Appendix).

2. Start customizing the form for the **ProjectManagers** SharePoint list as described in recipe *1 Customize a SharePoint list form from within SharePoint*.

3. In InfoPath, add an **Action** rule that has the following two actions to the **ID** field that is located under the **my:SharePointListItem_RW** group node under the **dataFields** group node:

   ```
   Set a field's value: ID = ID
   Query using a data connection: Main Data Connection
   ```

   where the first **ID** is the **ID** field that is located under the **q:SharePointListItem_RW** group node under the **queryFields** group node and the second **ID** is the **ID** field that is located under the **my:SharePointListItem_RW** group node under the **dataFields** group node. This rule sets up the query fields for the SharePoint list form to retrieve data for a particular ID and then queries the SharePoint list for this data. This will ensure that the SharePoint list form refreshes when you select a manager for viewing from within the SharePoint form library form. The SharePoint form library form will send a selected ID of a manager to the ID field that is located under the **my:SharePointListItem_RW** group node under the **dataFields** group node in the Main data source of the SharePoint list form.

4. Publish the SharePoint list form to SharePoint.

5. In InfoPath, create a new SharePoint form library form template or use an existing one.

6. Add a **Receive** data connection to the **ProjectManagers** SharePoint list (also see *Use a SharePoint list data connection* in recipe *43 3 Ways to retrieve data from a SharePoint list*). Ensure you select the **ID** and **ManagerName** fields as fields to include in the secondary data source and that you leave the **Automatically retrieve data when form is opened** check box selected.

InfoPath 2010 Cookbook 2

7. Add a **Repeating Table** with two columns to the view of the form template. Change the first text box in the repeating table into a **Drop-Down List Box** control, and replace the second text box with a **Button** control (also delete the field that is bound to the second text box control from the Main data source). Name the field bound to the drop-down list box **managerID** and label the button **Open Manager Form**.

8. Populate the drop-down list box with entries from the **ProjectManagers** secondary data source. Select the **ID** for the **Value** property and the **ManagerName** for the **Display name** property.

Figure 94. Populating the drop-down list box with data from the ProjectManagers list.

9. Add a hidden **Field (element)** of type **Text (string)** named **selectedManagerID** to the Main data source of the form. This field will store the ID of any manager that is selected from the repeating table when you click the **Open Manager Form** button.

10. Add an **Action** rule to the **Open Manager Form** button that has the following action:

```
Set a field's value: selectedManagerID = managerID
```

where **selectedManagerID** is the hidden field and **managerID** is the field bound to the drop-down list box in the repeating table.

Chapter 2: SharePoint Form Library Forms

11. Add an **Action** rule to the **selectedManagerID** hidden field that has the following action:

    ```
    Send data to Web Part
    ```

    and then on the **Rule Details** dialog box, click **Property Promotion**.

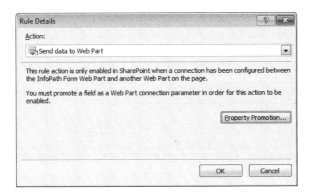

Figure 95. Adding a Send data to Web Part action in InfoPath Designer 2010.

12. On the **Form Options** dialog box, click **Add** in the section for managing SharePoint web part connection parameters (the bottom section).

13. On the **Select a field** dialog box, select **selectedManagerID** in the tree view, enter **SelectedManagerID** as the **Parameter name**, select the **Output** option, and click **OK**.

Figure 96. Promoting the selectedManagerID field as an output web part parameter.

With this you have set the **selectedManagerID** to send data to a web part whenever its value changes.

115

14. On the **Form Options** dialog box, click **OK**.

15. On the **Rule Details** dialog box, click **OK**.

16. Publish the form template to a SharePoint form library named **ProjectsLib**.

17. In SharePoint, navigate to the site where you published the form template, and click **Site Actions ➤ More Options**.

18. On the **Create** page, select **Page** under **Filter By**, select **Web Part Page**, and click **Create**.

19. On the **New Web Part Page** page, enter **ProjectAndManagers** in the **Name** text box, select **Header, Footer, 4 Columns, Top Row** from the **Choose a Layout Template** list box, select **Site Pages** from the **Document Library** drop-down list box, and click **Create**.

20. When the web part page opens, click **Add a Web Part** in the **Center-Left Column** web part zone.

21. At the top of the page, select **Forms** in the **Categories** list, select **InfoPath Form Web Part** in the **Web Parts** list, and click **Add**.

22. Click **Add a Web Part** in the **Center-Right Column** web part zone.

23. At the top of the page, select **Forms** in the **Categories** list, select **InfoPath Form Web Part** in the **Web Parts** list, and click **Add**.

24. Once you have added the two web parts to the page, you must configure them to display InfoPath forms from the **ProjectsLib** form library and **ProjectManagers** SharePoint list. So on the left web part, click on the text that says **Click here to open the tool pane**.

25. On the web part tool pane on the right-hand side of the page, select the **ProjectsLib** form library from the **List or Library** drop-down list box, expand the **Appearance** section, change the **Title** to **Project**, and then click **OK**.

26. On the right web part, click on the text that says **Click here to open the tool pane**.

27. On the web part tool pane on the right-hand side of the page, select the **ProjectManagers** SharePoint list from the **List or Library** drop-down list box, expand the **Appearance** section, change the **Title** to **Project Manager**, and then click **OK**.

28. Hover over the left web part, click the drop-down arrow that appears in the upper right-hand corner of the web part, and then select **Connections ➤ Send Data To ➤ Project Manager** from the drop-down menu that appears.

Chapter 2: SharePoint Form Library Forms

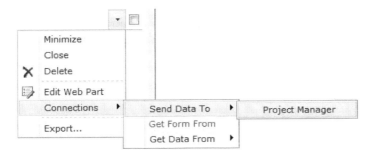

Figure 97. Configuring web part connections in SharePoint 2010.

29. On the **Configure Connection** webpage dialog, leave **SelectedManagerID** selected in the **Provider Field Name** drop-down list box, select **ID** from the **Consumer Field Name** drop-down list box, and then click **Finish**.

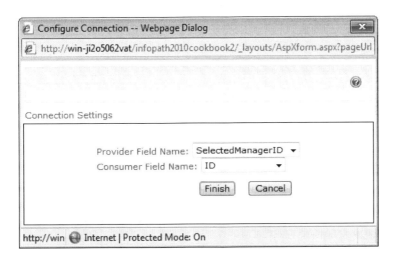

Figure 98. The Configure Connection webpage dialog in SharePoint 2010.

With this you have configured the **Project** web part to send data from the **SelectManagerID** field to the **ID** field of the **Project Manager** web part.

30. Click **Page** ➤ **Edit** ➤ **Stop Editing**.

In SharePoint, navigate to the **ProjectAndManagers** web part page. Select a manager from the drop-down list box in the repeating table. Add a second row to the repeating table and select a different manager. Click the **Open Manager Form** button behind the second drop-down list box. The SharePoint list form should display the details for the manager you selected. Edit the manager details in the SharePoint list form and then click **Save** on the toolbar. Finish entering data in the project form and then click **Save** on the toolbar.

117

InfoPath 2010 Cookbook 2

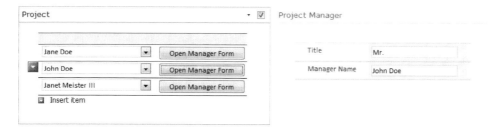

Figure 99. Passing data between a form library form and a list form on a SharePoint web part page.

Discussion

In the solution described above you learned how you can connect a SharePoint form library form with a SharePoint list form to be able to modify data that is used as read-only data in the SharePoint form library form. You also used a hidden field as a temporary storage location for a selected ID and to enable passing this ID as an output web part connection parameter, because fields inside repeating groups are not supported as web part connection parameters.

There are three types of web part connection parameters you can define:

1. Input
2. Output
3. Input and Output

A field that has been configured as an **Input** parameter can receive data from a field in another web part. A field that has been configured as an **Output** parameter can send data to a field in another web part. And a field that has been configured as an **Input and Output** parameter can both send and receive data.

You can configure web part connection parameters via the **Form Options** dialog box, when you add a **Send data to Web Part** action to a rule by clicking the **Property Promotion** button, or when you publish a form template through the **Publishing Wizard**. While you cannot configure web part connection parameters on a SharePoint list form template, you can still configure an InfoPath Form Web Part that hosts a SharePoint list form to send or receive data as you have seen in the solution described above.

And finally, you used a **Send data to Web Part** action in a rule on the hidden field to send a selected ID to any consumer web parts, in this case to an InfoPath Form Web Part containing a SharePoint list form, whenever the value of the **selectedManagerID** field changed.

35 Pass data from a selected row in a repeating table to another form

Problem

You have two InfoPath forms that are embedded on the same page in SharePoint. You want to select data from a row in a repeating table on the first form, click a button, and then have this data passed to the second form.

Solution

You can set up web part connection parameters in the InfoPath form templates and use a **Send data to Web Part** action in the first form to send data to the second form. In addition, you must use SharePoint Designer 2010 to set up the web part connections.

For this recipe, you will create two form templates. The first form template sends data and the second form template receives data.

To design the first form template:

1. In InfoPath, create a new SharePoint form library form template or use an existing one.

2. Add a **Repeating Table** with two columns to the view of the form template. Name the first text box in the repeating table **title**, and the second text box **color**.

3. Add two hidden fields of type **Text (string)** to the Main data source of the form. Name the fields **selectedTitle** and **selectedColor**, respectively.

4. Click anywhere in the second column of the repeating table, and then select **Table Tools ▸ Layout ▸ Rows & Columns ▸ Insert Right**. This should insert a column to the right of the second column. If a third text box was added to the repeating table, delete it both from the view and from the Main data source.

5. Add a **Button** control to the third column of the repeating table and label it **Select**.

6. Add an **Action** rule to the button that has the following 3 actions:

   ```
   Set a field's value: selectedTitle = title
   Set a field's value: selectedColor = color
   Send data to Web Part
   ```

   This action rule sets the values of the **selectedTitle** and **selectedColor** hidden fields to be equal to the values of the **title** and **color** fields that are located in the same row in which the **Select** button was clicked, and then sends the data to any consumer web parts.

7. To be able to have a form send data to another web part, you must set up **Output** web part connection parameters. So click **File ▸ Info ▸ Form Options**.

119

8. On the **Form Options** dialog box, select **Property Promotion** under **Category**, and then in the section to add SharePoint web part connection parameters (the bottom section), click **Add**.

9. On the **Select a field** dialog box, select **selectedTitle** from the fields section, enter **Selected Title** as the **Parameter name**, select **Output** as the **Parameter type**, and click **OK**.

10. Repeat steps 8 and 9 to add a **Selected Color** parameter that is linked to the **selectedColor** field as an **Output** web part connection parameter.

11. On the **Form Options** dialog box, click **OK**.

12. Publish the form template to a SharePoint form library named **SourceFormLib**.

To design the second form template:

1. In InfoPath, create a new SharePoint form library form template or use an existing one.

2. Add two **Text Box** controls to the view of the form template and name them **title** and **color**, respectively. The values of these two fields will be set by the other form.

3. To be able to have a form receive data from another web part, you must set up **Input** web part connection parameters. So click **File ➤ Info ➤ Form Options**.

4. On the **Form Options** dialog box, select **Property Promotion** under **Category**, and then in the section to add SharePoint web part connection parameters (the bottom section), click **Add**.

5. On the **Select a field** dialog box, select **title** from the fields section, enter **Title** as the **Parameter name**, select **Input** as the **Parameter type**, and click **OK**.

6. Repeat steps 4 and 5 to add a **Color** parameter that is linked to the **color** field as an **Input** web part connection parameter.

7. On the **Form Options** dialog box, click **OK**.

8. Publish the form template to a SharePoint form library named **DestinationFormLib**.

Once you have designed and published the form templates, you must embed them either in a SharePoint web part page or wiki page.

To embed the forms in a SharePoint web part page:

1. In SharePoint, navigate to the site where you published the form templates, and click **Site Actions ➤ More Options**.

Chapter 2: SharePoint Form Library Forms

2. On the **Create** page, select **Page** under **Filter By**, select **Web Part Page**, and click **Create**.

3. Enter **PassMultipleParams** in the **Name** text box, select **Header, Footer, 4 Columns, Top Row** from the **Choose a Layout Template** list box, select **Site Pages** from the **Document Library** drop-down list box, and click **Create**.

4. When the web part page opens, click **Add a Web Part** in the **Center-Left Column** web part zone.

5. At the top of the page, select **Forms** in the **Categories** list, select **InfoPath Form Web Part** in the **Web Parts** list, and click **Add**.

6. Click **Add a Web Part** in the **Center-Right Column** web part zone.

7. At the top of the page, select **Forms** in the **Categories** list, select **InfoPath Form Web Part** in the **Web Parts** list, and click **Add**.

8. Once the two web parts have been added to the page, you must configure them to display InfoPath forms from the **SourceFormLib** and **DestinationFormLib** form libraries. On the left web part, click on the text that says **Click here to open the tool pane**.

9. On the web part tool pane on the right-hand side of the page, select the **SourceFormLib** form library from the **List or Library** drop-down list box, expand **Appearance**, change the **Title** to **Source Form Web Part**, and click **OK**.

10. On the right web part, click on the text that says **Click here to open the tool pane**.

11. On the web part tool pane on the right-hand side of the page, select the **DestinationFormLib** form library from the **List or Library** drop-down list box, expand **Appearance**, change the **Title** to **Destination Form Web Part**, and click **OK**.

12. Click **Page** ➤ **Edit** ➤ **Stop Editing**.

Once you have embedded the InfoPath forms on a web part page, you must set up the web part connections for the forms from within SharePoint Designer 2010, because you can only set up single connections from within SharePoint's browser interface.

To set up web part connections in SharePoint Designer 2010:

1. In SharePoint Designer 2010, click **File** ➤ **Sites** ➤ **Open Site**.

2. On the **Open Site** dialog box, browse to and select the site on which the **PassMultipleParams** web part page is located, and click **Open**.

3. Once the site has opened, click **Site Pages** in the left **Navigation** pane.

4. On the **Site Pages** page, click **PassMultipleParams.aspx**.

5. On the **PassMultipleParams.aspx** page under **Customization**, click **Edit file**.

6. On the page editor, click the left web part to select it, and then on the Ribbon, click **Web Part Tools ➤ Format ➤ Connections ➤ Add Connection**.

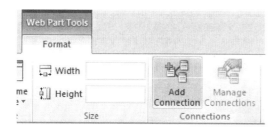

Figure 100. Add Connection button on the Ribbon in SharePoint Designer 2010.

7. On the **Web Part Connections Wizard**, select **Send Data To**, and click **Next**.

Figure 101. Web Part Connections Wizard in SharePoint Designer 2010.

8. On the **Web Part Connections Wizard**, leave the **Connect to a Web Part on this page** option selected, and click **Next**.

Chapter 2: SharePoint Form Library Forms

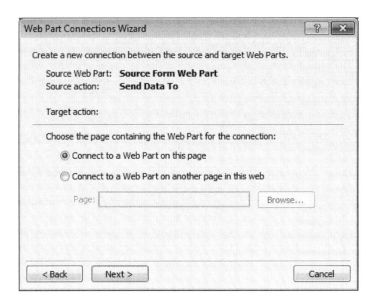

Figure 102. Selecting to connect to a web part on the same page.

9. On the **Web Part Connections Wizard**, leave **Destination Form Web Part** selected in the **Target Web Part** drop-down list box, leave **Get Data From** selected in the **Target action** drop-down list box, and click **Next**.

Figure 103. Selecting the web part to connect to.

123

10. On the **Web Part Connections Wizard**, select **Selected Color** from the **Columns in Source Form Web Part** list and select **Color** from the **Inputs to Destination Form Web Part** list on the same row, select **Selected Title** from the **Columns in Source Form Web Part** list and select **Title** from the **Inputs to Destination Form Web Part** list on the same row, and then click **Next**.

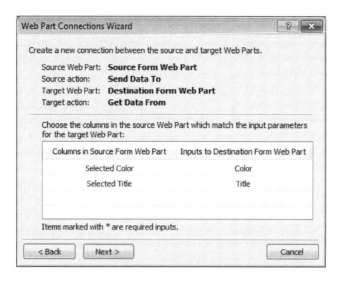

Figure 104. Setting up the parameters for the web part connections in SharePoint Designer.

11. On the **Web Part Connections Wizard**, review the information, and click **Finish**.

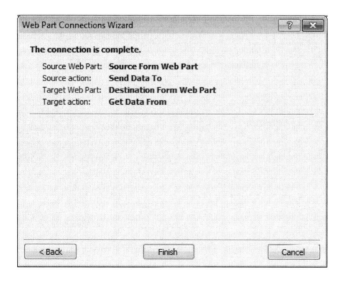

Figure 105. Last screen of the Web Part Connections Wizard.

12. Click **Save** to save the page.

Chapter 2: SharePoint Form Library Forms

In SharePoint, navigate to the **PassMultipleParams** web part page. Populate the repeating table with a couple of rows of data. Click the **Select** button in one of the rows and verify that the data from the fields in the row in which the **Select** button is located is copied over to the second form.

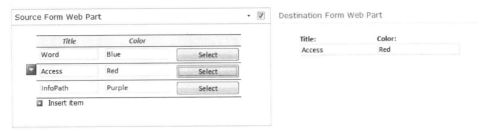

Figure 106. Passing data between two form library forms on a SharePoint web part page.

Discussion

While the solution described above used a repeating table in the Main data source of a form to pass a row of data to another form, you could have also retrieved data from a secondary data source such as a SharePoint list, bound this secondary data source to a repeating table and then added a select button to each row (see *Use a Select button in a repeating table* in recipe *45 3 Ways to copy SharePoint list data to form fields*) to be able to select and pass data from a row of the repeating to the other form.

In recipe *34 Master/detail across two forms linked through one field* you used SharePoint's browser interface to set up web part connections between two InfoPath Form Web Parts. However, whenever you want to set up more than one web part connection, you must use SharePoint Designer 2010 to do so, because SharePoint's browser interface allows you to set up only one web part connection between two web parts, and not multiple.

36 Create an InfoPath form as part of a document set

Problem

You have an InfoPath form which you want to include as a document in a document set whenever a new instance of that Document Set is created.

Solution

You can publish an InfoPath form template as a site content type, create a sample form that is based on that content type, and include the content type for the form as well as the sample InfoPath form in the content type for the document set.

Before you can use document sets in SharePoint 2010, a site collection administrator must activate the **Document Sets** feature on the site collection. To activate this feature:

InfoPath 2010 Cookbook 2

1. Navigate to the top-level site in the site collection, and click **Site Actions** ➤ **Site Settings**.

2. On the **Site Settings** page under **Site Collection Administration**, click **Site collection features**.

3. On the **Features** page, click **Activate** behind the **Document Sets** feature.

Document sets are based on a **Document Set** content type. If you do not already have a **Document Set** content type at your disposal, you can follow the instructions below to create a new one:

1. In SharePoint, navigate to the site where you want to create a new **Document Set** content type, and click **Site Actions** ➤ **Site Settings**.

2. On the **Site Settings** page under **Galleries**, click **Site content types**.

3. On the **Site Content Types** page, click **Create**.

4. On the **New Site Content Type** page, enter a **Name** for the content type (for example **Employee Assessment Document Set**), select **Document Set Content Types** from the **Select parent content type from** drop-down list box, leave **Document Set** selected in the **Parent Content Type** drop-down list box, and click **OK**.

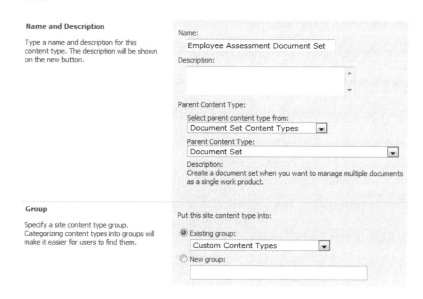

Figure 107. Creating a new Document Set content type in SharePoint 2010.

Once you have a **Document Set** content type, you must associate it with a SharePoint document library just like you would associate any other type of content type with a library so that it can be used to create document sets.

Chapter 2: SharePoint Form Library Forms

To add a **Document Set** content type to a document library:

1. In SharePoint, create a new document library in much the same way you created a form library in recipe *16 Create a form library and edit its form template* (use the **Document Library** template instead of the **Form Library** template) or use an existing one.

2. Navigate to the document library and via the **Document Library Settings** page, add the **Employee Assessment Document Set** content type as a content type to the document library in much the same way you added a content type to a form library in recipe *27 Enable different types of forms to be created in one form library*.

To have users be able to create certain types of InfoPath forms within a document set, you must add the content type(s) that those forms are created from to the **Document Set** content type you created earlier. In addition, you can add a default InfoPath form (XML file) to the **Document Set** content type, so that whenever a new document set is created using the **Document Set** content type, the InfoPath form is included in the new document set by default.

To enable creating an InfoPath form as part of a document set:

1. In InfoPath, create a new SharePoint form library form template or use an existing one.

2. Publish the form template as a site content type as described in recipe *26 Publish a form template as a site content type* to the same SharePoint site or a parent site of the site where the **Document Set** content type is located. Name the content type for the form template **Employee Assessment Form**.

3. In SharePoint, navigate to the site where the **Document Set** content type is located, and click **Site Actions** ▶ **Site Settings**.

4. On the **Site Settings** page under **Galleries**, click **Site content types**.

5. On the **Site Content Types** page under **Custom Content Types** (if you created the **Document Set** content type by following the steps earlier in this solution), click **Employee Assessment Document Set**.

6. On the **Employee Assessment Document Set** page under the **Settings** section, click **Document Set settings**.

7. On the **Document Set Settings** page, select the **Employee Assessment Form** content type from the list of **Available Site Content Types**, click **Add** to add it to the list of **Content types allowed in the Document Set**, and then click **OK**.

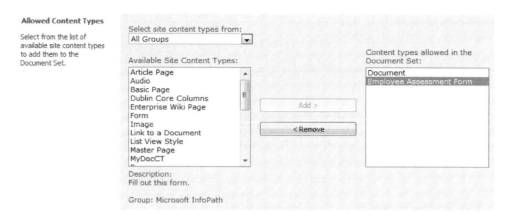

Figure 108. Adding the content type for the InfoPath form to the Document Set content type.

With this you have added the form as a type of document that can be created in any document set that is based on the **Employee Assessment Document Set** content type.

8. Navigate to the document library to which you added the **Employee Assessment Document Set** as a content type, and click **Library Tools** ➤ **Documents** ➤ **New** ➤ **New Document** ➤ **Employee Assessment Document Set** to create a new document set.

9. On the **New Document Set** dialog box, enter a **Name** for the Document Set (for example **Assessment Document Set - John Doe**), and click **OK**. With this you have created a new document set that is based on the **Employee Assessment Document Set**.

10. When the new document set opens, click **Library Tools** ➤ **Documents** ➤ **New** ➤ **New Document** ➤ **Employee Assessment Form**.

11. When the InfoPath form opens, leave all of the fields blank or fill in default data that should be included in a sample form when a new document set is created, and then click **Save**.

12. On the **Save As** dialog box, enter a **File name** for the form (for example **Sample Assessment Form**), and click **Save**. After this, the form is saved as a document in the document set. Close the form when you are done.

13. Back in the **Assessment Document Set - John Doe** document set, select the check box in front of the form you just saved, click **Library Tools** ➤ **Documents** ➤ **Copies** ➤ **Download a Copy**, and save the form as **Sample_Assessment_Form.xml** somewhere locally on disk. You may delete the **Assessment Document Set - John Doe** document set if you wish by clicking **Document Set** ➤ **Manage** ➤ **Actions** ➤ **Delete** on the Ribbon, or by going back to the root folder of the document library, selecting the check box in front of the

Chapter 2: SharePoint Form Library Forms

document set and clicking **Delete document** under the **Manage** group on the **Documents** tab on the Ribbon.

14. Repeat steps 3 through 6 to navigate to the **Document Set Settings** page.

15. On the **Document Set Settings** page under **Default Content**, click the **Add new default content** link. This should add a second row for default content.

16. Select **Employee Assessment Form** from the **Content Type** drop-down list box in the new row you just added, and then click **Browse** on the same row.

17. On the **Choose File to Upload** dialog box, browse to and select the **Sample_Assessment_Form.xml** file, and click **Open**.

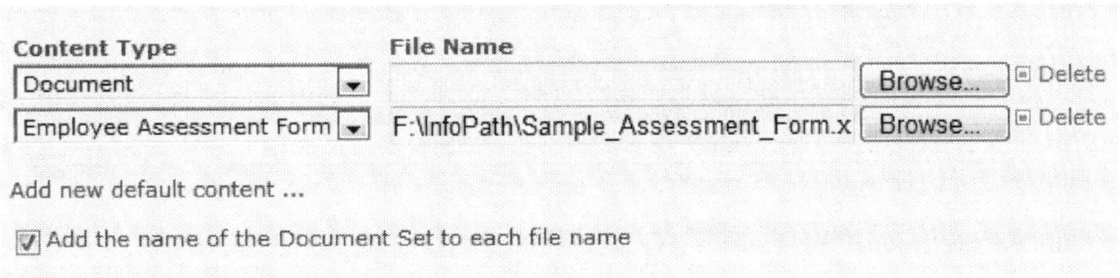

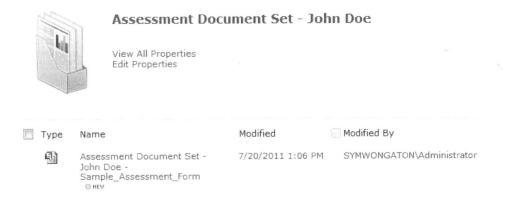

Figure 109. The sample InfoPath form added as default content to add to the document set.

18. On the **Document Set Settings** page, click **OK**. With this you have configured a sample InfoPath form to be automatically added as a default document to a document set when you create a new document set that is based on the **Employee Assessment Document Set** content type.

In SharePoint, repeat steps 8 and 9 listed above. Verify that the sample InfoPath form has automatically been added to the new document set you created.

Figure 110. Newly created document set containing automatically created sample InfoPath form.

129

Discussion

Document sets are a new document management feature in SharePoint 2010. Conceptually, a document set is a container or folder that holds a related set of documents. These documents could be anything ranging from Word and Excel documents to PowerPoint presentations and even InfoPath forms as shown in the solution above. A document set is based on the **Document Set** parent content type, which inherits from the **Document Collection Folder** content type, which in turn inherits from the **Folder** content type in SharePoint.

A document set can help streamline the use of documents and increase consistency in deliverables (documents) across recurring activities that require the same set of documents to be generated every single time. A few examples of recurring activities include assessing the performance of employees every year or starting a new project every quarter. These two scenarios are highly indicative that you may require the same types of documents to be created repeatedly over a period of time. For example, assessment InfoPath forms and a summary Word document template in the case of an employee assessment; and project Word document templates, PowerPoint templates for customer presentations, Excel templates for time and budget estimates, etc. in the case of a new project.

To be able to create a document set that holds different types of documents, you must:

1. Create a new **Document Set** content type that inherits from the **Document Set** parent content type.
2. Add all of the content types that correspond to the types of documents you want to create (Word, Excel, PowerPoint, etc.) to the **Document Set** content type as allowable content types, and define any default documents for the content types you allowed.
3. Associate the newly created **Document Set** content type with a document library.
4. Create new document sets that are based on the **Document Set** content type in the same way you would create any new document in a document library.

When you allow users to add InfoPath forms as documents in a document set, the InfoPath forms should generally be stored within the document set itself and not within a separate form library. Therefore, you should not set up submit connections for the form templates of such forms, but instead, enable such forms to be saved in the document set rather than submitted elsewhere. You can read more about the difference between saving and submitting forms in the introduction of the *Configure forms for submit to a form library* section of this Chapter on page 58.

Merge InfoPath forms in SharePoint

When you merge InfoPath forms, you consolidate the data from several forms that are based on the same XML schema into one form. The data in the original forms is not deleted, but rather a new form with the merged data is created. Merging can be useful for example when you want to provide a summary of data or when you want to compare data from several forms. A good example is the collation of responses to a survey as is demonstrated in the following three recipes.

37 Create an InfoPath survey form suitable for merging

Problem

You want to be able to have users fill out a list of single choice, multiple choice, and free text questions on a survey form in SharePoint.

Solution

You can use repeating sections, option buttons, multiple-selection list boxes, and text boxes to display survey questions in a format that can be used later for merging the forms in InfoPath Filler 2010.

To create an InfoPath survey form that is suitable for merging:

1. In InfoPath, create a new SharePoint form library form template.

2. Add a **Repeating Section** control to the view of the form template, and then open the **Repeating Section Properties** dialog box.

3. On the **Repeating Section Properties** dialog box on the **Data** tab, deselect the **Allow users to insert and delete the sections** check box, and then click the **Advanced** tab.

4. On the **Repeating Section Properties** dialog box on the **Advanced** tab under **Merging forms**, click **Merge Settings**.

5. On the **Merge Settings** dialog box, accept all of the default settings, but also select the **Remove blank groups (recommended)** check box, and click **OK**.

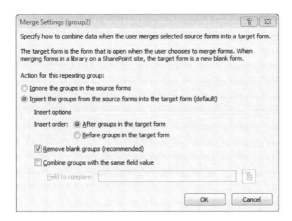

Figure 111. Merge Settings dialog box in InfoPath Designer 2010.

By selecting this check box, you will prevent blank responses from appearing in the results when the survey forms are merged.

6. On the **Repeating Section Properties** dialog box, click **OK**.

7. Repeat steps 2 through 6 three times to add an additional 3 repeating sections for a total of 4 repeating sections on the view of the form template.

8. The first question you are going to add is a single choice question. You can use option buttons to add single choice questions to the survey form. So click inside the first repeating section, and then add an **Option Button** control with 3 choices to the repeating section. Rename the field bound to the option button control to **question1** and label the option buttons **A**, **B**, and **C**, respectively.

9. Open the **Option Button Properties** dialog box for each individual option button and on the **Data** tab change the value of the **Value when selected** property to **A**, **B**, or **C**, respectively. Note that if the question is about rating something on a scale of 1 to 3, you could keep the default values of 1, 2, and 3 for the buttons. And if the question is about choosing the best option out of 3 options, you could change the values to for example, A, B, and C. The choice is yours, but always keep the merging of the data in the forms in mind, and remember that if you use numbers (for example for ratings), you get the added benefit of being able to use aggregate functions such as **avg** and **sum** to display an aggregated result for all forms merged. You will use this for the fourth question.

10. The second question you are going to add is a multiple choice question. You can use multiple-selection list boxes to add multiple choice questions to the survey form. So click inside the second repeating section, and then add a **Multiple-Selection List Box** control to the repeating section. Rename the repeating field bound to the multiple-selection list box to **question2**.

11. Open the **Multiple-Selection List Box Properties** dialog box, manually add 4 choices (**A**, **B**, **C**, and **D**), and then click **OK**. These will be static choices a user can select from.

12. With the multiple-selection list box still selected on the view of the form template, click **Properties ➤ Color ➤ Borders**.

13. On the **Borders and Shading** dialog box on the **Borders** tab under **Presets**, click **None** to remove all borders, and then click **OK**.

14. The third question you are going to add is a free text question. You can use multi-line text boxes to add free text questions to the survey form. So click inside the third repeating section, and then add a **Text Box** control to the repeating section. Rename the field bound to the text box control to **question3**.

15. Open the **Text Box Properties** dialog box, click the **Display** tab, select **Mutli-line** to make the text box accept multiple lines of text, and click **OK**.

Chapter 2: SharePoint Form Library Forms

16. The fourth question you are going to add is a single choice question. So click inside the fourth repeating section, and then add an **Option Button** control with 3 choices to the repeating section. Rename the field bound to the option button control to **question4** and label the option buttons **1**, **2**, and **3**, respectively.

17. Open the **Option Button Properties** dialog box for each individual option button and on the **Data** tab ensure the **Value when selected** property has a value of **1**, **2**, or **3**, respectively. Because you are going to calculate the average of all answers to this question in all of the forms, you need their values to be numeric.

18. Publish the form template to a SharePoint form library.

In SharePoint, navigate to the form library where you published the form template and add a couple of forms to it by filling out the survey and varying the responses for the different survey forms.

Discussion

Before you can merge forms, merging must be enabled on the form template. This setting is enabled by default when you create a new form template, but if it has been disabled, you can enable it by opening the **Form Options** dialog box (**File ➤ Info ➤ Form Options**) and then selecting the **Enable form merging** check box via the **Advanced** category.

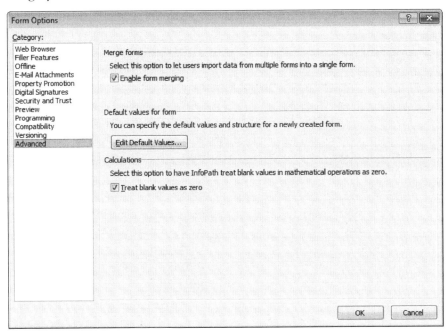

Figure 112. Enabling form merging in InfoPath Designer 2010.

Once you have enabled merging, you can configure how a control merges data via the **Merge forms** section on the **Advanced** tab of the **Properties** dialog box of that control.

133

InfoPath 2010 Cookbook 2

For example, for text boxes you can specify whether you would like to add a prefix to the text when it is merged and whether a character should be used to separate the text from the individual text boxes.

Before you start to design a form template for merging, take a moment to think about how you may want to have the fields in the merged form appear. The way fields on forms are combined when merged depends on the structure of the Main data source of the form. While you can enable merging on most controls in InfoPath, the best controls to use to combine data from multiple forms are repeating tables and repeating sections.

There are basically three ways you can set up repeating tables or repeating sections for merging:

1. Use one repeating section or table that contains the fields to be merged.

Figure 113. An InfoPath form and its Main data source for the first way of merging forms.

2. Use a separate repeating section or table for each field that should be merged.

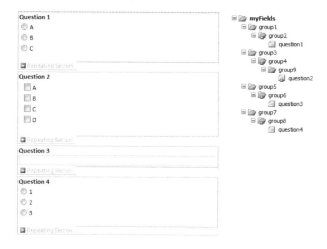

Figure 114. An InfoPath form and its Main data source for the second way of merging.

Chapter 2: SharePoint Form Library Forms

3. Use a combination of options 1 and 2.

The solution described in this recipe made use of the second type of form structure for merging. Where surveys are concerned, the second type of form structure allows you to group responses by question (with each question being a field in a repeating section), while the first type of form structure would be useful if you wanted to group responses by the persons taking the survey. In the latter case, all of the responses from one particular person would be listed on the merged form before the next batch of responses from the next person is listed and so forth.

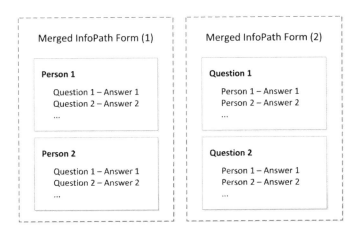

Figure 115. The resulting merged InfoPath forms for methods 1 and 2.

You could extend this recipe further by:

- Configuring a submit connection so that the form can be submitted to a form library (see recipe *18 Submit a form to a form library and then close it*).

- Configuring the form to be left open and to switch to a view that displays a piece of text such as for example "Thank you for taking the survey" instead of closing the form (see recipe *20 Submit a form and switch to a 'Thank You' view*).

- Embed the form in an InfoPath Form Web Part (see recipe *33 Embed an InfoPath form on a SharePoint page*) and place this on a separate page for users to fill out instead of having users access the form library to fill out the survey form.

Once you have created and published your merge-ready InfoPath survey form template, you are now ready to merge the survey forms people have filled out. But before you do, you may want to enhance the display of the aggregated survey results by adding a 'Summary' view to the form template as you will do in the next recipe.

38 Design an InfoPath form to summarize merged data

Problem

You have created an InfoPath form that can be used as a survey form in SharePoint, and now you want to be able to summarize all of the responses of the survey forms on a separate view.

Solution

You can use aggregate functions to summarize data from a survey that contains repeating fields.

To design an InfoPath form to summarize merged data:

1. Design a form template as described in recipe *37 Create an InfoPath survey form suitable for merging*.

2. Click **Page Design** ➤ **Views** ➤ **New View** to add a second view to the form template and name it **MergedSurveyResultsView**.

3. Open the **View Properties** dialog box, deselect the **Show on the View menu when filling out this form** check box, and click **OK**.

4. Type the text **Question 1** on the view, and then type the responses **A:**, **B:**, and **C:**; each on a separate line.

5. Behind each response you are going to add a total. This total should indicate how many people chose a particular response. So click behind the text that says **A:**, and then click **Home** ➤ **Controls** ➤ **Calculated Value** to add a calculated value control that is not bound to any field on the form, but that is rather based on a formula.

6. On the **Insert Calculated Value** dialog box, click the formula button behind the **XPath** text box.

7. On the **Insert Formula** dialog box, construct a formula that says:

   count(group2[question1 = "A"])

   or

   count(my:group1/my:group2[my:question1 = "A"])

   if you have the **Edit XPath (advanced)** check box selected. Note that you will have to use the **Filter Data** option on the **Select a Field or Group** dialog box when constructing the formula or manually type in the filter expression. What this formula does is count the amount of **group2** group nodes that contain a **question1** field that has a value of **A**. When all of the forms are merged together, the **group1** group node in the Main data source will contain all of the **group2** group nodes with the **question1** fields for all of the forms. So by setting up the form structure as you did with repeating sections, you can now easily perform aggregate calculations (**count**,

avg, **sum**, **min**, **max**) on each question when merging the data of all of the forms together. Note: The group node numbers in your form template may differ from what is shown in the formula listed above.

8. On the **Insert Formula** dialog box, click **OK**.
9. On the **Insert Calculated Value** dialog box, click **OK**.
10. Repeat steps 5 through 9 for the **B** and **C** responses of **question 1**, but then change the filter value in the formula to **B** or **C** instead of **A**.
11. Repeat steps 4 through 10 for question 2, but change the text to **Question 2** and the responses to **A**, **B**, **C**, and **D**. The formula for the calculated value control for the first response should look something like the following:

    ```
    count(question2[. = "A"])
    ```

    or

    ```
    count(my:group3/my:group4/my:group9/my:question2[. = "A"])
    ```

    if you have the **Edit XPath (advanced)** check box selected. Here **question2** is the repeating field bound to the multiple-selection list box and **group9** the group node containing **question2**. Remember that you can apply the same techniques to repeating fields and repeating groups in InfoPath. Note: The group node numbers in your form template may differ from what is shown in the formula listed above.

12. Because question 3 is a free text question, you will not summarize anything for it on the **MergedSurveyResultsView** view. You should use **View 1** to analyze the textual responses.

13. For question 4, you are going to take the average of all of the responses. So type the text **Question 4** on the view, add a second line with the text **Average:**, and then add a calculated value control behind the text **Average** as you have done previously in this solution. The formula for the calculated value should take the average of all **question4** fields and should say:

    ```
    avg(question4)
    ```

    or

    ```
    xdMath:Avg(my:group7/my:group8/my:question4)
    ```

    if you have the **Edit XPath (advanced)** check box selected. Note: The group node numbers in your form template may differ from what is shown in the formula listed above.

14. Select **Page Design** ▶ **Views** ▶ **View 1 (default)** to switch back to **View 1**, add a **Button** control with a label of **Merged Survey Results** to the view, add an **Action** rule that switches to the **MergedSurveyResultsView** view to the button, and add a **Formatting** rule to the button that **Hides this control** when the **Number of**

occurrences of group2 ≤ 1.

To construct the formula for the condition on the formatting rule, you can use the **The expression** option on the **Condition** dialog box with the following expression:

```
count(my:group1/my:group2) <= 1
```

What the formatting rule does is count the amount of **group2** group nodes that are present in the form. If this amount is greater than 1 it means that the form is a merged form, so the button should be shown on the **View 1** view so that you can switch to see the aggregated results on the **MergedSurveyResultsView** view.

15. Publish the form template to a SharePoint form library.

In SharePoint, navigate to the form library where you published the form template and merge the forms as described in recipe *39 Merge InfoPath forms from a SharePoint form library*. Click the **Merged Survey Results** button to switch to the view that displays a summary of all of the data in the forms that were merged.

Discussion

In the solution described above you saw that once you have set up a form that has a repeating node structure, you are able to use this structure to your advantage to summarize data using aggregate functions such as **count**, **min**, **max**, **sum**, and **avg** on the repeating fields in the InfoPath form.

39 Merge InfoPath forms from a SharePoint form library

Problem

You have created and published a merge-ready InfoPath survey form as described in the previous two recipes. Now you want to collect all of the responses to the survey and display them in one InfoPath form that contains the data of all of the forms merged together.

Solution

You can use the **Merge** functionality of a form library to merge several InfoPath forms into one form.

To merge InfoPath forms from a SharePoint form library:

1. In SharePoint, navigate to the form library that contains the forms you want to merge, and select **Library Tools ➤ Library ➤ Manage Views ➤ Current View ➤ Merge Documents**.

Chapter 2: SharePoint Form Library Forms

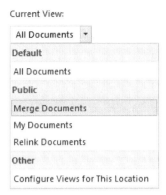

Figure 116. Menu item to access the Merge Documents page in SharePoint 2010.

2. On the **Merge Documents** page, select the check box under the **Merge** column for each form you want to add to the final merged form. As you start to select the forms to include in the merged form, the contextual Ribbon for merging documents should appear.

Figure 117. Selecting InfoPath forms for merging in SharePoint 2010.

3. Click **Library Tools** ➤ **Documents** ➤ **Actions** ➤ **Merge** to open InfoPath Filler 2010 and merge the forms. Note that while the forms are stored in a SharePoint form library, the merging itself takes place outside of SharePoint using InfoPath Filler 2010.

4. In InfoPath Filler 2010, click **Save** on the **Quick Access Toolbar** and save the form to a location in SharePoint.

5. Close InfoPath Filler 2010.

In SharePoint, navigate to the location where you saved the merged form and open the form. When the form opens, the **Merged Survey Results** button should be visible on the form. Click the **Merged Survey Results** button to access the **MergedSurveyResultsView** view and analyze the merged data.

139

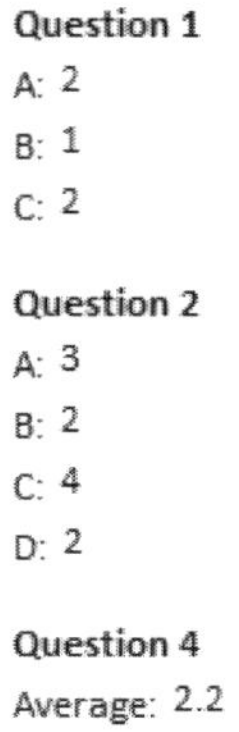

InfoPath 2010 Cookbook 2

Question 1
A: 2
B: 1
C: 2

Question 2
A: 3
B: 2
C: 4
D: 2

Question 4
Average: 2.2

Figure 118. The merged InfoPath form displaying aggregated responses to a survey.

Discussion

When you merge InfoPath forms, SharePoint sends the forms to InfoPath Filler 2010 to be merged (even if the forms are based on a browser-enabled form template and stored in SharePoint). The **Merge Documents** view (or page) in SharePoint allows you to select multiple InfoPath forms for which you want to merge the data they contain into one InfoPath form. SharePoint form libraries come by default with two types of views that are unique to them. These views are the **Merge Documents** and the **Relink Documents** views. You can access these views from the **Current View** drop-down list box in the **Manage Views** group on the **Library** tab on the Ribbon of a form library. These views also appear on document libraries whenever you associate the document libraries with content types with which you can create InfoPath forms. For example, if you have a **Document Set** content type that can create InfoPath forms (also see recipe *36 Create an InfoPath form as part of a document set*) and you add this content type to a document library, the two aforementioned views will automatically appear in the **Current View** drop-down list box on the Ribbon.

To be able to use the merge functionality in SharePoint, the forms you want to merge must have the same XML schema, the form template for the forms must have merging enabled, and the forms must contain data that can be merged. Form merging is enabled by default when you create a new form template, but it can be disabled by deselecting the **Enable form merging** check box on the **Form Options** dialog box. If a form template has not been enabled for merging and you try to merge forms that are based on that form template, you will receive the following warning message:

The merge cannot be started, because the merge feature is disabled for the selected form template. To fix this problem, contact the form designer.

If you see this message, open the form template and enable the merge functionality if required as follows:

1. In InfoPath, click **File ➤ Info ➤ Form Options**.
2. On the **Form Options** dialog box, select **Advanced** in the **Category** list.

3. On the **Form Options** dialog box under **Merge forms**, select the **Enable form merging** check box, and click **OK**.

After you enable form merging, you must republish the form template for the form template to be updated in SharePoint and for the forms to use the merge-enabled form template.

Move InfoPath forms between form libraries

Moving documents in general involves copying them to a new location and then deleting them from the old location. Where InfoPath forms are concerned, you can move forms or form libraries containing forms. But before moving any InfoPath forms or form libraries it is worthwhile to consider what the impact of the move would be and whether you would break any links to published form templates. While the move itself may not seem like much work initially, fixing broken forms might involve quite a bit of work.

One of the more important questions to ask when moving forms is whether those forms would still be able to access the form templates that are linked to the content types they are associated with. In addition, you should also verify that moving forms would not break any external data connections used by the forms, and that any other settings that have been defined on a form library such as for example workflows, would still function properly.

There are many scenarios possible when moving forms and form libraries in SharePoint. This section takes a look at a few of the most common scenarios you could encounter and provides background information that should help you come up with solutions if you have scenarios that have not been discussed in the next three recipes.

40 Move a form to another form library on the same site

Problem

You have an InfoPath form in a form library and want to move the form to another form library on the same site.

Solution

You can use the **Send To** functionality in SharePoint to move a form from one form library to another form library that is located on the same site.

To move a form to another form library on the same site:

1. In SharePoint, ensure that the form library to which you want to move the form has a default content type associated with it (also see recipe *28 Change the default form template of a form library*) that uses the same form template as the form template the form you want to move is linked to.

InfoPath 2010 Cookbook 2

2. Navigate to the form library where the form that you want to move is located, select the check box in front of the form, and then select **Library Tools** ➤ **Documents** ➤ **Copies** ➤ **Send To** ➤ **Other Location**; or hover over the name of the form until the drop-down arrow appears on the right-hand side of the form's name, click the drop-down arrow, and then select **Send To** ➤ **Other Location** from the drop-down menu that appears.

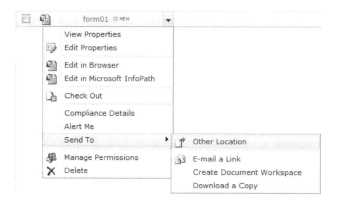

Figure 119. Selecting to send a form to a particular location in SharePoint 2010.

3. On the **Copy** page, enter the URL of the **Destination document library or folder**, and click the **Click here to test** link to ensure that the destination is reachable.

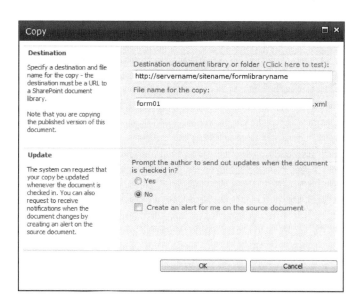

Figure 120. The Copy page in SharePoint 2010.

4. On the **Copy** page, change the **File name for the copy** if you wish, and then click **OK**.

142

5. On the **Copy Progress** dialog box, verify that the information is correct, and then click **OK**.

6. Once the file has been copied, click **Done** on the **Copy Progress** dialog box.

7. Optionally, back in the form library, select the check box in front of the form you just copied, and then click **Library Tools ➤ Documents ➤ Manage ➤ Delete Document** to delete the form from the form library. With this you have moved the form to another form library.

If you want to move multiple forms at the same time from one form library to another form library, you can use the **Open with Explorer** functionality in SharePoint.

To move multiple forms from one form library to another form library:

1. In SharePoint, navigate to the source form library where the forms that you want to move are located, and click **Library Tools ➤ Library ➤ Connect & Export ➤ Open with Explorer**. This should open Windows Explorer.

Figure 121. The Open with Explorer command on the Ribbon in SharePoint 2010.

2. In Windows Explorer, select the InfoPath forms (XML files) you want to move, and press **Ctrl+X** to cut and place them on the Windows clipboard. Note: If you want to copy forms, but not delete them from the source form library, use **Ctrl+C** instead of **Ctrl+X**.

3. In Windows Explorer, use the network folder structure to navigate to the destination form library, and once there, press **Ctrl+V** to paste the forms you cut or copied earlier.

4. Close Windows Explorer.

In SharePoint, navigate to the destination form library and verify that the forms you moved or copied are present in the form library. Note that if you moved forms that are not based on a site content type, you may have to relink the forms to the correct form templates as described in recipe *42 Relink InfoPath forms in a form library*, after you have moved the forms.

Discussion

Moving a form is a two-step process that involves copying the form to a destination form library and then deleting the form from the source form library. In the solution described above, you used the **Send To** command to move one form and the **Open with Explorer** command to move multiple forms from one form library to another. If you wanted to move all of the forms that are located in a form library to a different location, you could use the technique described in recipe *41 Move a form library to another site*.

It is recommended that you plan ahead and take the scope of content types (see the discussion section of *Create a new site content type* in the Appendix) into consideration when you know that you will be moving forms between form libraries in the future. For example, if you have a form library on site A1, which is a child site of site A, and you suspect or know that you will want to or have to move the form library to site A2, which is also a child site of site A, you could publish the form template for the form library as a site content type (see recipe *26 Publish a form template as a site content type*) on site A (or any site higher up in the site hierarchy), rather than publish it directly to the form library (see recipe *21 Publish a form template to a form library*). This should make moving forms to another form library on the same site or to another form library on a different site in the same site collection easier to carry out. This also applies to cases where you want to use a workflow to move forms as described in recipe *87 Move a form from one form library to another using a workflow*.

Before moving a form, you should find out the following two things:

1. The form template the form is linked to.
2. The form template the content type of the form is linked to.

The two aforementioned form templates should be one and the same before and after you move the form. If you do not ensure that this is the case, you will not be able to open a form after you have moved it.

You can easily use SharePoint's browser interface to find out which form template a form is linked to by using the **Relink Documents** view. Navigate to a form library that contains a few InfoPath forms and select **Library Tools** ➤ **Library** ➤ **Manage Views** ➤ **Current View** ➤ **Relink Documents**. Once you are on the **Relink Documents** page, you will see two columns: **Content Type** and **Template Link**. The **Content Type** column contains the name of the content type SharePoint has identified as the content type the form is based on and the **Template Link** column contains the URL of the form template the form is linked to.

Content Type	Template Link
My Form	http://win-ji2o5062vat/infopath2010cookbook2/FormsLib/Forms/template.xsn
My Form	http://win-ji2o5062vat/infopath2010cookbook2/FormsLib/Forms/template.xsn
My Form	http://win-ji2o5062vat/infopath2010cookbook2/FormsLib/Forms/template.xsn

Figure 122. Content Type and Template Link columns on the Relink Documents page in SharePoint.

Note that the **Relink Documents** page only tells you what the form is linked to, and not which form template the content type is linked to. You must go to the **Advanced Settings** page of the content type via the form library settings page and the details page of the content type to find out which form template (document template) is assigned to the

Chapter 2: SharePoint Form Library Forms

content type that is listed in the **Content Type** column on the **Relink Documents** page. This is an important step to carry out, because as you will learn in recipe *42 Relink InfoPath forms in a form library*, SharePoint links a form to the document template of the content type listed in the **Content Type** column on the **Relink Documents** page when you use the relink functionality. So if the wrong content type is listed in the **Content Type** column or the form template assigned to the content type listed in the **Content Type** column is not the correct form template for the form, you must fix either the content type assigned to the form or the form template assigned to the content type before relinking documents, otherwise the forms will be incorrectly relinked. And this is exactly what is stated at the top of the **Relink Documents** page in the following sentence:

Before using this page, ensure that the "New" button works for each content type, and that each document is assigned to the correct content type, otherwise this page will link the documents incorrectly.

```
Use this page to relink documents that are not correctly linked to their content type's document
template. To relink all documents in this library, click Relink All Documents. To relink specific
documents, select the Relink check box for each document you want to relink, and then click Relink
Selected Documents. Before using this page, ensure that the "New" button works for each content
type, and that each document is assigned to the correct content type, otherwise this page will link
the documents incorrectly.
```

Figure 123. Informational text at the top of the Relink Documents page in SharePoint 2010.

Also bear in mind that when you move a form to a form library, SharePoint automatically assigns a content type to that form. In most cases this should be the default content type that is associated with the form library if a form library is associated with only one content type. But in the cases where you have multiple content types defined on a form library (also see recipe *27 Enable different types of forms to be created in one form library*), the automatic content type assignment may not work as intended, which again may result in relink errors.

Tip:

> It is best to move a form to a form library that is associated with only one content type, rather than to a form library that is associated with multiple content types to avoid erroneous reassignment of content types to forms.

Important:

> Always test whether connections to external data sources that a form depends on will continue working at the destination location before moving any forms.

41 Move a form library to another site

Problem

You have InfoPath forms stored in a form library on a site and you want to move all of the forms in the form library to a new form library on the same site or a site in the same site collection.

Solution

The quickest way to move all forms to a new form library is to export the form library as a list template, create a new form library based on the list template, and then delete all of the forms in the source form library or delete the source form library itself.

To save a SharePoint form library as a list template:

1. In SharePoint, navigate to the form library that contains the forms you want to move, and click **Library Tools** ➤ **Library** ➤ **Settings** ➤ **Library Settings**.

2. On the **Form Library Settings** page under **Permissions and Management**, click **Save form library as template**.

3. On the **Save as Template** page, enter a **File name** and a **Template name**, select the **Include Content** check box, and click **OK**. The form library and all of its forms should be stored as a list template in the **List Template Gallery** of the site collection. To access the **List Template Gallery** of a site collection, you can either click on the **list template gallery** link that appears on a page after you have successfully saved a list template, or you can click **Site Actions** ➤ **Site Settings** ➤ **Galleries** ➤ **List templates** on the top-level site of the site collection.

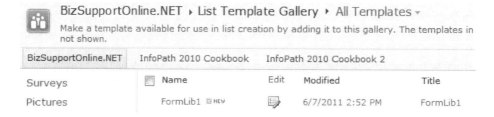

Figure 124. New list template named FormLib1 in the List Template Gallery in SharePoint.

Once you have saved a list template, it should appear as a selectable template on the **Create** page, which you can access via **Site Actions** ➤ **More Options** or via **Site Actions** ➤ **View All Site Content** ➤ **Create** in SharePoint.

To move or copy the form library with its contents to a new form library on the same site or a site in the same site collection:

Chapter 2: SharePoint Form Library Forms

1. Navigate to the site where you want to create the new form library.

2. Follow the first set of instructions in recipe *16 Create a form library and edit its form template*, but when you are on the **Create** page for libraries, select the list template you saved earlier instead of the standard **Form Library** template to create the new form library.

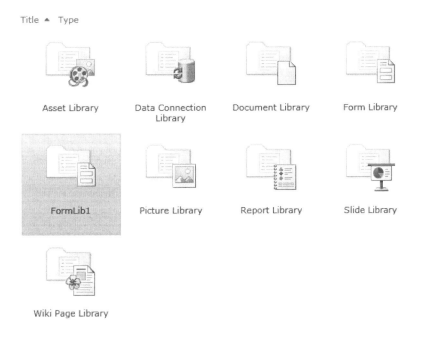

Figure 125. Selecting a saved list template named FormLib1 on the Create page in SharePoint.

3. Click **Library Tools** ➤ **Library** ➤ **Settings** ➤ **Library Settings** to navigate to the **Form Library Settings** page of the newly created form library.

4. If the **Content Types** section is not visible on the **Form Library Settings** page, enable management of content types as described in steps 3 and 4 of recipe *27 Enable different types of forms to be created in one form library*.

5. On the **Form Library Settings** page under the **Content Types** section, click on each content type and go through their advanced settings to ensure that they are linked to the correct form templates. If necessary, correct the document template URL for each content type as follows:

    a. If the source form library was associated with a default **Form** list content type, this content type should have automatically been correctly created on the new form library, but if it was not:

        i. In SharePoint, ensure that the **Form** list content type is set as the default content type on the new form library, and if it is not, set it to be the default

147

content type as described in recipe *28 Change the default form template of a form library*.

   ii. In InfoPath, republish the form template to the new form library by choosing the **Form Library** option and updating the form template of the new form library you created in SharePoint (also see recipe *21 Publish a form template to a form library*).

   b. If the form library was associated with any site content types that are not accessible from the site where the new form library is located:

   i. In InfoPath, republish the form templates for each content type as a site content type on the site where the new form library is located or on a parent site of the site where the new form library is located (also see recipe *26 Publish a form template as a site content type*).

   ii. In SharePoint, manually correct the document template URL for each content type that is associated with the form library by entering the URL that points to the location of the newly published form template in the **Enter the URL of an existing document template** text box on the content type's **Advanced Settings** page, which you can access via **Library Tools ➤ Library ➤ Settings ➤ Library Settings ➤ [Content Type Name] ➤ Advanced settings**.

6. If necessary, relink the forms in the form library as described in recipe *42 Relink InfoPath forms in a form library*.

Discussion

When moving a form library to another site, you must consider the impact this would have on the links between the forms and the content types that are associated with the form library. For example, if you move a form library that makes use of content types that were defined on another site, these content types may have to be recreated on the new site or a parent site that is shared by both sites, so that you can properly relink the forms in the destination form library.

The technique of using a list template to move forms to a form library on another site can also be used to move forms to a form library on a site in a different site collection or on a different server. Note that you would first have to download a copy of the list template and save it locally on disk and then upload it to the **List Template Gallery** (also see *Upload a list template to a List Template Gallery* in the Appendix) of the other site collection, or move it to another server before uploading it to the destination **List Template Gallery**.

You can also use the list template technique to archive InfoPath forms stored in a form library to disk or storage media, and then restore the form library containing the forms at a later point in time using the solution described above. Note that you would also have to archive the original form templates used to create the forms, so that content types can be recreated and/or corrected if necessary when the form library is restored.

Chapter 2: SharePoint Form Library Forms

42 Relink InfoPath forms in a form library

Problem

You moved a few InfoPath forms to a new form library and want to relink them to the form template that is the document template of their content type.

Solution

You can use the **Relink Documents** functionality of a form library to relink forms in the form library.

To relink InfoPath forms in a form library:

1. In SharePoint, navigate to the form library that contains the forms you want to relink, and select **Library Tools** ➤ **Library** ➤ **Manage Views** ➤ **Current View** ➤ **Relink Documents**. SharePoint should open the **Relink Documents** page. The **Content Type** column on this page displays which content type a particular form is linked to, and the **Template Link** column displays the URL of the form template the form is linked to.

2. For each form you want to relink, ensure that:

   a. The content type listed in the **Content Type** column is the correct content type that should be used for that form.

   b. The content type listed in the **Content Type** column has the form template that you want to relink the form to, assigned as its document template. If the content type is linked to an incorrect form template, you must first correct that link before relinking the forms to the form library. You can correct the document template URL as follows:

      i. If the form library has not been set to allow management of content types:

         1. On the **Form Library Settings** page under **General Settings**, click **Advanced settings**.

         2. On the **Advanced Settings** page under **Document Template**, correct the URL of the form template that has been set in the **Template URL** text box.

      ii. If the form library has been set to allow management of content types:

         1. On the **Form Library Settings** page under **Content Types**, click on the content type you want to correct.

         2. On the details page of the content type under **Settings**, click **Advanced settings**.

         3. On the **Advanced Settings** page under **Document Template** correct the URL of the form template that has been set in the **Enter the URL of an existing document template** text box.

149

3. On the **Relink Documents** page, select the check box in the **Relink** column for each form you want to relink, and then on the Ribbon, click **Library Tools ▶ Documents ▶ Actions ▶ Relink**. If you want to relink all of the forms in a form library, you can select one form and then click **Library Tools ▶ Documents ▶ Actions ▶ Relink All**.

Figure 126. The Relink and Relink All commands on the Ribbon in SharePoint 2010.

The forms should now be linked to the form templates that correspond to the content types listed on the **Relink Documents** page.

Discussion

The **Relink Documents** page allows you to relink forms to the form template that corresponds to a particular content type. When a form is saved or submitted, it contains a reference to the form template that was used to create it. If you move a form (XML file) to a different form library or perform an operation that may have broken this link, you should be able to fix the link via the **Relink Documents** page. You can access the **Relink Documents** page by switching to the **Relink Documents** view of the form library or by clicking **Relink documents to this library** under the **Permissions and Management** section of the **Form Library Settings** page. When you are on the **Relink Documents** page, you should see two columns named **Content Type** and **Template Link**. You can use these two columns to check whether a form is correctly linked to a content type and form template. Another way of checking which template a form is linked to is by downloading a copy of the form by clicking **Library Tools ▶ Documents ▶ Copies ▶ Download a Copy** on the Ribbon, opening the XML file in Notepad, and then checking the URL of the form template (XSN file) listed in the `mso-infoPathSolution` processing instruction.

When you relink a form, SharePoint relinks the form to the form template that has been defined as the document template of the content type listed in the **Content Type** column for that form on the **Relink Documents** page. So you must ensure that the content type that is listed for the form on the **Relink Documents** page indeed corresponds to the content type of the form template you want to relink the form to, because if it does not, SharePoint may incorrectly relink the form and you will get an error when you try to open the form.

Always remember that the content type of a form leads the relinking process and that if that content type is linked to the wrong form template, SharePoint will also relink the form to the wrong form template (also see page 144 for more information on the **Relink Documents** page in SharePoint). In some cases, when you move forms to a form library that has multiple content types associated with it, SharePoint may also assign the forms to

Chapter 2: SharePoint Form Library Forms

an incorrect content type. To prevent such incorrect assignments of content types to forms, always try to move forms to a form library that has only one content type associated with it. This way SharePoint will have no choice but to link the forms you move to that one content type on the form library.

The following figure explains how the relinking process works when you move forms from one site collection to another.

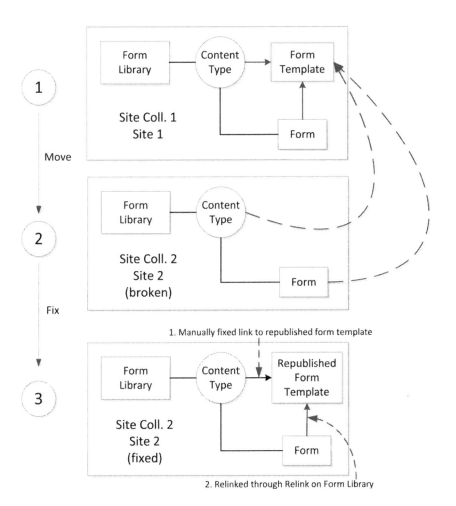

Figure 127. Moving InfoPath forms from one site collection to another.

In the figure above:

1. InfoPath forms are located in a form library on Site 1 in Site Collection 1. The forms are based on a content type, which has the form template that the forms are linked to, defined as its document template.

151

2. The form library is moved to Site 2 in Site Collection 2. At this stage, both the content type and the forms are still pointing to the form template on Site 1 in Site Collection 1, and because cross-site collection access is not possible, the forms cannot be opened, so you must relink them.

3. You can fix the forms in the form library on Site 2 in Site Collection 2 by first manually republishing the form template to Site 2 in Site Collection 2, changing the document template for the content type to point to the republished form template, and then using the relink functionality of the form library to relink the forms to the newly published form template through their relationship with the content type.

Chapter 3: Retrieve SharePoint List Data

A common task when designing InfoPath forms is to retrieve and display data from SharePoint lists. InfoPath 2010 comes with 3 data connections you can use to connect to and retrieve data from SharePoint lists:

1. SharePoint list data connections
2. Web Service data connections
3. XML data connections

The commands to create the aforementioned types of data connections can be found under the **Get External Data** group on the **Data** tab on the Ribbon in InfoPath Designer 2010.

Figure 128. Ribbon commands to add data connections to retrieve data in InfoPath 2010.

You will learn several ways to retrieve, sort, filter, and work with SharePoint list or library data as you progress through the recipes in this chapter.

Retrieve and display SharePoint list data

SharePoint list data connections are probably the easiest to use when it comes to retrieving data from a SharePoint list or library. They offer simple sort functionality and you can use them to retrieve data from Excel, Access, or SQL Server through SharePoint. REST Web Service data connections are probably the most flexible to use as they offer filter and sort functionality that is not available on the other types of data connections.

The recipes in this section will show you how to use SharePoint list data connections, REST Web Service data connections, and XML data connections to retrieve data from SharePoint lists, and also discuss when it would make sense to use each method.

43 3 Ways to retrieve data from a SharePoint list

Use a SharePoint list data connection

Problem

You have a SharePoint list which contains data you want to display as read-only on an InfoPath form.

Solution

You can use a SharePoint list data connection to retrieve data from a SharePoint list and use this data within an InfoPath form.

Suppose you have a SharePoint list named **OfficeApplications** as described in *Create a SharePoint list form for an existing SharePoint list* of recipe *2 Customize a SharePoint list form from within InfoPath*.

To get data from this SharePoint list using a SharePoint list data connection:

1. In InfoPath, create a new browser-compatible template or use an existing one.
2. Click **Data** ➤ **Get External Data** ➤ **From SharePoint List**.
3. On the **Data Connection Wizard**, enter the URL of the SharePoint site where the SharePoint list you want to connect to is located, and click **Next**.

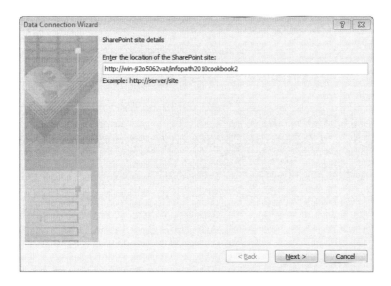

Figure 129. Entering the URL of the SharePoint site where the list is located.

4. On the **Data Connection Wizard**, select the list you want to connect to (**OfficeApplications** in this case) from the **Select a list or library** list box, and click

Chapter 3: Retrieve SharePoint List Data

Next.

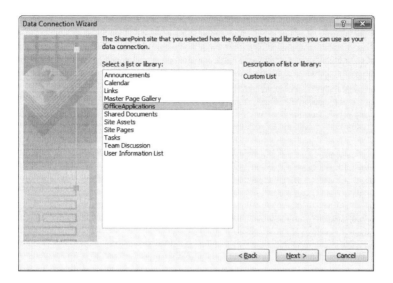

Figure 130. Selecting the SharePoint list to connect to.

5. On the **Data Connection Wizard**, select any fields (for example, **Title** and **Color**) from the SharePoint list that you want to include in the secondary data source that will be created for the SharePoint list in InfoPath, and click **Next**.

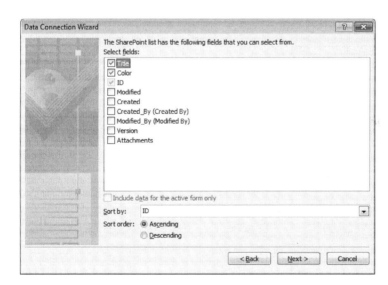

Figure 131. Selecting the fields to include in the data source.

6. On the **Data Connection Wizard**, click **Next**. Note that if you wanted to save data from the SharePoint list within the form template for offline use, you could select the **Store a copy of the data in the form template** check box before clicking **Next**.

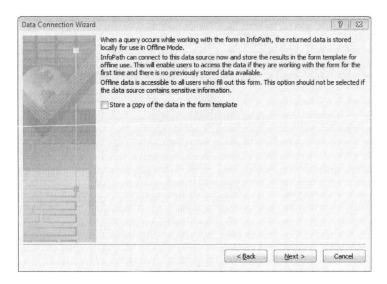

Figure 132. Choosing not to store a copy of the data in the form template.

7. On the **Data Connection Wizard**, enter a name for the data connection or accept the default name InfoPath generates based on the name of the SharePoint list, leave the **Automatically retrieve data when form is opened** check box selected, and click **Finish**.

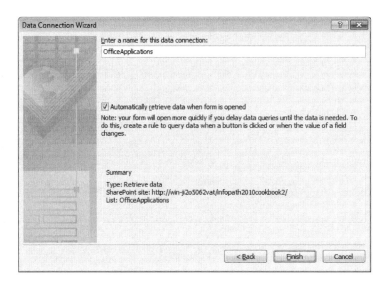

Figure 133. The last screen of the Data Connection Wizard in InfoPath Designer 2010.

You should now be able to use the data connection to get data from the SharePoint list and use it in your InfoPath form for example to populate a drop-down list box. The data

Chapter 3: Retrieve SharePoint List Data

is returned in the **SharePointListItem_RW** repeating group node that is located under the **dataFields** group node in the secondary data source for the SharePoint list.

Figure 134. The data source for the SharePoint list on the Fields task pane in InfoPath Designer 2010.

Discussion

If you click **Data ➤ Get External Data ➤ Data Connections**, you should see the data connection listed on the **Data Connections** dialog box. At the bottom of the **Data Connections** dialog box you can get more details about the data connection, such as for example that its type is **Retrieve data**, that it is a **Secondary data source**, and that it connects to a SharePoint site.

Figure 135. Data Connections dialog box in InfoPath Designer 2010.

157

InfoPath 2010 Cookbook 2

In the solution described above, you left the **Automatically retrieve data when form is opened** check box selected on the last screen of the **Data Connection Wizard**. It is not a best practice to leave this check box selected especially if you expect a SharePoint list to contain many items, since loading all of the data from the SharePoint list when the form opens could negatively impact the performance of the form.

Just like the Main data source of SharePoint list forms (see the discussion section of *Create a SharePoint list form for an existing SharePoint list* in recipe *2 Customize a SharePoint list form from within InfoPath*), a secondary data source for a SharePoint list consists of a **queryFields** and a **dataFields** group node. The **queryFields** group node contains the fields that can be used to query (look up) data in the SharePoint list, while the **dataFields** group node contains fields that can be used to display data from the SharePoint list.

In cases where you want to retrieve data on-demand instead of automatically when a form opens, it is best to deselect the **Automatically retrieve data when form is opened** check box on the last screen of the **Data Connection Wizard** and then use the fields under the **queryFields** group node of the secondary data source for the SharePoint list to retrieve data as shown in recipe *50 Filter SharePoint list data using an exact match*.

Use the ListData REST web service

Problem

You have a SharePoint list which contains data you want to display as read-only on an InfoPath form.

Solution

You can use a data connection to SharePoint's **ListData** REST web service to retrieve data from a SharePoint list and display this data within an InfoPath form.

Suppose you have a SharePoint list named **OfficeApplications** as described in *Create a SharePoint list form for an existing SharePoint list* of recipe *2 Customize a SharePoint list form from within InfoPath*.

To get data from this SharePoint list using the **ListData** REST web service:

1. In InfoPath, create a new browser-compatible form template or use an existing one.

2. Select **Data** ➤ **Get External Data** ➤ **From Web Service** ➤ **From REST Web Service**.

3. On the **Data Connection Wizard**, enter the URL of the **ListData** REST web service, for example:

   ```
   http://servername/sitename/_vti_bin/ListData.svc/OfficeApplications
   ```

   and click **Next**. Here, **servername** is the name of the SharePoint server and **sitename** is the name of the site where the **OfficeApplications** SharePoint list is located. Tip: Always test a REST Web Service URL in a browser to see whether it returns valid XML data before using the URL in InfoPath.

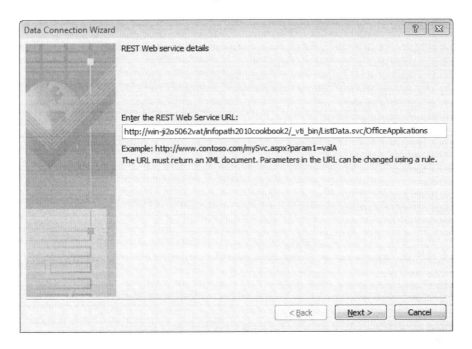

Figure 136. Entering the REST Web Service URL on the Data Connection Wizard.

4. On the **Data Connection Wizard**, enter a name for the data connection (for example **OfficeApplicationsREST**), leave the **Automatically retrieve data when form is opened** check box selected, and click **Finish**.

You should now be able to use the data connection to get data from the SharePoint list and use it in your InfoPath form for example to populate a drop-down list box. The data returned for each item in the data source is located under the **entry** repeating group node and the **m:properties** group node in the secondary data source for the REST web service.

Discussion

The advantage of using a REST web service data connection compared to using a SharePoint list data connection as described in *Use a SharePoint list data connection* in this recipe is the ability to perform exact as well as wildcard match filtering, and to sort SharePoint list data dynamically and on multiple fields instead of just one field. (also see recipe *49 Dynamically sort SharePoint list data on one or more fields* and recipe *51 Filter SharePoint list data using a BETWEEN match*).

InfoPath 2010 Cookbook 2

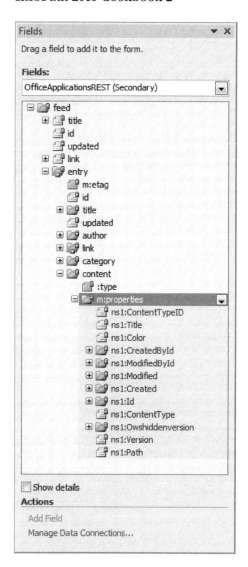

Figure 137. The data source for the REST web service on the Fields task pane in InfoPath 2010.

Tip:

> If you do not know where the data you want to use is located in the data source for a REST web service, enter the REST URL in a browser and check the data there to find the corresponding XML nodes to use in InfoPath.

Chapter 3: Retrieve SharePoint List Data

Use an XML data connection

Problem

You have a SharePoint list which contains data you want to display as read-only on an InfoPath form. You do not want to show all of the items from the SharePoint list, but rather only those items that were created by the user who opens the form.

Solution

You can specify a view that filters list items on the current user in an XML data connection that makes use of the URL protocol to retrieve data from a SharePoint list.

Suppose you have a SharePoint list named **OfficeApplications** as described in *Create a SharePoint list form for an existing SharePoint list* of recipe *2 Customize a SharePoint list form from within InfoPath*.

To get data from this SharePoint list using an XML data connection and the URL protocol:

1. In SharePoint, navigate to the **OfficeApplications** SharePoint list for which you want to show data on an InfoPath form and click **List Tools ➤ List ➤ Manage Views ➤ Create View**.

2. On the **Create View** page under the **Choose a view format** section, click **Standard View**.

3. On the **Create View** page, enter **CurrentUserItems** as the **View Name**, select the **Display** check box for all of the columns you would like to display in the list, under **Filter** select the **Show items only when the following is true** option, select **Created By** from the **Show the items when column** drop-down list box, leave **is equal to** selected in the following drop-down list box, and type **[Me]** in the text box that follows before clicking **OK**.

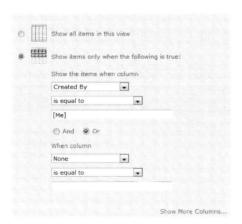

Figure 138. Settings under the Filter section on the Create View page in SharePoint 2010.

161

InfoPath 2010 Cookbook 2

This should display only those items that the current user created in the SharePoint list.

4. Click on the drop-down arrow on the right-hand side of the view name in the breadcrumb trail at the top of the page, and then select **Modify this view** from the drop-down menu that appears.

Figure 139. Selecting to modify the view.

5. On the **Edit View** page, copy the GUID that is listed behind the **View** query string parameter in the URL in the browser's address bar and paste it in Notepad. It should resemble the following:

%7B5EB10707%2D8F4B%2D42E9%2DBC45%2D779A51ABE7F7%7D

And while you are at it, also copy the GUID that is listed behind the **List** query string parameter in the URL in the browser's address bar and paste it in Notepad. It should resemble the following:

%7B66004C03%2D9FB5%2D4D83%2DAC83%2DFA90CC679662%7D

Click **Cancel** when you are done.

Figure 140. GUIDs for the List and View query string parameters in the browser's address bar.

6. In InfoPath, create a new SharePoint form library form template or use an existing one.

7. Select **Data ➤ Get External Data ➤ From Other Sources ➤ From XML File**.

8. On the **Data Connection Wizard**, enter the URL that points to the SharePoint list, for example:

```
http://servername/sitename/_vti_bin/owssvr.dll?Cmd=Display&List={GUID}&View
={GUID}&XMLDATA=TRUE&noredirect=true
```

and click **Next**. Here, **servername** is the name of the SharePoint server and **sitename** is the site where the SharePoint list is located. In addition, replace the **{GUID}** pieces of text listed in the URL with the actual GUIDs you copied earlier to Notepad. A sample URL that includes the GUIDs resembles the following:

Chapter 3: Retrieve SharePoint List Data

```
http://win-
ji2o5062vat/infopath2010cookbook2/_vti_bin/owssvr.dll?Cmd=Display&List=%7BC
52FFB09%2D9186%2D4C19%2DA3A9%2DF974F0AE2819%7D&View=%7B64A303B0%2DEDD1%2D4F
9D%2D8F92%2D0D6A056A1D4A%7D&XMLDATA=TRUE&noredirect=true
```

Figure 141. Entering the URL for the XML data connection on the Data Connection Wizard.

9. On the **Data Connection Wizard**, select the **Access the data from the specified location** option, leave the **Store a copy of the data for offline use** check box deselected, and click **Next**.

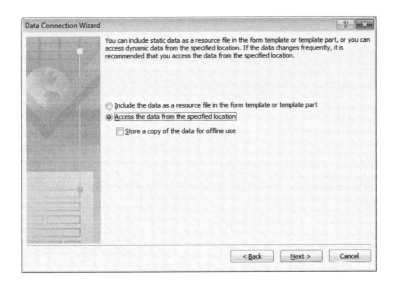

Figure 142. Setting the connection to get the data from SharePoint instead of the form template.

InfoPath 2010 Cookbook 2

Because you want fresh data to be retrieved from the server every time you query the data connection, you must select the option to access the data from the specified location and not store it in the form template.

10. On the **Data Connection Wizard**, rename the data connection to **GetListData**, leave the **Automatically retrieve data when form is opened** check box selected, and click **Finish**.

11. On the **Fields** task pane, select **GetListData (Secondary)** from the **Fields** drop-down list box, expand the **rs:data** group node, and then drag-and-drop the **z:row** repeating field to the view of the form template. When you drop it, select **Repeating Table** from the context menu that appears.

Figure 143. Groups and fields in the secondary data source.

12. Publish the form template to a SharePoint form library.

In SharePoint, navigate to the form library where you published the form template and add a new form. When the form opens, verify that only those items that were created by you appear in the repeating table on the form. Sign in as a different user, add a new form, and verify again that the items that were created by the user you signed in as appear in the repeating table on the form.

Discussion

SharePoint supports the URL protocol with which you can send commands to SharePoint by using an URL that contains a command and (optionally) parameters. You can learn more about the URL protocol on the MSDN web site.

The syntax for the URL to send to SharePoint is:

Chapter 3: Retrieve SharePoint List Data

```
http://servername/sitename/_vti_bin/owssvr.dll?Cmd=MethodName[&Parameter1=Value1
&Parameter2=Value2...]
```

where **servername** is the name of the SharePoint server and **sitename** is the name of the SharePoint site. For example, in the solution described above, you used the following URL:

```
http://servername/sitename/_vti_bin/owssvr.dll?Cmd=Display&List={GUID}&View={GUID}&XMLDATA=TRUE&noredirect=true
```

where **Display** is the command to send to SharePoint. The **Display** command runs a database query and returns XML or HTML. You used it in the solution described above to retrieve data (as XML) from a SharePoint list (for which you specified its GUID through the **List** query string parameter in the URL) using a specific view (for which you specified its GUID through the **View** query string parameter in the URL) that was defined on that list.

While there is little benefit to using the URL protocol to retrieve data from a SharePoint list, because you can use a standard SharePoint list data connection to do almost everything you can do using the URL protocol, there are a few exceptions. For example, if you want to specify a specific view to use when retrieving data as you have done in the solution described above, or if you want to retrieve data from columns of a SharePoint list that are not shown when you use a standard SharePoint list data connection in InfoPath, you could use the URL protocol to retrieve data instead of the standard SharePoint list data connection. Other than the two aforementioned exceptions, the URL protocol offers sorting and filtering similar to the standard SharePoint list data connection, that is, you can perform exact match filtering on one or multiple fields, and you can perform sorting on one field unless you retrieve data by using a SharePoint view and define additional sort fields on that view.

In recipe *58 Retrieve a list of forms created by the current user from a form library* you will see an example of using the standard SharePoint list data connection to retrieve forms the current user has created. There is a caveat to using that method, which could warrant using the method in the solution described above instead.

Tip:

> Always test the URL for a data connection that makes use of the URL protocol in a browser to see whether it returns valid XML data before using that URL in an XML data connection in InfoPath.

InfoPath 2010 Cookbook 2

44   Display SharePoint list data in a repeating table

Problem

You have added a SharePoint list connection to a form template and now want to display the data from the SharePoint list in a repeating table.

Solution

You can bind the secondary data source for the SharePoint list to a repeating table to be able to display the data in the repeating table.

Suppose you have a SharePoint list named **OfficeApplications** as described in recipe *2 Customize a SharePoint list form from within InfoPath*.

To display data from this SharePoint list in a repeating table:

1. In InfoPath, create a new SharePoint form library form template or use an existing one.

2. Add a SharePoint list data connection to the form template as described in *Use a SharePoint list data connection* of recipe *43 3 Ways to retrieve data from a SharePoint list*.

3. On the **Fields** task pane, select **OfficeApplications (Secondary)** from the **Fields** drop-down list box.

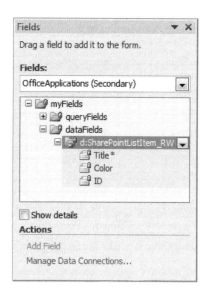

Figure 144. The OfficeApplications secondary data source in InfoPath Designer 2010.

4. On the **Fields** task pane, expand the **dataFields** group node, click the **d:SharePointListItem_RW** repeating group node, drag it to the view of the form

166

Chapter 3: Retrieve SharePoint List Data

template, drop it, and select **Repeating Table** from the context menu that appears when you drop it.

5. Publish the form template to a SharePoint form library.

In SharePoint, navigate to the form library where you published the form template and add a new form. When the form opens, all of the data from the SharePoint list should be displayed in the repeating table.

Discussion

In the solution described above, you bound a repeating group node under the **dataFields** group node of the secondary data source for the SharePoint list to a repeating table control. Note that if you used one of the other two methods for retrieving SharePoint list data as described in recipe *43 3 Ways to retrieve data from a SharePoint list*, you would have had to bind the repeating table fields to different repeating group nodes or repeating fields within the secondary data source for the SharePoint list.

If you look at the structure of the secondary data source for the SharePoint list on the **Fields** task pane, you will see that there are two group nodes under the **myFields** root node:

1. queryFields
2. dataFields

The **queryFields** group node contains fields that can be used to query (look up and/or filter) data in the SharePoint list, while the **dataFields** group node contains fields that contain the data from the SharePoint list after you have run a query on the data connection. You can use the fields under the **dataFields** group node to display data from the SharePoint list on the InfoPath form.

Unlike the **dataFields** group node in the Main data source of a SharePoint list form (see the discussion section of *Create a SharePoint list form for an existing SharePoint list* in recipe *2 Customize a SharePoint list form from within InfoPath*), in the case of a **Receive** data connection for a SharePoint list, you can only use the fields under the **dataFields** group node to display data, and not to add or edit data in the SharePoint list. The data in the fields under the **dataFields** group node is read-only. This also means that when you bind these fields to controls in a repeating table, you cannot modify the data that is displayed in the repeating table. For example, if you click on any of the text box controls within the repeating table and try to set their default value, you will see that the **Default Value** option has been disabled. So if you want to work with and change data that comes from a **Receive** data connection for a SharePoint list, you must find a way to copy the data from the secondary data source over to other fields on the InfoPath form that are modifiable. The next recipe shows you ways to copy data from a SharePoint list to fields in the Main data source of a form.

45 3 Ways to copy SharePoint list data to form fields

Auto-populate fields when an item in a drop-down list box is selected

Problem

You have added a SharePoint list data connection to a form template and populated a drop-down list box with the data from the SharePoint list data source. You want users to be able to select an item from the drop-down list box and then have other fields on the form automatically populate with data corresponding to the selected item in the drop-down list box.

Solution

You can use filters on the data in the secondary data source for the SharePoint list to lookup and copy the information you require to other fields on the InfoPath form.

Suppose you have a SharePoint list named **OfficeApplications** as described in recipe *2 Customize a SharePoint list form from within InfoPath*.

To copy data from this SharePoint list when an item in a drop-down list box is selected:

1. In InfoPath, create a new SharePoint form library form template or use an existing one.

2. Add a **Receive** data connection to the **OfficeApplications** SharePoint list to the form template as described in *Use a SharePoint list data connection* of recipe *43 3 Ways to retrieve data from a SharePoint list*. Ensure you select **Title** and **Color** as the fields to include in the data source, and that you leave the **Automatically retrieve data when form is opened** check box selected.

3. Add a **Drop-Down List Box** control to the view of the form template, name it **selectedOfficeApplication**, and populate it with entries from the **OfficeApplications** secondary data source. Use the **ID** for the **Value** and the **Title** for the **Display name** of the items in the drop-down list box.

Chapter 3: Retrieve SharePoint List Data

Figure 145. Populating the drop-down list box with SharePoint list items.

4. Add two **Text Box** controls to the view of the form template and name them **title** and **color**, respectively.

5. Add an **Action** rule to the drop-down list box that has the following two actions:

   ```
   Set a field's value: title = Title[ID = selectedOfficeApplication]
   Set a field's value: color = Color[ID = selectedOfficeApplication]
   ```

   where **title**, **color**, and **selectedOfficeApplication** are fields located in the Main data source of the form; and **ID**, **Title**, and **Color** are fields located under the **d:SharePointListItem_RW** repeating group node under the **dataFields** group node in the **OfficeApplications (Secondary)** data source. The values of both the **Title** and **Color** fields in the secondary data source are filtered on the value of the **ID** field in the secondary data source being equal to the selected value in the drop-down list box (**[ID = selectedOfficeApplication]**). You can use the **Filter Data** option on the **Select a Field or Group** dialog box to set up the filter for both fields. This rule performs data lookups in the secondary data source of the SharePoint list

InfoPath 2010 Cookbook 2

based on the selected item in the drop-down list box, and then sets the values of the text box controls accordingly.

6. Publish the form template to a SharePoint form library.

In SharePoint, navigate to the form library where you published the form template and add a new form. When the form opens, select an item from the drop-down list box, and verify that the corresponding values for title and color are populated in the text boxes.

Select Office Application:	InfoPath
Title:	InfoPath
Color:	Purple

Figure 146. The InfoPath form displaying the title and color for a selected Office application.

Discussion

In the solution described above, all of the data from the secondary data source was retrieved as soon as the form opened. This is mainly because you needed to populate the drop-down list box with initial data, so that users would have something to select from. But if your scenario entails a user knowing an **ID** or **Title** they could enter, you could change the solution to allow users to explicitly enter this data into a text box, and then run a query that makes use of that **ID** or **Title** to retrieve corresponding data. In such a solution you would first have to set the value of the **ID** or **Title** field under the **queryFields** group node in the secondary data source to be equal to the value the user typed into the text box, run a **Query for data** action on the secondary data source, and then use a **Set a field's value** action to populate form fields based on the data that was returned in the fields located under the **dataFields** group node in the secondary data source. You would not have to use the **Filter Data** option for such a solution, since filtering would have already taken place when you ran the query (also see recipe *50 Filter SharePoint list data using an exact match*).

Use a Select button in a repeating table

Problem

You have bound a secondary data source for a SharePoint list to a repeating table control on an InfoPath form. Now you want to be able to copy the data from one of the rows of the repeating table to other fields on the InfoPath form.

Solution

You can add an extra column with a button to the repeating table that is bound to the secondary data source for the SharePoint list and then use action rules on the button to set values of other fields on the form.

Chapter 3: Retrieve SharePoint List Data

Suppose you have a SharePoint list named **OfficeApplications** as described in recipe *2 Customize a SharePoint list form from within InfoPath*.

To copy data from this SharePoint list using a button to select data from a repeating table row:

1. In InfoPath, create a new SharePoint form library form template or use an existing one.

2. Add a **Receive** data connection to the **OfficeApplications** SharePoint list to the form template as described in *Use a SharePoint list data connection* of recipe *43 3 Ways to retrieve data from a SharePoint list*. Ensure you select **Title** and **Color** as the fields to include in the data source, and that you leave the **Automatically retrieve data when form is opened** check box selected.

3. Bind the **d:SharePointListItem_RW** repeating group node under the **dataFields** group node in the **OfficeApplications** secondary data source to a repeating table on the view of the form template as described in recipe *44 Display SharePoint list data in a repeating table*.

4. Click anywhere in the header of the right-most column to place the cursor, and then select **Table Tools ➤ Layout ➤ Rows & Columns ➤ Insert Right** to add a new column to the repeating table.

5. Add a **Button** control to the cell of the new column in the repeating table and label the button **Select**.

6. Add two **Text Box** controls to the view of the form template and name them **title** and **color**, respectively.

7. Add an **Action** rule to the **Select** button that has the following two actions:

   ```
   Set a field's value: title = Title
   Set a field's value: color = Color
   ```

   where **title** and **color** are the fields that are bound to the text box controls and are located in the Main data source of the form, while **Title** and **Color** are located under the **d:SharePointListItem_RW** repeating group node under the **dataFields** group node in the **OfficeApplications (Secondary)** data source.

8. Publish the form template to a SharePoint form library.

In SharePoint, navigate to the form library where you published the form template and add a new form. When the form opens, click on the **Select** button in any row of the repeating table. The values of the **Title** and **Color** fields in the same row of the repeating table in which the **Select** button is located, should appear in the corresponding **title** and **color** text boxes on the form.

InfoPath 2010 Cookbook 2

Title	Color	ID	
Word	Blue	1	Select
Excel	Green	2	Select
Access	Red	3	Select
PowerPoint	Orange	4	Select
OneNote	Purple	5	Select
InfoPath	Purple	6	Select
Publisher	Blue	12	Select

Title: Access
Color: Red

Figure 147. The InfoPath form with the title and color of Access selected.

Discussion

A repeating table that is bound to a secondary data source is not modifiable, meaning that you cannot add any fields to it. The data source is locked; you can see that it is at the padlocks that have been placed on the fields and groups in the secondary data source on the **Fields** task pane. However, you are allowed to add buttons to rows of the repeating table, because buttons do not have to be bound to fields in the data source. The solution described above makes use of the latter.

By adding a button to each row of the repeating table, you enable the data in each individual row to be selected through the button that is located in the same row. Copying data from the secondary data source for the SharePoint list then simply becomes a matter of adding an action rule to the button to set the values of fields that are located elsewhere on the form.

Copy data to a row in a repeating table on insert

Problem

You have a repeating table control on an InfoPath form. Every time a user clicks to add a row to the repeating table, you want to copy values that correspond to an item selected in a drop-down list box to that specific row of the repeating table.

Solution

You can set the default value of the fields in the repeating table to pull data from the SharePoint list whenever a new row is added to the repeating table.

Suppose you have a SharePoint list named **OfficeApplications** as described in recipe *2 Customize a SharePoint list form from within InfoPath*.

Chapter 3: Retrieve SharePoint List Data

To copy data from this SharePoint list when a new row is added to the repeating table:

1. In InfoPath, create a new SharePoint form library form template or use an existing one.

2. Add a **Receive** data connection to the **OfficeApplications** SharePoint list to the form template as described in *Use a SharePoint list data connection* of recipe *43 3 Ways to retrieve data from a SharePoint list*. Ensure you select **Title** and **Color** as the fields to include in the data source, and that you leave the **Automatically retrieve data when form is opened** check box selected.

3. Add a **Drop-Down List Box** control to the view of the form template, name it **selectedOfficeApplication**, and populate it with entries from the **OfficeApplications** secondary data source. Use the **ID** for the **Value** and the **Title** for the **Display name** of the items in the drop-down list box.

4. Add a **Repeating Table** control with 3 columns to the view of the form template, and rename the fields in the repeating table to **id**, **title**, and **color**, respectively.

5. Click **Data** ➤ **Form Data** ➤ **Default Values**, and then on the **Edit Default Values** dialog box, deselect the check box in front of the **group2** repeating group node. This should remove the first empty row from the repeating table when the repeating table is shown for the first time.

Figure 148. A cleared check box in front of the group2 node.

6. Set the **Default Value** of the **id** field in the repeating table to the following formula:

   ```
   xdXDocument:GetDOM("OfficeApplications")/dfs:myFields/dfs:dataFields/d:Shar
   ePointListItem_RW/d:ID[. = xdXDocument:get-
   DOM()/my:myFields/my:selectedOfficeApplication]
   ```

   What this formula does is filter the secondary data source for the SharePoint list on the **ID** of the selected Office Application in the drop-down list box, and then returns the **ID** of the item found. Note: You must deselect the **Refresh value when formula is recalculated** check box on the **Field or Group Properties** dialog box, so that the **id** fields in all of the other rows in the repeating table are not refreshed every time a new row is added to the repeating table.

7. Set the **Default Value** of the **title** field in the repeating table to the following formula:

   ```
   xdXDocument:GetDOM("OfficeApplications")/dfs:myFields/dfs:dataFields/d:Shar
   ePointListItem_RW/d:Title[../d:ID = xdXDocument:get-
   DOM()/my:myFields/my:selectedOfficeApplication]
   ```

   What this formula does is filter the secondary data source for the SharePoint list on the **ID** of the selected Office Application in the drop-down list box, and then returns the **Title** of the item found. Note: You must deselect the **Refresh value when formula is recalculated** check box on the **Field or Group Properties** dialog box, so that the **title** fields in all of the other rows in the repeating table are not refreshed every time a new row is added to the repeating table.

8. Set the **Default Value** of the **color** field in the repeating table to the following formula:

   ```
   xdXDocument:GetDOM("OfficeApplications")/dfs:myFields/dfs:dataFields/d:Shar
   ePointListItem_RW/d:Color[../d:ID = xdXDocument:get-
   DOM()/my:myFields/my:selectedOfficeApplication]
   ```

   What this formula does is filter the secondary data source for the SharePoint list on the **ID** of the selected Office Application in the drop-down list box, and then returns the **Color** of the item found. Note: You must deselect the **Refresh value when formula is recalculated** check box on the **Field or Group Properties** dialog box, so that the **color** fields in all of the other rows in the repeating table are not refreshed every time a new row is added to the repeating table.

9. Publish the form template to a SharePoint form library.

In SharePoint, navigate to the form library where you published the form template and add a new form. When the form opens, select an item from the drop-down list box, and click **Insert item** on the repeating table. A row that contains SharePoint list data that corresponds to the selected item in the drop-down list box should appear in the newly added row of the repeating table.

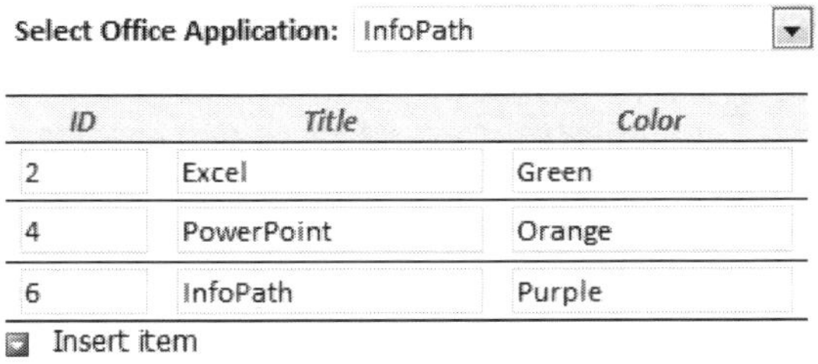

Figure 149. The InfoPath form with 3 applications selected and inserted into the repeating table.

Discussion

In the solution described above you saw how you can use default values on fields in a repeating table to pull data from a secondary data source for a SharePoint list. In the next recipe you will learn how you can use a similar technique of 'pulling data' to populate rows of a repeating table with data from a SharePoint list.

46 Map rows of a repeating table to SharePoint list items

Problem

You want to copy data from a SharePoint list to a repeating table on an InfoPath form.

Solution

You can pre-add a number of rows to a repeating table (as many rows as you think you would need or that would be suitable for displaying items from the SharePoint list), and then automatically map the fields in the repeating table to the corresponding items in the SharePoint list by using the **count** function and **preceding-sibling** XPath axis in an XPath filter expression.

Suppose you have a SharePoint list named **OfficeApplications** as described in recipe *2 Customize a SharePoint list form from within InfoPath*.

To copy data from this SharePoint list to a repeating table that has 5 fixed rows:

1. In InfoPath, create a new SharePoint form library form template or use an existing one.

2. Add a **Receive** data connection to the **OfficeApplications** SharePoint list to the form template as described in *Use a SharePoint list data connection* of recipe *43 3 Ways to retrieve data from a SharePoint list*. Ensure you select **Title** and **Color** as the fields to include in the data source, and that you leave the **Automatically retrieve data when form is opened** check box selected.

3. Add a **Repeating Table** control with 3 columns to the view of the form template, and rename the fields in the repeating table to **id**, **title**, and **color**, respectively.

4. Click **Data** ▸ **Form Data** ▸ **Default Values** and add 4 additional default rows (**group2** nodes) to the repeating table for a total of 5 default rows.

5. Set the **Default Value** of the **id** field in the repeating table to the following formula:

```
xdXDocument:GetDOM("OfficeApplications")/dfs:myFields/dfs:dataFields/d:SharePointListItem_RW[count(current()/../preceding-sibling::my:group2) + 1]/d:ID
```

What this formula does is count the amount of **group2** group nodes that precede the **group2** group node of the current context node, which is the **id** field in the current row of the repeating table, and then uses this amount as a filter on the **OfficeApplications** secondary data source to find the one item in the SharePoint list that is positioned at the same index number as the current row is. For example, **[1]** corresponds to the first item, **[2]** to the second item, etc. That is the trick to make this solution work. Note: You must leave the **Refresh value when formula is recalculated** check box on the **Field or Group Properties** dialog box selected for the default value to be refreshed.

6. Set the **Default Value** of the **title** field in the repeating table to the following formula (Tip: You can copy the formula from the **id** field and change **d:ID** to **d:Title** to save time):

```
xdXDocument:GetDOM("OfficeApplications")/dfs:myFields/dfs:dataFields/d:SharePointListItem_RW[count(current()/../preceding-sibling::my:group2) + 1]/d:Title
```

Note: You must leave the **Refresh value when formula is recalculated** check box on the **Field or Group Properties** dialog box selected for the default value to be refreshed.

7. Set the **Default Value** of the **color** field in the repeating table to the following formula (Tip: You can copy the formula from the **id** field and change **d:ID** to **d:Color** to save time):

```
xdXDocument:GetDOM("OfficeApplications")/dfs:myFields/dfs:dataFields/d:SharePointListItem_RW[count(current()/../preceding-sibling::my:group2) + 1]/d:Color
```

Note: You must leave the **Refresh value when formula is recalculated** check box on the **Field or Group Properties** dialog box selected for the default value to be refreshed.

8. Publish the form template to a SharePoint form library.

In SharePoint, navigate to the form library where you published the form template and add a new form. When the form opens, data from the first 5 items of the SharePoint list should appear in the first 5 rows in the repeating table. Click **Insert item** to insert a new row in the repeating table. The new row should be populated with data from the 6th item in the SharePoint list, if there is a 6th item present in the SharePoint list.

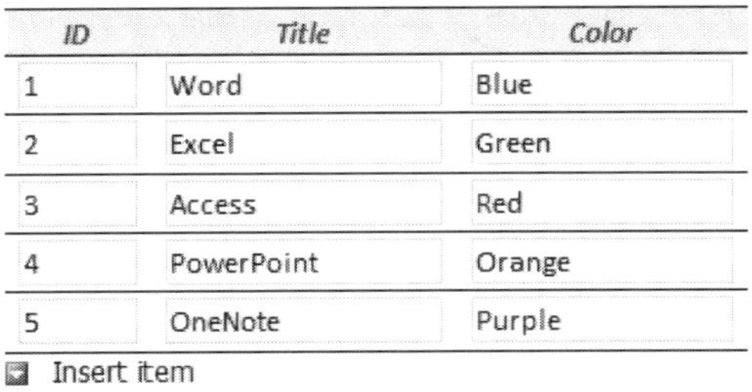

ID	Title	Color
1	Word	Blue
2	Excel	Green
3	Access	Red
4	PowerPoint	Orange
5	OneNote	Purple

Insert item

Figure 150. The InfoPath form displaying the first 5 items from the SharePoint list.

Discussion

As mentioned in step 5 of the solution described above, the trick for making this solution work lies in having a reference number for each row in the repeating table and then using this number as a filter on the data in the SharePoint list to find the correct data for each row in the repeating table. Because there are currently no rules in InfoPath with which you can set values in a repeating table, you can use this technique where a repeating table pulls its own data in from another data source to set the values of its fields. And because there are also no rules in InfoPath with which you can add rows to a repeating table, you must pre-add a fixed amount of rows by adding default rows to the repeating table. So while the solution described above is not the perfect solution for copying data to a repeating table or a repeating section, it provides you with a couple of techniques to work around a few limitations of InfoPath.

Sort and filter SharePoint list data

Filtering SharePoint list data is particularly useful when you have SharePoint lists that contain a large amount of data, and you want to use this data in an InfoPath form, but do not want the data retrieval to negatively impact the performance of the form. InfoPath 2010 offers direct filtering on SharePoint list data connections through fields that are located under the **queryFields** group node of the secondary data source for a SharePoint list. However, since fields under the **queryFields** group node only accept values but not additional operators to query a list on, you can only use them to perform filtering that returns exact match data. If you want to filter data and return LIKE matches or matches between two values, you must use other methods to retrieve and filter SharePoint list data. The recipes in this section discuss several ways to sort and filter SharePoint list data in InfoPath.

47 Statically sort SharePoint list data on one field

Problem

You want to retrieve data from a SharePoint list and have the data appear sorted when it is displayed on an InfoPath form.

Solution

You can use the **Sort by** option on the **Data Connection Wizard** when setting up the data connection for the SharePoint list to sort the list's data by a chosen field in the list in an ascending or a descending order.

To sort SharePoint list data statically on one field:

1. In InfoPath, create a new browser-compatible form template or use an existing one.
2. Click **Data** ➤ **Get External Data** ➤ **From SharePoint List**.
3. On the **Data Connection Wizard**, enter the URL of the SharePoint site where the SharePoint list you want to connect to is located, and click **Next**.
4. On the **Data Connection Wizard**, select the list you want to connect to from the **Select a list or library** list box, and click **Next**.
5. On the **Data Connection Wizard**, select any fields from the SharePoint list that you want to include in the data source. Below the list of fields, you will see a **Sort by** drop-down list box and **Sort order** options.

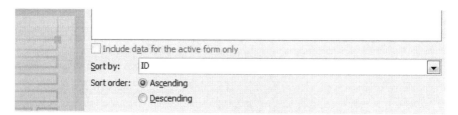

Figure 151. Sort by and Sort order options on the Data Connection Wizard in InfoPath 2010.

Use the drop-down list box to select the field you want to use to sort the list data by and use the option buttons to select whether to sort the data in an ascending or a descending order.

6. Click **Next**, and finish creating the data connection.

If you now use the data connection to retrieve data from the SharePoint list, the data returned should be sorted by the field you specified through the **Data Connection Wizard**. For example, you could bind the secondary data source for the SharePoint list to a repeating table control as described in recipe *44 Display SharePoint list data in a repeating table* or populate a drop-down list box control with this data, and then preview the form to see whether the data has been sorted.

Chapter 3: Retrieve SharePoint List Data

Discussion

Using the **Sort by** drop-down list box on the **Data Connection Wizard** is the quickest and easiest way to retrieve and sort data from a SharePoint list. However, there are two disadvantages to using this method for sorting SharePoint list data:

1. You can only set the field to sort the data by through the **Data Connection Wizard** at design time, which means that you cannot allow users to select a different field to sort the data by when they are filling out the form at runtime.
2. You can only choose one field to sort the data. If you want to use multiple fields to sort data, try the method described in recipe *49 Dynamically sort SharePoint list data on one or more fields*.

Note that sorting data through a SharePoint list data connection sorts the data on the server when it is retrieved and not locally in the InfoPath form.

48 Statically sort SharePoint list data on multiple fields

Problem

You want to retrieve data from a SharePoint list, but want to have the data appear sorted when it is displayed on an InfoPath form.

Solution

You can use the **View**, **SortField**, and **SortDir** query string parameters in an URL to send a command to SharePoint to sort and retrieve data from a SharePoint list.

Suppose you have a SharePoint list named **OfficeApplications** that contains items as specified in recipe *2 Customize a SharePoint list form from within InfoPath*, and you want to sort the items in this list by title and color.

To sort the data contained in the **OfficeApplications** SharePoint list statically on multiple fields:

1. In SharePoint, navigate to the **OfficeApplications** SharePoint list for which you want to sort data in an InfoPath form and click **List Tools** ➤ **List** ➤ **Manage Views** ➤ **Create View**.

2. You are going to use a SharePoint view to retrieve the data from the **OfficeApplications** SharePoint list sorted by the **Color** field, and then you will use the **Title** field in the URL of an XML data connection to sort the data retrieved in a descending order. You can create a new SharePoint view to sort the data by **Color** or set similar sorting options on the default view used by the SharePoint list. Here you are going to create a new view. So on the **Create View** page under the **Choose a view format** section, click **Standard View**.

InfoPath 2010 Cookbook 2

3. On the **Create View** page, enter **SortedDataView** as the **View Name**, select the **Display** check box for all of the columns you would like to display in the list, under **Sort** select **Color** from the **First sort by the column** drop-down list box, leave the **Show items in ascending order** option selected, and then click **OK**.

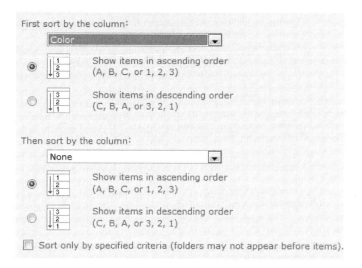

Figure 152. Settings under the Sort section on the Create View page in SharePoint 2010.

4. Click on the drop-down arrow on the right-hand side of the view name in the breadcrumb trail at the top of the page, and then select **Modify this view** from the drop-down menu that appears.

Figure 153. Selecting to modify the view.

5. On the **Edit View** page, copy the GUID that is listed behind the **View** query string parameter in the URL in the browser's address bar and paste it in Notepad. It should resemble something like the following:

`%7BF706A38B%2D1302%2D4C0C%2DA6F6%2D2A21FF52FB04%7D`

and while you are at it, also copy the GUID that is listed behind the **List** query string parameter in the URL in the browser's address bar and paste it in Notepad. It should resemble something like the following:

`%7BACFED261%2D5B80%2D47F2%2D9BD0%2DCDA38935AA59%7D`

Chapter 3: Retrieve SharePoint List Data

Click **Cancel** when you are done.

6. In InfoPath, create a new SharePoint form library form template or use an existing one.

7. Select **Data** ➤ **Get External Data** ➤ **From Other Sources** ➤ **From XML File**.

8. On the **Data Connection Wizard**, enter the URL that points to the **OfficeApplications** SharePoint list. For example:

```
http://servername/sitename/_vti_bin/owssvr.dll?Cmd=Display&List={GUID}&View={GUID}&XMLDATA=TRUE&noredirect=true&SortField=Title&SortDir=desc
```

and click **Next**. Here, **servername** is the name of the SharePoint server and **sitename** is the name of the site where the **OfficeApplications** SharePoint list is located. In addition, replace the **{GUID}** pieces of text listed in the URL with the actual GUIDs you copied earlier to Notepad. Note that the **SortDir** query string parameter in the URL listed above specifies that the items should be ordered in a descending order. A sample URL would resemble the following:

```
http://win-ji2o5062vat/infopath2010cookbook2/_vti_bin/owssvr.dll?Cmd=Display&List=%7BACFED261%2D5B80%2D47F2%2D9BD0%2DCDA38935AA59%7D&View=%7BF706A38B%2D1302%2D4C0C%2DA6F6%2D2A21FF52FB04%7D&XMLDATA=TRUE&noredirect=true&SortField=Title&SortDir=desc
```

9. On the **Data Connection Wizard**, select the **Access the data from the specified location** option, leave the **Store a copy of the data for offline use** check box deselected, and click **Next**.

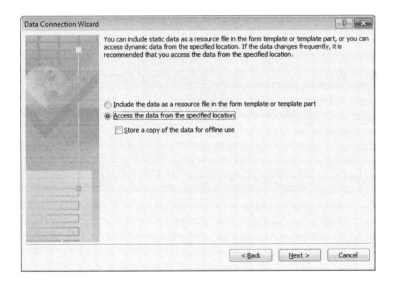

Figure 154. Selecting to access the data from SharePoint instead of storing it in the template.

Because you want fresh data to be retrieved from the server every time you query the data connection, you must select the option to access the data from the specified location and not store it in the form template.

10. On the **Data Connection Wizard**, rename the data connection to **GetOfficeApplications**, leave the **Automatically retrieve data when form is opened** check box selected, and click **Finish**.

11. Bind the **z:row** repeating field under the **rs:data** group node in the **GetOfficeApplications** secondary data source to a repeating table control on the view of the form template as described in recipe *44 Display SharePoint list data in a repeating table*. Note that **z:row** is a repeating field and not a field under a repeating group as in recipe *44 Display SharePoint list data in a repeating table*. However, it can still be bound to a repeating table control.

12. Publish the form template to a SharePoint form library.

In SharePoint, navigate to the form library where you published the form template and add a new form. When the form opens, verify that the titles for the applications have been ordered in a descending order in the repeating table.

Title	Color
Word	Blue
Publisher	Blue
PowerPoint	Orange
OneNote	Purple
InfoPath	Purple
Excel	Green
Access	Red

Figure 155. The InfoPath form displaying SharePoint list items in a descending order by 'Title'.

Discussion

You could consider using the URL protocol sorting method described in the solution above for example if you needed to retrieve SharePoint list data through a specific SharePoint view and also wanted to sort that data. Note that if you do not specify the **View** query string parameter in the URL, the default view of the SharePoint list would automatically be used. You can specify a specific SharePoint view to use by adding the **View** query string parameter to the URL as you have done in the solution above. The value of the **View** query string parameter must be set to the **GUID** of the SharePoint view you want to use.

Just like with a SharePoint list data connection, the URL protocol allows you to sort data statically and on only one field through the URL. However, because the URL protocol also uses a SharePoint view to retrieve data, you get the added benefit of being able to sort data on additional fields by specifying sort fields on the SharePoint view itself. When you combine the two (**View** query string parameter in the URL plus sort fields on the SharePoint view), the URL protocol first retrieves and sorts the data according to the sort fields specified on the SharePoint view, and then applies sorting according to the sort field (**SortField**) and sort direction (**SortDir**) you specified through the URL, which may override the sorting performed by the SharePoint view.

Note that sorting data through the URL protocol sorts the data on the server when it is retrieved and not locally in the InfoPath form.

49 Dynamically sort SharePoint list data on one or more fields

Problem

You want to retrieve data from a SharePoint list and give users the ability to dynamically sort the data when they are filling out the form.

Solution

You can use the **$orderby** query option in the REST URL of a SharePoint list to dynamically sort data on one or multiple fields.

Suppose you have a SharePoint list named **OfficeApplications** that contains items as specified in recipe *2 Customize a SharePoint list form from within InfoPath*, and you want to sort the items in this list by title and color.

To dynamically sort SharePoint list data on one or more fields:

1. In InfoPath, create a new SharePoint form library form template or use an existing one.

2. Add a **Drop-Down List Box** control to the form template and name it **orderByField**.

3. Open the **Drop-Down List Box Properties** dialog box, and manually add the following two items to the drop-down list box:

   ```
   Value: Title
   Display Name: Title

   Value: Color
   Display Name: Color
   ```

   The values of the items in the drop-down list box should be the same as the names of the fields by which you want to sort the SharePoint list. If you do not know what the correct field names are, perform steps 4 through 8 and then at step 8 you can look under the **m:properties** group node for the fields you want to use for sorting.

4. Select **Data ▶ Get External Data ▶ From Web Service ▶ From REST Web Service**.

183

InfoPath 2010 Cookbook 2

5. On the **Data Connection Wizard**, enter the REST Web Service URL for the SharePoint list:

   ```
   http://servername/sitename/_vti_bin/ListData.svc/OfficeApplications
   ```

   where **servername** is the name of the SharePoint server and **sitename** is the name of the site where the **OfficeApplications** SharePoint list is located. Click **Next**.

6. On the **Data Connection Wizard**, name the data connection **GetOfficeApplications**, deselect the **Automatically retrieve data when form is opened** check box, and click **Finish**.

7. On the **Fields** task pane, select **GetOfficeApplications (Secondary)** from the **Fields** drop-down list box, and then drag the **entry** repeating group node to the view of the form template, drop it, and select **Repeating Section** from the context menu that appears.

8. On the **Fields** task pane, expand the **entry**, **content**, and **m:properties** group nodes, and then under the **m:properties** group node, select the **Title** field and drag-and-drop it inside the repeating section. Repeat this step for the **Color** field.

9. Add an **Action** rule to the drop-down list box with an action that says:

   ```
   Change REST URL: GetOfficeApplications
   ```

   where you should change the **REST Web Service URL** to:

   ```
   concat("http://servername/sitename/_vti_bin/ListData.svc/OfficeApplications?$orderby=", .)
   ```

   where **servername** is the name of the SharePoint server, **sitename** is the name of the site where the **OfficeApplications** SharePoint list is located, and **.** refers to the **orderByField** field that is bound to the drop-down list box.

10. Add a second action that says:

    ```
    Query using a data connection: GetOfficeApplications
    ```

    to the same rule.

11. Publish the form template to a SharePoint form library.

In SharePoint, navigate to the form library where you published the form template and add a new form. When the form opens, select either **Title** or **Color** from the drop-down list box. The SharePoint list data should be loaded in the repeating section and then sorted by either **Title** or **Color**, depending on your selection.

Chapter 3: Retrieve SharePoint List Data

Sort by:	Title		
Title:	Access	Color:	Red
Title:	Excel	Color:	Green

Figure 156. The InfoPath form with sorting applied.

Discussion

When you use the **$orderby** query option in a REST web service URL, the SharePoint list items returned are ordered in an ascending (**asc**) order by default. If you want to sort list items in a descending order, you must append **desc** to the query string as follows:

```
concat("http://servername/sitename/_vti_bin/ListData.svc/OfficeApplications?$orderby=", ., " desc")
```

The advantage of using the **ListData** REST web service to sort SharePoint list items compared to other sorting methods is that it gives you the ability to sort data dynamically (when the form is being filled out) on one or multiple fields. For example, if you wanted to sort the list items in an ascending order on **Title** and in a descending order on **Color**, you could modify the formula that generates the REST web service URL as follows:

```
http://servername/sitename/_vti_bin/ListData.svc/OfficeApplications?$orderby=Title asc, Color desc
```

For more information about the use of query options refer to the article entitled *Open Data Protocol by Example* on the MSDN web site.

In the solution described above, you sorted SharePoint list data on only one field, but you could easily add a second drop-down list box to the view of the form template and modify the formula that generates the REST web service URL to allow users to sort data dynamically on multiple fields.

Note that when using a REST web service data connection, the data is sorted on the server when it is retrieved instead of locally in the InfoPath form.

50 Filter SharePoint list data using an exact match

Problem

You have a repeating table on a form that displays data from a SharePoint list. You want to be able to retrieve and display only those items from the SharePoint list that are an exact match for the data you are looking for.

Solution

You can use fields under the **queryFields** group node of a secondary data source and a **Refresh** button to look up and retrieve data from a SharePoint list you want to display in a repeating table.

Suppose you have a SharePoint list named **OfficeApplications** as described in recipe *2 Customize a SharePoint list form from within InfoPath* and you want to be able to type a color into a text box and return only those Office applications that have that color specified in their **Color** field.

To filter repeating table items from a SharePoint list on an exact match:

1. In InfoPath, create a new SharePoint form library form template or use an existing one.

2. Add a **Receive** data connection to the **OfficeApplications** SharePoint list (see *Use a SharePoint list data connection* in recipe *43 3 Ways to retrieve data from a SharePoint list*), but then deselect the **Automatically retrieve data when form is opened** check box on the last screen of the **Data Connection Wizard**.

3. Bind the **d:SharePointListItem_RW** repeating group node under the **dataFields** group node in the **OfficeApplications** secondary data source to a repeating table control on the view of the form template as described in recipe *44 Display SharePoint list data in a repeating table*.

4. On the **Fields** task pane, expand all of the nodes under the **queryFields** group node of the **OfficeApplications** secondary data source, select the **Color** field, and drag-and-drop it onto the view of the form template. It should automatically bind to a text box control.

5. Add a **Button** control to the view of the form template.

6. With the button control still selected, click the **Properties** tab on the Ribbon, and then under the **Button** group, select **Refresh** from the **Action** drop-down list box.

7. Publish the form template to a SharePoint form library.

In SharePoint, navigate to the form library where you published the form template and add a new form. When the form opens, type a color, for example **Purple**, into the color text box, and click **Refresh**. OneNote and InfoPath should be displayed in the repeating table. If you empty the color text box and click **Refresh**, all of the items from the **OfficeApplications** SharePoint list should be displayed in the repeating table.

Chapter 3: Retrieve SharePoint List Data

Color:	Purple		Refresh

Title	Color
OneNote	Purple
InfoPath	Purple

Figure 157. The InfoPath form displaying items with the color Purple.

Discussion

The **queryFields** group node contains fields that can be used to query (look up) data in a SharePoint list, and the **dataFields** group node contains fields that can be used to display data from the SharePoint list. In the solution described above, you used a field from under the **queryFields** group node to search for data that exactly matched the color you entered into a text box control. You also used the **Refresh** action on a button to query a data connection for a SharePoint list to retrieve items from that list. The **Refresh** button action can refresh one or all of the secondary data sources in an InfoPath form using the corresponding data connections.

If you want to specify only one secondary data source that should be refreshed:

1. Open the **Button Properties** dialog box via the Ribbon (**Properties** ➤ **Button** ➤ **Control Properties**) or by right-clicking the button and selecting **Button Properties** from the context menu that appears.
2. On the **Button Properties** dialog box on the **General** tab, click **Settings**.
3. On the **Refresh** dialog box, the **All secondary data sources** option should be selected by default.

Figure 158. The Refresh dialog box with default settings.

If you want to refresh only one specific secondary data source, select the **One secondary data source** option, select the data source you want to refresh from the **Choose the secondary data source** drop-down list box, and click **OK**.

InfoPath 2010 Cookbook 2

Figure 159. Selecting one specific data source to refresh.

4. On the **Button Properties** dialog box, click **OK**.

Instead of using the **Refresh** action on a button, you could have also used a **Query for data** action on a button instead as follows:

1. Add a **Button** control to the form template.
2. Select **Home ➤ Add Rule ➤ When This Button Is Clicked ➤ Query for Data**.
3. On the **Rule Details** dialog box, select **OfficeApplications** from the **Data connection** drop-down list box, and click **OK**.

The **Refresh** and **Query for data** actions offer similar functionality. The difference between these two actions is that you can use the **Refresh** action to refresh all of the secondary data sources in a form all at once, while to achieve the same thing using a **Query for data** action, you would have to add an individual **Query for data** action for each secondary data source to be able to refresh all of the secondary data sources in a form. Therefore, the **Refresh** button action is ideal and easier to use if you want to refresh all of the secondary data sources in a form all at once.

51 Filter SharePoint list data using a BETWEEN match

Problem

You have a SharePoint list and want to find all items with a first character that falls between two chosen characters of the alphabet.

Solution

You can use the **ListData** REST web service with a **$filter** query option to perform a BETWEEN search on data in a SharePoint list.

Chapter 3: Retrieve SharePoint List Data

Suppose you have a SharePoint list named **OfficeApplications** as described in recipe *2 Customize a SharePoint list form from within InfoPath* and you want to be able to find all applications of which the first character falls between A and P or between Q and Z.

To filter a SharePoint list using a BETWEEN match:

1. In InfoPath, create a new SharePoint form library form template or use an existing one.

2. Add two **Button** controls to the view of the form template and label them **A-P** and **Q-Z** respectively.

3. Select **Data** ➤ **Get External Data** ➤ **From Web Service** ➤ **From REST Web Service**.

4. On the **Data Connection Wizard**, enter the REST Web Service URL for the SharePoint list:

   ```
   http://servername/sitename/_vti_bin/ListData.svc/OfficeApplications?$select
   =Title,Color&$filter=Title ge 'A' and Title le 'P'
   ```

   and click **Next**. Here, **servername** is the name of the SharePoint server and **sitename** is the name of the site where the **OfficeApplications** SharePoint list is located. The initial URL selects only the **Title** and **Color** fields and returns only those items that fall between A and P.

5. On the **Data Connection Wizard**, name the data connection **GetOfficeApplications**, deselect the **Automatically retrieve data when form is opened** check box, and click **Finish**.

6. On the **Fields** task pane, select **GetOfficeApplications (Secondary)** from the **Fields** drop-down list box, drag the **entry** repeating group to the view of the form template, drop it, and select **Repeating Section** from the context menu when you drop it.

7. On the **Fields** task pane, expand the **entry**, **content**, and **m:properties** group nodes, and then select the **d:Title** field and drag-and-drop it inside the repeating section. Repeat this step for the **d:Color** field.

8. Add an **Action** rule to the **A-P** button with a **Change REST URL** action that changes the REST Web Service URL of the **GetOfficeApplications** data connection to:

   ```
   "http://servername/sitename/_vti_bin/ListData.svc/OfficeApplications?$selec
   t=Title,Color&$filter=Title ge 'A' and Title le 'P'&$orderby=Title"
   ```

   and a second action that says:

   ```
   Query using a data connection: GetOfficeApplications
   ```

   This rule queries the REST web service data connection to find all of the items from

InfoPath 2010 Cookbook 2

the **OfficeApplications** SharePoint list that have a **Title** that starts with a character that falls between A and P.

9. Add an **Action** rule to the **Q-Z** button with a **Change REST URL** that changes the REST Web Service URL of the **GetOfficeApplications** data connection to:

   ```
   "http://servername/sitename/_vti_bin/ListData.svc/OfficeApplications?$select=Title,Color&$filter=Title ge 'Q' and Title le 'Z'&$orderby=Title"
   ```

   and a second action that says:

   ```
   Query using a data connection: GetOfficeApplications
   ```

   This rule queries the REST web service data connection to find all of the items from the **OfficeApplications** SharePoint list that have a **Title** that starts with a character that falls between Q and Z.

10. Publish the form template to a SharePoint form library.

In SharePoint, navigate to the form library where you published the form template and add a new form. When the form opens, click on any of the two buttons and verify that the data has been filtered correctly, that is, clicking the **A-P** button should return only those applications that fall between A and P, and clicking the **Q-Z** button should return only those applications that fall between Q and Z.

Figure 160. The InfoPath form displaying list items that fall between A and P.

Discussion

The **ListData** REST web service allows you to perform filtering on the server to retrieve only the data you really want to retrieve, instead of retrieving all of the data and then filtering it locally in InfoPath. This method is ideal if you have SharePoint lists that contain a large amount of data.

In the solution described above you used the **$filter** query option, the conditional operator **and** and two comparison operators (**ge** and **le**) to perform a BETWEEN search. You also used the **$orderby** query option to sort the results alphabetically. This solution works, because when textual values are compared with each other, they are compared alphabetically.

For the full list of operations you can use with REST, refer to the article entitled *Open Data Protocol by Example* on the MSDN web site.

Chapter 3: Retrieve SharePoint List Data

52 Filter SharePoint list data using a LIKE match

Filter data on the server

Problem

You have a SharePoint list and want to find all items that contain a piece of text you enter into a text box on an InfoPath form.

Solution

You can use the **ListData** REST web service with the **$filter** query option and **substringof** filter method to perform a LIKE search on data in a SharePoint list.

Suppose you have a SharePoint list named **OfficeApplications** as described in recipe *2 Customize a SharePoint list form from within InfoPath* and you want to be able to enter a piece of text into a text box and return only those Office applications that contain that piece of text in their **Title** field.

To filter a SharePoint list using a LIKE match:

1. In InfoPath, create a new SharePoint form library form template or use an existing one.

2. Add a **Text Box** and **Button** control to the view of the form template. Name the text box control **queryText** and label the button control **Search**.

3. Select **Data** ▶ **Get External Data** ▶ **From Web Service** ▶ **From REST Web Service**.

4. On the **Data Connection Wizard**, enter the REST Web Service URL for the SharePoint list:

   ```
   http://servername/sitename/_vti_bin/ListData.svc/OfficeApplications?$select
   =Title,Color
   ```

   and click **Next**. Here, **servername** is the name of the SharePoint server and **sitename** is the name of the site where the **OfficeApplications** SharePoint list is located. The initial URL selects only the **Title** and **Color** fields.

5. On the **Data Connection Wizard**, name the data connection **GetOfficeApplications**, deselect the **Automatically retrieve data when form is opened** check box, and click **Finish**.

6. On the **Fields** task pane, select **GetOfficeApplications (Secondary)** from the **Fields** drop-down list box, drag the **entry** repeating group node to the view of the form template, drop it, and select **Repeating Section** from the context menu when you drop it.

InfoPath 2010 Cookbook 2

7. On the **Fields** task pane, expand the **entry**, **content**, and **m:properties** group nodes, select the **d:Title** field and drag-and-drop it inside the repeating section. Repeat this step for the **d:Color** field.

8. Add an **Action** rule to the button with a **Change REST URL** action that changes the REST Web Service URL of the **GetOfficeApplications** data connection to:

   ```
   concat("http://servername/sitename/_vti_bin/ListData.svc/OfficeApplications?$select=Title,Color&$filter=substringof('", queryText, "', Title)")
   ```

   and a second action that says:

   ```
   Query using a data connection: GetOfficeApplications
   ```

   This rule queries the REST web service data connection with a filter that filters the results on the value of the **queryText** field being present in the **Title** field of any item in the **OfficeApplications** SharePoint list.

9. Publish the form template to a SharePoint form library.

In SharePoint, navigate to the form library where you published the form template and add a new form. When the form opens, type a partial string that is contained in any of the titles of the Office applications, and click the **Search** button. The Office applications for which the text you entered is contained in their title should be displayed. For example, if you entered "w", the records for Word and PowerPoint should be displayed, since both titles contain a "w".

Figure 161. The InfoPath form displaying items containing a 'w'.

Discussion

The **ListData** REST web service allows you to perform filtering on the server to retrieve only the data you really want to retrieve, instead of retrieving all of the data from a SharePoint list and then filtering it locally in InfoPath. This method is ideal if you have SharePoint lists that contain a large amount of data.

In the solution described above you saw that when used with the **$filter** query option, the **substringof** filter method allowed you to search for list items that partially matched the title of Office applications. But you could also use filter methods that search for text at either the beginning or end of a title.

For example, if you wanted to perform a search on only the first part of the title, you could use the **startswith** filter method, and if you wanted to perform a search on only the last part of the title, you could use the **endswith** filter method.

Chapter 3: Retrieve SharePoint List Data

To use the **startswith** filter method, you would have to change the REST web service URL to the following:

```
concat("http://servername/sitename/_vti_bin/ListData.svc/OfficeApplications?$sel
ect=Title,Color&$filter=startswith(Title, '", queryText, "')")
```

And to use the **endswith** filter method, you would have to change the REST web service URL to the following:

```
concat("http://servername/sitename/_vti_bin/ListData.svc/OfficeApplications?$sel
ect=Title,Color&$filter=endswith(Title, '", queryText, "')")
```

For the full list of query options and filter methods you can use with REST, refer to the article entitled *Open Data Protocol by Example* on the MSDN web site.

Filter data locally in the InfoPath form

Problem

You have a SharePoint list and want to find all items that contain a piece of text you enter into a text box on an InfoPath form.

Solution

You can use conditional formatting along with the **contains** function to filter data from a SharePoint list.

Suppose you have a SharePoint list named **OfficeApplications** as described in recipe *2 Customize a SharePoint list form from within InfoPath* and you want to be able to enter a piece of text into a text box and return only those Office applications that contain that piece of text in their **Title** field.

To filter a SharePoint list using a LIKE match:

1. In InfoPath, create a new SharePoint form library form template or use an existing one.

2. Add a **Text Box** control to the view of the form template and name it **queryText**.

3. Add a **Receive** data connection to the **OfficeApplications** SharePoint list (see *Use a SharePoint list data connection* in recipe *43 3 Ways to retrieve data from a SharePoint list*), ensure you select **Title** and **Color** as the fields to include in the data source, name the data connection **GetOfficeApplications**, and leave the **Automatically retrieve data when form is opened** check box selected.

4. Bind the **GetOfficeApplications (Secondary)** data source to a repeating table on the view of the form template as described in recipe *44 Display SharePoint list data in a repeating table*.

5. Add a **Formatting** rule to the rows (**SharePointListItem_RW** repeating group node) of the repeating table with a **Condition** that says:

```
Title does not contain queryText
```

and that has a formatting of **Hide this control**. This rule hides all of the rows in the repeating table for which the **Title** field in the secondary data source does not contain the text entered into the **queryText** text box.

6. Publish the form template to a SharePoint form library.

In SharePoint, navigate to the form library where you published the form template and add a new form. When the form opens, all of the items in the SharePoint list should be displayed in the repeating table. Type the whole or part of the title of one of the Office applications into the text box and then tab or click away from the text box. The rows containing the text you entered should appear in the repeating table and all other rows should be hidden.

Search for:	oPath
Title	Color
InfoPath	Purple

Figure 162. The InfoPath form with a local filter applied on SharePoint list items.

Discussion

In the solution described above, you used the **contains** function in a formatting rule to filter rows of a repeating table based on a LIKE search. The **contains** function takes two arguments and returns **true** if the first field or text string contains the second; otherwise, it returns **false**.

The difference between this solution and the previous solution is that in the previous solution, not all of the SharePoint list data was downloaded before it was filtered, but was rather filtered on the server before it was returned to the InfoPath form. In this solution however, all of the data is retrieved from the SharePoint list, so all of the data is downloaded, and then it is filtered locally in the form rather than on the server. Needless to say, the method described in this solution should be used for SharePoint lists that contain a limited amount of items, and should be avoided if you have a SharePoint list that contains a large amount of data, since it may negatively impact the performance of the form.

Remember that filter conditions that make use of the **contains** function are case-sensitive, so for example, a search for "oPath" would return different results than a search for "opath". If you want to make the filtering case-insensitive, you must use the **translate** function to convert the fields on both sides of the comparison operator to either lowercase or uppercase before comparing the fields with each other (see for example step 6 of recipe *9 Perform wildcard searches with a SharePoint list form*).

Chapter 3: Retrieve SharePoint List Data

53 Display master/detail data from linked lists

Problem

You have two SharePoint lists that are linked to each other through a lookup column. You want to be able to display data from the master list in a drop-down list box on an InfoPath form, select an item from the drop-down list box, and then have the related detail items appear in a repeating table.

Solution

You can use fields under the **queryFields** group node of a SharePoint list data source to query and retrieve data on demand, including related data.

Suppose you have two SharePoint lists named **ShoeBrands** and **RunningShoes** as described in recipe *13 Use an InfoPath form for a master/detail view on two linked SharePoint lists*.

To display master/detail data from two linked SharePoint lists:

1. In InfoPath, create a browser-compatible form template or use an existing one.

2. Add a **Receive** data connection to the **ShoeBrands** SharePoint list (also see *Use a SharePoint list data connection* in recipe *43 3 Ways to retrieve data from a SharePoint list*). Ensure you select **Title** to be included as a field in the data source, and that you leave the **Automatically retrieve data when form is opened** check box selected.

3. Add a **Receive** data connection to the **RunningShoes** SharePoint list. Ensure you select **Title** and **ShoeBrand** as fields to include in the data source, and that you deselect the **Automatically retrieve data when form is opened** check box.

4. Add a **Drop-Down List Box** control to the view of the form template, name it **shoeBrand**, and populate it with entries from the **ShoeBrands** secondary data source. Select the **ID** field for the **Value** property and the **Title** field for **Display name** property of the drop-down list box.

5. Bind the **RunningShoes** secondary data source to a repeating table control on the view of the form template as described in recipe *44 Display SharePoint list data in a repeating table*.

6. Add an **Action** rule to the **shoeBrand** drop-down list box that has the following actions:

    ```
    Set a field's value: ShoeBrand = .
    Query using a data connection: RunningShoes
    ```

    where **ShoeBrand** is the **ShoeBrand** field that is located under the **q:SharePointListItem_RW** group node under the **queryFields** group node in the **RunningShoes (Secondary)** data source, and **.** refers to the **shoeBrand** field in the

195

Main data source. This rule sets up a query for the **RunningShoes** secondary data source and then executes that query to retrieve filtered data.

7. Publish the form template to a SharePoint form library.

In SharePoint, navigate to the form library where you published the form template and add a new form. When the form opens, select a shoe brand from the drop-down list box. The corresponding running shoes should appear in the repeating table.

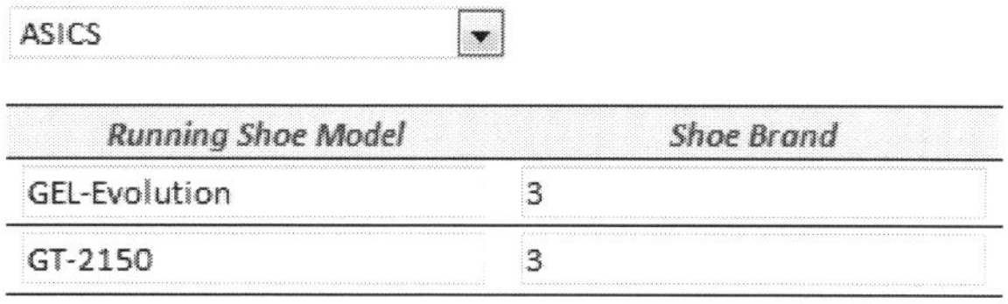

Running Shoe Model	Shoe Brand
GEL-Evolution	3
GT-2150	3

Figure 163. The InfoPath form filtered on ASICS running shoes.

Discussion

In the solution described above, you learned how to use the query fields of a SharePoint list data connection to filter and retrieve related SharePoint list items. This technique works well if you have large lists from which you want to retrieve data.

54 Display a list of people from the current user's department

Problem

You want to be able to display a list of users who are in the same department as the user who is currently filling out the form.

Solution

You can use the **User Information List** SharePoint list to look up the department of the current user and then perform a second search to find all of the people who are in that same department. The **Department** property in SharePoint user profiles must have already been populated with values for this solution to work.

To display a list of people who are in the same department as the current user:

1. In InfoPath, create a new SharePoint form library form template or use an existing one.

2. Add a **Text Box** control to the view of the form template and name it **myDepartment**.

Chapter 3: Retrieve SharePoint List Data

3. Add a **Receive** data connection to the **User Information List** SharePoint list,

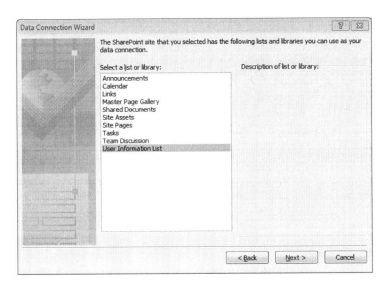

Figure 164. Selecting to connect to the User Information List in InfoPath Designer 2010.

ensure you select **Department** and **User_name (User name)** as fields to include in the data source, deselect the **Automatically retrieve data when form is opened** check box, and accept the default name for the data connection (**User Information List**).

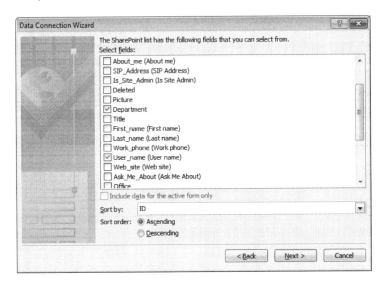

Figure 165. Selecting the fields to include in the data source.

4. Bind the **d:SharePointListItem_RW** repeating group node under the **dataFields** group node of the **User Information List (Secondary)** data source to a repeating

197

table on the view of the form template as described in recipe *44 Display SharePoint list data in a repeating table*.

5. You can either add a button to the view to query the User Information List or as in this solution, query the User Information List when the form loads. So click **Data ▶ Rules ▶ Form Load** to open the **Rules** task pane, and add an **Action** rule that has the following 6 actions:

   ```
   Set a field's value: UserName = userName()
   ```

   where **UserName** is the **User name** field under the **q:SharePointListItem_RW** group node under the **queryFields** group node in the **User Information List** secondary data source and **userName()** is the InfoPath function that retrieves the name of the person filling out the form.

   ```
   Query using a data connection: User Information List
   ```

   This action queries the secondary data source to retrieve the user profile information for the current user.

   ```
   Set a field's value: myDepartment = Department
   ```

   where **myDepartment** is the field that is bound to the text box and that is located in the Main data source of the form, while **Department** is the **Department** field that is located under the **d:SharePointListItem_RW** repeating group node under the **dataFields** group node in the **User Information List** secondary data source. This action rule retrieves the results of the query that just ran and stores it in the **myDepartment** field.

   ```
   Set a field's value: UserName = ""
   ```

   where **UserName** is the **User name** field under the **q:SharePointListItem_RW** group node under the **queryFields** group node in the **User Information List** secondary data source. This action clears the value you set earlier so that you can retrieve the user profile information for all users instead of just one.

   ```
   Set a field's value: Department = myDepartment
   ```

   where **Department** is the **Department** field under the **q:SharePointListItem_RW** group node under the **queryFields** group node in the **User Information List** secondary data source and **myDepartment** is located in the Main data source. This action rule sets the value of the department for which all users must be retrieved by the query.

   ```
   Query using a data connection: User Information List
   ```

   This action queries the **User Information List** data connection to retrieve the user profile information for all users who have the same department as the current user.

6. Add a **Formatting** rule to the repeating table that is bound to the **User Information List** secondary data source (the **d:SharePointListItem_RW** repeating

Chapter 3: Retrieve SharePoint List Data

group node) with a **Condition** that says:

```
translate(d:UserName, "ABCDEFGHIJKLMNOPQRSTUVWXYZ",
"abcdefghijklmnopqrstuvwxyz") = translate(xdUser:get-UserName(),
"ABCDEFGHIJKLMNOPQRSTUVWXYZ", "abcdefghijklmnopqrstuvwxyz")
```

where **d:UserName** is the **User name** field under the **d:SharePointListItem_RW** repeating group node under the **dataFields** group node in the **User Information List** secondary data source and **xdUser:get-UserName()** is the **userName()** InfoPath function that retrieves the name of the person filling out the form. Note that the **translate** function is used in the formula above to ensure that both user names are in lowercase when they are compared with each other and for the comparison not the fail finding records due to non-matching cases.

Select a formatting of **Hide this control**. This formatting rule hides the row in the repeating table that corresponds to the current user, so that the current user is excluded from the list of users in the department.

7. Publish the form template to a SharePoint form library.

In SharePoint, navigate to the form library where you published the form template and add a new form. When the form opens, check whether the people who are listed in the repeating table have the same department as the currently logged on user. Log on as a different user who is in a different department. Add a new form and check whether the list of users is correct.

Department:	Accounting	

Department	User name
Accounting	john.doe
Accounting	jane.doe

Figure 166. InfoPath form displaying users who are in the same department as the current user.

Discussion

In the solution described above you used fields under the **queryFields** group node of the data source for the SharePoint list to first query the User Information List to find the department of the person who is filling out the form, and then used the department returned to query the User Information List for a second time to find all of the users from that department.

The User Information List displays the users on a particular SharePoint site and gets its information from SharePoint user profiles. When you add a user or a group of users to a SharePoint site, the first time an individual user logs onto the site, that user is automatically added to the User Information List for that site. You can use the User Information List to lookup a limited amount of information for a particular user such as for example her first and last name, email address, phone number, department, etc. Since

InfoPath 2010 Cookbook 2

the User Information List does not contain all of the properties of a user's profile, if you want to retrieve properties that are not contained in the User Information List, you can use the User Profile Service to retrieve that information (see recipe *68 Get the details of the manager of a selected person in a person/group picker* for an example of how to use the User Profile Service).

55 Retrieve the top X items from a SharePoint list

Problem

You have a SharePoint list and want to retrieve and display the top X amount of items from the list in a drop-down list box on an InfoPath form.

Solution

You can use the **$top** query option in the REST web service URL of the SharePoint list to filter data and return only the top X amount of entries from the feed.

Suppose you have a SharePoint list named **OfficeApplications** as described in recipe *2 Customize a SharePoint list form from within InfoPath*.

To retrieve the top X amount of items from that SharePoint list:

1. In InfoPath, create a new SharePoint form library form template or use an existing one.

2. Select **Data** ▶ **Get External Data** ▶ **From Web Service** ▶ **From REST Web Service**.

3. On the **Data Connection Wizard**, enter the REST Web Service URL for the SharePoint list:

   ```
   http://servername/sitename/_vti_bin/ListData.svc/OfficeApplications?$select=Title,Color
   ```

   and click **Next**. Here, **servername** is the name of the SharePoint server and **sitename** is the name of the site where the **OfficeApplications** SharePoint list is located. The initial URL selects only the **Title** and **Color** fields.

4. On the **Data Connection Wizard**, name the data connection **GetOfficeApplications**, deselect the **Automatically retrieve data when form is opened** check box, and click **Finish**.

5. Add a **Drop-Down List Box** control to the view of the form template, and set its items to come from the **GetOfficeApplications** data source. Select the **entry** repeating group node for the **Entries** property of the drop-down list box, and the **Title** field under the **m:properties** group node under the **content** group node for both the **Value** and the **Display name** properties of the drop-down list box.

Chapter 3: Retrieve SharePoint List Data

Figure 167. Drop-down list box populated from REST Web Service secondary data source.

6. Add a **Text Box** control with the data type **Whole Number (integer)** to the view of the form template and name it **amountOfItems**.

7. Add a **Button** control to the view of the form template and label it **Fetch Items**.

8. Add an **Action** rule to the button control with an action that says:

```
Change REST URL: GetOfficeApplications
```

that sets the **REST Web Service URL** to the following formula:

```
concat("http://servername/_vti_bin/ListData.svc/OfficeApplications?$select=
Title,Color&$top=", string(amountOfItems))
```

where **amountOfItems** is the field that is bound to the text box control. Note that the **string** function is used within the **concat** function to convert the number into a string.

Add a second action that says:

InfoPath 2010 Cookbook 2

```
Query using a data connection: GetOfficeApplications
```

This rule changes the REST web service URL to include a filter that returns the amount of items specified in the **amountOfItems** field, and then queries the data connection for the REST web service.

9. Publish the form template to a SharePoint form library.

In SharePoint, navigate to the form library where you published the form template and add a new form. When the form opens, the drop-down list box should be empty. Click the **Fetch Items** button. The drop-down list box should now contain all of the items from the SharePoint list. Enter a **3** in the text box and click the button again. The drop-down list box should contain only the first 3 items from the SharePoint list.

Figure 168. The InfoPath form displaying the first 3 items in the SharePoint list.

Discussion

In the solution described above, you used the **$top** query option to return the top X amount of items from a SharePoint list. The **$top** query option returns entries from the top of the feed. For example:

```
http://servername/sitename/_vti_bin/ListData.svc/OfficeApplications?$select=Title,Color&$top=2
```

returns the first two items starting from the top of the feed. And if you entered no number or a number greater than the total amount of items in the SharePoint list, all of the items from the SharePoint list would be returned.

Note that if your scenario does not call for returning a dynamic amount of items from a SharePoint list or you are unable to use REST for one reason or another, you could also use the URL protocol with a SharePoint view (also see *Use an XML data connection* in recipe *43 3 Ways to retrieve data from a SharePoint list*) and set the SharePoint view to display a static amount of items.

56 Paginate and navigate through a SharePoint list using previous and next buttons

Problem

You have a SharePoint list and want to sequentially navigate through all of the items in the list by clicking on previous and next buttons.

Chapter 3: Retrieve SharePoint List Data

Solution

You can use the **$inlinecount**, **$top**, and **$skip** query options in the REST web service URL of the SharePoint list to filter and paginate data.

Suppose you have a SharePoint list named **OfficeApplications** as described in recipe *2 Customize a SharePoint list form from within InfoPath*.

To paginate and navigate through SharePoint list data using previous and next buttons:

1. In InfoPath, create a new SharePoint form library form template or use an existing one.

2. Add two **Button** controls to the view of the form template. Label the first button **Previous** and the second button **Next**.

3. Select **Data** ➤ **Get External Data** ➤ **From Web Service** ➤ **From REST Web Service**.

4. On the **Data Connection Wizard**, enter the REST Web Service URL for the SharePoint list:

   ```
   http://servername/sitename/_vti_bin/ListData.svc/OfficeApplications?$select
   =Title,Color&$inlinecount=allpages&$top=2
   ```

   and click **Next**. Here, **servername** is the name of the SharePoint server and **sitename** is the name of the site where the **OfficeApplications** SharePoint list is located. What this REST web service URL does is retrieve the **Title** and **Color** fields of items in the **OfficeApplications** SharePoint list, in addition to the total number of entries without a filter applied as a **count** element in the feed, and restrict the amount of items returned to 2. You will be showing 2 items per page.

5. On the **Data Connection Wizard**, name the data connection **GetOfficeApplications**, leave the **Automatically retrieve data when form is opened** check box selected, and click **Finish**.

6. On the **Fields** task pane, select **GetOfficeApplications (Secondary)** from the **Fields** drop-down list box, drag-and-drop the **entry** repeating group node onto the view of the form template, and select **Repeating Section** when you drop it.

7. On the **Fields** task pane, expand the **entry**, **content**, and **m:properties** group nodes, and then drag-and-drop the **d:Title** and **d:Color** fields inside the repeating section.

8. Add a **Field (element)** with the name **position**, the data type **Whole Number (integer)**, and a default value equal to **0** to the Main data source of the form. This field will be used to keep track of the current position in the secondary data source while navigating through the pages of items.

9. Add a **Formatting** rule to the **Previous** button with a **Condition** that says:

   ```
   position ≤ 0
   ```

203

and with a **Formatting** of **Disable this control**. This rule disables the **Previous** button if the value of the **position** field is less than or equal to **0**.

10. Add a **Formatting** rule to the **Next** button with a **Condition** that says:

    ```
    position ≥ count - 2
    ```

    and with a **Formatting** of **Disable this control**. **count** is the **m:count** field under the **feed** group node in the **GetOfficeApplications** secondary data source. This rule disables the **Next** button if the value of the **position** field is greater than or equal to the total amount of items in the secondary data source minus 2. 2 is the amount of items you are going to display per page. This amount should be the same as the amount you chose for the **$top** query option. Note: You must use the **Use a formula** option on the **Condition** dialog box and then select the **m:count** field in the **GetOfficeApplications** secondary data source when constructing the formula for the condition.

11. Add an **Action** rule to the **Previous** button that has the following 3 actions:

    ```
    Set a field's value: position = position - 2
    Change REST URL: GetOfficeApplications
    Query using a data connection: GetOfficeApplications
    ```

    The **REST Web Service URL** for the **Change REST URL** action should be set to:

    ```
    concat("http://servername/sitename/_vti_bin/ListData.svc/OfficeApplications?$select=Title,Color&$inlinecount=allpages&$top=2&$skip=", position)
    ```

    using the **Insert Formula** dialog box. This REST web service URL uses the **$skip** query option to skip the amount of items specified in the **position** field and then returns the first 2 items that are located immediately after the items that were skipped in the secondary data source. The **concat** function is used to dynamically construct the REST web service URL.

12. Add an **Action** rule to the **Next** button that has the following 3 actions:

    ```
    Set a field's value: position = position + 2
    Change REST URL: GetOfficeApplications
    Query using a data connection: GetOfficeApplications
    ```

    The **REST Web Service URL** for the **Change REST URL** action should be set to:

    ```
    concat("http://servername/sitename/_vti_bin/ListData.svc/OfficeApplications?$select=Title,Color&$inlinecount=allpages&$top=2&$skip=", position)
    ```

    using the **Insert Formula** dialog box. This REST web service URL uses the **$skip** query option to skip the amount of items specified in the **position** field and then returns the first 2 items that are located immediately after the items that were skipped in the secondary data source. The **concat** function is used to dynamically construct the REST web service URL.

Chapter 3: Retrieve SharePoint List Data

13. Publish the form template to a SharePoint form library.

In SharePoint, navigate to the form library where you published the form template and add a new form. When the form opens, the first two items in the SharePoint list should be displayed in the repeating section and the **Previous** button should be disabled. Click the **Next** button. The **Previous** button should be enabled and the next 2 items in the list should be displayed in the repeating section. Continue clicking the **Next** button until you reach the last item in the list. The **Next** button should then be disabled. Click the **Previous** button and navigate backwards until you reach the first item in the list. The **Previous** button should then be disabled.

Previous	Next

Title:	Word
Color:	Blue
Title:	Excel
Color:	Green

Figure 169. The InfoPath form displaying the first two items in the SharePoint list.

Previous	Next

Title:	OneNote
Color:	Purple
Title:	InfoPath
Color:	Purple

Figure 170. The InfoPath form displaying items 5 and 6 in the SharePoint list.

Previous	Next

Title:	Publisher
Color:	Blue

Figure 171. The InfoPath form displaying the last item in the SharePoint list.

Discussion

In the solution described above, you used the following query options in the REST web service URL:

- **$select**

  Limits the properties on each entry to just those requested. Example:

  ```
  http://servername/sitename/_vti_bin/ListData.svc/OfficeApplications?$select=Title,Color
  ```

  returns the **Title** and **Color** fields for each item.

- **$inlinecount**

  Includes the number of entries without a filter applied as a **count** element in the feed. Example:

  ```
  http://servername/sitename/_vti_bin/ListData.svc/OfficeApplications?$top=2&$inlinecount=allpages
  ```

  returns a **count** of 7 for a SharePoint list that contains a total of 7 items.

- **$top**

  Returns entries from the top of the feed. Example:

  ```
  http://servername/sitename/_vti_bin/ListData.svc/OfficeApplications?$top=2
  ```

  returns the first two items starting from the top of the feed.

- **$skip**

  Skips a specified amount of entries. Example:

  ```
  http://servername/sitename/_vti_bin/ListData.svc/OfficeApplications?$skip=2
  ```

  skips the first two items starting from the top of the feed.

Note that **$top** is always applied after **$skip**. For example, on page 2, Access and PowerPoint are displayed. Here, **$skip=2** would be applied first to the SharePoint list meaning that Word and Excel (the first 2 items in the list starting from the top) would be skipped. The item that comes after Excel is Access, so when **$top=2** is applied, Access and PowerPoint are returned and displayed on the page. On page 3, OneNote and InfoPath are displayed. Here, **$skip=4** would be applied first to the list meaning that all items in the SharePoint list up to and including PowerPoint (the first 4 items in the list starting from the top) would be skipped. The item that comes after PowerPoint is OneNote, so when **$top=2** is applied, OneNote and InfoPath are returned and displayed on the page.

A hidden field named **position** was used in the solution described above as a 'cursor' to keep track of the position within the SharePoint list during page navigation. Because 2 items were displayed on each page, the value of **$top** was set to a static value of 2 and the value of **$skip** was dynamically set in the REST web service URL to the value of the **position** field, which was decreased or increased every time you clicked on either the **Previous** or **Next** button.

Retrieve and display forms from a form library

A SharePoint form library is a specialized type of SharePoint list, so you can use similar methods to retrieve and display InfoPath forms as you did for retrieving and displaying SharePoint list items.

The recipes in this section are meant to guide you through a few scenarios for retrieving and working with InfoPath forms from within an InfoPath form.

57 Retrieve a list of forms from a form library

Problem

You want to display a list of all of the forms that are present in a SharePoint form library.

Solution

You can create a **Receive** data connection to a SharePoint list, but connect it to the SharePoint form library instead of the SharePoint list to retrieve a list of the forms from the form library.

To retrieve a list of forms from a form library:

1. In InfoPath, create a new SharePoint form library form template or use an existing one.

2. Add a **Receive** data connection to a SharePoint list to the form template as described in *Use a SharePoint list data connection* of recipe *43 3 Ways to retrieve data from a SharePoint list*. Ensure you select the SharePoint form library that contains the forms you want to display from the list of SharePoint lists or libraries you can connect to, select the **Title** field to be included in the data source, and leave the **Automatically retrieve data when form is opened** check box selected. Note that the **Title** field contains the file name (including the XML extension) of an InfoPath form in the form library.

3. Bind the secondary data source for the SharePoint form library to a repeating table on the view of the form template as described in recipe *44 Display SharePoint list data in a repeating table*.

4. Publish the form template to a SharePoint form library.

In SharePoint, navigate to the form library where you published the form template and add a new form. When the form opens, all of the file names for the InfoPath forms in the SharePoint form library should be displayed in the **Title** column of the repeating table.

InfoPath 2010 Cookbook 2

Discussion

In the solution described above you saw that you can connect a SharePoint list data connection to a SharePoint document library or SharePoint form library instead of a SharePoint list, to be able to retrieve data from a library instead of a list.

One reason to connect to a SharePoint form library instead of a SharePoint list would be to open InfoPath forms from within another InfoPath form. But for this you would have to use URLs of the forms contained in the form library. InfoPath does not allow you to modify fields that are located in a secondary data source. This includes setting the **Default Value** of such fields. So while you can retrieve data from a form library, you cannot do much with this data unless you copy values from the secondary data source to other fields on the form (see recipes *45 3 Ways to copy SharePoint list data to form fields* or *46 Map rows of a repeating table to SharePoint list items*) where you can for example prepend the URL of the form library to the file name of the form, so that you can set the constructed full URL of the form as the value of a hyperlink field to be able to click and open a form from the form library from within the InfoPath form (see for example the technique described in recipe *59 Open a form in the browser from another form*).

When you connect a SharePoint list data connection to a library instead of a list, you will see a check box with the label **Include data for the active form only** enabled on the screen of the **Data Connection Wizard** where you select the fields that should be included in the data source.

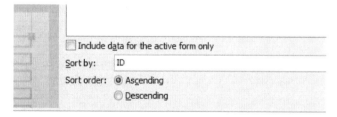

Figure 172. The Include data for the active form only check box on the Data Connection Wizard.

It only makes sense to select this check box if you have created a SharePoint list data connection to the form library to which the current form will be saved or submitted, and you would like to have the ability to access form library field values for the current form only. For example if you want to retrieve the value of the status of a workflow that is running or has run on a form and use this value in the form to for example show/hide fields, or if you want to retrieve the name of the person who created the (existing) form in the form library, you could select the **Include data for the active form only** check box on the **Data Connection Wizard** when you are setting up the data connection to the form library in which the form is stored, to get access to that status or **CreatedBy** field for that specific form from within the form itself.

58 Retrieve a list of forms created by the current user from a form library

Problem

You want to create an InfoPath form that displays a list of InfoPath forms that are stored in another form library and that were created by the user who opened the form.

Solution

You can use the **userName** function in InfoPath to retrieve the logon name of the user who is filling out a form, use this logon name to lookup a corresponding account name in the **User Information List** SharePoint list, and then use the account name found as a filter to query the SharePoint list data connection for the form library containing the user's forms.

To retrieve and display InfoPath forms created by the current user from a form library:

1. In InfoPath, create a new SharePoint form library form template or use an existing one.

2. Add a **Receive** data connection to the **User Information List** SharePoint list (also see *Use a SharePoint list data connection* of recipe *43 3 Ways to retrieve data from a SharePoint list*), ensure you select **Name**, **Account**, and **Work_e-mail** as fields to include in the data source, accept the default data connection name of **User Information List**, and deselect the **Automatically retrieve data when form is opened** check box.

3. Add a **Receive** data connection to the SharePoint form library that contains the forms you want to display on the InfoPath form (also see recipe *57 Retrieve a list of forms from a form library*), ensure you select **Title** and **Created_By** as fields to include in the data source, give the data connection a suitable name such as for example **GetUserForms**, and deselect the **Automatically retrieve data when form is opened** check box.

4. Bind a repeating table control to the data from the **GetUserForms** secondary data source as described in recipe *44 Display SharePoint list data in a repeating table*.

5. To retrieve only those forms that were created by the user who opened the form, you must use the **userName** function to retrieve the logon name of the user who opened the form, use this logon name to search for a corresponding display name in the **User Information List** SharePoint list, and then use the display name found to filter the data from the **GetUserForms** secondary data source on the value of its **Created By** field. So click **Data** ➤ **Rules** ➤ **Form Load** and add an **Action** rule to the **Form Load** event with the following 4 actions:

```
Set a field's value: Name = concat("DOMAIN\", translate(userName(),
"ABCDEFGHIJKLMNOPQRSTUVWXYZ", "abcdefghijklmnopqrstuvwxyz"))
```

where **Name** refers to the **Account** field under the **q:SharePointListItem_RW** group node under the **queryFields** group node in the **User Information List (Secondary)** data source, and **DOMAIN** is the domain name used for logon names. This action sets up a query for the **User Information List** secondary data source to be able to retrieve the **User Information List** record for the one user where the account ID of the user in the **User Information List** is equal to the user name (the value returned by the **userName()** function).

```
Query using a data connection: User Information List
```

This action populates the **User Information List** secondary data source based on the logon name of the current user that was passed to it through its query fields.

```
Set a field's value: Author = Title
```

where **Author** refers to the **CreatedBy** field under the **q:SharePointListItem_RW** group node under the **queryFields** group node in the **GetUserForms (Secondary)** data source, and **Title** refers to the **Name** field under the **d:SharePointListItem_RW** repeating group node under the **dataFields** group node in the **User Information List (Secondary)** data source. This action sets up a query for the **GetUserForms** secondary data source to be able to retrieve only those forms where the display name of the person who created the form in the **GetUserForms** secondary data source is equal to the display name of the user in the **User Information List**.

```
Query using a data connectionL GetUserForms
```

This action populates the **GetUserForms** secondary data source based on the value of the **CreatedBy** field that was passed to it through its query fields.

6. Publish the form template to a SharePoint form library.

In SharePoint, navigate to the form library where you published the form template and add a new form. When the form opens, verify that only the forms you created are displayed in the repeating table on the form. Logon as a different user, add a new form again, and verify that only the forms for the user you are signed in as are displayed on the form.

Discussion

In the solution described above you used a standard SharePoint list data connection to retrieve the forms that were created by the current user, instead of using the method described in *Use an XML data connection* of recipe *43 3 Ways to retrieve data from a SharePoint list*. If you compare the two methods with each other, you will notice that had you used the XML data connection method from recipe *43 3 Ways to retrieve data from a SharePoint list*, you would have had to make only one call to SharePoint to retrieve data instead of two calls (the two times you used the **Query for data** action in a rule). The

Chapter 3: Retrieve SharePoint List Data

reason why the double querying was required in the solution described above is because the **CreatedBy** field under the **queryFields** group node of the **GetUserForms** secondary data source takes the display name of an account rather than the actual username as its value. And because the **userName** function in InfoPath returns the user name (logon name) of the person filling out the form (excluding a domain name), you must use this user name to lookup the display name in the **User Information List** (see the discussion section of recipe *54 Display a list of people from the current user's department* for more information on the **User Information List** SharePoint list) data source, and then pass this to the fields under the **queryFields** group node of the **GetUserForms** secondary data source to retrieve the forms that were created by the current user.

While querying twice is insignificant compared to once, especially if you only retrieve the data once, remember that InfoPath Forms Services is by default configured to allow 75 postbacks per session before it displays an error. So whatever you can do to keep the amount of postbacks down is a bonus. A second benefit of using the URL protocol method as described in *Use an XML data connection* of recipe *43 3 Ways to retrieve data from a SharePoint list* as opposed to the standard SharePoint list data connection method is that in the case of the URL protocol you let SharePoint take care of filtering on the current user through the use of a view on the list, while in the solution described above, you are dependent on values being passed from InfoPath to SharePoint to be able to filter on the current user. The less dependency you can build into any solution, the fewer weak links and defects you will ultimately create.

59 Open a form in the browser from another form

Problem

You want to retrieve all of the forms contained in a form library, be able to select one of those forms, and then open the selected form in the browser.

Solution

You can use SharePoint's REST interface to paginate data and retrieve forms from a form library along with a hyperlink control to set the link of each form to an appropriate link that can open the form in the browser.

To open an InfoPath form in the browser by clicking on a link in another form:

1. In InfoPath, create a new SharePoint form library form template or use an existing one.

2. Add a **Repeating Table** control with 1 column to the view of the form template.

3. Open the **Repeating Table Properties** dialog box, and deselect the **Allow users to insert and delete rows** check box.

4. Click **Data** ▶ **Form Data** ▶ **Default Values**, and add 4 additional **group2** nodes under the **group1** node for a total of 5 default rows.

5. Delete the text box control from the first column of the repeating table (as well as its corresponding field from the Main data source) and add a **Hyperlink** control in its place. Name the hyperlink field element **formUrl** and the field attribute under it **formTitle**.

Figure 173. Main data source of the form in InfoPath Designer 2010.

6. Add a **Formatting** rule to the repeating table (**group2** repeating group node) with a **Condition** that says:

   ```
   formTitle is blank
   ```

   and with a **Formatting** of **Hide this control**. This formatting rule hides any rows in the repeating table when the **formTitle** field in that row is blank.

7. In this solution, you are going to use SharePoint's **ListData** REST web service to retrieve the forms from a form library. So select **Data ➤ Get External Data ➤ From Web Service ➤ From REST Web Service**.

8. On the **Data Connection Wizard**, enter the REST Web Service URL for the SharePoint form library:

   ```
   http://servername/sitename/_vti_bin/ListData.svc/FormLibraryName?$select=Name,Path&$inlinecount=allpages&$top=5
   ```

   where **servername** is the name of the SharePoint server and **sitename** the name of the site where the form library **FormLibraryName** is located. Also note that the fields **Name** and **Path** are retrieved and that the top 5 results are returned.

9. On the **Data Connection Wizard**, name the data connection **GetForms**, leave the **Automatically retrieve data when form is opened** check box selected, and click **Finish**.

10. Add a **Field (element)** with the name **position**, the data type **Whole Number (integer)**, and a default value equal to **0** to the Main data source of the form. This field will be used to keep track of the current position in the SharePoint form library while navigating through the pages of forms.

11. Add two **Button** controls to the view of the form template, and label the buttons **Previous** and **Next**, respectively.

12. Add a **Formatting** rule to the **Previous** button with a **Condition** that says:

Chapter 3: Retrieve SharePoint List Data

```
position ≤ 0
```

and with a **Formatting** of **Disable this control**. This rule disables the **Previous** button if **position** is less than or equal to 0.

13. Add a **Formatting** rule to the **Next** button with a **Condition** that says:

    ```
    position ≥ count - 5
    ```

    and with a **Formatting** of **Disable this control**. Here, **count** is the **m:count** field in the **GetForms** secondary data source. This rule disables the **Next** button if **position** is greater than or equal to the total amount of forms in the SharePoint form library minus 5, where 5 is the amount of rows you want to display in the repeating table. This amount should be the same as the amount you chose for the **$top** query option in the REST web service URL. Note: You must use the **Use a formula** option on the **Condition** dialog box and then select the **m:count** field in the **GetForms** secondary data source when constructing the formula for the condition. If you do not see the **m:count** field listed in the secondary data source, ensure that the REST web service URL you used contains the **$inlinecount=allpages** query option.

14. Add an **Action** rule to the **Previous** button that has the following 3 actions:

    ```
    Set a field's value: position = position - 5
    Change REST URL: GetForms
    Query using a data connection: GetForms
    ```

    Use the **Insert Formula** dialog box to set the **REST Web Service URL** for the **Change REST URL** action to the following formula:

    ```
    concat("http://servername/sitename/_vti_bin/ListData.svc/FormLibraryName?$s
    elect=Name,Path&$inlinecount=allpages&$top=5&$skip=", position)
    ```

    This action rule moves 5 places backwards in the SharePoint form library starting from the current **position** and then retrieves the first 5 forms starting from the new **position**.

15. Add an **Action** rule to the **Next** button that has the following 3 actions:

    ```
    Set a field's value: position = position + 5
    Change REST URL: GetForms
    Query using a data connection: GetForms
    ```

    Use the **Insert Formula** dialog box to set the **REST Web Service URL** for the **Change REST URL** action to the following formula:

    ```
    concat("http://servername/sitename/_vti_bin/ListData.svc/FormLibraryName?$s
    elect=Name,Path&$inlinecount=allpages&$top=5&$skip=", position)
    ```

    This action rule moves 5 places forward in the SharePoint form library starting from the current **position** and then retrieves the first 5 forms starting from the new **position**.

16. Set the **Default Value** of the **formTitle** field to the following formula:

    ```
    entry[count(current()/../../preceding-sibling::group2) + 1]/properties/Name
    ```

    or

    ```
    xdXDocument:GetDOM("GetForms")/ns1:feed/ns1:entry[count(current()/../../preceding-sibling::my:group2) + 1]/m:properties/d:Name
    ```

    if you have the **Edit XPath (advanced)** check box selected on the **Insert Formula** dialog box. Leave the **Refresh value when formula is recalculated** check box selected on the **Properties** dialog box for the field. In the formula above, **current()** refers to the **formTitle** attribute (context node) in the current row of the repeating table. From the **formTitle** attribute, you must move upwards twice (**/../../**) to get to the **group2** group node of the **formTitle** context node, and then use the **preceding-sibling** XPath axis and the **count** function to count the amount of **group2** nodes preceding the current row. Once found, you must add a 1 to accommodate the fact that there are never any rows before the first row in the repeating table and because counting in XPath filters must start at 1 and not 0. The filter is used to return the one row in the **GetForms** secondary data source that corresponds to the same row in the repeating table position-wise.

17. Repeat the previous step for the **formUrl** field, but use the following formula instead:

    ```
    concat(SharePointSiteUrl(), "_layouts/FormServer.aspx?", "XmlLocation=",
    SharePointServerRootUrl(), substring(entry[count(current()/../preceding-
    sibling::group2) + 1]/properties/Path, 2), "/",
    entry[count(current()/../preceding-sibling::group2) + 1]/properties/Name,
    "&OpenIn=Browser&Source=", SharePointSiteUrl())
    ```

    or

    ```
    concat(xdServerInfo:get-SharePointSiteUrl(), "_layouts/FormServer.aspx?",
    "XmlLocation=", xdServerInfo:get-SharePointServerRootUrl(),
    substring(xdXDocument:GetDOM("GetForms")/ns1:feed/ns1:entry[count(current()
    /../preceding-sibling::my:group2) + 1]/m:properties/d:Path, 2), "/",
    xdXDocument:GetDOM("GetForms")/ns1:feed/ns1:entry[count(current()/../preced
    ing-sibling::my:group2) + 1]/m:properties/d:Name,
    "&OpenIn=Browser&Source=", xdServerInfo:get-SharePointSiteUrl())
    ```

    if you have the **Edit XPath (advanced)** check box selected on the **Insert Formula** dialog box. Note that you must use both the **Name** and **Path** fields when constructing the value for the **formUrl** field (the URL of a form).

18. Publish the form template to a SharePoint form library.

In SharePoint, navigate to the form library where you published the form template and add a new form. When the form opens, the repeating table should be populated with 5 forms from the form library if the form library contains 5 or more items. If the form library contains less than 5 forms, the repeating table should be populated with the amount of forms contained in the form library and both buttons should be disabled. Click

Chapter 3: Retrieve SharePoint List Data

on the link of any of the forms. The InfoPath form should open in a new browser window.

Figure 174. The InfoPath form displaying the first 5 forms in the form library and the URL of form03.

Discussion

Because the data contained in a secondary data source is locked, you are unable to add any fields to it. Therefore, if you want to use data from a secondary data source within a repeating table, you must use a mechanism that copies the data from the secondary data source to a repeating table in the Main data source. And since you cannot dynamically add rows to a repeating table through rules, you must pre-add a certain amount of rows to the repeating table as shown in the solution above.

SharePoint's **ListData** REST web service allows you to retrieve a specific amount of rows from a SharePoint list without having to download all of the data as you would have to do when using a standard SharePoint list data connection without any query parameters defined on it. In addition, because this solution makes use of a fixed amount of rows in a repeating table, you also have to retrieve a fixed amount of rows from the SharePoint list for display, while maintaining the ability to go through all of the forms in the SharePoint form library. The **ListData** REST web service allows you to do this through a combination of query options, which results in pagination functionality as was first described in recipe *56 Paginate and navigate through a SharePoint list using previous and next buttons*.

In the solution described above you also used a couple of new functions in InfoPath 2010 with which you can retrieve URLs of a SharePoint server or site. InfoPath 2010 has the following functions you can use to retrieve SharePoint-related URL information:

- **SharePointListUrl** – Returns the address of the SharePoint list where the form is hosted.

- **SharePointServerRootUrl** – Returns the address of the SharePoint server where the form is hosted.

215

- **SharePointSiteCollectionUrl** – Returns the address of the SharePoint site collection where the form is hosted.
- **SharePointSiteUrl** – Returns the address of the SharePoint site where the form is hosted.

Note that these functions only work in browser forms and not in forms that are filled out through InfoPath Filler 2010. If you want your forms to work in both a browser and InfoPath Filler 2010, use static URLs instead of the aforementioned functions.

And finally, the URL of each form was constructed using the **concat** function to generate a valid URL that included the **FormServer.aspx** page of InfoPath Forms Services and the **OpenIn=Browser** query string parameter to be able to force the forms to open in the browser (also see the discussion section of recipe *31 Add a link to open a form from a SharePoint page*).

60 Use SharePoint Search in InfoPath to search for documents – method 1

Problem

You want to be able to perform a search query on a SharePoint site from within an InfoPath form to find other forms or documents on the site.

Solution

You can use the **Query** operation of the SharePoint Search Service to search for and retrieve documents and pages that match a specific search term on one or more SharePoint sites that have been configured for search.

Before proceeding, an administrator must ensure that the SharePoint Search Service is running and that content sources have been configured and crawled. Consult the SharePoint documentation for information about configuring SharePoint Search.

To search for forms on SharePoint sites from within an InfoPath form:

1. In InfoPath, create a new SharePoint form library form template or use an existing one.

2. Add a **Text Box** control and a **Button** control to the view of the form template. Name the text box control **searchQuery** and label the button control **Find**. The **searchQuery** text box will be used to enter a search term, and the **Find** button will be used to perform an initial search.

3. Add a **Custom Table** with 1 column and 3 rows to the view of the form template. You will use this table to show pages of search results with each page displaying only 3 items, that is, 3 hyperlinks.

Chapter 3: Retrieve SharePoint List Data

4. Place a **Hyperlink** control in each one of the 3 rows of the custom table. Name the hyperlink controls **linkurl1**, **linkurl2**, and **linkurl3**, respectively. And name their corresponding attributes **title1**, **title2**, and **title3**, respectively. These hyperlink controls will contain the titles and URLs of 3 documents and document locations found after performing the search or paging through the search results.

5. Add two **Button** controls above the custom table and label them **Fetch Previous** and **Fetch Next**. These two buttons will be used to navigate through the search results.

6. Add a hidden **Field (element)** with the name **available** and the data type **Whole Number (integer)** to the Main data source of the form. This field will be used to store the total amount of search items found.

7. Add a hidden **Field (element)** with the name **startAt** and the data type **Whole Number (integer)** to the Main data source of the form. This field will be used to store the number of the item to start retrieving search results from when paging through the search results. The value of this field should be set to **1** when performing a new search, that is, when you click the **Find** button.

Figure 175. The Main data source of the form.

8. To be able to call the SharePoint Search Service, you must add a data connection for it to the form template. So select **Data ▶ Get External Data ▶ From Web Service ▶ From SOAP Web Service**.

9. On the **Data Connection Wizard**, enter the URL of the Search Service on a SharePoint site or site collection. For example:

    http://servername/_vti_bin/Search.asmx

    In the URL above, the Search Service on a SharePoint site collection would be

217

called. To call the Search Service on a SharePoint site, enter an URL such as for example:

```
http://servername/sitename/_vti_bin/Search.asmx
```

10. On the **Data Connection Wizard**, select **Query** from the list of operations, and click **Next**.

11. On the **Data Connection Wizard**, leave the parameter as is, and click **Next**. You will be setting the **queryXml** parameter later.

12. On the **Data Connection Wizard**, leave the **Store a copy of the data in the form template** check box deselected, and click **Next**.

13. On the **Data Connection Wizard**, accept the default name for the data connection (**Query**), deselect the **Automatically retrieve data when form is opened** check box, and click **Finish**. With this you have created a data connection to call the SharePoint Search web service.

14. When a user clicks the **Find** button, an initial search must be performed. So add an **Action** rule to the **Find** button that has the following 3 actions:

    ```
    Set a field's value: startAt = 1

    Set a field's value: queryXml = concat("<QueryPacket
    xmlns='urn:Microsoft.Search.Query'><Query><Range><StartAt>",
    string(startAt), "</StartAt></Range><Context><QueryText language='en-US'
    type='STRING'>", searchQuery,
    "</QueryText></Context></Query></QueryPacket>")

    Query using a data connection: Query
    ```

    queryXml in the second action is located under the **queryFields** group node under the **s0:Query** group node in the **Query (Secondary)** data source. The second action uses the **concat** function to construct a query string based on the values of the **startAt** and **searchQuery** fields in the Main data source. In addition, the **string** function is used to convert the value of the **startAt** field from a number into a string. The third action calls the web service to perform the search.

15. The **Fetch Previous** button should be disabled if the navigation position is on the first page of search results. So add a **Formatting** rule to the **Fetch Previous** button with a **Condition** that says:

    ```
    available = 0
    or
    available is blank
    or
    startAt ≤ 1
    ```

    and that has a formatting of **Disable this control**. This rule disables the button if there are no search results or if the first page of search results is being shown.

Chapter 3: Retrieve SharePoint List Data

16. When the user clicks the **Fetch Previous** button, the previous 3 search results must be retrieved and shown in the hyperlink controls in the custom table. So add an **Action** rule to the **Fetch Previous** button that has the following 3 actions:

    ```
    Set a field's value: startAt = startAt - 3

    Set a field's value: queryXml = concat("<QueryPacket
    xmlns='urn:Microsoft.Search.Query'><Query><Range><StartAt>",
    string(startAt), "</StartAt></Range><Context><QueryText language='en-US'
    type='STRING'>", searchQuery,
    "</QueryText></Context></Query></QueryPacket>")

    Query using a data connection: Query
    ```

    queryXml in the second action is located under the **queryFields** group node under the **s0:Query** group node in the **Query (Secondary)** data source. The second action uses the **concat** function to construct a query XML string based on the values of the **startAt** and **searchQuery** fields in the Main data source. In addition, the **string** function is used to convert the value of the **startAt** field from a number into a string. The third action calls the web service to perform the search. Because you will be displaying 3 search result items per page, you must subtract 3 from the value of the **startAt** field every time the **Fetch Previous** button is clicked.

17. The **Fetch Next** button should be disabled if the navigation position has reached the last page of search results. So add a **Formatting** rule to the **Fetch Next** button with a **Condition** that says:

    ```
    available = 0
    or
    available is blank
    or
    startAt > available - 3
    ```

    and that has a formatting of **Disable this control**. This rule disables the button if there are no search results or if the current navigation position has reached the last page of search results.

18. When the user clicks the **Fetch Next** button, the next 3 search results must be retrieved and shown in the hyperlink controls in the custom table. So add an **Action** rule to the **Fetch Next** button that has the following 3 actions:

    ```
    Set a field's value: startAt = startAt + 3

    Set a field's value: queryXml = concat("<QueryPacket
    xmlns='urn:Microsoft.Search.Query'><Query><Range><StartAt>",
    string(startAt), "</StartAt></Range><Context><QueryText language='en-US'
    type='STRING'>", searchQuery,
    "</QueryText></Context></Query></QueryPacket>")

    Query using a data connection: Query
    ```

    queryXml in the second action is located under the **queryFields** group node under the **s0:Query** group node in the **Query (Secondary)** data source. The second action uses the **concat** function to construct a query XML string based on the values of the **startAt** and **searchQuery** fields in the Main data source. In addition, the **string** function is used to convert the value of the **startAt** field from a number into a string. The third action calls the web service to perform the search. Because you will be displaying 3 search result items per page, you must add 3 to the value of the **startAt** field every time the **Fetch Next** button is clicked.

19. Add a **Formatting** rule to the **linkurl1** hyperlink with a **Condition** that says:

    ```
    linkurl1 is blank
    ```

    and that has a formatting of **Hide this control**. This rule hides the hyperlink control if it does not contain any data.

20. Add a **Formatting** rule to the **linkurl2** hyperlink with a **Condition** that says:

    ```
    linkurl2 is blank
    ```

    and that has a formatting of **Hide this control**. This rule hides the hyperlink control if it does not contain any data.

21. Add a **Formatting** rule to the **linkurl3** hyperlink with a **Condition** that says:

    ```
    linkurl3 is blank
    ```

    and that has a formatting of **Hide this control**. This rule hides the hyperlink control if it does not contain any data.

22. On the **Fields** task pane, double-click the **available** field to open its **Field or Group Properties** dialog box, and then set its **Default Value** to the following formula:

    ```
    substring-before(substring-after(QueryResult, "<TotalAvailable>"),
    "</TotalAvailable>")
    ```

    This formula parses the **QueryResult** field that is located under the **dataFields** group node under the **s0:QueryResponse** group node in the **Query (Secondary)** data source to find the value of the **TotalAvailable** XML element in the search results. Leave the **Refresh value when formula is recalculated** check box selected on the **Field or Group Properties** dialog box, and click **OK** to close the dialog box.

23. On the **Fields** task pane, double-click the **linkurl1** field to open its **Field or Group Properties** dialog box, and then set its **Default Value** to the following formula:

    ```
    substring-after(substring-before(substring-after(QueryResult, "LinkUrl"),
    "</LinkUrl>"), ">")
    ```

    This formula parses the **QueryResult** field that is located under the **dataFields** group node under the **s0:QueryResponse** group node in the **Query (Secondary)** data source to find the value of the first **LinkUrl** XML element in the search results. Leave the **Refresh value when formula is recalculated** check box selected on the **Field or Group Properties** dialog box, and click **OK** to close the dialog box.

Chapter 3: Retrieve SharePoint List Data

24. On the **Fields** task pane, double-click the **title1** field to open its **Field or Group Properties** dialog box, and then set its **Default Value** to the following formula:

```
substring-after(substring-before(substring-after(QueryResult, "Title"),
"</Title>"), ">")
```

This formula parses the **QueryResult** field that is located under the **dataFields** group node under the **s0:QueryResponse** group node in the **Query (Secondary)** data source to find the value of the first **Title** XML element in the search results. Leave the **Refresh value when formula is recalculated** check box selected on the **Field or Group Properties** dialog box, and click **OK** to close the dialog box.

25. On the **Fields** task pane, double-click the **linkurl2** field to open its **Field or Group Properties** dialog box, and then set its **Default Value** to the following formula:

```
substring-after(substring-before(substring-after(substring-
after(QueryResult, concat(linkurl1, "</LinkUrl>")), "LinkUrl"),
"</LinkUrl>"), ">")
```

This formula parses the **QueryResult** field that is located under the **dataFields** group node under the **s0:QueryResponse** group node in the **Query (Secondary)** data source and uses the location of the first **LinkUrl** XML element to find the value of the second **LinkUrl** XML element in the search results. Leave the **Refresh value when formula is recalculated** check box selected on the **Field or Group Properties** dialog box, and click **OK** to close the dialog box.

26. On the **Fields** task pane, double-click the **title2** field to open its **Field or Group Properties** dialog box, and then set its **Default Value** to the following formula:

```
substring-after(substring-before(substring-after(substring-
after(QueryResult, concat(@title1, "</Title>")), "Title"), "</Title>"),
">")
```

This formula parses the **QueryResult** field that is located under the **dataFields** group node under the **s0:QueryResponse** group node in the **Query (Secondary)** data source and uses the location of the first **Title** XML element to find the value of the second **Title** XML element in the search results. Leave the **Refresh value when formula is recalculated** check box selected on the **Field or Group Properties** dialog box, and click **OK** to close the dialog box.

27. On the **Fields** task pane, double-click the **linkurl3** field to open its **Field or Group Properties** dialog box, and then set its **Default Value** to the following formula:

```
substring-after(substring-before(substring-after(substring-
after(QueryResult, concat(linkurl2, "</LinkUrl>")), "LinkUrl"),
"</LinkUrl>"), ">")
```

This formula parses the **QueryResult** field that is located under the **dataFields** group node under the **s0:QueryResponse** group node in the **Query (Secondary)** data source and uses the location of the second **LinkUrl** XML element to find the value of the third **LinkUrl** XML element in the search results. Leave the **Refresh**

InfoPath 2010 Cookbook 2

value when formula is recalculated check box selected on the **Field or Group Properties** dialog box, and click **OK** to close the dialog box.

28. On the **Fields** task pane, double-click the **title3** field to open its **Field or Group Properties** dialog box, and then set its **Default Value** to the following formula:

```
substring-after(substring-before(substring-after(substring-
after(QueryResult, concat(@title2, "</Title>")), "Title"), "</Title>"),
">")
```

This formula parses the **QueryResult** field that is located under the **dataFields** group node under the **s0:QueryResponse** group node in the **Query (Secondary)** data source and uses the location of the second **Title** XML element to find the value of the third **Title** XML element in the search results. Leave the **Refresh value when formula is recalculated** check box selected on the **Field or Group Properties** dialog box, and click **OK** to close the dialog box.

29. Publish the form template to a SharePoint form library.

In SharePoint, navigate to the form library where you published the form template and add a new form. When the form opens, type a search term into the text box and click **Find**. The results should be returned. If there are no results, the hyperlinks should remain invisible. If there are results, click on any link to open the document or page.

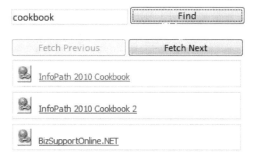

Figure 176. A search for the search term 'cookbook' returned links to site pages.

Figure 177. A search for the search term 'S.Y.M.' within documents returned one InfoPath form.

Discussion

The SharePoint Search Service allows you to search for documents in SharePoint from client applications (such as InfoPath) and web applications outside of the context of a

Chapter 3: Retrieve SharePoint List Data

SharePoint site. The SharePoint Search Service has two methods for retrieving search results: **Query** and **QueryEx**. While **Query** returns the results as a string in XML format, **QueryEx** returns the search results as a **DataSet** object. Unless you are writing code, you should use the **Query** method with InfoPath.

The XML format of the search query is defined by the **Microsoft.Search.Query** schema, which looks like the following:

```
<QueryPacket>
    <Query>
        <QueryId />
        <SupportedFormats>
            <Format />
         </SupportedFormats>
        <Context>
            <QueryText />
            <OriginatorContext />
        </Context>
        <Range>
            <StartAt />
            <Count />
        </Range>
        <Properties>
            <Property />
        </Properties>
        <SortByProperties>
            <SortByProperty />
        </SortByProperties>
        <EnableStemming />
        <TrimDuplicates />
        <IgnoreAllNoiseQuery />
        <IncludeRelevantResults />
    </Query>
</QueryPacket>
```

You can consult the MSDN documentation to find more details about this schema. The solution above kept things simple by including only the **Context** and **Range** XML elements in the **Query** XML element. But you could fine tune the search query by adding more elements if you wish.

The type of search you performed in the solution above made use of the keyword query syntax. You can get more information about this syntax on MSDN (search for *Keyword Query Syntax Reference* on the MSDN web site). When you use the keyword query syntax, each item in the search result is returned in a **Document** XML element, which contains a **Title** element and a **LinkUrl** element you can use with hyperlink controls on an InfoPath form. The following XML fragment is an example of the results for one item from the search results.

```
<Document relevance="62916773" xmlns="urn:Microsoft.Search.Response.Document">
  <Title>doc.xml</Title>
  <Action>
    <LinkUrl size="783" fileExt="xml">
      http://servername/sitename/libname/doc.xml
    </LinkUrl>
  </Action>
  <Description />
```

223

InfoPath 2010 Cookbook 2

```
  <Date>2011-03-11T10:07:13</Date>
</Document>
```

Tip:

> You can see what the full XML that is returned by the SharePoint Search Service looks like by dragging the **QueryResult** field that is located under the **dataFields** group node under the **s0:QueryResponse** group node in the **Query** secondary data source, and then binding it to a multi-line text box on the form. You can use this text box for debugging purposes and then delete it once the form is working properly.

The solution described above also made use of the **substring-before** and **substring-after** functions to parse the XML returned by the web service. Let us take a look at how these functions work when retrieving the value of the **TotalAvailable** XML element from the search results.

If the first part of the **QueryResult** search results looks as follows

```
<ResponsePacket xmlns="urn:Microsoft.Search.Response"><Response><Range><StartAt>1</StartAt><Count>4</Count><TotalAvailable>4</TotalAvailable><Results>...
```

then **substring-after(QueryResult, "<TotalAvailable>")** would return

```
4</TotalAvailable><Results>...
```

because the first occurrence of the **<TotalAvailable>** text is searched for in the **QueryResult** XML string and then all of the text after that is returned. And then **substring-before(substring-after(QueryResult, "<TotalAvailable>"), "</TotalAvailable>")** would return

4

which includes all of the text before the **</TotalAvailable>** text in the text returned by **substring-after(QueryResult, "<TotalAvailable>")**.

This is how you can use the **substring-before** and **substring-after** functions in a nested way to parse a piece of text and arrive at the formula shown in step 22 of the solution. This technique was used repeatedly in this recipe to find the values of the **Title** and **LinkUrl** XML elements.

The keyword query syntax does not offer much flexibility or the possibility to perform specific enough searches on SharePoint, so the next recipe will show you how to use the SQL query syntax to perform more specific searches on SharePoint via InfoPath.

61 Use SharePoint Search in InfoPath to search for documents – method 2

Problem

You want to be able to perform a search query on InfoPath forms stored in one or more form libraries on a SharePoint site from within an InfoPath form.

Solution

You can use the **Query** operation of the SharePoint Search Service, the SQL query syntax, and a search scope to search for InfoPath forms stored in one or more specific SharePoint form libraries.

Before proceeding, an administrator must ensure that the SharePoint Search Service is running and that content sources have been configured and crawled. Consult the SharePoint documentation for information about configuring SharePoint Search.

You must also ensure that at least one search scope that includes one or more SharePoint form libraries has been defined. Search scopes can be defined either at the Search Service Application level (in SharePoint Central Administration) or at the site administration level. To define a search scope at the site administration level:

1. In SharePoint, navigate to the **Site Settings** page of the top-level site in the site collection.

2. On the **Site Settings** page under **Site Collection Administration**, click **Search scopes**.

3. On the **View Scopes** page, click **New Scope**.

4. On the **Create Scope** page, enter a **Title** for the scope (for example, **FormLibraries**), and click **OK**.

5. On the **View Scopes** page, click **Add rules** under the **Update Status** column for the scope you just created.

6. On the **Add Scope Rule** page, leave **Web Address** selected as the **Scope Rule Type**, enter the URL of the form library you want to search in the **Folder** text box, and click **OK**.

7. If you want to include more form libraries in the search scope, on the **View Scopes** page, click on the scope title, and then on the **Scope Properties and Rules** page under **Rules**, click **New Rule** to add a rule for another form library you want to include in the scope.

SharePoint should automatically schedule an update for the new scope. Once the text **Ready** appears in the **Update Status** column on the **View Scopes** page and a number greater than 0 appears in the **Items** column, you can start using the scope in search queries.

InfoPath 2010 Cookbook 2

To search for forms in one or more form libraries from within an InfoPath form:

1. Follow steps 1 through 13 of recipe *60 Use SharePoint Search in InfoPath to search for documents – method 1*

2. When a user clicks the **Find** button, an initial search must be performed. So add an **Action** rule to the **Find** button that has the following 3 actions:

    ```
    Set a field's value: startAt = 1

    Set a field's value: queryXml = concat("<QueryPacket
    xmlns='urn:Microsoft.Search.Query'><Query><Range><StartAt>",
    string(startAt), "</StartAt></Range><Context><QueryText language='en-US'
    type='MSSQLFT'>SELECT rank, title, path, author FROM Scope() WHERE
    CONTAINS('", '"', searchQuery, '"', "') AND", ' "scope"', "='FormLibraries'
    AND NOT CONTAINS('.aspx')</QueryText></Context></Query></QueryPacket>")

    Query using a data connection: Query
    ```

    queryXml in the second action is located under the **queryFields** group node under the **s0:Query** group node in the **Query (Secondary)** data source. The second action uses the **concat** function to construct a query XML string based on the values of the **startAt** and **searchQuery** fields in the Main data source. In addition, the **string** function is used to convert the value of the **startAt** field from a number into a string. The third action calls the web service to perform the search.

3. The **Fetch Previous** button should be disabled if the navigation position is on the first page of search results. So add a **Formatting** rule to the **Fetch Previous** button with a **Condition** that says:

    ```
    available = 0
    or
    available is blank
    or
    startAt ≤ 1
    ```

    and that has a formatting of **Disable this control**. This rule disables the button if there are no search results or if the first page of search results is being shown.

4. When the user clicks the **Fetch Previous** button, the previous 3 search results must be retrieved and shown in the hyperlink controls in the custom table. So add an **Action** rule to the **Fetch Previous** button that has the following 3 actions:

    ```
    Set a field's value: startAt = startAt - 3

    Set a field's value: queryXml = concat("<QueryPacket
    xmlns='urn:Microsoft.Search.Query'><Query><Range><StartAt>",
    string(startAt), "</StartAt></Range><Context><QueryText language='en-US'
    type='MSSQLFT'>SELECT rank, title, path, author FROM Scope() WHERE
    CONTAINS('", '"', searchQuery, '"', "') AND", ' "scope"', "='FormLibraries'
    AND NOT CONTAINS('.aspx')</QueryText></Context></Query></QueryPacket>")

    Query using a data connection: Query
    ```

    queryXml in the second action is located under the **queryFields** group node under

Chapter 3: Retrieve SharePoint List Data

the **s0:Query** group node in the **Query (Secondary)** data source. The second action uses the **concat** function to construct a query XML string based on the values of the **startAt** and **searchQuery** fields in the Main data source. In addition, the **string** function is used to convert the value of the **startAt** field from a number into a string. The third action calls the web service to perform the search. Because you will be displaying 3 search result items per page, you must subtract 3 from the value of the **startAt** field every time the **Fetch Previous** button is clicked.

5. The **Fetch Next** button should be disabled if the navigation position has reached the last page of search results. So add a **Formatting** rule to the **Fetch Next** button with a **Condition** that says:

```
available = 0
or
available is blank
or
startAt > available - 3
```

and that has a formatting of **Disable this control**. This rule disables the button if there are no search results or if the current navigation position has reached the last page of search results.

6. When the user clicks the **Fetch Next** button, the next 3 search results must be retrieved and shown in the hyperlink controls in the custom table. So add an **Action** rule to the **Fetch Next** button that has the following 3 actions:

```
Set a field's value: startAt = startAt + 3

Set a field's value: queryXml = concat("<QueryPacket
xmlns='urn:Microsoft.Search.Query'><Query><Range><StartAt>",
string(startAt), "</StartAt></Range><Context><QueryText language='en-US'
type='MSSQLFT'>SELECT rank, title, path, author FROM Scope() WHERE
CONTAINS('"', '"', searchQuery, '"', '"') AND", ' "scope"', "='FormLibraries'
AND NOT CONTAINS('.aspx')</QueryText></Context></Query></QueryPacket>")

Query using a data connection: Query
```

queryXml in the second action is located under the **queryFields** group node under the **s0:Query** group node in the **Query (Secondary)** data source. The second action uses the **concat** function to construct a query XML string based on the values of the **startAt** and **searchQuery** fields in the Main data source. In addition, the **string** function is used to convert the value of the **startAt** field from a number into a string. The third action calls the web service to perform the search. Because you will be displaying 3 search result items per page, you must add 3 to the value of the **startAt** field every time the **Fetch Next** button is clicked.

7. Add a **Formatting** rule to the **linkurl1** hyperlink with a **Condition** that says:

```
linkurl1 is blank
```

and that has a formatting of **Hide this control**. This rule hides the hyperlink control if it does not contain any data.

8. Add a **Formatting** rule to the **linkurl2** hyperlink with a **Condition** that says:

   ```
   linkurl2 is blank
   ```

   and that has a formatting of **Hide this control**. This rule hides the hyperlink control if it does not contain any data.

9. Add a **Formatting** rule to the **linkurl3** hyperlink with a **Condition** that says:

   ```
   linkurl3 is blank
   ```

   and that has a formatting of **Hide this control**. This rule hides the hyperlink control if it does not contain any data.

10. On the **Fields** task pane, double-click the **available** field to open its **Field or Group Properties** dialog box, and then set its **Default Value** to the following formula:

    ```
    substring-before(substring-after(QueryResult, "<TotalAvailable>"),
    "</TotalAvailable>")
    ```

    This formula parses the **QueryResult** field that is located under the **dataFields** group node under the **s0:QueryResponse** group node in the **Query (Secondary)** data source to find the value of the **TotalAvailable** XML element in the search results. Leave the **Refresh value when formula is recalculated** check box selected on the **Field or Group Properties** dialog box, and click **OK** to close the dialog box.

11. On the **Fields** task pane, double-click the **linkurl1** field to open its **Field or Group Properties** dialog box, and then set its **Default Value** to the following formula:

    ```
    substring-after(substring-before(substring-after(QueryResult, "LinkUrl"),
    "</LinkUrl>"), ">")
    ```

    This formula parses the **QueryResult** field that is located under the **dataFields** group node under the **s0:QueryResponse** group node in the **Query (Secondary)** data source to find the value of the first **LinkUrl** XML element in the search results. Leave the **Refresh value when formula is recalculated** check box selected on the **Field or Group Properties** dialog box, and click **OK** to close the dialog box.

12. On the **Fields** task pane, double-click the **title1** field to open its **Field or Group Properties** dialog box, and then set its **Default Value** to the following formula:

    ```
    substring-after(substring-before(substring-after(QueryResult,
    "<Name>TITLE</Name>"), "</Value>"), "<Value>")
    ```

    This formula parses the **QueryResult** field that is located under the **dataFields** group node under the **s0:QueryResponse** group node in the **Query (Secondary)** data source to find the value of the **Value** XML element that corresponds to the first title (**Name** XML element that has a value of **TITLE**) in the search results. Leave the **Refresh value when formula is recalculated** check box selected on the **Field or Group Properties** dialog box, and click **OK** to close the dialog box.

13. On the **Fields** task pane, double-click the **linkurl2** field to open its **Field or Group Properties** dialog box, and then set its **Default Value** to the following formula:

   ```
   substring-after(substring-before(substring-after(substring-
   after(QueryResult, concat(linkurl1, "</LinkUrl>")), "LinkUrl"),
   "</LinkUrl>"), ">")
   ```

   This formula parses the **QueryResult** field that is located under the **dataFields** group node under the **s0:QueryResponse** group node in the **Query (Secondary)** data source and uses the location of the first **LinkUrl** XML element to find the value of the second **LinkUrl** XML element in the search results. Leave the **Refresh value when formula is recalculated** check box selected on the **Field or Group Properties** dialog box, and click **OK** to close the dialog box.

14. On the **Fields** task pane, double-click the **title2** field to open its **Field or Group Properties** dialog box, and then set its **Default Value** to the following formula:

   ```
   substring-after(substring-before(substring-after(substring-
   after(QueryResult, concat(@title1, "</Value>")), "<Name>TITLE</Name>"),
   "</Value>"), "<Value>")
   ```

   This formula parses the **QueryResult** field that is located under the **dataFields** group node under the **s0:QueryResponse** group node in the **Query (Secondary)** data source and uses the location of the **Value** XML element for the first title to find the value of the **Value** XML element for the second title in the search results. Leave the **Refresh value when formula is recalculated** check box selected on the **Field or Group Properties** dialog box, and click **OK** to close the dialog box.

15. On the **Fields** task pane, double-click the **linkurl3** field to open its **Field or Group Properties** dialog box, and then set its **Default Value** to the following formula:

   ```
   substring-after(substring-before(substring-after(substring-
   after(QueryResult, concat(linkurl2, "</LinkUrl>")), "LinkUrl"),
   "</LinkUrl>"), ">")
   ```

   This formula parses the **QueryResult** field that is located under the **dataFields** group node under the **s0:QueryResponse** group node in the **Query (Secondary)** data source and uses the location of the second **LinkUrl** XML element to find the value of the third **LinkUrl** XML element in the search results. Leave the **Refresh value when formula is recalculated** check box selected on the **Field or Group Properties** dialog box, and click **OK** to close the dialog box.

16. On the **Fields** task pane, double-click the **title3** field to open its **Field or Group Properties** dialog box, and then set its **Default Value** to the following formula:

   ```
   substring-after(substring-before(substring-after(substring-
   after(QueryResult, concat(@title2, "</Value>")), "<Name>TITLE</Name>"),
   "</Value>"), "<Value>")
   ```

   This formula parses the **QueryResult** field that is located under the **dataFields** group node under the **s0:QueryResponse** group node in the **Query (Secondary)** data source and uses the location of the **Value** XML element for the second title to find the value of the **Value** XML element for the third title in the search results. Leave the **Refresh value when formula is recalculated** check box selected on the **Field or Group Properties** dialog box, and click **OK** to close the dialog box.

17. Publish the form template to a SharePoint form library.

In SharePoint, navigate to the form library where you published the form template and add a new form. When the form opens, type a search term or an asterisk (*) into the text box and click **Find**. The results should be returned. If there are no results, the hyperlinks should remain invisible. If there are results, click on any link to open the document.

Figure 178. Search results for searching on an asterisk (*), i.e. for all forms in the search scope.

Figure 179. Search results for searching on specific text contained within forms in the search scope.

Discussion

The SharePoint Search Service allows you to search for documents in SharePoint from client applications (such as InfoPath) and web applications outside of the context of a SharePoint site. The SharePoint Search Service has two methods for retrieving search results: **Query** and **QueryEx**. While **Query** returns the results as a string in XML format, **QueryEx** returns the search results as a **DataSet** object. Unless you are writing code, you should use the **Query** method with InfoPath.

A search scope defines a subset of information in the search index. In the solution described above you used a search scope to limit your search to only one or more SharePoint form libraries that you defined as rules on the scope. You also used the SQL query syntax in a search query to be able to perform complex searches on forms stored in form libraries. You can get more information about the SQL syntax for SharePoint Search on MSDN (search for *SharePoint Search SQL Syntax Reference* on the MSDN web site).

Chapter 3: Retrieve SharePoint List Data

Let us take a brief look at a few key parts of the formula that is used to set the value of the **queryXml** field under the **queryFields** and **Query** group nodes in the secondary data source.

```
concat("<QueryPacket 
xmlns='urn:Microsoft.Search.Query'><Query><Range><StartAt>", string(startAt), 
"</StartAt></Range><Context><QueryText language='en-US' type='MSSQLFT'>SELECT 
rank, title, path, author FROM Scope() WHERE CONTAINS('", '"', searchQuery, '"', 
"') AND", ' "scope"', "='FormLibraries' AND NOT 
CONTAINS('.aspx')</QueryText></Context></Query></QueryPacket>")
```

FormLibraries is the name of the search scope used in the search query in the formula displayed above. The first thing you will notice is that the type of search being performed makes use of **MSSQLFT**, which indicates that the type of query is a SQL Full Text syntax query.

The second thing to note is that on several places within the **concat** function, you must trade double quotes for single quotes so that the final SQL query is of an acceptable format for the web service. For example, when specifying the scope to use in the following search query

```
SELECT rank, title, path, author FROM Scope() WHERE CONTAINS(' "your search 
query goes here" ') AND "scope"='FormLibraries' AND NOT CONTAINS('.aspx')
```

you must place the word **scope** between double quotes instead of single quotes for the search query to be valid. But because you are also using double quotes to concatenate strings in the formula, this would result in an error in InfoPath. So you must use single quotes for concatenation instead of double quotes. Note that you can mix double and single quotes when concatenating strings using the **concat** furnction in InfoPath, so for example

```
' "scope" '
```

would work as well as

```
" 'scope' "
```

inside of the **concat** function. However, the SQL syntax requires you to use the first.

The third thing to note is that the first search condition in the WHERE clause is placed between double quotes inside of the CONTAINS Full-Text predicate. This allows you to not only search on single words, but also on sentences, and even use the wildcard character (*) to return all of the forms in the form libraries you added to the search scope.

```
CONTAINS(' "your search query goes here" ')
```

The last thing to note is that the second search condition in the WHERE clause excludes all files in the form libraries that end on **.aspx**.

231

InfoPath 2010 Cookbook 2

```
AND NOT CONTAINS('.aspx')
```

The solution described above uses the same parsing technique (with the **substring-before** and **substring-after** functions to display the results) you used in recipe *60 Use SharePoint Search in InfoPath to search for documents – method 1*. However, because the XML that is returned by the SharePoint Search Service is slightly different, you had to use different formulas to retrieve the URLs and titles of the documents.

When you use the SharePoint Search SQL syntax, each item in the search result is returned in a **Document** XML element, which contains a **LinkUrl** element and several **Property** elements depending on the fields you specify in the SELECT clause. The following XML fragment is an example of the results for one item in the search results.

```
<Document xmlns="urn:Microsoft.Search.Response.Document">
  <Action>
    <LinkUrl fileExt="xml">http://servername/sitename/libname/doc.xml</LinkUrl>
  </Action>
  <Properties xmlns="urn:Microsoft.Search.Response.Document.Document">
    <Property>
      <Name>RANK</Name>
      <Type>Int64</Type>
      <Value>100000000</Value>
    </Property>
    <Property>
      <Name>TITLE</Name>
      <Type>String</Type>
      <Value>doc.xml</Value>
    </Property>
    <Property>
      <Name>PATH</Name>
      <Type>String</Type>
      <Value>http://servername/sitename/libname/doc.xml</Value>
    </Property>
    <Property>
      <Name>AUTHOR</Name>
      <Type>Object</Type>
      <Value>...</Value>
    </Property>
  </Properties>
</Document>
```

Chapter 4: Use InfoPath Controls with Data from SharePoint

Drop-Down List Box

A drop-down list box is a control that takes up the space of only one row in a list and can be temporarily expanded to display a list of items from which a user can select one item. Cascading or dependent drop-down list boxes are paired drop-down list boxes, where you select an item from one drop-down list box and then a second drop-down list box is automatically populated with items that depend on the selection made in the first drop-down list box.

The recipes in this section take you through a couple of scenarios for creating cascading drop-down list boxes that are populated with data from one or several SharePoint lists.

62 Cascading drop-down list boxes using one SharePoint list

Problem

You have a SharePoint list that contains the names, types, and models of running shoes. You want to add three drop-down list boxes to an InfoPath form and have the first drop-down list box populated with all of the running shoe brand names, the second drop-down list box with only the running shoe types belonging to the selected brand in the first drop-down list box, and the third drop-down list box with only the running shoe models belonging to the selected brand in the first drop-down list box and the selected type in the second drop-down list box.

Solution

You can use the **Filter Data** option on the data source for the SharePoint list used to populate the drop-down list boxes to filter the data based on values that are entered or selected in the Main data source of the form.

Suppose you have a SharePoint list named **RunningShoesBrandsTypes** that contains the following data:

Title (Text)	ShoeBrand (Text)	ShoeType (Text)
Wave Alchemy	Mizuno	Control
Wave Renegade	Mizuno	Control

Title (Text)	ShoeBrand (Text)	ShoeType (Text)
Wave Nirvana	Mizuno	Stability
Wave Inspire	Mizuno	Stability
GEL-Evolution	ASICS	Control
GEL-Foundation	ASICS	Control
GEL-Kayano	ASICS	Stability
Ariel	Brooks	Control
Addiction	Brooks	Control
Adrenaline	Brooks	Stability
ProGrid Stabil CS	Saucony	Control

Note:

> You can use the **RunningShoesBrandsTypesList.stp** file, which you can download from www.bizsupportonline.com, to load the **RunningShoesBrandsTypes** SharePoint list into a SharePoint test environment (also see *Upload a list template to a List Template Gallery* in the Appendix).

To create cascading drop-down list boxes using data from one SharePoint list:

1. In InfoPath, create a new SharePoint form library form template or use an existing one.

2. Add a **Receive** data connection to the **RunningShoesBrandsTypes** SharePoint list to the form template (also see *Use a SharePoint list data connection* in recipe *43 3 Ways to retrieve data from a SharePoint list*). Include the **Title**, **ShoeBrand**, and **ShoeType** fields in the data source, leave the **Automatically retrieve data when form is opened** check box selected, and name the data connection **RunningShoesBrandsTypes**.

3. Add a **Drop-Down List Box** control to the view of the form template and name it **shoeBrand**.

4. Open the **Drop-Down List Box Properties** dialog box.

5. On the **Drop-Down List Box Properties** dialog box on the **Data** tab, select **Get choices from an external data source**, and select **RunningShoesBrandsTypes** from the **Data source** drop-down list box. The **SharePointListItem_RW** repeating group should automatically be populated in the **Entries** text box.

6. On the **Drop-Down List Box Properties** dialog box, click the button behind the **Value** text box.

7. On the **Select a Field or Group** dialog box, select **ShoeBrand**, and click **OK**.

8. Repeat the previous two steps for the **Display name** text box on the **Drop-Down List Box Properties** dialog box.

9. On the **Drop-Down List Box Properties** dialog box, select the **Show only entries with unique display names** check box, and click **OK**. This should prevent duplicate brand names from appearing in the drop-down list box.

10. Add a second **Drop-Down List Box** control to the view of the form template and name it **shoeType**.

11. Open the **Drop-Down List Box Properties** dialog box of the **shoeType** drop-down list box.

12. On the **Drop-Down List Box Properties** dialog box on the **Data** tab, select **Get choices from an external data source**, select **RunningShoesBrandsTypes** from the **Data source** drop-down list box, and click the button behind the **Entries** text box.

13. On the **Select a Field or Group** dialog box, select the **SharePointListItem_RW** repeating group node if it has not already been selected, and then click **Filter Data**.

14. On the **Filter Data** dialog box, click **Add**.

15. You must add a filter that will return only the **ShoeType** fields that fall under the same repeating group node as the selected **shoeBrand** in the first drop-down list box. For this you must add a filter that compares the **ShoeBrand** from the SharePoint list to the **shoeBrand** value selected in the first drop-down list box on the form. So select **ShoeBrand** from the first drop-down list box on the **Specify Filter Conditions** dialog box. This **ShoeBrand** field is located in the secondary data source for the SharePoint list.

16. On the **Specify Filter Conditions** dialog box, leave **is equal to** selected in the second drop-down list box, and then select **Select a field or group** from the third drop-down list box.

17. On the **Select a Field or Group** dialog box, select **Main** from the **Fields** drop-down list box, select **shoeBrand**, and then click **OK**. Note: The **shoeBrand** in the Main data source corresponds to the selected shoe brand in the first drop-down list box.

18. On the **Specify Filter Conditions** dialog box, click **OK**.

19. On the **Filter Data** dialog box, click **OK**.
20. On the **Select a Field or Group** dialog box, click **OK**. The XPath expression in the **Entries** text box on the **Drop-Down List Box Properties** dialog box should now say:

    ```
    /dfs:myFields/dfs:dataFields/d:SharePointListItem_RW[d:ShoeBrand =
    xdXDocument:get-DOM()/my:myFields/my:shoeBrand]
    ```

21. On the **Drop-Down List Box Properties** dialog box, click the button behind the **Value** text box.
22. On the **Select a Field or Group** dialog box, select **ShoeType**, and click **OK**.
23. Repeat the previous two steps for the **Display name** text box on the **Drop-Down List Box Properties** dialog box.
24. On the **Drop-Down List Box Properties** dialog box, select the **Show only entries with unique display names** check box, and click **OK**. This should prevent duplicate shoe types from appearing in the second drop-down list box.
25. Before you continue, preview the form to see whether the types for each brand are automatically being populated in the **shoeType** drop-down list box when you select a shoe brand from the first drop-down list box.
26. Add a third **Drop-Down List Box** control to the view of the form template and name it **shoeModel**.
27. Open the **Drop-Down List Box Properties** dialog box for the third drop-down list box.
28. On the **Drop-Down List Box Properties** dialog box on the **Data** tab, select **Get choices from an external data source**, select **RunningShoesBrandsTypes** from the **Data source** drop-down list box, and then click the button behind the **Entries** text box.
29. On the **Select a Field or Group** dialog box, select the **d:SharePointListItem_RW** repeating group node if it has not already been selected, and then click **Filter Data**.
30. On the **Filter Data** dialog box, click **Add**.
31. You must add a filter that will return only the **ShoeModel** fields that fall under the same repeating group node as the selected **shoeBrand** in the first drop-down list box and the selected **shoeType** in the second drop-down list box. For this you must add a filter that compares the **ShoeBrand** from the SharePoint list to the **shoeBrand** value selected in the first drop-down list box, and that compares the **ShoeType** from the SharePoint list to the **shoeType** value selected in the second drop-down list box. So select **ShoeBrand** from the first drop-down list box on the **Specify Filter Conditions** dialog box. This **ShoeBrand** field is located in the secondary data source for the SharePoint list.

Chapter 4: Use InfoPath Controls with Data from SharePoint

32. On the **Specify Filter Conditions** dialog box, leave **is equal to** selected in the second drop-down list box, and then select **Select a field or group** from the third drop-down list box.

33. On the **Select a Field or Group** dialog box, select **Main** from the **Fields** drop-down list box, select **shoeBrand**, and then click **OK**. Note: The **shoeBrand** in the Main data source corresponds to the selected shoe brand in the first drop-down list box.

34. On the **Specify Filter Conditions** dialog box, click the **And** button behind the third drop-down list box to add a second filter condition. The button should automatically become a drop-down list box with the **and** operator as its selected item.

35. On the **Specify Filter Conditions** dialog box, select **ShoeType** from the first drop-down list box for the second condition. This **ShoeType** field is located in the secondary data source for the SharePoint list.

36. On the **Specify Filter Conditions** dialog box, leave **is equal to** selected in the second drop-down list box for the second condition, and then select **Select a field or group** from the third drop-down list box for the second condition.

37. On the **Select a Field or Group** dialog box, select **Main** from the **Fields** drop-down list box, select **shoeType**, and click **OK**. Note: The **shoeType** in the Main data source corresponds to the selected shoe type in the second drop-down list box.

38. On the **Specify Filter Conditions** dialog box, click **OK**.

39. The filter on the **Filter Data** dialog box, should now say:

    ```
    ShoeBrand = shoeBrand and ShoeType = shoeType
    ```

    Click **OK**.

40. On the **Select a Field or Group** dialog box, click **OK**. The XPath expression in the **Entries** text box on the **Drop-Down List Box Properties** dialog box should now say:

    ```
    /dfs:myFields/dfs:dataFields/d:SharePointListItem_RW[d:ShoeBrand =
    xdXDocument:get-DOM()/my:myFields/my:shoeBrand and d:ShoeType =
    xdXDocument:get-DOM()/my:myFields/my:shoeType]
    ```

41. On the **Drop-Down List Box Properties** dialog box, click the button behind the **Value** text box.

42. On the **Select a Field or Group** dialog box, select **Title** (the shoe model is stored in this field), and click **OK**.

43. Repeat the previous two steps for the **Display name** text box on the **Drop-Down List Box** properties dialog box.

44. On the **Drop-Down List Box Properties** dialog box, click **OK**. Note that because the shoe model names are expected to be unique in the SharePoint list, you do not have to select the **Show only entries with unique display names** check box.

45. Add an **Action** rule to the **shoeBrand** drop-down list box that has the following two actions:

```
Set a field's value: shoeType = ""
Set a field's value: shoeModel = ""
```

where both **shoeType** and **shoeModel** are located in the Main data source of the form. This rule ensures that any previously selected values in the **shoeType** and **shoeModel** drop-down list boxes are cleared when the drop-down list boxes are populated again with items.

46. Add an **Action** rule to the **shoeType** drop-down list box that has the following action:

```
Set a field's value: shoeModel = ""
```

where **shoeModel** is located in the Main data source of the form. This rule ensures that any previously selected value in the **shoeModel** drop-down list box is cleared when the drop-down list box is populated again with items.

47. Publish the form template to a SharePoint form library.

In SharePoint, navigate to the form library where you published the form template and add a new form. When the form opens, verify that the second and third drop-down list boxes are empty. Select a brand from the first drop-down list box. The second drop-down list box should now contain items and the third drop-down list box should still be empty. Select a type from the second drop-down list box. The third drop-down list box should contain the running shoe models for the selected shoe brand and shoe type in the first and second drop-down list boxes.

Figure 180. The InfoPath form displaying the cascading drop-down list boxes.

Discussion

To create cascading drop-down list boxes that make use of SharePoint list data in InfoPath, you must apply filtering. And as you have already seen from the recipes in Chapter 3, there are two basic ways to filter SharePoint list data in InfoPath when you make use of rules:

Chapter 4: Use InfoPath Controls with Data from SharePoint

1. Use the **Filter Data** option on a secondary data source.
2. Use fields under the **queryFields** group node in the secondary data source.

If you use the first method, you must retrieve all of the data from SharePoint and then filter it locally in the InfoPath form. And if you use the second method, you generally filter the data as you retrieve it from SharePoint. The solution described above uses the first method and works best for populating drop-down list boxes from SharePoint lists that contain a small amount of data.

Because the data from all three drop-down list boxes are coming from the same SharePoint list, you must pre-fetch all of the data from the SharePoint list and then use the **Filter Data** option on the secondary data source for the SharePoint list to filter the data and display it in the drop-down list boxes. The pre-fetching of data takes place when the form opens, because you set the secondary data source to automatically retrieve the data when the form opened. However, you could also set the SharePoint list data to be retrieved on demand by deselecting the **Automatically retrieve data when form is opened** check box on the data connection and then adding a **Query for data** action in a rule on another control that should trigger populating the first drop-down list box.

You could have also used the second filter method in the solution above by adding three separate data connections to the same SharePoint list (instead of just one data connection) to the form template and then using query fields to filter and populate the data in each drop-down list box with each drop-down list box using its own (filtered) secondary data source. You will learn how to use query fields to filter SharePoint list data in cascading drop-down list boxes in the next recipe.

63 Cascading drop-down list boxes using linked SharePoint lists

Problem

You have two SharePoint lists that are linked to each other through a lookup column and you want to use these lists to create cascading drop-down list boxes on an InfoPath form.

Solution

You can use fields under the **queryFields** group node of the data source for the SharePoint list and rules to filter data and populate cascading drop-down list boxes.

Suppose you have two SharePoint lists that are linked to each other through a lookup column. The first SharePoint list is named **ShoeBrands** and has the following contents:

ID	Title
1	Saucony
2	Brooks
3	ASICS
4	Mizuno
5	New Balance

Note:

> You can use the **ShoeBrandsList.stp** file, which you can download from www.bizsupportonline.com, to load the **ShoeBrands** SharePoint list into a SharePoint test environment (also see *Upload a list template to a List Template Gallery* in the Appendix).

The second SharePoint list is named **RunningShoes** and has the following contents:

ID	Title	ShoeBrand (Lookup)
1	Wave Alchemy	Mizuno
2	Wave Renegade	Mizuno
3	GEL-Evolution	ASICS
4	GT-2150	ASICS
5	Ariel	Brooks
6	ProGrid Stabil CS	Saucony
7	New Balance 1012	New Balance

Chapter 4: Use InfoPath Controls with Data from SharePoint

Note:

> You can use the **RunningShoesList.stp** file, which you can download from www.bizsupportonline.com, to load the **RunningShoes** SharePoint list into a SharePoint test environment. You must then manually add a **ShoeBrand** lookup column and link it to the **Title** column in the **ShoeBrands** SharePoint list as shown below.

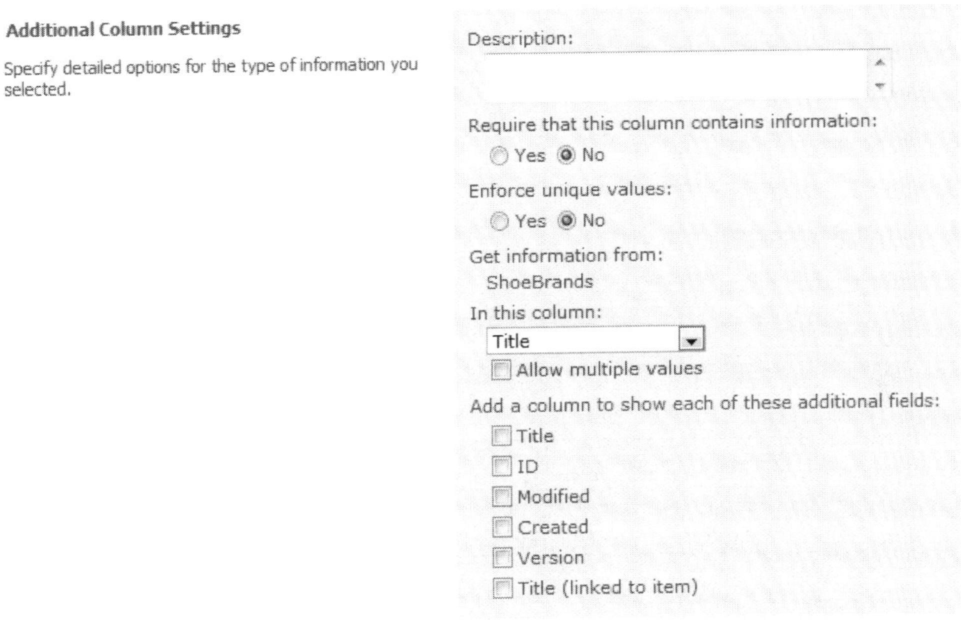

Figure 181. Additional column settings for the ShoeBrand lookup column in the RunningShoes list.

To create cascading drop-down list boxes by querying linked SharePoint lists:

1. In InfoPath, create a new SharePoint form library form template or use an existing one.

2. Add a **Receive** data connection to the **ShoeBrands** SharePoint list to the form template (also see *Use a SharePoint list data connection* in recipe *43 3 Ways to retrieve data from a SharePoint list*). Include the **ID** and **Title** fields in the data source, select **Title** as the field to sort the list by, leave the **Automatically retrieve data when form is opened** check box selected, and name the data connection **ShoeBrands**.

3. Add a **Drop-Down List Box** control to the view of the form template and name it **shoeBrand**.

241

4. Populate the **shoeBrand** drop-down list box with items from the **ShoeBrands** secondary data source, use **ID** as the **Value**, and use **Title** as the **Display name** for the drop-down list box.

5. Add a **Receive** data connection to the **RunningShoes** SharePoint list to the form template. Include the **ID**, **Title**, and **ShoeBrand** fields in the data source, select **Title** as the field to sort the list by, deselect the **Automatically retrieve data when form is opened** check box, and name the data connection **RunningShoes**.

6. Add a second **Drop-Down List Box** control to the view of the form template and name it **runningShoe**.

7. Populate the **runningShoe** drop-down list box with items from the **RunningShoes** secondary data source, use **ID** as the **Value**, and use **Title** as the **Display name** for the drop-down list box.

8. The **runningShoe** drop-down list box should be populated with items when an item is selected from the **shoeBrand** drop-down list box, so you have to add a rule that uses the selected value from the **shoeBrand** drop-down list box to query the **RunningShoes** secondary data source, so that the **runningShoe** drop-down list box can be populated with filtered items. So add an **Action** rule to the **shoeBrand** drop-down list box that has the following 3 actions:

```
Set a field's value: runningShoe = ""
Set a field's value: ShoeBrand = .
```

where **ShoeBrand** is the **ShoeBrand** field under the **q:SharePointListItem_RW** group node under the **queryFields** group node in the **RunningShoes** secondary data source, and which contains the ID of the shoe brand that is linked to the running shoe. . represents the **shoeBrand** field in the Main data source.

```
Query using a data connection: RunningShoes
```

The first action clears any previously selected value in the **runningShoe** drop-down list box. The second action sets the value of the **ShoeBrand** query field in the **RunningShoes** secondary data source to be equal to the value of the selected item in the **shoeBrand** drop-down list box. The third action sends the query to SharePoint to filter and retrieve the data for the **RunningShoes** secondary data source and then populate the **runningShoe** drop-down list box with this data.

9. Publish the form template to a SharePoint form library.

In SharePoint, navigate to the form library where you published the form template and add a new form. When the form opens, the first drop-down list box should contain shoe brands and the second drop-down list box should be empty. Select a shoe brand from the first drop-down list box. The second drop-down list box should be populated with the running shoes for the brand you selected in the first drop-down list box. Select another shoe brand from the first drop-down list box. The second drop-down list box should be first cleared and then refilled with the running shoes corresponding to the newly selected shoe brand.

Chapter 4: Use InfoPath Controls with Data from SharePoint

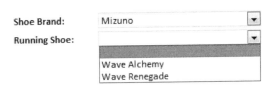

Figure 182. The InfoPath form displaying the cascading drop-down list boxes.

Discussion

The solution described above works best for populating drop-down list boxes from SharePoint lists that contain large amounts of data or which you want to populate on demand. Filtering data through query fields of a data connection is a two-step process:

1. You must set the value of one or more query fields of the data connection to the value(s) you want to filter the data on.
2. You must (re)query the data connection to retrieve the filtered data.

These two steps were performed in step 8 through the use of actions in a rule.

To initiate the process of cascading the data, you must have some data to start with. So in the solution described above the data for the **ShoeBrands** secondary data source was automatically retrieved when the form opened. You could have also set this data to be retrieved on demand by deselecting the **Automatically retrieve data when form is opened** check box on the first data connection and then adding a **Query for data** action in a rule on an extra button or another field that should trigger populating the first drop-down list box.

Whether you use filtering within InfoPath (as described in recipe *62 Cascading drop-down list boxes using one SharePoint list*) or filtering in SharePoint (through querying as described in the solution above) for setting up cascading drop-down list boxes depends largely on your scenario and how you want to deal with data retrieval.

The advantage of using filtering within InfoPath is that the data is retrieved only once to populate the data sources and subsequently used for the rest of the session in the form and filtered to populate drop-down list boxes. So this method reduces the amount of queries sent to SharePoint to retrieve data. However, note that postbacks may still take place to be able to properly render the controls on the view whenever you select an item from a drop-down list box that affects the data in another drop-down list box. The disadvantage of using filtering within InfoPath is that the initial loading of data may take a long while, so affect the responsiveness and performance of the form, especially if the SharePoint lists being queried contain large amounts of data.

The advantage of using query fields of a data connection to create cascading drop-down list boxes is that only a subset of the data is retrieved, since it is filtered on the server. This positively affects the responsiveness and performance of forms. The disadvantage of using query fields of a data connection is that you must repeatedly make calls to SharePoint to retrieve the data to populate the drop-down list boxes. This may increase the amount of requests and load on the server.

If you have relatively small SharePoint lists that you want to use for populating cascading drop-down list boxes, you could choose to use the filtering within InfoPath method. However, if you have very large SharePoint lists to filter, it might be best to choose the query and filter on SharePoint method for creating cascading drop-down list boxes in InfoPath.

Combo Box

A combo box combines the functionality of a drop-down list box, which contains read-only items, with a text box in which you can enter a new item that does not yet exist in the list. However, entering a new item in a combo box does not permanently add that item to the underlying data source of the combo box.

The recipe described in this section shows you a trick for dynamically (and permanently) adding items to a combo box that is being populated with data from a SharePoint list.

64 Dynamically add an item to a combo box populated by a SharePoint list

Problem

You have a combo box, which you have populated with items from a SharePoint list. You want to be able to enter a new item in the combo box and have that new item automatically and permanently added to the underlying data source of the combo box while you are still filling out the form.

Solution

You can use SharePoint's **Lists** web service to add a new item to a SharePoint list that is being used to populate a combo box.

Suppose you have a SharePoint list named **Countries**. This SharePoint list currently contains only one item named **New Zealand**.

Note:

> You can use the **CountriesList.stp** file, which you can download from www.bizsupportonline.com, to load the **Countries** SharePoint list into a SharePoint test environment (also see *Upload a list template to a List Template Gallery* in the Appendix).

Chapter 4: Use InfoPath Controls with Data from SharePoint

To dynamically and permanently add an item to a combo box that is being populated by a SharePoint list:

1. In SharePoint, navigate to the **Countries** SharePoint list, and click **List Tools ▶ List ▶ Settings ▶ List Settings**.

2. When the **List Settings** page opens, copy the GUID from the browser's address bar. It should look something like:

   ```
   %7BADFA2558%2DB237%2D491B%2D8E86%2D1F8A7ADFF3E0%7D
   ```

3. Convert the **%7B** characters to **{**, **%2D** to **-**, and **%7D** to **}**. The resulting list GUID should now resemble:

   ```
   {ADFA2558-B237-491B-8E86-1F8A7ADFF3E0}
   ```

   Copy it to the clipboard.

4. In Notepad, create an XML file named **CountriesBatch.xml** that has the following contents:

   ```
   <Batch>
   <Method ID="1" Cmd="New">
   <Field Name="Title">Country Name</Field>
   </Method>
   </Batch>
   ```

   or use the **CountriesBatch.xml** file, which you can download from www.bizsupportonline.com. You will use this XML file to add a new country name to the **Countries** SharePoint list through the **Lists** web service.

5. In InfoPath, create a new SharePoint form library form template or use an existing one.

6. Add a hidden **Field (element)** of type **Text (string)** and named **listName** to the Main data source of the form template, and set its **Default Value** to be equal to the list GUID from step 3.

7. Select **Data ▶ From Other Sources ▶ From XML File**, add an XML data connection for the **CountriesBatch.xml** file to the InfoPath form template, and leave the **Automatically retrieve data when form is opened** check box on the last screen of the **Data Connection Wizard** selected.

8. To be able to add an item to the **Countries** SharePoint list whenever you enter a non-existent item into the combo box, you must set up a submit data connection to the **Lists** web service to submit the newly added item to the SharePoint list. So click **Data ▶ Submit Form ▶ To Other Locations ▶ To Web Service**.

9. On the **Data Connection Wizard**, enter the URL of the **Lists** web service, for example:

   ```
   http://servername/sitename/_vti_bin/Lists.asmx
   ```

and click **Next**. Here, **servername** is the name of the SharePoint server and **sitename** is the name of the site where the **Countries** SharePoint list is located.

10. On the **Data Connection Wizard**, select the **UpdateListItems** operation from the list of operations, and click **Next**.

11. On the **Data Connection Wizard**, select **tns:listName** in the **Parameters** list and then click the button behind the **Field or group** text box.

12. On the **Select a Field or Group** dialog box, select **listName**, and click **OK**. With this you have set the **listName** parameter of the web service operation to be equal to the value of the **listName** field in the Main data source of the form, which has the **Countries** SharePoint list GUID as its default value.

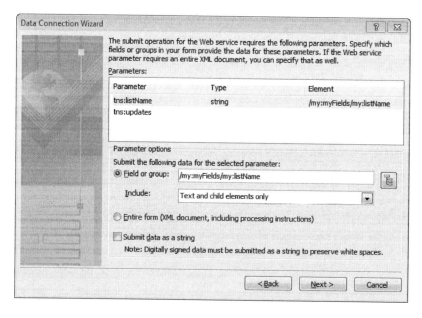

Figure 183. Setting the value of the first parameter of the web service operation.

13. On the **Data Connection Wizard**, select **tns:updates** in the **Parameters** list, and then click the button behind the **Field or group** text box.

14. On the **Select a Field or Group** dialog box, select **CountriesBatch (Secondary)** from the **Fields** drop-down list box, select the **Batch** group node, and then click **OK**. With this you have set the **updates** parameter of the web service operation to be equal to the contents of the entire **Batch** group node in the secondary data source for the XML file you added earlier.

15. On the **Data Connection Wizard**, select **XML subtree, including selected element** from the **Include** drop-down list box, and click **Next**. This setting will submit the entire XML contents of the **Batch** node including its child nodes and their values to the web service.

Chapter 4: Use InfoPath Controls with Data from SharePoint

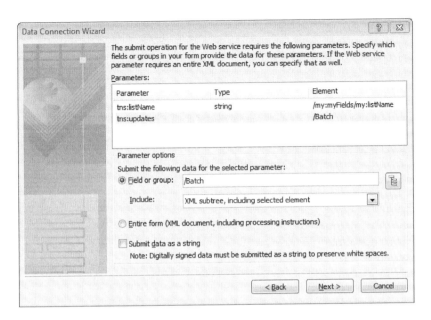

Figure 184. Setting the value of the second parameter of the web service operation.

16. On the **Data Connection Wizard**, name the data connection **UpdateListItems**, deselect the **Set as the default submit connection** check box, and click **Finish**.

17. Add a **Combo Box** control to the view of the form template and name it **country**.

18. Add a **Receive** data connection to the **Countries** SharePoint list to the form template (also see *Use a SharePoint list data connection* in recipe *43 3 Ways to retrieve data from a SharePoint list*), ensure you include the **Title** field in the data source and that you also select **Title** from the **Sort by** drop-down list box when you add the data connection. Name the data connection **Countries** and leave the **Automatically retrieve data when form is opened** check box selected.

19. Populate the combo box with the entries from the **Countries** secondary data source, and bind both the **Value** and **Display name** of the combo box to the **Title** field in the secondary data source.

20. Add an **Action** rule to the combo box with an action that says:

```
Query using a data connection: Countries
```

This rule is meant to refresh the data in the **Countries** secondary data source by retrieving the data again from SharePoint whenever you select or type an item in the combo box. This ensures that the combo box is filled with the most recent items from the SharePoint list including any items that another user may have added to the list after you opened the form.

247

21. Add a second **Action** rule to the combo box with a **Condition** that has two expressions that say:

    ```
    count(xdXDocument:GetDOM("Countries")/dfs:myFields/dfs:dataFields/d:SharePo
    intListItem_RW[d:Title = xdXDocument:get-DOM()/my:myFields/my:country]) = 0
    ```

    and

    ```
    country is not blank
    ```

    This condition ensures that the rule only runs if the piece of text that was entered into the combo box does not already exist in the **Countries** secondary data source. To construct the condition for the rule:

    a. Click the text **None – Rule runs when field changes** under **Condition**.
    b. On the **Condition** dialog box, select **Use a formula** from the third drop-down list box.
    c. On the **Insert Formula** dialog box, click **Insert Field or Group**.
    d. On the **Select a Field or Group** dialog box, select **Countries** from the **Fields** drop-down list box, expand the **dataFields** group node, select **d:SharePointListItem_RW**, and click **Filter Data**.
    e. On the **Filter Data** dialog box, click **Add**.
    f. On the **Specify Filter Conditions** dialog box, select **Title** from the first drop-down list box, leave **is equal to** selected in the second drop-down list box, and then select **Select a field or group**.
    g. On the **Select a Field or Group** dialog box, select **Main** from the **Fields** drop-down list box, select **country**, and click **OK**.
    h. On the **Specify Filter Conditions** dialog box, click **OK**. This filter will return all of the items in the **Countries** secondary data source where the **Title** is the same as the text entered into field in the **Main** data source that is bound to the combo box.
    i. On the **Filter Data** dialog box, click **OK**.
    j. On the **Select a Field or Group** dialog box, click **OK**.
    k. On the **Insert Formula** dialog box, add

    ```
    count(
    ```

    in front of the constructed formula and

    ```
    ) = 0
    ```

    behind the constructed formula. What this formula will now do is count the amount of items in the **Countries** secondary data source where the **Title** is the same as the text entered into the field in the **Main** data source that is bound to the combo box, and check whether this amount is equal to **0**. If the amount is

Chapter 4: Use InfoPath Controls with Data from SharePoint

equal to **0**, it means that the item that was entered into the combo box does not yet exist in the SharePoint list.

l. On the **Insert Formula** dialog box, select the **Edit XPath (advanced)** check box, press **Ctrl+A** to select the entire text for the formula, press **Ctrl+C** to copy the formula to the Windows clipboard, and click **Cancel**.

m. On the **Condition** dialog box, select **The expression** from the first drop-down list box, replace the entire text in the text box by pressing **Ctrl+A** and then **Ctrl+V** to paste the formula you just copied, and click **OK**.

22. Add the following 3 actions to the **Action** rule you added in the previous step:

    ```
    Set a field's value: Field = .
    ```

    where **Field** refers to the **Field** field in the **CountriesBatch** secondary data source and **.** refers to the **country** field in the Main data source.

    ```
    Submit using a data connection: UpdateListItems
    Query using a data connection: Countries
    ```

    The first action sets the value of the **Field** field in the **CountriesBatch** XML file that has to be submitted to the web service to add a new item to the **Countries** SharePoint list, the second action submits the data to the web service, and the third action requeries the **Countries** data connection to refresh the data in the combo box.

23. Publish the form template to a SharePoint form library.

In SharePoint, navigate to the form library where you published the form template and add a new form. When the form opens, type a country name that does not exist in the combo box and tab or click away from the combo box. Save the form in the form library. Navigate to the **Countries** list and check whether the new country was added. Navigate back to the form library and add a second form, but this time select an existing item from the combo box, and then save the form. Navigate once more to the **Countries** SharePoint list and verify that no duplicate country was created.

Figure 185. The InfoPath form after 'United States' was entered and saved as a new item.

Discussion

In the solution described above, you populated a combo box with items from a SharePoint list. And to be able to add and permanently store any new items that were entered into the combo box, you made use of SharePoint's **Lists** web service to submit and add new items to the SharePoint list while the form was being filled out.

249

You added two rules to the combo box to be able to add a new item to the SharePoint list when the combo box loses focus (when you tab or click away from the combo box):

1. The first rule requeries the data source used to populate the combo box, so that it contains the latest data from the SharePoint list.
2. The second rule sets the value (**Title** of the new item) of a field in the secondary data source for the XML file that is passed via an input parameter to the **Lists** web service. The last action in the second rule requeries the data connection used to populate the combo box again, so that the data source contains the latest data from the SharePoint list.

Note that both the **Value** and **Display name** properties of the combo box were configured to get their values from the **Title** field in the **Countries** secondary data source, and that the **Value** property was not configured to come from the **ID** field. The **ID** of the new item is automatically generated by SharePoint when you call the **UpdateListItems** operation of the **Lists** web service. And because you want to pass the actual country name to the web service, so have to set the value of the **Field** element that has a **Name** attribute with a value of **Title** in the **CountriesBatch** secondary data source equal to the country name (and not an ID), you must configure the **Value** property of the combo box to get its value from the **Title** field in the **Countries** secondary data source instead of from the **ID** field.

What this also means is that you could potentially wind up with duplicate items in the combo box, for example if someone manually adds a country name to the SharePoint list directly in SharePoint a split second before you enter and add that same country name to the combo box via the InfoPath form. You can prevent duplicate items from appearing in the combo box by selecting the **Show only entries with unique display names** check box on the **Properties** dialog box of the combo box. But remember that by doing this you would only be preventing items that have the same **Title** in the SharePoint list from appearing multiple times in the combo box, while they still exist in the SharePoint list. So if you do not want such a visual "fix", you would have to go to the **Countries** SharePoint list in SharePoint and manually delete any duplicate items.

Picture

Picture controls are used to display images on an InfoPath form. You can add an image to a picture control on an InfoPath form either as an embedded base64 encoded string or as a hyperlink.

Figure 186. Dialog box that pops up when you add a Picture control to an InfoPath form template.

Chapter 4: Use InfoPath Controls with Data from SharePoint

When you retrieve an image from a SharePoint picture library, it is easier to store the URL of that image in a picture control that is configured to accept a hyperlink than it is to embed that image in a picture control. If you want to embed images from a SharePoint picture library on an InfoPath form, the most likely way to do this would be to write code to provide such functionality. So if you do not want to or cannot write code, always look for a way to link to images rather than embed them in InfoPath forms.

The following recipes discuss a few scenarios for retrieving and working with images that are stored in a SharePoint picture library.

65 3 Ways to get an image from a picture library

Method 1: Get an image through a REST web service

Problem

You have a SharePoint picture library from which you want to retrieve images by first searching for all images that contain a specific piece of text in their name, and then from the images found, select one through a drop-down list box on an InfoPath form.

Solution

You can use the **ListData** REST web service to retrieve images from a SharePoint picture library, thereby performing a LIKE search.

To get an image from a SharePoint picture library using the **ListData** REST web service:

1. In InfoPath, create a new SharePoint form library form template or use an existing one.
2. Add a **Text Box** and a **Button** control to the view of the form template. Name the text box control **searchForImage** and label the button control **Search**.
3. Add a **Drop-Down List Box** control to the view of the form template and name it **imageSelected**.
4. Add a **Picture** control **As a link** to the view of the form template and name it **image**.
5. With the picture control still selected, select **Control Tools** ▶ **Properties** ▶ **Modify** ▶ **Read-Only** to make the picture control read-only.
6. Select **Data** ▶ **Get External Data** ▶ **From Web Service** ▶ **From REST Web Service**.
7. On the **Data Connection Wizard**, enter the URL of the **ListData** REST web service, for example:

    `http://servername/sitename/_vti_bin/ListData.svc/MyPics`

251

and click **Next**. Here, **servername** is the name of the SharePoint server and **sitename** is the name of the site where a picture library named **MyPics** is located.

8. On the **Data Connection Wizard**, enter a name for the data connection (for example **GetPictures**), deselect the **Automatically retrieve data when form is opened** check box, and click **Finish**.

9. Add an **Action** rule to the **Search** button that has the following action:

```
Change REST URL: GetPictures
```

where the value of the **REST Web Service URL** should be set to the following formula:

```
concat("http://servername/sitename/_vti_bin/ListData.svc/MyPics?$filter=sub
stringof('", searchForImage, "', Name)")
```

where **servername** is the name of the SharePoint server, **sitename** is the name of the SharePoint site where a picture library named **MyPics** is located, **searchForImage** is the field bound to the text box control, and **Name** is a static piece of text that represents the name of the column in the picture library that contains the name of the image. You must add the **substringof** filter method to the REST web service URL to find only those images where the text you enter into the text box can be found in the **Name** field of the image. Note that **Name** is the static name of the field the **substringof** filter method should use and not the **d:Name** node in the **GetPictures** secondary data source.

Add a second action to the rule that says:

```
Query using a data connection: GetPictures
```

This second action requeries the **GetPictures** secondary data connection using the REST web service URL you modified.

Add a third action to the rule that says:

```
Set a field's value: imageSelected = ""
```

This third action sets the value of the **imageSelected** field, which is bound to the drop-down list box, to be equal to an empty string. This action ensures that any previously selected image is cleared from the drop-down list box when performing a new search.

10. Populate the drop-down list box control with items from the **GetPictures** secondary data source by selecting the **entry** repeating group node for the **Entries** property and the **d:Name** field under the **m:properties** group node under the **entry** repeating group node for both the **Value** and the **Display name** properties of the drop-down list box.

Chapter 4: Use InfoPath Controls with Data from SharePoint

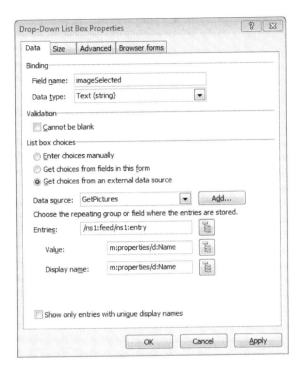

Figure 187. Settings on the Drop-Down List Box Properties dialog box in InfoPath 2010.

11. Add an **Action** rule to the drop-down list box that says:

    ```
    Set a field's value: image = concat("http://servername/sitename/MyPics/",
    .)
    ```

    where **servername** is the name of the SharePoint server, **sitename** is the name of the site where a picture library named **MyPics** is located, and **.** represents the value of the **imageSelected** field bound to the drop-down list box.

12. Publish the form template to a SharePoint form library.

In SharePoint, navigate to the form library where you published the form template and add a new form. When the form opens, enter part of the name of any image into the text box and click the **Search** button. If images are found, the drop-down list box should contain items. Select an image from the drop-down list box. The corresponding image should appear in the picture control.

Figure 188. The InfoPath form displaying a selected image from the picture library.

253

Discussion

When you create a SharePoint list data connection to a SharePoint picture library in InfoPath, it does not normally offer a field that contains the URL to an image within the picture library, unless you enable the **Document ID Service** (see method 3 later in this recipe).

In the solution described above, you used the **ListData** REST web service to retrieve the file name of an image to be able to construct an URL and use this in a picture control to display an image on an InfoPath form. The resulting XML of a call to this web service has a **Name** element that contains the file name (including the file extension) and a **Path** element in which the URL of the picture library where the file is located is stored. So instead of using a static URL like you did in step 11, you could have used the value of the **Path** element in the **concat** function to concatenate the URL of the picture library with the file name for the image, and then set the value of the picture control to this resulting URL. And instead of using a static server and site URL, you could have used the **SharePointServerRootUrl** function in the **concat** function to dynamically generate the URL. The formula from step 11 would have then become:

```
concat(SharePointServerRootUrl(), Path, "/", .)
```

Note that the **SharePointServerRootUrl** function only works when the form is being viewed or filled out through a browser; it does not work in InfoPath Filler 2010. So the use of static URLs allows you to preview or fill out the form in InfoPath Filler 2010. But if you are going to publish the form template to the same site where the picture library is located and the form is going to be filled out exclusively through a browser, you may want to specify dynamic URLs in the **concat** function. Refer to the discussion section of recipe *59 Open a form in the browser from another form* for a description of the four InfoPath functions that return SharePoint URLs.

Method 2: Get an image through the URL protocol

Problem

You have a SharePoint picture library from which you want to retrieve all images and then click a button to select one of those images.

Solution

You can use the URL protocol to retrieve images from a SharePoint picture library.

To get an image from a picture library using the URL protocol:

1. In InfoPath, create a new SharePoint form library form template or use an existing one.
2. Select **Data** ▸ **Get External Data** ▸ **From Other Sources** ▸ **From XML File**.

Chapter 4: Use InfoPath Controls with Data from SharePoint

3. On the **Data Connection Wizard**, enter the URL that points to the SharePoint picture library that contains the images, for example:

   ```
   http://servername/sitename/_vti_bin/owssvr.dll?Cmd=Display&List={GUID}&XMLD
   ATA=TRUE&noredirect=true
   ```

   and click **Next**. Here, **servername** is the name of the SharePoint server and **sitename** is the name of the site where the SharePoint picture library is located. In addition, you must look up and enter the GUID of the picture library in the URL. You can retrieve the GUID from the browser's address bar when you navigate to the settings page of the picture library in SharePoint. The GUID is listed as the value of the **List** query string parameter (see the discussion section for more information on how to find the GUID). A sample URL would resemble the following:

   ```
   http://win-
   ji2o5062vat/infopath2010cookbook2/_vti_bin/owssvr.dll?Cmd=Display&List=%7B8
   95102C8%2D3027%2D4E99%2DA885%2DA91C15FFCD3C%7D&XMLDATA=TRUE&noredirect=true
   ```

4. On the **Data Connection Wizard**, select the **Access the data from the specified location** option, leave the **Store a copy of the data for offline use** check box deselected, and click **Next**.

5. On the **Data Connection Wizard**, rename the data connection to **GetPictures**, leave the **Automatically retrieve data when form is opened** check box selected, and click **Finish**.

6. On the **Fields** task pane, select **GetPictures (Secondary)** from the **Fields** drop-down list box, and expand the **rs:data** group node.

Figure 189. The GetPictures secondary data source on the Fields task pane.

7. Drag-and-drop the **z:row** repeating field onto the view of the form template. When you drop it, select **Repeating Section** from the context menu that appears.
8. Click **Insert ▶ Tables ▶ Custom Table** and add a custom table with 1 row and 2 columns inside the repeating section you just added.
9. On the **Fields** task pane, select the **:ows_NameOrTitle** field (attribute) that is located under the **z:row** repeating field (element), and then drag-and-drop it in the first cell of the custom table you just added.
10. Add a **Button** control to the second cell of the custom table and label it **Select**. This button will be used to select the link to an image from the repeating section and set the value of a picture control.
11. Add a **Picture** control **As a link** to the view of the form template (below the repeating section control) and name it **image**.
12. Open the **Picture Properties** dialog box, and then on the **Data** tab, select the **Read-Only** check box.
13. On the **Picture Properties** dialog box, click the **Size** tab, ensure that the **Height** and **Width** are both set to **auto**, and then click **OK**. This should allow the picture control to dynamically resize itself to the size of any image that is placed in it.
14. Add an **Action** rule to the button control with an action that says:

    ```
    Set a field's value: image = concat("http://servername/",
    @ows_RequiredField)
    ```

    where **servername** is the name of the SharePoint server, **image** is the field bound to the picture control, and **@ows_RequiredField** is the field (attribute) under the **z:row** repeating field (element) in the **GetPictures** secondary data source. The **@ows_RequiredField** field contains the URL of the image. This URL includes the site and library in which the image is located. Note that you could also use the **ows_NameOrTitle** field (attribute) under the **z:row** repeating field (element) in the **GetPictures** secondary data source to construct the URL of the image. The **:ows_NameOrTitle** field returns the file name of the image.

15. Publish the form template to a SharePoint form library.

In SharePoint, navigate to the form library where you published the form template and add a new form. When the form opens, the names of the images should automatically be retrieved from the picture library and displayed in the repeating section. Click on any of the **Select** buttons in the repeating section. The corresponding image should appear in the picture control.

Chapter 4: Use InfoPath Controls with Data from SharePoint

greenbullet.png	Select
redbullet.png	Select

Figure 190. The InfoPath form displaying a selected image from the picture library.

Discussion

When you create a SharePoint list data connection to a SharePoint picture library, by default the data source does not contain a field that contains the URL of an image unless you are running the **Document ID Service**, in which case the **Document ID** field should contain the URL to retrieve the image (see method 3 in this recipe).

If you do not want to or cannot activate the **Document ID Service**, you can make use of the URL protocol to retrieve images from a SharePoint picture library. The URL protocol returns a field called **ows_RequiredField** that contains a relative URL of an image in a picture library. It also returns a field called **ows_NameOrTitle** field that contains the file name of an image in a picture library. Neither the **ows_RequiredField** field or the **ows_NameOrTitle** field returns a full URL to an image, so you must use the **concat** function to construct the full URL of the image you select, so that you can use that URL as the value of a picture control that is configured to use a hyperlink.

In the solution described above, you also had to retrieve the GUID of the picture library to be able to use the URL protocol. To retrieve the GUID of a SharePoint picture library:

1. In SharePoint, navigate to the SharePoint picture library you want to use.
2. Select **Settings** ➤ **Picture Library Settings**.
3. On the **Picture Library Settings** page, copy the GUID that comes after

   `List=`

   from the URL in the browser's address bar. The GUID should resemble:

   `%7BC0948B8E%2D5E76%2D49EB%2DBF6F%2D9FCF5AC8F3ED%7D`

And finally, just like in method 1 of this recipe, you could use the **SharePointServerRootUrl** function in the **concat** function to dynamically generate the URL instead of using a static server URL. The formula from step 14 would then become:

`concat(SharePointServerRootUrl(), @ows_RequiredField)`

Method 3: Get an image through a Document ID

Problem

You have a SharePoint picture library from which you want to retrieve an image.

Solution

You can use the document ID of an image in a picture control that is configured to use a hyperlink to display images on an InfoPath form. To be able to use document IDs, an administrator must first activate the **Document ID Service**.

Important:

> Consult the SharePoint documentation on the use and consequences of activating the **Document ID Service** on a SharePoint site collection before implementing the solution described in this method of this recipe.

To get an image from a picture library using a document ID:

1. In InfoPath, create a new SharePoint form library form template or use an existing one.

2. Add a **Receive** SharePoint list data connection to the picture library that contains the images you want to retrieve (also see *Use a SharePoint list data connection* in recipe *43 3 Ways to retrieve data from a SharePoint list*). When creating the data source, ensure you select **Title** and **Document_ID** as the fields to include in the data source. The **Document_ID** field contains the URL of an image.

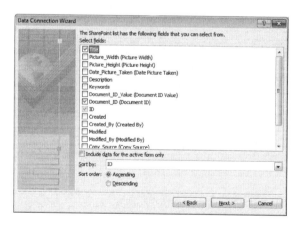

Figure 191. Selecting the fields to include in the data source.

3. On the **Fields** task pane, select the secondary data source for the picture library you just added from the **Fields** drop-down list box, expand the entire **dataFields** group

Chapter 4: Use InfoPath Controls with Data from SharePoint

node, and then drag-and-drop the **d:SharePointListItem_RW** repeating group node to the view of the form template. Select **Repeating Table** from the context menu that appears when you drop repeating group node onto the view.

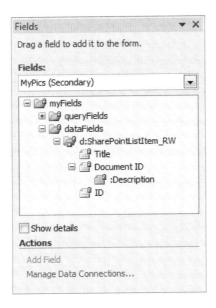

Figure 192. The secondary data source for the picture library on the Fields task pane.

4. InfoPath should have automatically bound the **Document ID** field to a hyperlink control. Right-click the hyperlink control and select **Change Control ➤ Picture** from the context menu that appears to change the hyperlink control into a picture control.

5. Publish the form template to a SharePoint form library.

In SharePoint, navigate to the form library where you published the form template and add a new form. When the form opens, it should display all of the images in the **Document ID** column of the repeating table.

Title	Document ID	ID
Green Bullet	●	3
Red Bullet	●	4

Figure 193. The InfoPath form displaying the images from the picture library.

259

InfoPath 2010 Cookbook 2

Discussion

When you create a **Receive** SharePoint list data connection to a SharePoint picture library, by default the data source does not contain a field that stores the URL of an image unless you are running the **Document ID Service**, in which case the **Document ID** field should contain the URL to retrieve the image.

A document ID is a unique identifier for a document or document set within a site collection. A document ID comes with a static redirect URL with which you can open the document or document set that is linked to the document ID, no matter where that document is located. When a user requests a document, the **Document ID Service** redirects the user to the static redirect URL of the document, which resembles the following URL:

```
http://servername/sitename/_layouts/DocIdRedir.aspx?ID=BIZSUPPORT-132-4
```

Here, **servername** is the name of the SharePoint server, **sitename** is the name of the SharePoint site, **DocIdRedir.aspx** is the ASPX page that is used for URL redirection, and **ID** is the document ID that is unique to each document.

When you activate the **Document ID Service** feature on a site collection, document IDs are automatically generated for all documents within that site collection and which inherit from the **Document** or **Document Set** content types.

An administrator can activate the **Document ID Service** as follows:

1. In SharePoint, navigate to the top-level site in the SharePoint site collection, and click **Site Actions ▶ Site Settings**.

2. On the **Site Settings** page under **Site Collection Administration**, click **Site collection features**.

3. On the **Features** page, click the **Activate** button behind the **Document ID Service** feature if it is not currently active. Once activated, a job for the assignment of IDs to documents will be scheduled, so it may take a while before all documents in the site collection have unique document IDs.

Figure 194. Document ID Service feature activated in SharePoint 2010.

In the solution described above you retrieved all images and displayed them in a repeating table. You could extend or change the solution to provide a list of images a user could choose from either by selecting an image from a drop-down list box as described in method 1, clicking a button in the repeating table to select an image as described in method 2, or browsing through images as described in the next recipe.

Chapter 4: Use InfoPath Controls with Data from SharePoint

66 Browse through images in a SharePoint picture library

Problem

You want to be able to select an image from a SharePoint picture library by sequentially clicking through all of the images in the picture library until you find the one you are looking for.

Solution

You can use the document IDs of images to sequentially navigate through a list of images that are located in a picture library. To be able to use document IDs, an administrator must first activate the **Document ID Service**.

Important:

> Consult the SharePoint documentation on the use and consequences of activating the **Document ID Service** on a SharePoint site collection before implementing the solution described in this recipe.

To browse through images in a SharePoint picture library:

1. In InfoPath, create a new SharePoint form library form template or use an existing one.

2. Add a **Receive** SharePoint list data connection to the picture library (also see *Use a SharePoint list data connection* in recipe *43 3 Ways to retrieve data from a SharePoint list*) that contains the images you want to retrieve. Include the **Document_ID** field in the data source, leave the **Automatically retrieve data when form is opened** check box selected, and name the data connection **MyPics**.

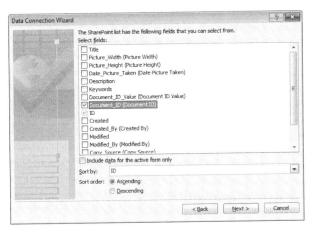

Figure 195. Selecting the Document_ID field on the Data Connection Wizard in InfoPath.

261

3. Add a **Picture** control **As a link** to the view of the form template and name it **selectedImage**.

4. Add a hidden **Field (element)** of type **Whole Number (integer)** to the Main data source, name it **position**, and set its **Default Value** to be equal to **1**. This field will serve as a counter for navigating through the images in the picture library.

5. Add two **Button** controls to the view of the form template and label them **Previous** and **Next**, respectively.

6. Add an **Action** rule to the **Previous** button with a **Condition** that says:

   ```
   position > 1
   ```

   and an action that says:

   ```
   Set a field's value: position = position - 1
   ```

   This rule decreases the value of the **position** field by 1 every time the **Previous** button is clicked and only if the value of the **position** field is greater than 1.

7. Add an **Action** rule to the **Next** button with a **Condition** that says:

   ```
   position < count(SharePointListItem_RW)
   ```

   where **SharePointListItem_RW** is the repeating group node under the **dataFields** group node in the **MyPics** secondary data source.

   And add an action that says:

   ```
   Set a field's value: position = position + 1
   ```

   This rule increases the value of the **position** field by 1 every time the **Next** button is clicked and only if the value of the **position** field is less than the total amount of items in the SharePoint picture library.

8. Set the **Default Value** of the **selectedImage** field to

   ```
   xdXDocument:GetDOM("MyPics")/dfs:myFields/dfs:dataFields/d:SharePointListIt
   em_RW[count(preceding-sibling::d:SharePointListItem_RW) + 1 =
   xdXDocument:get-DOM()/my:myFields/my:position]/d:_dlc_DocIdUrl
   ```

   where **MyPics** is the name of the data source for the SharePoint picture library. This formula returns the value of the **Document ID** field (**d:_dlc_DocIdUrl**) in the **MyPics** secondary data source with a filter on the value specified in the **position** field. The formula uses the **preceding-sibling** XPath axis and the **count** function to count the amount of list items preceding the list item that is currently the context node.

9. Publish the form template to a SharePoint form library.

In SharePoint, navigate to the form library where you published the form template and add a new form. When the form opens, the first image in the library should be displayed,

Chapter 4: Use InfoPath Controls with Data from SharePoint

and when you click on the previous and next buttons, you should be able to sequentially navigate through the images in the picture library.

Figure 196. The InfoPath form displaying an image from the picture library.

Discussion

See the discussion section of method 3 in the previous recipe for an explanation of document IDs and how to activate the **Document ID Service**. If you do not want to or cannot activate the **Document ID Service**, you can still retrieve images by using one of the first two image retrieval methods described in recipe *65 3 Ways to get an image from a picture library*.

Person/Group Picker

The person/group picker control in InfoPath allows you to select one or more people from a SharePoint site.

Figure 197. Person/Group Picker control in InfoPath 2010.

The way the person/group picker control works is that you can either type in values that represent users or groups into the text box of the person/group picker control or click the **Browse** button (the second button behind the text box) to open a dialog box to search for and select users or groups.

If you type names directly into the text box without performing a search through the dialog box, you can check whether those names are valid by clicking on the **Check Names** button (the first button behind the text box) of the person/group picker control.

When you place a person/group picker control on an InfoPath browser-compatible form template without explicitly configuring the control, publish the form template to SharePoint, and then open forms in the browser, the person/group picker control automatically uses the context of the SharePoint site where the form is located to find users and groups. However, if you want to use the person/group picker control on a form in InfoPath Filler 2010, you must explicitly configure it to get its list of users and groups from a specific SharePoint site. You can specify the SharePoint site the person/group picker control should retrieve its list of users and groups from via the **SharePoint Server** tab on the **Person/Group Picker Properties** dialog box.

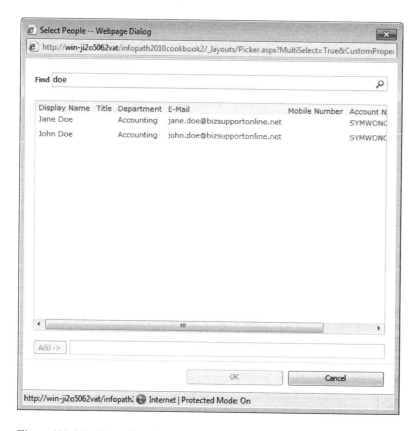

Figure 198. The Select People web page dialog in SharePoint 2010.

Figure 199. SharePoint Server tab of the Person/Group Picker Properties dialog box in InfoPath 2010.

Chapter 4: Use InfoPath Controls with Data from SharePoint

The person/group picker control allows you to select only one user or group by default, but you can specify whether the control should allow multiple users/groups to be entered or selected by selecting the **Allow multiple sections** check box on the **General** tab of the **Person/Group Picker Properties** dialog box.

Figure 200. General tab of the Person/Group Picker Properties dialog box in InfoPath 2010.

Other configuration options include:

- Specifying whether the control should display users only or a combination of users and groups.
- Specifying whether all users should be shown or only users from a specific group.

And finally, to make a person/group picker control mandatory, you can select the **Cannot be blank** check box, which is located on the **Data** tab of the **Person/Group Picker Properties** dialog box or that is part of the **Modify** group on the **Properties** tab on the Ribbon.

67 Get email addresses from a person/group picker

Problem

You have a person/group picker control on an InfoPath form and want to use it to select one or more users and then store the email address(es) of the selected user(s) in a hidden field that can be used in an email data connection to send emails to the selected user(s).

Solution

You can use the **eval** function and the **User Information List** SharePoint list to lookup email addresses for a selected group of people and concatenate them into a string

InfoPath 2010 Cookbook 2

separated by semi-colons. Note that email addresses must have already been populated in SharePoint user profiles for this solution to work.

To generate a list of email addresses from a person/group picker control:

1. In InfoPath, create a new SharePoint form library form template or use an existing one.

2. Add a **Person/Group Picker** control to the view of the form template.

3. Open the **Person/Group Picker Properties** dialog box and then on the **General** tab, select the **Allow multiple selections** check box and leave the **People Only** option selected. With this you have configured the person/group picker control to allow multiple users to be selected. Click **OK** to close the dialog box.

4. On the **Fields** task pane, add a hidden **Field (element)** with the data type **Text (string)** and the name **emailAddresses** to the Main data source.

5. Click **Data** ➤ **Get External Data** ➤ **From SharePoint List** (also see *Use a SharePoint list data connection* in recipe *43 3 Ways to retrieve data from a SharePoint list*) and add a **Receive** data connection to the **User Information List** SharePoint list on the site from which the person/group picker control should get its information.

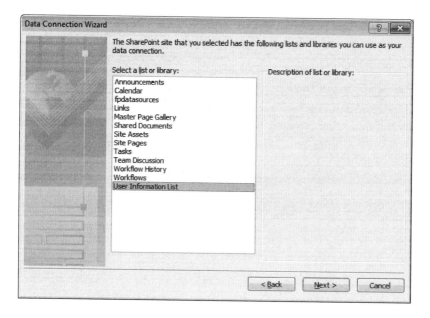

Figure 201. Selecting the User Information List on the Data Connection Wizard in InfoPath.

When you are configuring the data connection, ensure you select **Account** and **Work_e-mail** as the fields to include in the data source, and that you leave the **Automatically retrieve data when form is opened** check box selected. You will use this data connection later to set the default value of the **emailAddresses** field.

Chapter 4: Use InfoPath Controls with Data from SharePoint

When the **emailAddresses** field retrieves its data from the **User Information List**, which takes place immediately after you select users from the person/group picker control, the **User Information List** should already contain data so that lookups can be performed. This is why you must populate the secondary data source for the **User Information List** either when the form is opened (as you have done in this step) or ensure that you run a **Query for data** action rule before any users are selected from the person/group picker control.

6. Set the **Default Value** of the **emailAddresses** field to the following formula:

   ```
   eval(eval(EMail[Name = AccountId and . != ""], 'concat(., ";")'), "..")
   ```

   or

   ```
   xdMath:Eval(xdMath:Eval(xdXDocument:GetDOM("User Information
   List")/dfs:myFields/dfs:dataFields/d:SharePointListItem_RW/d:EMail[../d:Nam
   e = xdXDocument:get-DOM()/my:myFields/my:group/pc:Person/pc:AccountId and .
   != ""], 'concat(., " ;")'), "..")
   ```

   if you have the **Edit XPath (advanced)** check box selected on the **Insert Formula** dialog box. Here, the outer **eval** function returns all of the **Work e-mail** fields in the **User Information List** secondary data source where the **Account** field in the secondary data source is equal to the **AccountId** field of the person/group picker in the Main data source and where the value of the **Work e-mail** field is not blank:

   ```
   eval(EMail[Name = AccountId and . != ""], "..")
   ```

   You can construct this expression using the dialog boxes with the **Filter Data** option in InfoPath. The inner **eval** function works on each one of the **Work e-mail** fields that is returned by the outer **eval** function and uses the **concat** function to append a semi-colon to each email address:

   ```
   eval(eval(EMail[Name = AccountId and . != ""], 'concat(., ";")'), "..")
   ```

   You must manually alter the outer **eval** function to add the inner **eval** function with the **concat** function. Leave the **Refresh value when formula is recalculated** check box selected on the **Field or Group Properties** dialog box when you are configuring the default value for the **emailAddresses** field.

7. On the **Fields** task pane, drag-and-drop the **emailAddresses** field onto the view to temporarily bind it to a text box control, so that you can display and check its value.

8. Publish the form template to a SharePoint form library.

In SharePoint, navigate to the form library where you published the form template and add a new form. When the form opens, enter a few usernames in the person/group picker control and click the button that checks names. The email addresses of the users you entered should appear as a concatenated string of email addresses separated by semi-colons in the **emailAddresses** field.

InfoPath 2010 Cookbook 2

Select People:	Jane Doe ; John Doe ; Clovis Carvalho ;	
Email Addresses:	john.doe@bizsupportonline.net ;jane.doe@bizsupportonline.net ;clov	

Figure 202. The InfoPath form displaying the email addresses of the selected users.

Now you should be able to use the concatenated string of email addresses as the value for the **To** field in for example an email data connection.

Discussion

In the solution described above, you made use of the **User Information List** (see the discussion section of recipe *54 Display a list of people from the current user's department* for more information about the **User Information List** SharePoint list) SharePoint list to lookup email addresses of users. You also used the **eval** function to generate a list of email addresses. The **eval** function returns the values of a field or group. It takes two arguments, of which the second argument defines the expression to calculate for the field or group. You can use it on a repeating group or a repeating field to concatenate values of all of the fields or fields within the group. In the solution described above, it was used in a nested way to be able to not only concatenate email addresses, but also add semi-colons to separate those email addresses. This technique was extensively explained in *InfoPath 2010 Cookbook: 101 Codeless Recipes for Beginners*.

68 Get the details of the manager of a selected person in a person/group picker

Problem

You have a person/group picker control on an InfoPath form and want to retrieve the first name, last name, and email address of the manager of a user when you click a button.

Solution

You can use the **GetUserPropertyByAccountName** and the **GetUserProfileByName** operations of SharePoint's User Profile Service to retrieve the details of a person's manager. You can use the **GetUserPropertyByAccountName** operation to retrieve the value of the **Manager** property for a particular user, and then use the **GetUserProfileByName** operation to retrieve the first name, last name, and email address properties of the manager.

To get the details of the manager of a selected person in a person/group picker control:

1. In InfoPath, create a new SharePoint form library form template or use an existing one.

Chapter 4: Use InfoPath Controls with Data from SharePoint

2. Add a **Person/Group Picker** control to the view of the form template. Do not configure the control to **Allow multiple selections**; the control should allow only one user to be selected.

3. Add a **Button** control to the view of the form template and label it **Get Manager Details**.

4. Add a **Text Box** control to the view of the form template and name it **manager**.

5. Select **Data ▶ Get External Data ▶ From Web Service ▶ From SOAP Web Service** to add a **Receive** data connection for the User Profile Service.

6. On the **Data Connection Wizard**, enter the URL of the User Profile Service on a SharePoint site. For example:

   `http://servername/sitename/_vti_bin/UserProfileService.asmx`

   where **servername** is the name of the SharePoint server, **sitename** is the name of a SharePoint site, and **UserProfileService.asmx** is the User Profile Service ASMX page. Click **Next**.

7. On the **Data Connection Wizard**, select **GetUserPropertyByAccountName** from the list of operations, and click **Next**.

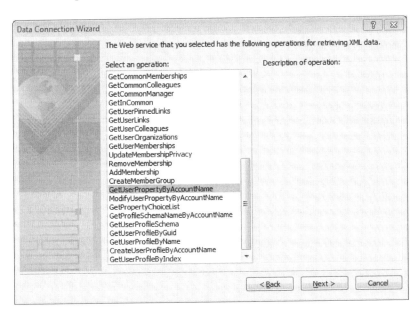

Figure 203. Selecting the GetUserPropertyByAccountName operation.

8. On the **Data Connection Wizard**, leave the parameter values empty, and click **Next**. You will be setting these values later through the use of rules.

9. On the **Data Connection Wizard**, leave the **Store a copy of the data in the form template** check box deselected, and click **Next**.

269

InfoPath 2010 Cookbook 2

10. On the **Data Connection Wizard**, leave the name of the data connection as **GetUserPropertyByAccountName**, deselect the **Automatically retrieve data when form is opened** check box, and click **Finish**.

11. Repeat steps 5 through 10 to add a second SOAP web service data connection, but this time, select **GetUserProfileByName** as the operation and name the data connection **GetUserProfileByName**.

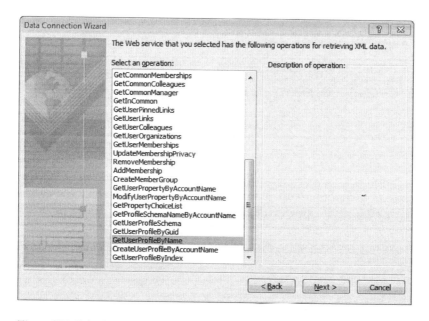

Figure 204. Selecting the GetUserProfileByName operation.

12. Add an **Action** rule to the **Get Manager Details** button with a **Condition** that says:

    `AccountId is not blank`

    where **AccountId** is the **AccountId** field of the person/group picker control.

    And add the following 5 actions to the rule:

    `Set a field's value: accountName = AccountId`

    where **accountName** is located under the **queryFields** group node of the **GetUserPropertyByAccountName** secondary data source, and **AccountId** is the **AccountId** field of the person/group picker control. This action sets the value of the **accountName** parameter of the **GetUserPropertyByAccountName** operation to be equal to the value of the **accountId** field of the person/group picker control.

    `Set a field's value: propertyName = "Manager"`

    where **propertyName** is located under the **queryFields** group node of the **GetUserPropertyByAccountName** secondary data source, and **Manager** is a static

Chapter 4: Use InfoPath Controls with Data from SharePoint

piece of text that represents the name of the property for which you want to retrieve a value. This action sets the value of the **propertyName** parameter of the **GetUserPropertyByAccountName** operation to be equal to the text **Manager**, which is the name of the property that should be retrieved.

```
Query using a data connection: GetUserPropertyByAccountName
```

This action calls the **GetUserPropertyByAccountName** operation of the User Profile Service and passes the values of the **accountName** and **propertyName** parameters to it to be able to retrieve the value of the **Manager** property, which when returned should be located under the **dataFields** group node of the **GetUserPropertyByAccountName** secondary data source.

```
Set a field's value: AccountName = Value
```

where **AccountName** is located under the **queryFields** group node of the **GetUserProfileByName** secondary data source, and **Value** is located under the **dataFields** group node of the **GetUserPropertyByAccountName** secondary data source. This action sets the value of the **AccountName** parameter of the **GetUserProfileByName** operation to be equal to the value of the **Manager** property you just retrieved when you queried the **GetUserPropertyByAccountName** data connection. Note that while **Value** is contained in a repeating group node named **ValueData**, you queried the User Profile Service to retrieve only one property (Manager), so **ValueData** should contain only one row of data and the formula should return the value of the **Value** field in the first row of data.

```
Query using a data connection: GetUserProfileByName
```

This action calls the **GetUserProfileByName** operation of the User Profile Service and passes the value of the **AccountName** you just set to it to be able to retrieve the values of all of the properties of the manager.

13. Once the **GetUserProfileByName** operation has returned results, you can use filters on the values of properties you want to use. In this case, you want to extract the values of the **FirstName**, **LastName**, and **WorkEmail** properties, so set the **Default Value** of the **manager** text box to the following formula:

```
normalize-space(concat(Value[Name = "FirstName"], " ", Value[Name =
"LastName"], " [", Value[Name = "WorkEmail"], "]"))
```

or

```
normalize-
space(concat(xdXDocument:GetDOM("GetUserProfileByName")/dfs:myFields/dfs:da
taFields/tns:GetUserProfileByNameResponse/tns:GetUserProfileByNameResult/tn
s:PropertyData/tns:Values/tns:ValueData/tns:Value[../../../tns:Name =
"FirstName"], " ",
xdXDocument:GetDOM("GetUserProfileByName")/dfs:myFields/dfs:dataFields/tns:
GetUserProfileByNameResponse/tns:GetUserProfileByNameResult/tns:PropertyDat
a/tns:Values/tns:ValueData/tns:Value[../../../tns:Name = "LastName"], " [",
xdXDocument:GetDOM("GetUserProfileByName")/dfs:myFields/dfs:dataFields/tns:
```

InfoPath 2010 Cookbook 2

```
GetUserProfileByNameResponse/tns:GetUserProfileByNameResult/tns:PropertyDat
a/tns:Values/tns:ValueData/tns:Value[../../../tns:Name = "WorkEmail"],
"]"))
```

if you have the **Edit XPath (advanced)** check box selected. Here, all of the fields are located under the **dataFields** group node of the **GetUserProfileByName** secondary data source. Note that the **Value** field is filtered on the **Name** of a property for each property you want to retrieve (**FirstName**, **LastName**, and **WorkEmail**).

14. Publish the form template to a SharePoint form library.

In SharePoint, navigate to the form library where you published the form template and add a new form. When the form opens, type the account name of a user that has a manager in the person/group picker control, and click the button that checks names. Click the **Get Manager Details** button. The manager's first name, last name, and email address should appear in the text box.

Figure 205. Organization Chart showing that Jane Doe has Clovis Carvalho as her manager.

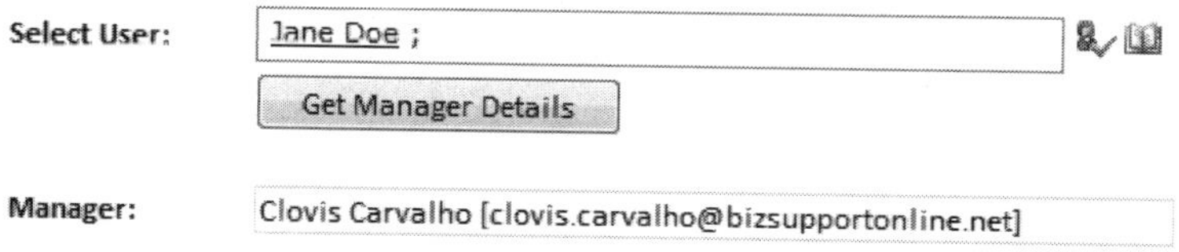

Figure 206. The InfoPath form showing the details of Jane Doe's manager.

Discussion

The solution described above used the User Profile Service of SharePoint to retrieve the details of a manager assigned to a particular user. Before you can call the User Profile Service, you must ensure that user profiles have been populated with data in SharePoint. An administrator must configure the population of user profiles in SharePoint through SharePoint Central Administration.

In the solution described above, you also saw that before you make a call to a web service operation, you must set the values of parameters. These parameters are located under the **queryFields** group node of the data source for the web service.

Chapter 4: Use InfoPath Controls with Data from SharePoint

Figure 207. The queryFields group node of the GetUserPropertyByAccountName data source.

And to retrieve the results of the call made to a web service operation, you have to retrieve the values of fields that are located under the **dataFields** group node of the data source for the web service.

Making a call to a web service is a 3-step process:

1. Set parameter values of the web service operation by setting the values of fields that are located under the **queryFields** group node of the secondary data source for the web service.
2. Use a **Query for data** action in an **Action** rule to call the web service operation.
3. Retrieve the results of the call from fields that are located under the **dataFields** group node of the secondary data source for the web service.

In the solution described above, you performed this 3-step process twice: Once to call the **GetUserPropertyByAccountName** operation and a second time to call the **GetUserProfileByName** operation of the User Profile Service.

You also retrieved the values of three properties: **FirstName**, **LastName**, and **WorkEmail**. While these are three well-known properties in a user's profile, you may not know the exact names of all of the properties returned by the **GetUserProfileByName** operation of the User Profile Service. If you do not know the exact property names, you can temporarily bind the **PropertyData** repeating group node that is located under the **dataFields** group node of the secondary data source for the web service to a repeating table on the form, preview the form, and then copy the names of the properties you want to use in your form.

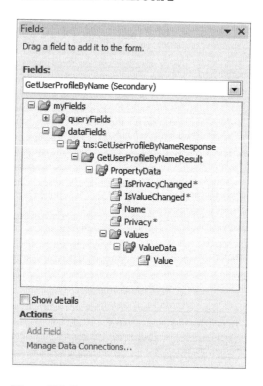

Figure 208. **PropertyData** repeating group node on the Fields task pane.

By temporarily binding the **PropertyData** repeating group node to a repeating table or repeating section control (also see recipe *44 Display SharePoint list data in a repeating table*), you should get a list of all of the properties that are available for use. The **Name** field under the **PropertyData** repeating group node contains the property's name and the **Value** field under the **ValueData** repeating group node contains the property's values.

Note that you could have also used the **User Information List** SharePoint list to retrieve the first name, last name, and email address of the manager (also see recipe *67 Get email addresses from a person/group picker*) instead of making a call to the **GetUserProfileByName** operation, because the User Information List contains all of those properties.

If you want to use the User Information List instead of the User Profile Service, you must follow a similar procedure of adding a **Receive** data connection to the User Information List SharePoint list, leaving the **Automatically retrieve data when form is opened** check box deselected when creating the data connection, and then using rules for the 3-step process mentioned earlier to:

1. Set the value of the **Account** field under the **queryFields** group node of the User Information List secondary data source to be equal to the value of the manager you retrieved when you called the **GetUserPropertyByAccountName** operation.

Chapter 4: Use InfoPath Controls with Data from SharePoint

2. Query the User Information List data connection to populate the User Information List secondary data source with data.
3. Retrieve the values of the **First name**, **Last name**, and **Work e-mail** fields from under the **dataFields** group node of the User Information List secondary data source.

In summary: You could make two web service calls to the User Profile Service as described in the solution above, or one web service call to the User Profile Service to first retrieve the manager of a person and then query the User Information List to retrieve the details of the manager.

In the solution described above, the manager of a person was retrieved when the form was being filled out. If your scenario defers retrieving the manager of a person until after the form has been saved or submitted, you could make use of a SharePoint Designer 2010 workflow to retrieve the manager of a person (see recipe *81 Send an email to the manager of a selected person* for an example of how to retrieve a manager through a workflow) instead of making calls to the User Profile Service.

Multiple-Selection List Box

A multiple-selection list box combines the functionality of a normal list box control with check box controls. Instead of being able to select only one item as is the case with a list box control, a multiple-selection list box allows you to select and store multiple items in one field.

The recipes in this section discuss a few scenarios for combining multiple-selection list boxes with SharePoint lists and person/group picker controls.

69 Fill a multi-select list box on a SharePoint list form with SharePoint list data

Problem

You have a SharePoint list that contains a choice column. You customized the form for this SharePoint list in InfoPath and now you want to use a multiple-selection list box to fill the value of the choice column. The multiple-selection list box should get its values from another SharePoint list.

Solution

You can add a field of type **Choice (allow multiple selections)** to the SharePoint list form template from within InfoPath and then bind it to a multiple-selection list box that gets its entries from an external data source.

InfoPath 2010 Cookbook 2

Suppose you have a SharePoint list named **OfficeApplications** as described in recipe *2 Customize a SharePoint list form from within InfoPath* which you want to use to populate a multiple-selection list box on the SharePoint list form.

To populate a multiple-selection list box on a SharePoint list form with data from another SharePoint list:

1. In SharePoint, create a new custom SharePoint list or use an existing one. The SharePoint list need not contain any other columns than the **Title** column.

2. Start the customization of the SharePoint list form either from within SharePoint or from within InfoPath as described in recipe *1 Customize a SharePoint list form from within SharePoint* or recipe *2 Customize a SharePoint list form from within InfoPath*.

3. In InfoPath, on the **Fields** task pane, click **Show advanced view**.

4. On the **Fields** task pane, expand the **dataFields** group node, right-click the **my:SharePointListItem_RW** group node, and select **Add** from the drop-down menu that appears.

5. On the **Add Field or Group** dialog box, enter a **Display Name** and **Name** for the field (for example, **My Choices** and **MyChoices**), select **Choice (allow multiple selections)** from the **Data type** drop-down list box, and click **OK**.

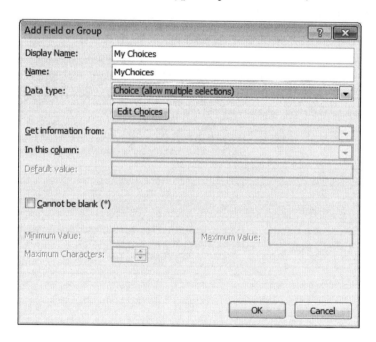

Figure 209. Adding a Choice field to a SharePoint list form in InfoPath Designer 2010.

6. On the **Fields** task pane, drag-and-drop the **:Value** repeating field from under the **My Choices** group node onto the view. InfoPath should automatically bind it to a multiple-selection list box.

Chapter 4: Use InfoPath Controls with Data from SharePoint

7. Right-click the multiple-selection list box and select **Multiple-Selection List Box Properties** from the context menu that appears.

8. On the **Multiple-Selection List Box Properties** dialog box on the **Data** tab, select **Get choices from an external data source**, and then click **Add** behind the **Data source** drop-down list box.

9. On the **Data Connection Wizard**, follow the steps to add a **Receive** data connection to the **OfficeApplications** SharePoint list. Ensure you select **ID** and **Title** as the fields to include in the data source and that you leave the **Automatically retrieve data when form is opened** check box selected.

10. On the **Multiple-Selection List Box Properties** dialog box on the **Data** tab, ensure **d:ID** is selected for the **Value** property and **d:Title** for the **Display name** property, and then click **OK**.

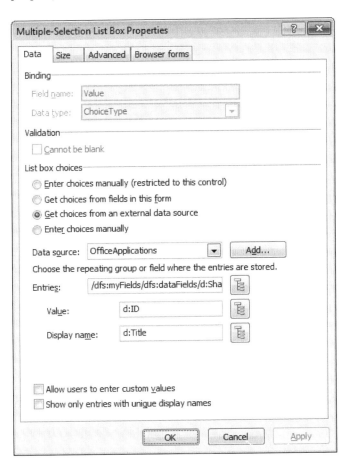

Figure 210. The multiple-selection list box configured to get entries from an external list.

11. Publish the form template to SharePoint.

277

In SharePoint, navigate to the SharePoint list for which you customized its form, and click **Add new item**. When the **New Item** page opens, ensure that the multiple-selection list box is displaying entries from the **OfficeApplications** SharePoint list.

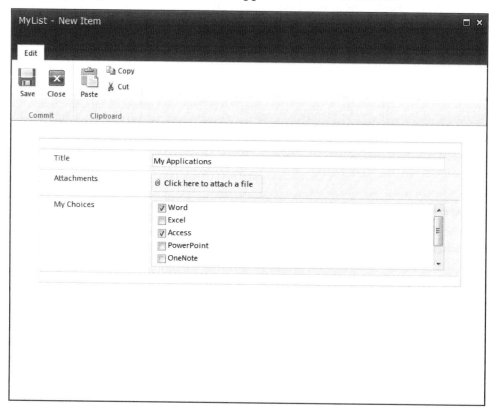

Figure 211. The New Item page with a multiple-selection list box in SharePoint 2010.

Fill out the form and then save the item. Click on the item you just created and verify that the form is displaying only the items you selected from the multiple-selection list box. Click **Edit Item** to edit the item and verify that the multiple-selection list box displays the items you already selected previously along with all of the other items from the **OfficeApplications** SharePoint list.

Discussion

In the solution described above you learned how to add a multiple-selection list box to a SharePoint list form to allow users to set the value for a choice column in a SharePoint list. You could have also first added a **Choice** column with a display type of **Checkboxes (allow multiple selections)** to the SharePoint list from within SharePoint and then bound this column to a multiple-selection list box in InfoPath to create functionality similar to the one described above.

Chapter 4: Use InfoPath Controls with Data from SharePoint

SharePoint list forms come with the following **Choice** data types you can choose from when selecting the data type for a field you are adding to the Main data source of a SharePoint list form:

- Choice (menu to choose from)
- Choice (allow multiple selections)
- Choice with Fill-in (menu to choose from or text)
- Choice with Fill-in (allow multiple selections)

From these four data types, you can only bind the **Choice (allow multiple selections)** and **Choice with Fill-in (allow multiple selections)** to a multiple-selection list box. Because of the structure of the other two data types, you can only bind them to controls that accept a single value such as for example a drop-down list box. The difference between the **Choice (allow multiple selections)** and **Choice with Fill-in (allow multiple selections)** data types lies in whether you want to allow a user to be able to manually add items to the multiple-selection list box or not. This option can also be switched on or off by selecting or deselecting the **Allow users to enter custom values** check box on the **Multiple-Selection List Box Properties** dialog box.

70 Get a list of email addresses from selected users in a multi-select list box

Problem

You have a person/group picker control and a multiple-selection list box control on an InfoPath form. You want to be able to select one or more users from the person/group picker control and have their account IDs appear as selectable choices in the multiple-selection list box control. Then you want to click a button and have the email addresses of only those users you selected from the multiple-selection list box appear in a text box as a concatenated string of email addresses separated by semi-colons.

Solution

You can use the repeating group node of a person/group picker control as the data source for a multiple-selection list box to populate the multiple-selection list box with the values that were selected through the person/group picker control. You can then use the **User Information List** SharePoint list and the **eval** function to retrieve and concatenate the email addresses of the users you select from the multiple-selection list box.

To populate a multiple-selection list box with users from a person/group picker and then lookup and concatenate the email addresses of selected users into a semi-colon separated string:

1. In InfoPath, create a new SharePoint form library form template or use an existing one.

InfoPath 2010 Cookbook 2

2. Add a **Person/Group Picker** control to the view of the form template.

3. Open the **Person/Group Picker Properties** dialog box and then on the **General** tab, select the **Allow multiple selections** check box and leave the **People Only** option selected. With this you have configured the person/group picker control to allow multiple users to be selected.

4. Add a **Button** control to the view of the form template and set its **Action** property to **Update Form**.

5. Add a **Multiple-Selection List Box** control to the view of the form template and name the repeating field under its group node **user**.

6. Open the **Multiple-Selection List Box Properties** dialog box, and then on the **Data** tab, select **Get choices from fields in this form**, configure the **Entries** to come from the **pc:Person** repeating group node of the person/group picker control, and set both the **Value** and **Display name** properties to **AccountId**.

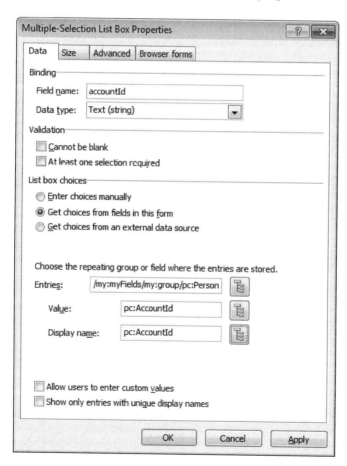

Figure 212. Configuring the multiple-selection list box to get entries from the people picker.

280

Chapter 4: Use InfoPath Controls with Data from SharePoint

Click **OK** to close the dialog box.

7. Click **Data** ➤ **Form Data** ➤ **Default Values**.

8. On the **Edit Default Values** dialog box, expand the node for the multiple-selection list box, deselect the **user** check box, and click **OK**. This should clear the check box for the first empty item in the multiple-selection list box when the form opens.

9. Add a **Button** control and a **Text Box** control to the view of the form template. Name the text box control **emailAddresses** and label the button control **Get E-mail Addresses**.

10. Click **Data** ➤ **Get External Data** ➤ **From SharePoint List** (also see *Use a SharePoint list data connection* in recipe *43 3 Ways to retrieve data from a SharePoint list*) and add a **Receive** data connection to the **User Information List** SharePoint list for the site from which the person/group picker control should get its information. When you are configuring the data connection, ensure you select **Account** and **Work_e-mail** as the fields to include in the data source, and that you leave the **Automatically retrieve data when form is opened** check box selected. You will use this SharePoint list data connection to lookup the email addresses of users.

11. Add a **Set a field's value** action rule to the **Get E-mail Addresses** button that sets the value of the **emailAddresses** field to the following formula:

    ```
    eval(eval(EMail[. != "" and count(Name[. = user]) > 0], 'concat(., "; ")'),
    "..")
    ```

    or

    ```
    xdMath:Eval(xdMath:Eval(xdXDocument:GetDOM("User Information
    List")/dfs:myFields/dfs:dataFields/d:SharePointListItem_RW/d:EMail[. != ""
    and count(../d:Name[. = xdXDocument:get-
    DOM()/my:myFields/my:group1/my:user]) > 0], 'concat(., "; ")'), "..")
    ```

    if you have the **Edit XPath (advanced)** check box selected on the **Insert Formula** dialog box. What this formula does is lookup the non-blank email addresses of each user that was selected in the multiple-selection list box, and then loops through all of them to concatenate them into a string separated by semi-colons.

12. Publish the form template to a SharePoint form library.

In SharePoint, navigate to the form library where you published the form template and add a new form. When the form opens, use the person/group picker to lookup one or more users, and then click the **Check names** button. Click the **Update Form** button. The multiple-selection list box should be populated with the account IDs of the users you selected through the person/group picker control. Select one of more accounts from the multiple-selection list box, and then click the **Get E-mail Addresses** button. The email addresses of the people you selected should appear in the text box as a concatenated string of email addresses separated by semi-colons.

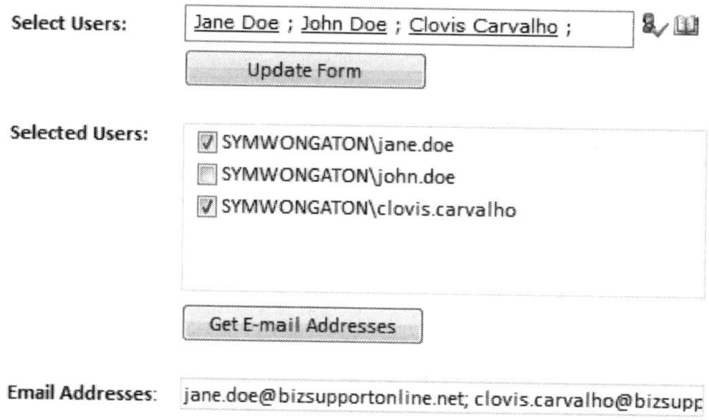

InfoPath 2010 Cookbook 2

Select Users: Jane Doe ; John Doe ; Clovis Carvalho ;
Update Form

Selected Users:
☑ SYMWONGATON\jane.doe
☐ SYMWONGATON\john.doe
☑ SYMWONGATON\clovis.carvalho

Get E-mail Addresses

Email Addresses: jane.doe@bizsupportonline.net; clovis.carvalho@bizsupp

Figure 213. The InfoPath form displaying selected users and their email addresses.

Discussion

The solution described above consists of two techniques: The first is binding a multiple-selection list box to data from a person/group picker control, and the second is using the **eval** function to extract and filter email addresses from a secondary data source and display them as a concatenated string.

Because the data structure of a person/group picker control is a repeating structure, you can not only bind it to a repeating table or repeating section control instead of a person/group picker control, but you can also use it to populate lists such as drop-down list boxes, multiple-selection list boxes, combo boxes, and normal list boxes.

The technique of using the **eval** function twice to create a concatenated string has already been used several times in this book and explained extensively in *InfoPath 2010 Cookbook: 101 Codeless Recipes for Beginners*. Nonetheless, its usage in this recipe requires a bit more explaining, since an extra trick was used in the filter. So let us break down the formula and see how it works.

The final formula looks as follows:

```
eval(eval(EMail[. != "" and count(Name[. = user]) > 0], 'concat(., "; ")'),
"..")
```

To construct this formula, you should start by creating a formula such as:

```
eval(EMail[. != "" and count(Name[. = user]) > 0], "..")
```

This formula performs a lookup in the **User Information List** secondary data source by retrieving all of the **Work e-mail** fields

```
EMail[ ... ]
```

282

Chapter 4: Use InfoPath Controls with Data from SharePoint

where **EMail** represents the **Work e-mail** field under the **d:SharePointListItem_RW** repeating group node under the **dataFields** group node of the **User Information List** secondary data source and **[...]** is a filter you can construct by clicking the **Filter Data** button on the **Select a Field or Group** dialog box. The filter consists of two conditions. The first filter condition uses the following expression:

```
Work e-mail is not blank
```

and the second filter condition says:

```
count(../d:Name[. = xdXDocument:get-DOM()/my:myFields/my:group1/my:user]) > 0
```

where **d:Name** is the **Account** field under the **d:SharePointListItem_RW** repeating group node under the **dataFields** group node of the **User Information List** secondary data source, and **my:user** is the repeating field bound to the multiple-selection list box in the Main data source.

The trick in the final formula lies in the second filter condition where you use the **count** function to count the amount of accounts in the **User Information List** secondary data source that have the same value as any one of the selected users in the multiple-selection list box. And if that amount is greater than zero (0), you know that a user was selected in the multiple-selection list box and that the email address for that user should be included in the results.

A multiple-selection list box consists of a repeating field under a group node. Whenever you select an item in a multiple-selection list box, a field element with the selected value is added under the group node of the multiple-selection list box. So if a particular item has not been selected, a field element for that item will be missing from under the group. Therefore, if you want to know whether an item that has a value of 'A' was selected in a multiple-selection list box, you must count how many fields there are under the group node of the multiple-selection list box that have a value of 'A'. And to do this, you must filter the repeating fields on their value being equal to 'A'. If the result is 0, the item that has a value of 'A' was not selected. In the solution described above, a similar technique was used, but then the secondary data source was filtered on the value of an account being present under the group node of the multiple-selection list box:

```
count(Name[. = user]) > 0
```

where **Name** represents the **Account** field in the **User Information List** secondary data source and **user** represents the repeating field of the multiple-selection list box. Note that you do not have to construct the expression for the filter condition by hand, but that you can use the cheating method I wrote about in recipe 30 of *InfoPath 2010 Cookbook: 101 Codeless Recipes for Beginners*.

Once you have the expression for the outer **eval** function constructed, you can add the inner **eval** function. Because you know that the outer **eval** function returns a list of email addresses:

```
eval(EMail[ ... ], "..")
```

and you want to separate those email addresses using semi-colons, you must use an expression such as:

```
concat(., "; ")
```

on each email address returned by the outer **eval** function where . represents an email address. The expression then becomes:

```
eval(EMail[ ... ], 'concat(., "; ")')
```

The filter has been replaced by an ellipsis (…) in the expression above to make the essential parts of the formula clearer. And when you combine the two **eval** functions, you get the following formula:

```
eval(eval(EMail[ ... ], 'concat(., "; ")'), "..")
```

This technique is not limited to using SharePoint lists as the data source to perform email lookups; you could also use a data source for the User Profile Service to perform similar lookups. See the discussion section of recipe *54 Display a list of people from the current user's department* to learn more about the User Information List.

71 Fill a multi-select list box with email addresses from a person/group picker

Problem

You have a person/group picker control and a multiple-selection list box control on an InfoPath form. You want to be able to select one or more users from the person/group picker control and have their email addresses appear as selectable choices in the multiple-selection list box control.

Solution

You can use the **User Information List** SharePoint list and the **Filter Data** option on a secondary data source to lookup the email addresses of users and then have those email addresses appear as items in a multiple-selection list box.

To populate a multiple-selection list box with email addresses from users who were selected from a person/group picker control.

1. In InfoPath, create a new SharePoint form library form template or use an existing one.

Chapter 4: Use InfoPath Controls with Data from SharePoint

2. Click **Data** ➤ **Get External Data** ➤ **From SharePoint List** (also see *Use a SharePoint list data connection* in recipe *43 3 Ways to retrieve data from a SharePoint list*) and add a **Receive** data connection to the **User Information List** SharePoint list for the site from which the person/group picker control should get its information. When you are configuring the data connection, ensure you select **Account** and **Work_e-mail** as the fields to include in the data source, and that you leave the **Automatically retrieve data when form is opened** check box selected. You will use this SharePoint list data connection to lookup the email addresses of users.

3. Add a **Person/Group Picker** control to the view of the form template.

4. Open the **Person/Group Picker Properties** dialog box and then on the **General** tab, select the **Allow multiple selections** check box and leave the **People Only** option selected. With this you have configured the person/group picker control to allow multiple users to be selected.

5. Add a **Button** control to the view of the form template and set its **Action** property to **Update Form**.

6. Add a **Multiple-Selection List Box** control to the view of the form template and name the repeating field under its group node **emailAddress**.

7. Click **Data** ➤ **Form Data** ➤ **Default Values**.

8. On the **Edit Default Values** dialog box, expand the node for the multiple-selection list box, deselect the **emailAddress** check box, and click **OK**.

Figure 214. Deselecting the emailAddress check box on the Edit Default Values dialog box.

InfoPath 2010 Cookbook 2

This should prevent an empty selected item from appearing in the multiple-selection list box when the form opens.

9. Open the **Multiple-Selection List Box Properties** dialog box and configure the multiple-selection list box to get its entries from the **User Information List** secondary data source. Use the **Filter Data** button on the **Select a Field or Group** dialog box to add two filter conditions that say:

```
Account = AccountId
and
Work e-mail is not blank
```

where **Account** and **Work e-mail** are fields that are located under the **d:SharePointListItem_RW** repeating group node under the **dataFields** group node of the **User Information List** secondary data source and **AccountId** is the field located under the repeating group node of the person/group picker control in the Main data source.

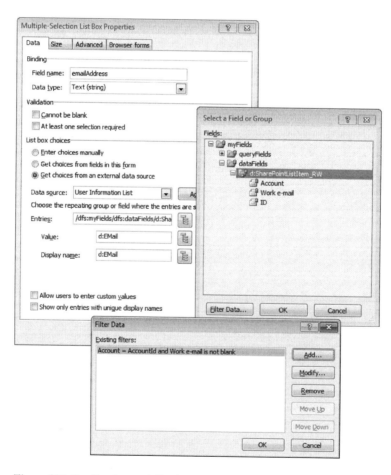

Figure 215. Configuring and filtering the items for the multiple-selection list box.

Chapter 4: Use InfoPath Controls with Data from SharePoint

The resulting XPath expression for the **Entries** property should resemble the following expression:

```
/dfs:myFields/dfs:dataFields/d:SharePointListItem_RW[d:Name =
xdXDocument:get-DOM()/my:myFields/my:group/pc:Person/pc:AccountId and
d:EMail != ""]
```

Set the values for the **Value** and **Display name** properties to both come from the **Work e-mail** field that is located under the **d:SharePointListItem_RW** repeating group node of the **User Information List** secondary data source.

10. Publish the form template to a SharePoint form library.

In SharePoint, navigate to the form library where you published the form template and add a new form. When the form opens, use the person/group picker to lookup one or more users, and then click the **Check names** button. Click the **Update Form** button. The multiple-selection list box should be populated with the email addresses of the people you selected.

Figure 216. The InfoPath form displaying selected users and email addresses.

Discussion

In the solution described above you saw how you can populate a multiple-selection list box by filtering a secondary data source on users that were selected through a person/group picker control on an InfoPath form. This technique is not limited to using SharePoint lists as data sources; you could also use a data source for the User Profile Service to populate the multiple-selection list box, for example, if you wanted to populate the multiple-selection list box with the names of the managers of the selected users (also see recipe *68 Get the details of the manager of a selected person in a person/group picker*), since the User Information List does not contain all SharePoint user profile information. See the discussion section of recipe *54 Display a list of people from the current user's department* to learn more about the User Information List.

You could extend the solution described above by adding a button and text box control named **emailAddresses** to the view, and then adding an **Action** rule to the button with the following action:

```
Set a field's value: emailAddresses = eval(eval(emailAddress, 'concat(., ";
")'), "..")
```

This action would set the value of the **emailAddresses** text box to a concatenated string for the email addresses that were selected from the **emailAddress** multiple-selection list box, separated by semi-colons. The resulting string would then be:

```
jane.doe@bizsupportonline.net; john.doe@bizsupportonline.net
```

when you select the email addresses for Jane Doe and John Doe from the multiple-selection list box.

Chapter 5: Use SharePoint Designer Workflows with InfoPath Forms

SharePoint Designer 2010 can be used to perform several modifications in SharePoint, one of which is create and publish codeless workflows that can run in SharePoint 2010.

You can use InfoPath 2010 forms in one of the following two ways with SharePoint Designer 2010 workflows:

1. As workflow initiation, association, or task forms to pass data to a SharePoint Designer 2010 workflow.
2. As list items or content types a SharePoint Designer 2010 workflow runs on or uses.

This chapter is not intended to give you an in-depth overview of how to create workflows in SharePoint Designer 2010, since an entire book could be written on the subject. However, because you do need some basic understanding of SharePoint Designer 2010 workflows before you move onto the InfoPath-related recipes in this chapter, I will first guide you through setting up a few simple workflows in SharePoint Designer 2010 and explain how to associate them with a list or content type before moving onto combining SharePoint Designer 2010 workflows with InfoPath 2010.

72 Create a workflow that runs on new forms in a specific form library

Problem

You want to have a workflow run whenever a new form is added to a specific form library on a SharePoint site.

Solution

You can create a list workflow in SharePoint Designer 2010 and associate it with the form library on which the workflow should run.

To create a workflow that runs on new forms in a specific form library:

1. In InfoPath, design a SharePoint form library form template or use an existing one, and publish it to either a form library or as a site content type. If published as a site content type, associate the content type with a form library as described in recipe *27 Enable different types of forms to be created in one form library*. We will call the form library you published the form template to **ListWorkflowLib**, so that we can easily refer to it in this recipe.

InfoPath 2010 Cookbook 2

2. Open SharePoint Designer 2010, and click **File ▶ Sites ▶ Open Site**.

Figure 217. Opening a site in SharePoint Designer 2010.

3. On the **Open Site** dialog box, browse to and select the site on which **ListWorkflowLib** is located or enter the URL of the site in the **Site name** text box, and click **Open**.

4. Once the site has been opened in SharePoint Designer 2010, click **Site ▶ New ▶ List Workflow** or select **Workflows** in the left **Navigation** pane and then click **Workflows ▶ New ▶ List Workflow** on the Ribbon, and select **ListWorkflowLib** from the drop-down menu that appears.

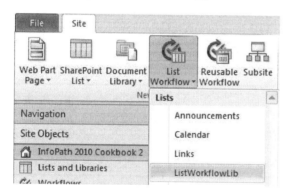

Figure 218. The List Workflow command on the Site tab in SharePoint Designer 2010.

5. On the **Create List Workflow** dialog box, type **ListWorkflowLibWF** in the **Name** text box, and click **OK**. Note that SharePoint Designer uses the name of the workflow to automatically create a column in the **ListWorkflowLib** form library, so ensure that the name you enter does not already exist in the form library as a column.

Chapter 5: Use SharePoint Designer Workflows with InfoPath Forms

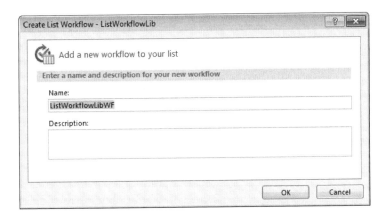

Figure 219. The Create List Workflow dialog box in SharePoint Designer 2010.

This should open the workflow editor with one step (**Step 1**) already added.

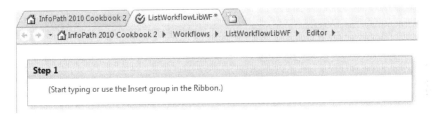

Figure 220. The workflow editor with one step in SharePoint Designer 2010.

6. You are going to keep this workflow very simple by just writing a message to the history list of the workflow whenever the workflow runs. This message will contain the date and time the workflow was started. So click on the text in **Step 1** to place the cursor inside of **Step 1**, click **Workflow ➤ Insert ➤ Action**, and select **Log to History List** under the **Core Actions** category.

Figure 221. Selecting the Log to History List action in SharePoint Designer 2010.

291

InfoPath 2010 Cookbook 2

7. Click **this message** in the sentence for the workflow action. A text box should appear in addition to two buttons behind the text box.

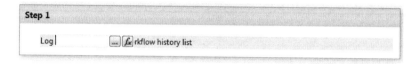

Figure 222. The workflow step after clicking this message in the workflow action sentence.

The first button allows you to build a string, while the second button allows you to lookup a string to set the message to. Click the second button (the formula button) behind the text box.

8. On the **Lookup for String** dialog box, select **Workflow Context** from the **Data source** drop-down list box, select **Date and Time Started** from the **Field from source** drop-down list box, leave **As String** selected in the **Return field as** drop-down list box, and click **OK**.

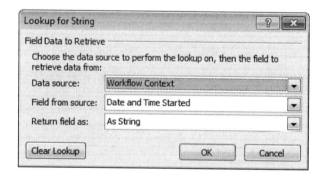

Figure 223. The Lookup for String dialog box in SharePoint Designer 2010.

The final sentence for the workflow action should say:

```
Log Workflow Context:Date and Time Started to the workflow history list
```

Note that the **Workflow Context** data source gives you access to the values of properties of the workflow that is running. SharePoint Designer 2010 has several data sources you can choose from, but the ones you are most likely to use are: **Current Item** (which gives you access to the item the workflow is running on), **Workflow Variables and Parameters** (which gives you access to the values of parameters and variables that have been defined and set in the workflow), and **Workflow Context**. Take a moment to go through the list of data sources to familiarize yourself with them.

9. Click **Workflow ➤ Save ➤ Check for Errors** to ensure that the workflow does not contain any errors.

Chapter 5: Use SharePoint Designer Workflows with InfoPath Forms

Figure 224. The Check for Errors command on the Workflow tab in SharePoint Designer 2010.

A message box saying that the workflow contains no errors should appear. If there are errors, you must fix them before publishing the workflow. Click **OK** to close the message box.

10. Click **Workflow** ➤ **Manage** ➤ **Workflow Settings**.

Figure 225. The Workflow Settings command under the Manage group on the Workflow tab.

11. On the workflow settings page under **Start Options**, select the **Start workflow automatically when an item is created** check box. This will allow the workflow to run whenever a new form is added to the form library. Leave the **Allow this workflow to be manually started** check box selected so that the workflow can also be manually started in case you want to run it again on a form or in case it failed to run.

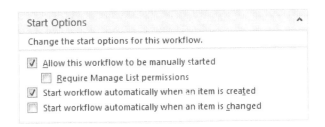

Figure 226. Configuring workflow start options in SharePoint Designer 2010.

12. Click **Workflow Settings** ➤ **Save** ➤ **Publish** to publish the workflow. Note: To go back to the workflow editor, you can click **Workflow Settings** ➤ **Edit** ➤ **Edit Workflow** or the **Edit workflow** link under the **Customization** section on the workflow settings page. And from the workflow editor, you can also publish the workflow by clicking **Workflow** ➤ **Save** ➤ **Publish** on the Ribbon.

In SharePoint, navigate to the **ListWorkflowLib** form library and add a new form to it. Save the form to the form library. Soon after you save the form to the form library, you should see a column named **ListWorkflowLibWF** containing the text **In Progress** appear behind the new form in the form library. Wait a few seconds and then refresh the page. You should see the text **Completed** appear in the aforementioned column when the workflow has run and successfully completed. Note that if an error occurs, you would see the text **Error Occurred** instead of **Completed**.

Figure 227. The text "Completed" appears in the workflow column after the workflow has run.

Click on the text **Completed** (or any other workflow status text that may have appeared). This should take you to the workflow status page where under the **Workflow History** section you should see a comment with the start time of the workflow listed in the **Description** column.

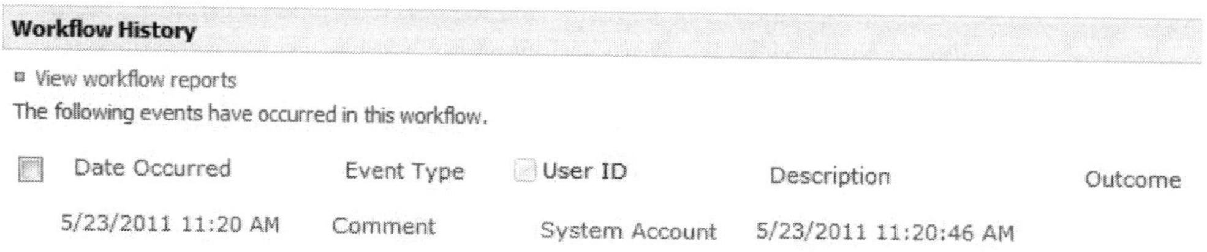

Figure 228. Workflow History on the Workflow Status page in SharePoint.

This start time corresponds to the start time you set the message of the **Log to History List** action to.

Discussion

The same way you use InfoPath Designer 2010 to design and publish an InfoPath form template and then create forms that are based on that form template, you use SharePoint Designer 2010 to design and publish a workflow template and then add workflows that are based on that workflow template to lists, libraries, or content types in SharePoint.

A workflow template defines what a workflow does. And like a form template, a workflow template consists of several parts (steps, actions, conditions, and forms), and can be configured so that any workflows that are based on that template are started automatically or manually. Figure 229 on the next page displays the general outline and components of a workflow template in SharePoint Designer 2010.

A workflow consists of one or more workflow steps, and each step consists of one or more workflow actions. Optionally, you can add workflow conditions around workflow actions to get a workflow to execute certain actions only under certain conditions.

Chapter 5: Use SharePoint Designer Workflows with InfoPath Forms

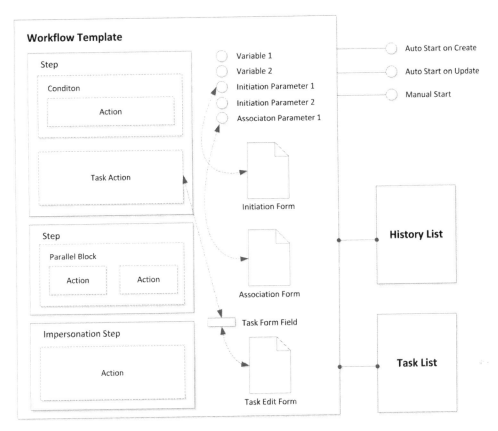

Figure 229. Components of a workflow template in SharePoint Designer 2010.

Actions can run in serial or in parallel. When run in serial, an action only runs when the previous action has completed. When run in parallel, actions run at the same time. By default, actions run in serial in a SharePoint Designer 2010 workflow. If you want actions to run in parallel, you must make use of a parallel block, which you can add to a step by clicking **Workflow ➤ Insert ➤ Parallel Block**.

Actions are ordered by category in SharePoint Designer 2010. Click **Workflow ➤ Insert Action** and take a moment to scroll through the list of all of the categories and actions in SharePoint Designer 2010. Note that the cursor must be located inside of a step for the **Action** command to be enabled on the Ribbon. The categories and actions are pretty self-explanatory and you will get a chance to work with several types of actions as you progress through this book.

In the solution described above, you used the **Log to History List** workflow action from the **Core Actions** category to write a date and time as the description of a message to the history list. You can use the **Log to History List** workflow action anytime this way to debug a SharePoint Designer workflow. For example, if a workflow you created is

295

showing unexpected behavior or producing incorrect values, you can add **Log to History List** workflow actions throughout the workflow to log the values of variables, parameters, etc. to the history list in order to verify that they are producing the values you expect them to produce.

Once you have created a workflow template in SharePoint Designer 2010, you must publish it. Depending on the type of workflow template you created, you may have to perform additional steps before the workflow that is based on that template can be used in SharePoint.

There are three types of workflows you can create using SharePoint Designer 2010:

1. List
2. Reusable
3. Site

List workflows are workflows that can run on a particular list or library, are tightly bound to that list or library, and cannot be reused across multiple lists or libraries.

Reusable workflows are workflows that can run on one particular content type or a content type named **All**, which represents all of the content types associated with a list or library. Reusable workflows, as the name suggests, can be reused across multiple lists or libraries, so they are not tightly bound to only one list or library as is the case with list workflows. You will learn more about reusable workflows in recipe *75 Create a workflow that runs on a specific type of form*.

Site workflows are not bound to any content type, list, or library, but run in the context of a site.

When you first create a list workflow template in SharePoint Designer 2010, you must choose a SharePoint list or library to associate the workflow with. Therefore, when you publish a list workflow template to SharePoint, a workflow that is based on that template is automatically added to the SharePoint list or library you selected when you created the workflow template; no further configuration is required in SharePoint and the workflow is ready to be started on items or documents in SharePoint. The same principle applies to site workflows, but reusable workflows are different. Reusable workflows require extra configuration steps, which you will learn more about in recipe *76 Add a workflow to a specific type of form in a form library*.

In the solution described above, you created a simple list workflow that ran whenever a new form was added to a form library. If you have a form library on which you enabled multiple content types, so which contains different types of forms (also see recipe *27 Enable different types of forms to be created in one form library*), associating a list workflow with the form library would have the effect of the workflow running on any type of form that is added to that form library. If you want a workflow to run on a specific type of form in the form library, you must create a reusable workflow as described in recipe *75 Create a workflow that runs on a specific type of form*.

Note that while you configured the workflow to automatically run whenever a new form is added to the form library, you can also manually start the workflow to run on a form in

Chapter 5: Use SharePoint Designer Workflows with InfoPath Forms

the form library (also see recipe *73 Manually start a workflow to run on a form*), because you left the **Allow this workflow to be manually started** option enabled on the workflow.

If you do not want a workflow to run anymore on a form library, you must delete it from the form library. To delete a list workflow from a form library:

1. In SharePoint, navigate to the settings page of the form library that has the workflow associated with it.

2. On the **Form Library Settings** page under **Permissions and Management**, click **Workflow Settings**.

3. On the **Workflow Settings** page, click **Remove a workflow**.

Figure 230. Workflow Settings page for a form library in SharePoint 2010.

4. On the **Remove Workflows** page, select the **Remove** option for the workflow you want to remove, and then click **OK**.

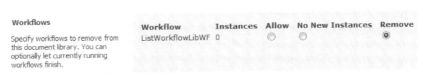

Figure 231. The Remove Workflows page for a form library in SharePoint 2010.

Note that deleting a workflow as described above only disassociates the workflow from the form library, but does not delete the actual workflow template that was used to associate the workflow to the form library. So if you wanted to, you could republish the workflow from within SharePoint Designer 2010 at a later stage to add the workflow back to the form library.

If you want to get the rid of all traces of the workflow, you must delete the workflow template from within SharePoint Designer 2010. This action removes the workflow from the form library, but also deletes the actual workflow template.

To delete a list workflow from a form library and its corresponding workflow template from within SharePoint Designer 2010:

1. In SharePoint Designer 2010, click **Workflows** in the left **Navigation** pane.
2. On the **Workflows** page, right-click the list workflow you want to delete, and select **Delete** from the context menu that appears.

Figure 232. Deleting a list workflow template in SharePoint Designer 2010.

3. On the **Confirm Delete** message box, click **Yes**.

73 Manually start a workflow to run on a form

Problem

You have configured a workflow that runs on forms in a form library to be manually started. Now you want to manually start the workflow on an existing form in the form library.

Solution

You must access the workflow start page to manually start a workflow on a form in a form library.

To manually start a workflow to run on a form:

1. If you have not already published a list workflow, follow the instructions in recipe *72 Create a workflow that runs on new forms in a specific form library* to create a list workflow that is associated with a form library named **ListWorkflowLib**.
2. In SharePoint, navigate to the **ListWorkflowLib** form library.
3. Select the check box in front of a form on which you want to start the workflow, and then click **Library Tools** ➤ **Documents** ➤ **Workflows** ➤ **Workflows**, or click on the drop-down arrow on the right-hand side of the name of the form when you hover over it, and select **Workflows** from the drop-down menu that appears.

Chapter 5: Use SharePoint Designer Workflows with InfoPath Forms

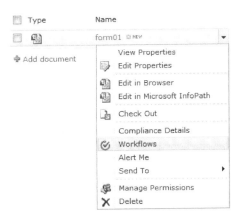

Figure 233. Accessing the Workflows page for an Infopath form in a SharePoint form library.

4. On the **Workflows** page for the form under the **Start a New Workflow** section, click **ListWorkflowLibWF**.

Figure 234. Manually starting a workflow on an InfoPath form in a form library in SharePoint.

5. On the **Start** page for the workflow, you will see a **Start** and a **Cancel** button. These buttons are located on an InfoPath form called a workflow initiation form, which you will learn how to customize in recipe *77 Pass data to a workflow at startup*.

Figure 235. Workflow initiation form with Start and Cancel buttons.

For now, click **Start** to manually start the workflow.

After you click the **Start** button, you should be redirected back to the form library. Wait a few seconds and then refresh the page. You should see the text **Completed** appear in the workflow column when the workflow has run and successfully completed. Click on the text **Completed**. This should take you to the workflow status page where under the **Workflow History** section you should see a comment with the start time of the workflow listed in the **Description** column.

Discussion

Once a workflow has been associated with a list or library, it can be started. A workflow can be started in one of three ways:

InfoPath 2010 Cookbook 2

1. Manually
2. Automatically when a new item is created
3. Automatically when an existing item is updated

For list workflows you must configure the start options when you create the workflow template in SharePoint Designer 2010. For reusable workflows you must define which start options should become available for a workflow when you create the workflow template and then configure the start options when you associate the workflow with a list or library (see recipe *75 Create a workflow that runs on a specific type of form* and recipe *76 Add a workflow to a specific type of form in a form library*). Note that site workflows can be started manually via the **Site Workflows** link on the **Site Actions** ▶ **View All Site Content** page.

If a workflow is manually started, you can allow the user who started the workflow to pass extra information to the workflow at startup using a workflow initiation form, which is an InfoPath form (also see recipe *77 Pass data to a workflow at startup*).

In the solution described above you saw that starting a workflow manually on an item is a 4-click process. You can reduce the amount of clicks to start a particular workflow on an InfoPath form in a form library by adding a custom action to the drop-down menu of forms in the form library as described in the next recipe.

74 Start a workflow from a custom action in a library

Problem

You want to be able to start a workflow on a form by selecting a menu item on the drop-down menu of an InfoPath form in a form library.

Solution

You can use SharePoint Designer 2010 to add a custom action to the drop-down menu of InfoPath forms in a form library, so that users can easily start a list workflow on a form.

To start a list workflow from a custom action on a form:

1. If you have not already published a list workflow, follow the instructions in recipe *72 Create a workflow that runs on new forms in a specific form library* to create a list workflow that is associated with a form library named **ListWorkflowLib**.
2. In SharePoint Designer 2010, in the left **Navigation** pane, click **Lists and Libraries**.

Chapter 5: Use SharePoint Designer Workflows with InfoPath Forms

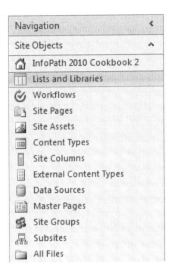

Figure 236. List and Libraries in the Navigation pane in SharePoint Designer 2010.

3. On the **Lists and Libraries** page under **Document Libraries**, click on the name of the form library to which you want to add a custom action.

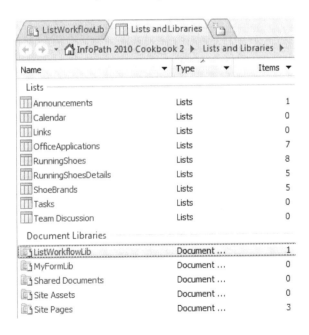

Figure 237. List and Libraries page in SharePoint Designer 2010.

301

InfoPath 2010 Cookbook 2

4. On the form library page under the **Custom Actions** section, click **New**.

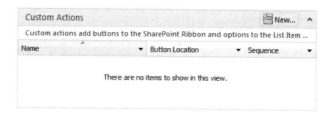

Figure 238. Custom Actions section in SharePoint Designer 2010.

5. On the **Create Custom Action** dialog box, enter a **Name** for the custom action (for example **Log Start Time**), select the **Initiate workflow** option, select the list workflow you want to start from the drop-down list box, and click **OK**.

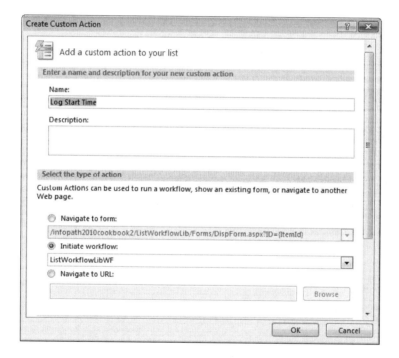

Figure 239. The Create Custom Action dialog box in SharePoint Designer 2010.

Note that you can also select an image to be used in front of the custom action in the form's drop-down menu and also specify where the menu item should appear in the form's drop-down menu by configuring the corresponding options under the **Advanced custom action options** section on the dialog box. If you leave the sequence number on **0**, the menu item will appear as the first menu item in the form's drop-down menu.

In SharePoint, navigate to the form library to which you added the custom action. Hover over a form in the form library, and then click the drop-down arrow that appears on the

Chapter 5: Use SharePoint Designer Workflows with InfoPath Forms

right-hand side of the name of the form to open the form's drop-down menu. The **Log Start Time** custom action you added should be listed as the first item in the menu.

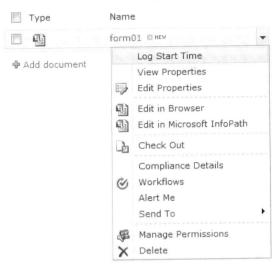

Figure 240. The newly added Log Start Time custom action in the menu of an InfoPath form.

Click the **Log Start Time** menu item. You should be taken directly to the workflow start page. Click **Start** to start running the workflow on the form.

Discussion

In the solution described above, you learned how to add a custom action to the drop-down menu of forms in a form library.

To delete the custom action you added:

1. In SharePoint Designer 2010, follow steps 2 and 3 of the solution described above.
2. On the form library page under the **Custom Actions** section, select the custom action you want to delete, and then click **Custom Actions ➤ Edit ➤ Delete** on the Ribbon.
3. On the **Confirm Delete** message box, click **Yes**.

In SharePoint, navigate to the form library from which you deleted the custom action. Hover over a form in the form library, and then click the drop-down arrow that appears on the right-hand side of the name of the form to open the form's drop-down menu. Verify that the custom action has been removed from the drop-down menu.

Note that custom actions as described in the solution above apply to list workflows and can only be added to all items in a list or library and not to individual items.

75 Create a workflow that runs on a specific type of form

Problem

You want to have a workflow run whenever a form that is based on a specific form template (a specific type of form) is added as a new form to a form library.

Solution

You must publish the form template as a site content type and then in SharePoint Designer 2010, create a reusable workflow that is associated with that content type.

To create a reusable workflow that can run on a specific type of form:

1. In InfoPath, design a SharePoint form library form template or use an existing one, and publish it as a site content type as described in recipe *26 Publish a form template as a site content type*. Name the content type **ReusableWFFormCT**.

2. Open SharePoint Designer 2010, and click **File ➤ Sites ➤ Open Site**.

3. On the **Open Site** dialog box, browse to and select the site on which the **ReusableWFFormCT** content type for the form template is located or enter the URL of the site in the **Site name** text box, and click **Open**.

4. Once the site has been opened, click **Site ➤ New ➤ Reusable Workflow**.

5. On the **Create Reusable Workflow** dialog box, type **ReusableWorkflowWF** in the **Name** text box, select the **ReusableWFFormCT** content type from the **Content Type** drop-down list box, and click **OK**. This should open the workflow editor with one step (**Step 1**) already added to the workflow.

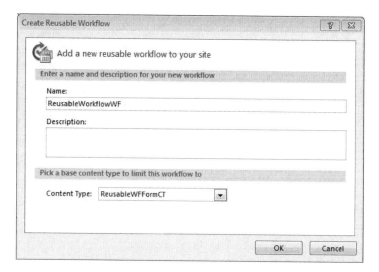

Figure 241. The Create Reusable Workflow dialog box in SharePoint Designer 2010.

Chapter 5: Use SharePoint Designer Workflows with InfoPath Forms

Note that if you already had SharePoint Designer 2010 open before you published the InfoPath form template as a site content type, the new content type may not be listed in the **Content Type** drop-down list box. If the content type is missing from the list of content types, close the dialog box, press **F5** or click the **Refresh** button on the **Quick Access Toolbar**, and then try creating the workflow again.

Figure 242. Refresh command on the Quick Access Toolbar in SharePoint Designer 2010.

6. In recipe *72 Create a workflow that runs on new forms in a specific form library*, you wrote the date and time the workflow started to the workflow history list. In this recipe, you are going to write the name of the item (form) on which the workflow is running to the workflow history list. Place the cursor inside of **Step 1**, click **Workflow ➤ Insert ➤ Action**, and select **Log to History List** under the **Core Actions** category.

7. Click **this message** in the sentence for the workflow action, and then click the formula button (second button) behind the text box that appears.

8. On the **Lookup for String** dialog box, select **Workflow Context** from the **Data source** drop-down list box, select **Item Name** from the **Field from source** drop-down list box, and click **OK**.

The final sentence for the workflow action should say:

```
Log Workflow Context:Item Name to the workflow history list
```

Figure 243. The configured action for the reusable workflow in SharePoint Designer 2010.

Note that the **Workflow Context** data source gives you access to the values of properties of the workflow that is running. SharePoint Designer 2010 has several data sources you can choose from, but the ones you are most likely to use are: **Current Item** (which gives you access to the item the workflow is running on), **Workflow Variables and Parameters** (which gives you access to the values of parameters and variables that have been defined and set in the workflow), and **Workflow Context**.

9. Click **Workflow ▶ Save ▶ Check for Errors** to ensure that the workflow does not contain any errors. A message box saying that the workflow contains no errors should appear. If there are errors, you must fix them before publishing the workflow. Click **OK** to close the message box.

10. Click **Workflow ▶ Manage ▶ Workflow Settings**.

11. On the workflow settings page under the **Start Options** section, select the **Disable automatic start on item change option** check box. This prevents the user who adds the workflow to a form library from selecting the option that allows the workflow to run whenever an existing form is resubmitted or resaved to the form library.

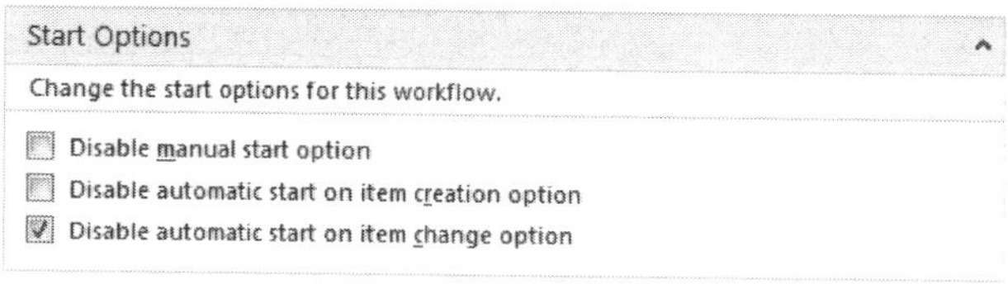

Figure 244. Start options for a reusable workflow in SharePoint Designer 2010.

Note that when you create a list workflow, you configure the way a user is allowed to start a workflow on an item by enabling start options on the workflow template (also see recipe *72 Create a workflow that runs on new forms in a specific form library*). On the other hand, when you create a reusable workflow and select start options for it, you merely disable the start options check boxes a user is allowed to select when she adds the workflow to a list or library (see recipe *76 Add a workflow to a specific type of form in a form library*); the start options on the reusable workflow template are not meant to actually specify how a workflow should be started, but rather what options a user can select when the workflow is associated with a list or library. So the start options on list and reusable workflow templates mean slightly different things.

The following figure shows what the configuration of the start options on the **Add a Workflow** page in SharePoint would look like after you have selected the **Disable automatic start on item change option** in SharePoint Designer 2010 and published the workflow template.

Figure 245. Start Options on the Add a Workflow page in SharePoint 2010.

As you can see from the figure above, the **Start this workflow when an item is changed** check box has been dimmed (disabled), as an indication that the user is not

Chapter 5: Use SharePoint Designer Workflows with InfoPath Forms

allowed to select this option. You will be going through the steps for adding a reusable workflow to a form library in the next recipe.

12. Click **Workflow Settings** ➤ **Save** ➤ **Publish** to publish the workflow.

Once you have created and published the workflow template in SharePoint Designer, you must then add a workflow that is based on that workflow template to the content type or to a form library that is associated with the content type (see recipe *76 Add a workflow to a specific type of form in a form library*) before the workflow can run on forms that are based on the content type associated with the workflow.

Discussion

When you create a reusable workflow template in SharePoint Designer 2010, you must choose a content type to associate the workflow with. In the solution described above, you chose to associate the workflow with a specific content type that had an InfoPath form template defined as its document template. And because content types are generally associated with a list or library in SharePoint, you must perform an extra step to manually attach a workflow that is based on the workflow template you created to lists or libraries on which you want the workflow to run. This step is called associating or adding a workflow to a list or library (see recipe *76 Add a workflow to a specific type of form in a form library*). And once you have added a workflow that is based on this workflow template to a form library, you should be able to run that workflow on forms that are based on the form template linked to the content type.

Because content types can be associated with one or multiple libraries, you can add a reusable workflow to one or multiple libraries without having to recreate the workflow template. Had you created a list workflow as described in recipe *72 Create a workflow that runs on new forms in a specific form library* instead of a reusable workflow, you would have had to recreate the list workflow template in SharePoint Designer 2010 for each form library on which you wanted to run the workflow. So a reusable workflow is recommended if you want to add a workflow to multiple lists or libraries instead of just one. There is where the term "reuse" comes from.

If you have a form library on which you enabled multiple content types, so which contains different types of forms (also see recipe *27 Enable different types of forms to be created in one form library*), associating a list workflow with the form library would have the effect of the workflow running on any type of form in that form library. If on the other hand you associated a reusable workflow with one specific type of form (content type) in that form library, the workflow would only run on those forms that were based on the form template that corresponded to the content type the workflow was associated with, and not on all of the types of forms in the form library.

If you want a reusable workflow to run on all types of forms in a form library as is the case with a list workflow, you would have to associate the workflow template with the **All** content type, which you can select from the **Content Type** drop-down list box on the **Create Reusable Workflow** dialog box when you create the workflow template in SharePoint Designer 2010.

InfoPath 2010 Cookbook 2

Tip:

> If you suspect that you will want to use a workflow on multiple form libraries in the future, consider creating a reusable workflow instead of a list workflow.

76 Add a workflow to a specific type of form in a form library

Problem

You have created a reusable workflow template in SharePoint Designer 2010 and published it. Now you want to run a workflow that is based on that workflow template on the type of form for which the workflow was created.

Solution

You must add a workflow that is based on the reusable workflow template you created to the content type that defines the type of form you want to run the workflow on.

To add a workflow to a specific type of form in a form library:

1. If you have not already created a reusable workflow, follow the instructions in recipe *75 Create a workflow that runs on a specific type of form* to create a reusable workflow that is associated with the content type that defines the type of form you want to run the workflow on.

2. In SharePoint, associate the content type with a form library as described in recipe *27 Enable different types of forms to be created in one form library*.

3. Navigate to the form library that is associated with the content type, and then click **Library Tools ▶ Library ▶ Settings ▶ Workflow Settings**, and select **Add a workflow** from the drop-down menu that appears.

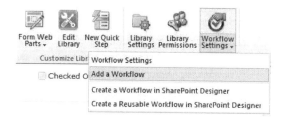

Figure 246. Add a Workflow drop-down menu item in SharePoint 2010.

Or click **Library Tools ▶ Library ▶ Settings ▶ Library Settings**, and then on the **Form Library Settings** page under **Permissions and Management**, click

Chapter 5: Use SharePoint Designer Workflows with InfoPath Forms

Workflow Settings. If you have previously added a workflow to the form library, you should be taken to the **Workflow Settings** page where you can select a content type from the drop-down list box and then click **Add a workflow** to add a workflow. If the form library does not yet have any workflows configured on it, you should be taken directly to the **Add a Workflow** page where you can add a workflow.

4. On the **Add a Workflow** page, select the content type you associated the workflow with in SharePoint Designer 2010 from the **Run on items of this type** drop-down list box, select the name of the workflow template from the **Select a workflow template** list box, enter a unique name for the workflow in the **Type a unique name for this workflow** text box, select the **Start this workflow when a new item is created** check box, and click **OK**. Note that the name you give the workflow need not be the same as the name of the workflow template.

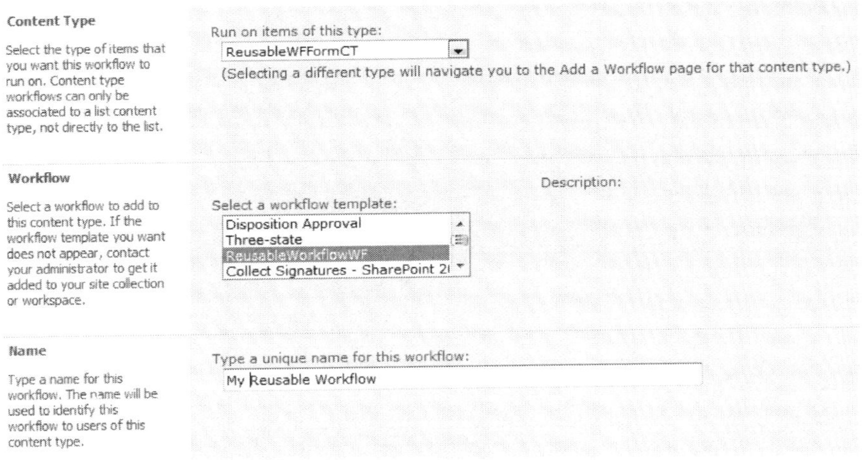

Figure 247. Adding a workflow to a content type of a form library in SharePoint 2010.

After you click **OK**, SharePoint should take you to the **Workflow Settings** page for the content type.

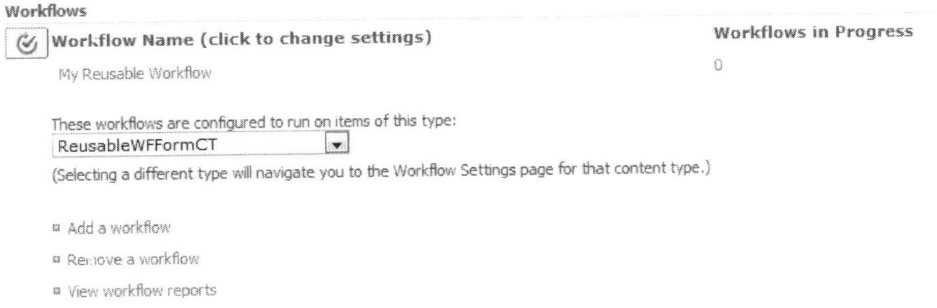

Figure 248. Workflow Settings page for the content type in SharePoint 2010.

309

On this page, you can also select any one of the other content types that have been associated with the form library from the **These workflows are configured to run on items of this type** drop-down list box to view the list of workflows that have been added to those content types.

In SharePoint, navigate to the form library that is associated with the content type and add a new form that is based on the content type the workflow is linked to, to the form library. Because you configured the workflow to start whenever a new item is added to the form library, the workflow should automatically start. Once the workflow has completed, navigate to the workflow history list and verify that the name of the InfoPath form was logged in the history list.

Discussion

In the solution described above, you added a reusable workflow indirectly to the list content type for a specific type of form in a form library by going through the workflow settings of the form library. But you can also add a reusable workflow directly to a list or site content type by going through the workflow settings of the content type itself.

When you add a workflow to a list content type, the workflow is added to only that one instance of the content type.

To add a reusable workflow directly to a list content type:

1. Navigate to the form library that is associated with the content type, and click **Library Tools ▶ Library ▶ Settings ▶ Library Settings**.

2. On the **Form Library Settings** page under the **Content Types** section, click the name of the content type to which you want to add a workflow. If the **Content Types** section is not visible on the page, you can follow steps 3 and 4 of recipe *27 Enable different types of forms to be created in one form library* to make it visible.

3. On the details page of the content type under **Settings**, click **Workflow settings**.

4. On the **Workflow Settings** page, which is the same page you eventually arrived on after performing step 4 in the solution described above, click **Add a workflow**.

5. On the **Add a Workflow** page, follow step 4 in the solution described above. As you can see, there are two entry points for the **Add a Workflow** page: You can get to this page via the workflow settings page of a form library or via the workflow settings page of a content type.

You can also add a workflow to a site content type. When you add a workflow to a site content type, the workflow is automatically added to any child content types (existing and new) that inherit from that content type if you select "Yes" for the **Update List and Site Content Types** option when you add the workflow. If you select "No" for the **Update List and Site Content Types** option, any child content types (existing and new) that inherit from that content type will not automatically get the workflow added to them.

Chapter 5: Use SharePoint Designer Workflows with InfoPath Forms

To add a reusable workflow directly to a site content type:

1. Navigate to the site where the content type is located, and click **Site Actions ➤ Site Settings**.
2. On the **Site Settings** page under **Galleries**, click **Site content types**.
3. On the **Site Content Types** page, click on the name of the site content type to which you want to add a workflow.
4. On the details page of the content type under **Settings**, click **Workflow settings**.
5. On the **Workflow Settings** page, click **Add a workflow**.
6. On the **Add a Workflow** page, you should notice that the **Run on items of this type** drop-down list box is absent. Select the name of the workflow template from the **Select a workflow template** list box, enter a unique name for the workflow in the **Type a unique name for this workflow** text box, select the **Start this workflow when a new item is created** check box, select **Yes** or **No** under **Update List and Site Content Types** depending on whether or not you want to update existing list and site content types that inherit from the current site content type (**Yes** is the recommended option), and then click **OK**.

To delete a reusable workflow that has been added to a content type:

1. In SharePoint, navigate to the settings page of the form library that has the workflow that you want to delete defined on one of its content types.
2. On the **Form Library Settings** page under the **Content Types** section, click the content type that has the workflow associated with it.
3. On the details page of the content type under **Settings**, click **Workflow settings**.
4. On the **Workflow Settings** page for the content type, you will notice that the content type has automatically been selected in the **These workflows are configured to run on items of this type** drop-down list box. You can also access the **Workflow Settings** page for the content type by going through the **Workflow Settings** page of the form library that the content type is associated with, and then selecting the content type from the aforementioned drop-down list box. Click the **Remove a workflow** link.
5. On the **Remove Workflows** page, select the **Remove** option for the workflow you want to remove, and then click **OK**.

Figure 249. Removing a workflow from a content type in SharePoint 2010.

InfoPath 2010 Cookbook 2

And just like you can delete a list workflow from a form library from within SharePoint Designer 2010 (see the discussion section of recipe *72 Create a workflow that runs on new forms in a specific form library*), you can also delete a reusable workflow from a site content type by deleting the reusable workflow template from within SharePoint Designer 2010.

Tip:

> If you want to delete a reusable workflow, it is best to delete that workflow from content types in SharePoint instead of deleting the workflow template for the workflow in SharePoint Designer to avoid having 'orphaned' workflows.

77 Pass data to a workflow at startup

Problem

You want to have a workflow run whenever a form that is based on a specific form template is added as a new form to a form library. You also want to allow the user who starts the workflow to specify a list of recipients to whom an email containing a link to the form the workflow is started on should be sent, and select a value for the urgency with which the form should be processed. The values for the urgency field should be retrieved from a SharePoint list.

Solution

You can create a list workflow or a reusable workflow in SharePoint Designer 2010 and then modify the workflow's initiation form in InfoPath Designer 2010 so that it retrieves a list of urgency values from a SharePoint list. The solution described here makes use of a reusable workflow.

To allow a user to pass data to a workflow at startup:

1. In InfoPath, create a new SharePoint form library form template or use an existing one, and publish it to SharePoint as a site content type (see recipe *26 Publish a form template as a site content type*). Name the content type **SendEmailCT**.

2. In SharePoint, create a custom list named **Urgency** that contains a list of urgency values, for example **Not Urgent**, **Semi-Urgent**, and **Very Urgent**; or download the **UrgencyList.stp** file from www.bizsupportonline.com and load it into your SharePoint test environment (also see *Upload a list template to a List Template Gallery* in the Appendix).

3. In SharePoint Designer 2010, create a reusable workflow as described in recipe *75 Create a workflow that runs on a specific type of form*, name it **SendEmailRWF**, and select the **SendEmailCT** content type from the **Content Type** drop-down list box.

312

Chapter 5: Use SharePoint Designer Workflows with InfoPath Forms

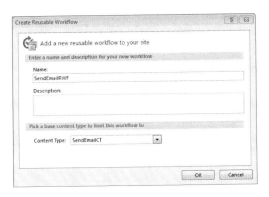

Figure 250. Creating the reusable workflow in SharePoint Designer 2010.

4. Click **Workflow ➤ Variables ➤ Initiation Form Parameters**. Initiation form parameters serve as input parameters for a workflow and are automatically hooked up by SharePoint Designer to controls on the initiation form you will modify later in InfoPath Designer 2010.

Figure 251. Initiation Form Parameters command on the Workflow tab in SharePoint Designer.

5. On the **Association and Initiation Form Parameters** dialog box, click **Add**.

6. On the **Add Field** dialog box, type **EmailRecipients** in the **Field name** text box, select **Person or Group** from the **Information type** drop-down list box, leave **Initiation (starting the workflow)** selected in the **Collect from parameter during** drop-down list box, and click **Next**.

Figure 252. Adding an initiation form parameter in SharePoint Designer 2010.

313

7. On the **Column Settings** dialog box, leave **Account** selected in the **Show Field** drop-down list box, select the **People Only** option, select the **All Users** option, select the **Allow multiple values** check box, and click **Finish**.

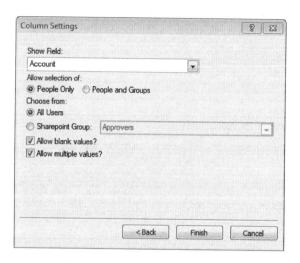

Figure 253. Configuring the properties for the initiation form parameter.

8. On the **Association and Initiation Form Parameters** dialog box, click **Add**.

9. On the **Add Field** dialog box, type **Urgency** in the **Field name** text box, leave **Single line of text** selected in the **Information type** drop-down list box, leave **Initiation (starting the workflow)** selected in the **Collect from parameter during** drop-down list box, and click **Next**. Note that you could have also selected **Choice (menu to choose from)** as the **Information type**, but this would have forced you to specify a fixed list of options. In this scenario, you do not want a fixed list of options, but rather want the values to come from a specific SharePoint list.

10. On the **Column Settings** dialog box, leave **Default value** empty, and click **Finish**.

11. On the **Association and Initiation Form Parameters** dialog box, click **OK**.

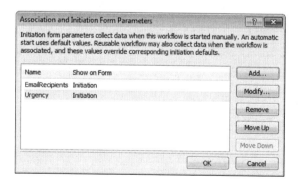

Figure 254. The Association and Initiation Form Parameters dialog with initiation parameters.

Chapter 5: Use SharePoint Designer Workflows with InfoPath Forms

12. The workflow must send an email to a list of recipients that is specified by the user at startup and that is stored in the **EmailRecipients** initiation parameter. The email must include the selected urgency that is stored in the **Urgency** parameter and a link to the form in the body of the email. So place the cursor inside of **Step 1**, click **Workflow ➤ Insert ➤ Action**, and then select **Send an Email** under the **Core Actions** category.

13. Click **these users** in the sentence for the workflow action.

14. On the **Define E-mail Message** dialog box, click the button behind the **To** text box.

15. On the **Select Users** dialog box, select **Workflow Lookup for a User** from the list of existing users and groups, and click **Add**.

16. On the **Lookup for Person or Group** dialog box, select **Workflow Variables and Parameters** from the **Data source** drop-down list box, select **Parameter: EmailRecipients** from the **Field from source** drop-down list box, select **Email Addresses, Semicolon Delimited** from the **Return field as** drop-down list box, and click **OK**.

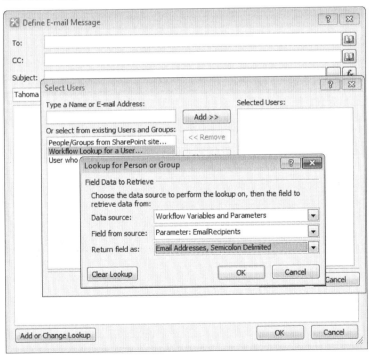

Figure 255. Configuring the email recipients to send an email to.

Note that you can always retrieve the value of any variable or parameter you have defined for the workflow from the **Workflow Variables and Parameters** data source. Here you are retrieving the value of an initiation parameter.

315

InfoPath 2010 Cookbook 2

17. On the **Select Users** dialog box, click **OK**.

18. On the **Define E-mail Message** dialog box, enter the text "InfoPath form requires your attention" as the **Subject**. Note that you can use the buttons behind the **Subject** text box to dynamically build a string for the subject line if your scenario calls for it. In this solution you should just type in the text as a static piece of text.

19. On the **Define E-mail Message** dialog box, click anywhere in the text box for the body of the email, type the text **InfoPath Form:**, and then click **Add or Change Lookup**.

20. On the **Lookup for String** dialog box, select **Workflow Context** from the **Data source** drop-down list box, select **Current Item URL** from the **Field from source** drop-down list box, and click **OK**.

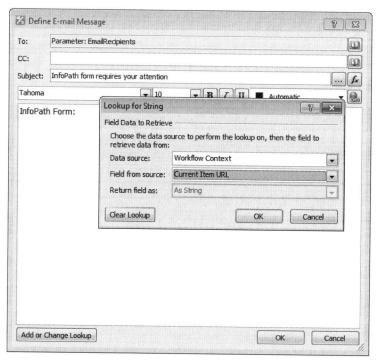

Figure 256. Constructing the body of the email message.

Note that the **Current Item URL** field contains the full URL of the InfoPath form (XML file). When a user clicks this URL in an email, it will not automatically open the form in the browser, but will rather prompt the user to download the file. If you want the form to open in the browser you must modify the URL to contain the **FormServer.aspx** page and the **OpenIn=Browser** query string parameter to have the form open in the browser when a user clicks the link (see the discussion section for more details). The text in the body of the email should now say:

Chapter 5: Use SharePoint Designer Workflows with InfoPath Forms

```
InfoPath Form: [%Workflow Context:Current Item URL%]
```

21. On the **Define E-mail Message** dialog box, type the text **Urgency:** on a new line, and then click **Add or Change Lookup**.

22. On the **Lookup for String** dialog box, select **Workflow Variables and Parameters** from the **Data source** drop-down list box, select **Parameter: Urgency** from the **Field from source** drop-down list box, leave **As String** selected in the **Return as field** drop-down list box, and click **OK**. The text in the body of the email should now say:

```
InfoPath Form: [%Workflow Context:Current Item URL%]
Urgency: [%Parameter: Urgency%]
```

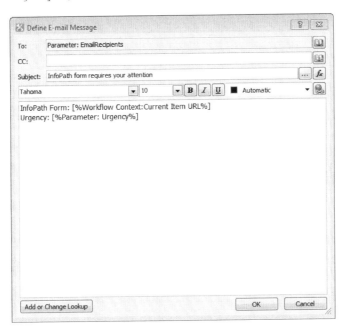

Figure 257. The completed Define E-Mail Message dialog box.

23. On the **Define E-mail Message** dialog box, click **OK**. The sentence for the workflow action should now say:

```
Email Parameter: EmailRecipients
```

Figure 258. The completed workflow step in SharePoint Designer 2010.

24. Click **Workflow** ➤ **Save** ➤ **Publish** to publish the workflow.

InfoPath 2010 Cookbook 2

25. Click **Workflow** ➤ **Manage** ➤ **Workflow Settings**.

26. Because a user must manually enter a list of email recipients and choose the urgency with which the form should be processed when she starts the workflow, the workflow must always be manually started; initiation parameters cannot be set for workflows that start automatically. So on the workflow settings page under the **Start Options** section, select the **Disable automatic start on item creation option** and the **Disable automatic start on item change option** check boxes.

27. On the workflow settings page under the **Forms** section, click **SendEmailRWF.xsn**. This should open the form template for the initiation form in InfoPath Designer 2010.

28. In InfoPath, you should see that SharePoint Designer already bound the **EmailRecipients** field to a person/group picker control and the **Urgency** field to a text box control. Because you want to select the **Urgency** from a SharePoint list, you must change the text box control into a drop-down list box control and then populate it with values from the SharePoint list. So right-click the text box control and select **Change Control** ➤ **Drop-Down List Box** from the context menu that appears.

29. Click **Data** ➤ **Get External Data** ➤ **From SharePoint List** and add a **Receive** data connection to the **Urgency** SharePoint list (also see *Use a SharePoint list data connection* in recipe *43 3 Ways to retrieve data from a SharePoint list*). Ensure you include the **Title** and **ID** fields in the secondary data source, sort the list by **Title**, leave the **Automatically retrieve data when form is opened** check box selected, and name the data connection **GetUrgency**.

30. Open the **Drop-Down List Box Properties** dialog box and configure the drop-down list box to get its entries from the **GetUrgency** external data source. Set both the **Value** and **Display name** properties to come from the **Title** field in the data source.

Figure 259. The completed InfoPath form template in InfoPath Designer 2010.

31. Preview the form to check whether the drop-down list box is being populated.

32. Click **Quick Publish** on the **Quick Access Toolbar** at the top of the screen in InfoPath Designer 2010, click **File** ➤ **Info** ➤ **Quick Publish**, or click **File** ➤ **Publish** ➤ **Workflow** to republish the form template. Note: InfoPath may prompt you to save the form template first.

Chapter 5: Use SharePoint Designer Workflows with InfoPath Forms

33. In SharePoint, add the workflow to the content type associated with a form library as described in recipe *76 Add a workflow to a specific type of form in a form library*.

In SharePoint, navigate to the form library to which you added the workflow, and add a new form that is based on the **SendEmailCT** content type to the form library. Once added, hover over the form, click on the drop-down arrow that appears on the right-hand side of the form's name, and select **Workflows** from the drop-down menu. On the **Workflows** page for the form under the **Start a New Workflow** section, click **SendEmailRWF** or the name you gave the workflow when you added it to the content type. On the **Start** page for the workflow, enter one or more user names, select a value for the urgency from the **Urgency** drop-down list box, and click **Start**. Once the workflow has run and completed, verify that the email message was sent.

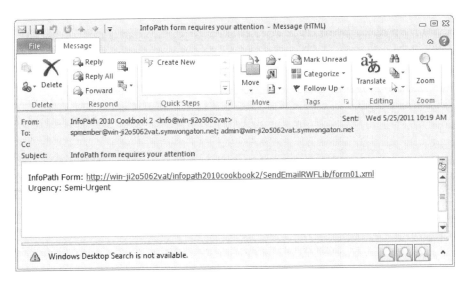

Figure 260. The email message as it appears in Outlook 2010 after the workflow has run.

Discussion

You can create three types of workflow forms in SharePoint Designer 2010: Association, initiation, and task forms. Association and initiation forms are combined into an **Association/Initiation** workflow form type. You can see what kind of workflow forms have been created for a SharePoint Designer 2010 workflow by looking at the value of the **Type** column under the **Forms** section on the workflow settings page. Workflow forms are InfoPath forms if you are creating workflows that run on SharePoint Server 2010 (not SharePoint Foundation) and they serve as input forms that may appear at different stages within a workflow's lifecycle.

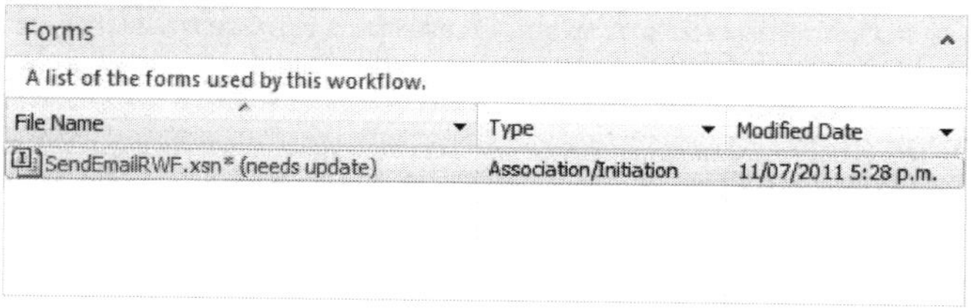

Figure 261. Workflow association/initiation form as listed in SharePoint Designer 2010.

In the figure above, the text **(needs update)** has been appended to the name of the InfoPath form template. This text generally appears after you have already created the form template in SharePoint Designer 2010 and customized it in InfoPath Designer 2010, but then modified something in the workflow that could have affected the validity of the form template. If you see the **(needs update)** text appear behind a form template, click on the form template to open it in InfoPath Designer 2010, make the necessary updates, and republish it.

In the solution described above you learned how to customize the initiation form of a SharePoint Designer workflow. The initiation form of a SharePoint Designer workflow is an InfoPath form that has an InfoPath form type of **Workflow Form**. You can verify this in InfoPath by looking at the **Form type** in the **Compatibility** section on the **Form Options** dialog box.

Workflow forms cannot be created from scratch from within InfoPath Designer 2010, because there is no **Workflow Form** template available when you open InfoPath Designer 2010 to create an InfoPath form template from scratch. However, workflow forms can be customized in InfoPath Designer 2010 after you have published a workflow from within SharePoint Designer 2010.

Workflow forms are similar to other types of forms in InfoPath in that you can add rules, conditional formatting, data connections, etc. to them just like you would do with any other type of form in InfoPath. You can even set multiple submit connections on the form, but should always ensure that there is at least one **Submit To Host** connection present that submits the form to SharePoint. This connection is added to the form template by default when the form template is created by SharePoint Designer 2010.

If you reopen the workflow initiation form in InfoPath, you will see that the initiation form is actually two workflow forms in one. If you open the **View** drop-down list box via **Page Design ▶ Views** on the Ribbon, you will see the following two views listed:

1. Start (default)
2. Associate

The **Start (default)** view is used to display the initiation form and the **Associate** view is used to display the association form for the workflow. You will learn more about association forms in the next recipe.

Controls on a workflow initiation form are automatically bound to initiation form parameters that you set up for the workflow in SharePoint Designer 2010, and you can

Chapter 5: Use SharePoint Designer Workflows with InfoPath Forms

retrieve the value of any parameter passed to the workflow from the **Workflow Variables and Parameters** data source of the workflow.

You also learned that you can dynamically retrieve the URL of the form a reusable workflow is running on from the **Current Item URL** field of the **Workflow Context** data source, and include this in an email to a list of email recipients. If you were creating a list workflow, you could retrieve the full path of the form the workflow is running on from the **Encoded Absolute URL** field in the **Current Item** data source instead of from the **Current Item URL** field in the **Workflow Context** data source as is the case when you create a reusable workflow.

The **Encoded Absolute URL** and **Current Item URL** fields always contain the full path of the XML file that represents the InfoPath form. Therefore, when a user clicks on a link that references this URL, an XML file is downloaded instead of the InfoPath form opened in the browser. If you want the InfoPath form to open in the browser, you must dynamically construct the URL to contain a reference to the **FormServer.aspx** page in addition to the **OpenIn** query string parameter. You can construct the URL the same way you did in steps 19 through 22 of the solution described above. The final text in the body of the email should say:

```
InfoPath Form: [%Workflow Context:Current Site
URL%]/_layouts/FormServer.aspx?XmlLocation=[%Workflow Context:Current Item
URL%]&OpenIn=Browser
Urgency: [%Parameter: Urgency%]
```

Note that the **Current Site URL** field in the **Workflow Context** data source is used to dynamically retrieve the URL of the site where the form is located.

78 Pass data to a workflow when attaching it to a library

Problem

You want to be able to enter comments and select a list of people when you add a workflow to a form library.

Solution

You must create a reusable workflow in SharePoint Designer 2010 and then modify its association form to include a field for selecting people and a field for entering comments.

To pass data to a workflow when adding the workflow to a library:

1. In InfoPath, use the form template you created and published in step 1 of the previous recipe.
2. In SharePoint Designer 2010, use the workflow you created in the previous recipe.
3. To be able to pass values from an association form to a workflow, you must setup association parameters. So open the workflow, click **Workflow ➤ Variables ➤**

Initiation Form Parameters, and add field named **Comments** of type **Multiple lines of text** that collects data during **Association (attaching to a list)**.

Figure 262. Adding the Comments association parameter in SharePoint Designer 2010.

Add a second field named **SelectedPeople** of type **Person or Group** that collects data during **Association (attaching to a list)** and that allows the selection of multiple values of **People Only** from the **All Users** group.

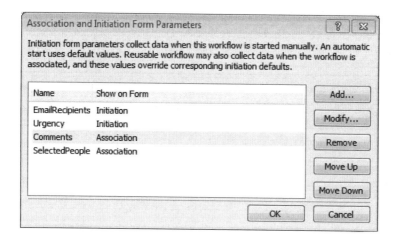

Figure 263. Comments and SelectedPeople association parameters in SharePoint Designer.

4. Publish the workflow and then click **Workflow ▶ Manage ▶ Workflow Settings** to go to the workflow settings page.

Chapter 5: Use SharePoint Designer Workflows with InfoPath Forms

5. On the workflow settings page under the **Forms** section, click the **Association/Initiation** form in the list. This should open the form template in InfoPath Designer 2010.

6. In InfoPath, select **Page Design ➤ Views ➤ View ➤ Associate** to switch to the view that is used for the association form.

7. The **Comments** and **SelectedPeople** fields should already be present on the **Associate** view, but if they are not, add them to the view from the **Fields** task pane.

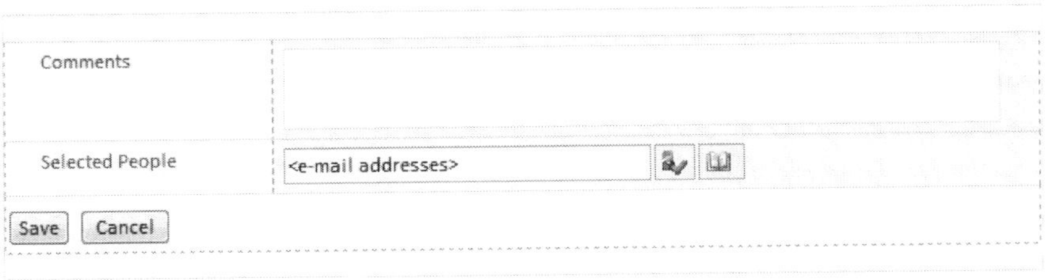

Figure 264. Associate view with controls in InfoPath Designer 2010.

8. Apply any other modifications you want, and then republish the form template.

9. In SharePoint Designer 2010, save and publish the workflow.

10. In SharePoint, you should have already added the content type to a form library as described in the previous recipe, but if you have not done so, create a new form library or use an existing one, and add the content type for the form template you published in step 1 to the form library as described in recipe *27 Enable different types of forms to be created in one form library*.

11. Navigate to the form library that is associated with the content type, click **Library Tools ➤ Library ➤ Settings ➤ Workflow Settings**, and then select **Add a Workflow** from the drop-down menu that appears.

12. On the **Add a Workflow** page, select the **SendEmailCT** content type from the **Run on items of this type** drop-down list box, select the **SendEmailRWF** workflow template from the **Select a workflow template** list box, enter a unique name for the workflow, and then click **Next**. After you click **Next**, the workflow association form should appear.

Figure 265. Association form in SharePoint 2010.

323

13. Enter some comments, select a few people, and click **Save**. The workflow is now all set up to be run on any form that is based on the **SendEmailCT** content type.

Discussion

There may be times when you require the user who adds (associates or attaches) a workflow to a list or library to pass extra information to the workflow to configure it, so that this information can be used by every workflow instance that is started afterwards. You can use a workflow association form to pass such configuration data to a workflow. This data is then stored in association parameters defined in the workflow and can be accessed inside of the workflow whenever the workflow is run on an item.

In the solution described above, you created association parameters, but did not do anything with them. Naturally, in a real-world scenario, you would then retrieve these parameters within the workflow and use them in workflow actions, for example to send emails to people or for logging purposes. This recipe was kept simple to illustrate the creation, modification, and use of an association form that is an InfoPath form.

Remember that association forms are used with reusable workflows to manually attach a workflow to a list or library after you have published the workflow. When you create a list or a site workflow, the association takes place when you create and publish the workflow from within SharePoint Designer 2010, so the use of association forms does not make sense for such types of workflows, although the **Associate** view is still present in InfoPath Designer 2010 for any workflow form template that is generated for a list or site workflow.

In addition, when you click the **Initiation Form Parameters** command on the **Workflow** or **Workflow Settings** tab in SharePoint Designer 2010 to add initiation or association parameters to a list or site workflow, you will notice that the **Collect from parameter during** drop-down list box is missing from the **Add Field** dialog box as an indication that you cannot add association parameters to a list or site workflow.

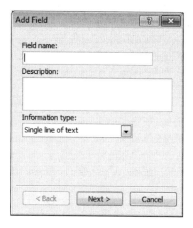

Figure 266. The Add Field dialog box in SharePoint Designer 2010 when creating a list workflow.

Chapter 5: Use SharePoint Designer Workflows with InfoPath Forms

79 Get the value of an InfoPath form field in a workflow

Problem

You want to be able to retrieve data from an InfoPath form field in a SharePoint Designer workflow and use this data to create a new item in a SharePoint list.

Solution

You can promote the form field from which you want to retrieve data, to a column in the form library when you publish the form template to SharePoint, and then use a lookup in the SharePoint Designer workflow to retrieve the value of the form field and use it to create a new SharePoint list item.

To get the value of an InfoPath form field from within a SharePoint Designer workflow:

1. In InfoPath, once you have designed a SharePoint form library form template that contains the field you want to access from within the workflow, publish the form template to SharePoint. While publishing the form template, promote the field you want to access either as a list column or a site column (see recipes *23 Promote form fields to columns of a form library* and *24 Promote form fields to existing site columns*). You do not have to select the **Allow users to edit data in this field by using a datasheet or properties page** check box when you promote the field, because in this case you only want to retrieve a value of a form field and not set the value of a form field. Name the promoted field **GetValueInWorkflow**.

2. In SharePoint, create a new SharePoint list named **Contacts** in which you can store names. The SharePoint list only needs to have a **Title** column.

3. In SharePoint Designer 2010, create a **List Workflow** and associate it with the form library where you published the form template that has the promoted field (also see recipe *72 Create a workflow that runs on new forms in a specific form library*). You are going to create a workflow that adds a new item to the **Contacts** SharePoint list and sets the value of the **Title** field of the new item to be equal to the value of the **GetValueInWorkflow** promoted field.

4. Select **Workflow ▶ Insert ▶ Action ▶ List Actions ▶ Create List Item** to add a **Create List Item** action to **Step 1** of the workflow, and then click **this list** in the sentence for the workflow action.

5. On the **Create New List Item** dialog box, select **Contacts** from the **List** drop-down list box, select **Title (*)** in the list of fields, and click **Modify**.

6. On the **Value Assignment** dialog box, click the formula button (second button) behind the **To this value** text box.

7. On the **Lookup for Single line of text** dialog box, leave **Current Item** selected in the **Data source** drop-down list box (**Current Item** represents the InfoPath form the workflow is running on), select **GetValueInWorkflow** from the **Field from**

source drop-down list box, and click **OK**.

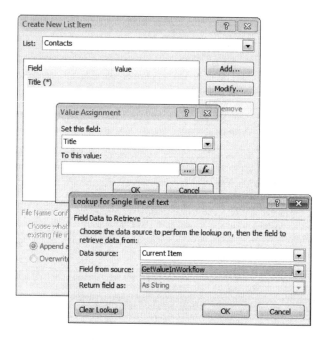

Figure 267. Configuring the creation of a new list item in SharePoint Designer 2010.

8. On the **Value Assignment** dialog box, click **OK**. With this you have set the value of the **Title** of the new item in the **Contacts** list to be equal to the value of the **GetValueInWorkflow** promoted field.

9. On the **Create New List Item** dialog box, click **OK**.

Figure 268. The completed workflow step in SharePoint Designer 2010.

10. Click **Workflow ➤ Manage ➤ Workflow Settings**.

11. On the workflow setting page under the **Start Options** section, select the **Start workflow automatically when an item is created** check box. You can leave the **Allow this workflow to be manually started** check box selected so that users are still able to rerun the workflow on the InfoPath form in case the workflow failed to create a new list item or if a list item needs to be created for forms that were created before the workflow was associated with the form library.

12. Click **Workflow Settings ➤ Save ➤ Publish** to publish the workflow.

Chapter 5: Use SharePoint Designer Workflows with InfoPath Forms

In SharePoint, navigate to the form library where you published the form template and add a new form. Fill out the form and then save or submit it to the form library. Once the workflow has run, navigate to the **Contacts** list and check whether a new item was created with a **Title** that has the same value as the one you entered into the **GetValueInWorkflow** promoted field while filling out the form.

Discussion

In the solution described above, you promoted a field to a column in a SharePoint form library to be able to run a workflow and retrieve the value of this field from within a SharePoint Designer workflow. The only requirement for a SharePoint Designer workflow to be able to retrieve the value of a field from an InfoPath form stored in a form library is that the field is a promoted field. It does not matter whether you use a list column or a site column to promote the field, neither does it matter whether you select the **Allow users to edit data in this field by using a datasheet or properties page** check box or not when your promote the field. You only need to select the **Allow users to edit data in this field by using a datasheet or properties page** check box if you want a SharePoint Designer workflow to write data to promoted InfoPath fields as demonstrated in the next recipe.

Note:

> Because you cannot promote all types of InfoPath fields to SharePoint (see the discussion section of recipe *23 Promote form fields to columns of a form library*), the solution described above is limited to the types of fields you can promote.

80 Set the value of an InfoPath form field through a workflow

Problem

You want to be able to select a person from a person/group picker control on an InfoPath form, have a SharePoint Designer workflow lookup the manager of the selected person, and then from within the workflow, write the name of the manager to a field on the InfoPath form.

Solution

You can promote the form field you want to write to from within the workflow, make it editable when you publish the form template to SharePoint, and then access the field from within the SharePoint Designer workflow to set its value to the manager's name. Note that users must have managers assigned to them and those values must have been populated in their SharePoint user profiles, otherwise manager lookups via the SharePoint

InfoPath 2010 Cookbook 2

Designer workflow you create in this solution will fail. Contact your administrator about the presence of manager information in SharePoint user profiles.

To set the value of an InfoPath form field from within a SharePoint Designer workflow:

1. In InfoPath, create a new SharePoint form library form template or use an existing one.

2. Add a **Person/Group Picker** control and a **Text Box** control to the view of the form template. Name the text box control **manager**. You will be using the person/group picker control to select a person, which the workflow will retrieve. The workflow should then lookup the manager of the selected person and write this value back to the **manager** field on the form. So the workflow must be able to get the value of the field bound to the person/group picker control and set the value of the **manager** field. Therefore, you need to promote both fields.

3. Publish the form template to a new SharePoint form library named **SetFormFieldValueLib**, promote the first **AccountId** field of the person/group picker as an **Employee** list column, promote the **manager** field as a **Manager** list column, and select the **Allow users to edit data in this field by using a datasheet or properties page** check box when you promote the **manager** field.

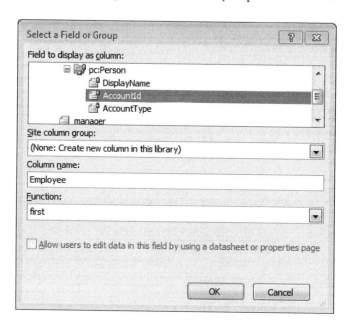

Figure 269. Promoting the AccountId field in InfoPath Designer 2010.

Chapter 5: Use SharePoint Designer Workflows with InfoPath Forms

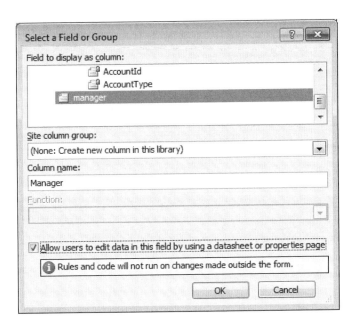

Figure 270. Promoting the manager field in InfoPath Designer 2010.

Also see recipe *23 Promote form fields to columns of a form library* for information on how to promote form fields.

4. In SharePoint Designer 2010, open the site where the **SetFormFieldValueLib** form library is located, create a new **List Workflow** named **SetFormFieldValueWF** and associate it with the **SetFormFieldValueLib** form library (also see recipe *72 Create a workflow that runs on new forms in a specific form library*). Note: If you already had the site open in SharePoint Designer when you published the form template and created the new form library, the new form library might not be listed in the list of lists or libraries you can associate the workflow with. If the form library is not listed in SharePoint Designer, click the **Refresh** button on the **Quick Access Toolbar** at the top of screen or press **F5**, and try again.

5. The workflow must retrieve the manager of the selected employee and then write the name of the manager to the **manager** field on the InfoPath form. So on the workflow editor, click to place the cursor inside of **Step 1**, and then select **Workflow ➤ Insert ➤ Action ➤ Relational Actions ➤ Lookup Manager of a User**.

6. Click **this user** in the sentence for the workflow action.

7. On the **Select Users** dialog box, select **Workflow Lookup for a User** in the existing users and groups list, and click **Add**.

8. On the **Lookup for Person or Group** dialog box, leave **Current Item** selected in the **Data source** drop-down list box, select **Employee** from the **Field from source** drop-down list box, and click **OK**.

329

InfoPath 2010 Cookbook 2

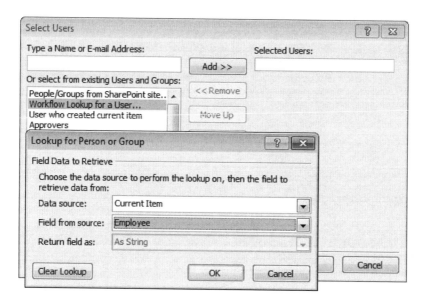

Figure 271. Dialog boxes to configure selecting a person to lookup a manager.

9. On the **Select Users** dialog box, click **OK**. The account ID for the manager of the person should automatically be stored in a variable that is listed after the **output to Variable** text in the sentence for the workflow action. By default, this should be a variable named **manager**. The sentence for the workflow action should now say:

   Find Manager of Current Item:Employee (output to Variable: manager)

10. Once you have retrieved the manager, you can use the value to set the manager field in the InfoPath form. So click to place the cursor below the previous workflow action, and then select **Workflow ➤ Insert ➤ Action ➤ List Actions ➤ Update List Item**.

11. Click **this list** in the sentence for the workflow action you just added.

12. On the **Update List Item** dialog box, leave **Current Item** selected in the **List** drop-down list box, and click **Add**.

13. On the **Value Assignment** dialog box, select **Manager** from the **Set this field** drop-down list box, and click the formula button (second button) behind the **To this value** text box.

14. On the **Lookup for Single line of text** dialog box, select **Workflow Variables and Parameters** from the **Data source** drop-down list box, select **Variable: manager** from the **Field from source** drop-down list box, select **Display Name** from the **Return field as** drop-down list box, and click **OK**.

330

Chapter 5: Use SharePoint Designer Workflows with InfoPath Forms

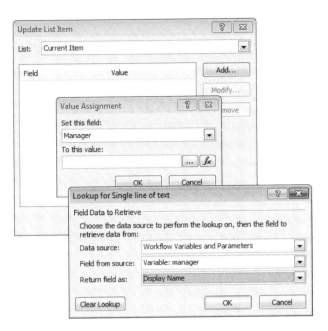

Figure 272. Dialog boxes to configure updating the manager field in the InfoPath form.

15. On the **Value Assignment** dialog box, click **OK**. With this you have set the value of the manager field in the InfoPath form to be equal to the value of the manager the workflow searched for based on the value of the field bound to the person/group picker control on the InfoPath form.

16. On the **Update List Item** dialog box, click **OK**.

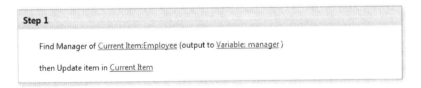

Figure 273. The completed workflow step in SharePoint Designer 2010.

17. Click **Workflow** ➤ **Manage** ➤ **Workflow Settings**.

18. On the workflow settings page under the **Start Options** section, select the **Start workflow automatically when an item is created** check box. You can leave the **Allow this workflow to be manually started** check box selected so that users are still able to rerun the workflow on the InfoPath form in case the workflow fails to update the form field.

19. Click **Workflow Settings** ➤ **Save** ➤ **Publish** to publish the workflow.

331

In SharePoint, navigate to the **SetFormFieldValueLib** form library where you published the form template and add a new form. When the form opens, select an employee from the person/group picker control, and then save or submit the form. Wait until the workflow has run and completed, and once it has, open the form and verify that the name of the manager was retrieved by the workflow and written to the **manager** form field. Note that users must have managers assigned to them and those values must have been populated in their SharePoint user profiles, otherwise manager lookups via the SharePoint Designer workflow will fail.

Discussion

If you want a SharePoint Designer workflow to be able to get as well as set the value of a field on an InfoPath form, you must:

1. Promote the field to a list column or site column (also see recipe *23 Promote form fields to columns of a form library* and recipe *24 Promote form fields to existing site columns*).
2. Select the **Allow users to edit data in this field by using a datasheet or properties page** check box for the field when you publish the form template.

Once a field has been promoted either as a list column or site column and made editable, it is automatically added to the view of the form library. However, the promoted field does not have to be part of the view of the form library for a SharePoint Designer workflow to have access to it; it must just be part of the schema of the form library (if you are creating a list workflow) or content type (if you are creating a reusable workflow) you associate the workflow with for the workflow to have read and/or write access to the field. So you could remove columns from the view of a form library and the workflow should still be able to get and set the values of those columns.

Note that you cannot set the values of all types of fields in InfoPath from within a SharePoint Designer workflow, because not all types of fields can be promoted as editable fields from within InfoPath to SharePoint. For example, the following types of fields cannot be promoted as editable fields:

- Rich text fields
- Date-only fields
- Repeating fields (e.g. fields of a multiple-selection list box or numbered list)
- Base64 encoded fields (e.g. a file attachment or embedded picture)
- Hyperlink fields

Chapter 5: Use SharePoint Designer Workflows with InfoPath Forms

81 Send an email to the manager of a selected person

Problem

You have a person/group picker control on an InfoPath form and you want to be able to select a person and then send an email to the manager of the selected person immediately after the form is saved or submitted to a form library.

Solution

You can promote the field bound to the person/group picker control, use a SharePoint Designer 2010 workflow to retrieve the value of that field, lookup the manager of the person, and then send an email to the manager.

To send an email to the manager of a selected person:

1. In InfoPath, create a new SharePoint form library form template or use an existing one.

2. Add a **Person/Group Picker** control to the view of the form template.

3. Publish the form template to a SharePoint form library named **SendEmailToManagerLib** and promote the first **AccountId** field of the person/group picker as described in recipe *23 Promote form fields to columns of a form library*. Name the promoted field **Employee**.

4. In SharePoint Designer 2010, open the site where the form library is located, create a new **List Workflow** and associate it with the **SendEmailToManagerLib** form library (also see recipe *72 Create a workflow that runs on new forms in a specific form library*). Note: If you already had the site open in SharePoint Designer when you published the form template and created the new form library, the new form library might not be listed in the list of lists or libraries you can associate the workflow with. If the form library is not listed in SharePoint Designer, click the **Refresh** button on the **Quick Access Toolbar** at the top of screen or press **F5**, and try again.

5. On the workflow editor, click to place the cursor inside of **Step 1**, and then select **Workflow ➤ Insert ➤ Action ➤ Relational Actions ➤ Lookup Manager of a User**.

6. Click **this user** in the sentence for the workflow action.

7. On the **Select Users** dialog box, select **Workflow Lookup for a User** in the existing users and groups list, and click **Add**.

8. On the **Lookup for Person or Group** dialog box, leave **Current Item** selected in the **Data source** drop-down list box, select **Employee** (the field you promoted earlier) from the **Field from source** drop-down list box, and click **OK**.

9. On the **Select Users** dialog box, click **OK**. The sentence for the workflow action should now say:

333

InfoPath 2010 Cookbook 2

```
Find Manager Current Item:Employee (output to Variable:manager)
```

The account ID for the manager of the person should automatically be stored in a variable that is listed after the **output to Variable** text in the sentence for the workflow action. By default, this should be a variable named **manager**.

10. Once you have retrieved the manager, you can use the value to send an email. Because a person may not have a manager, you should perform a check before sending an email. So click below the previous workflow action to place the cursor, and then click **Workflow ▶ Insert ▶ Condition** and select **If any value equals value** from the drop-down menu that appears.

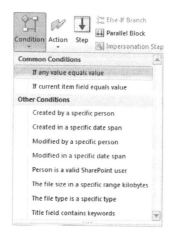

Figure 274. Adding a workflow condition in SharePoint Designer 2010.

11. Click **value** in the sentence for the workflow condition, and then click the formula button that appears behind the text box.

12. On the **Define Workflow Lookup** dialog box, select **Workflow Variables and Parameters** from the **Data source** drop-down list box, select **Variable: manager** from the **Field from source** drop-down list box, and click **OK**.

13. Click **equals** in the sentence for the workflow condition, and select **is not empty** from the drop-down menu that appears. The condition should now say:

```
If Variable: manager is not empty
```

14. Click within the if-block to place the cursor, and then select **Workflow ▶ Insert ▶ Action ▶ Core Actions ▶ Send an Email**.

15. Click **these users** in the sentence for the workflow action you just added.

16. On the **Define E-mail Message** dialog box, click the address book button behind the **To** text box.

Chapter 5: Use SharePoint Designer Workflows with InfoPath Forms

17. On the **Select Users** dialog box, select **Workflow Lookup for a User** in the existing users and groups list, and click **Add**.

18. On the **Lookup for Person or Group** dialog box, select **Workflow Variables and Parameters** from the **Data source** drop-down list box, select **Variable: manager** from the **Field from source** drop-down list box, select **Email Address** from the **Return field as** drop-down list box, and click **OK**.

19. On the **Select Users** dialog box, click **OK**. With this you have set the email to be sent to the email address of the manager.

20. On the **Define E-mail Message** dialog box, enter a **Subject** and define a body for the email message, and then click **OK**.

21. Repeat steps 10 through 20, but then add an **If** condition below the previous **If** condition (note that the second **If** statement should automatically change into an **Else if** statement) that says:

    ```
    Else if Variable: manager is empty
    ```

    and send an email to the administrator reporting that the user does not have a manager. Use the **Add or Change Lookup** button on the **Define E-mail Message** dialog box to construct a body with a text similar to the following:

    ```
    Cannot send an email, because [%Current Item:Employee%] does not have a manager.
    ```

    where **[%Current Item:Employee%]** performs a lookup for the account ID (**Employee** promoted field) of the selected person in the current form (**Current Item**).

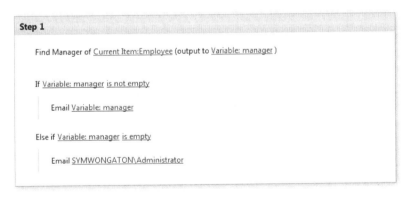

Figure 275. The completed workflow step in SharePoint Designer 2010.

22. Click **Workflow ➤ Manage ➤ Workflow Settings**.

23. On the workflow settings page under the **Start Options** section, select the **Start workflow automatically when an item is created** check box.

InfoPath 2010 Cookbook 2

24. Click **Workflow Settings** ➤ **Save** ➤ **Publish** to publish the workflow.

In SharePoint, navigate to the form library where you published the form template and add a new form. Select a person from the person/group picker control whose manager you want to send an email, and then save or submit the form. Wait until the workflow runs and completes, and then verify that the manager of the person you selected from the person/group picker control received an email. Also test the workflow for a person who does not have a manager and verify that the administrator received an email.

Discussion

In recipe *68 Get the details of the manager of a selected person in a person/group picker* you learned how to use the User Profile Service to retrieve the details of the manager of a selected person. While you could have used a similar technique to retrieve the email address in the InfoPath form itself and then use an email submit connection to send an email to the manager of the user, in the solution described above you let SharePoint take care of performing the lookup and sending the email.

If your scenario requires doing more with the details of the manager than just performing a lookup and sending an email, it would make sense to retrieve those details in the InfoPath form and not let the workflow do the work. In all other cases, it might be quicker, easier, and less error-prone to implement a SharePoint Designer workflow that takes care of performing the lookup and sending the email.

82 Set a task form field value from an initiation form in an approval workflow

Problem

You have a person/group picker control on a leave request form from which an employee name is selected. The leave request form is submitted to a form library and then a custom approval workflow is manually started on the form. When the approval workflow is started, the initiator of the workflow should be able to enter a textual request in a multi-line text box. A task should then be created and assigned to the manager of the employee, and when the manager opens the task form of the approval workflow, the request entered at startup of the workflow should appear on the task form for the manager to read. The manager should then be able to approve or reject the leave request.

Solution

You can use a combination of initiation parameters and task form fields to pass the value of an initiation parameter to a task form by using the workflow's Task list as an intermediary for the communication between the workflow's initiation and task forms.

To pass an initiation parameter value to a task form in a leave request approval workflow:

Chapter 5: Use SharePoint Designer Workflows with InfoPath Forms

1. In InfoPath, create a new SharePoint form library form template or use an existing one.

2. Add a **Person/Group Picker** control to the view of the form template.

3. Promote the first **AccountId** field of the person/group picker as a column named **Employee** as described in the discussion section of recipe *23 Promote form fields to columns of a form library*.

4. Publish the form template to a SharePoint form library named **LeaveRequestFormsLib**.

5. In SharePoint Designer 2010, create a new **List Workflow** named **GetManagerApprovalWF** and associate it with the **LeaveRequestFormsLib** form library (also see recipe *72 Create a workflow that runs on new forms in a specific form library*).

6. Because you want anyone who starts the workflow to have the ability to enter a textual request, you must create an initiation parameter to capture this request. So click **Workflow ➤ Variables ➤ Initiation Form Parameters** and add a parameter named **StartupRequest** of type **Multiple lines of text** to the workflow template.

7. Because an approval workflow assigns tasks to users and these tasks should have an expiration date, you will create a local variable that stores a date that is 7 days from the date the workflow was started. So click **Workflow ➤ Variables ➤ Local Variables**, and add a variable named **expirationDate** of type **Date/Time**.

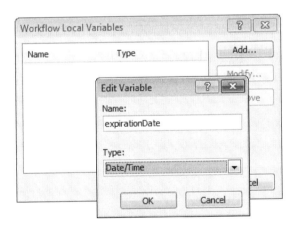

Figure 276. Adding a local variable to a workflow in SharePoint Designer 2010.

8. To set the **expirationDate** variable to a date in the future, you must perform a date calculation. So on the workflow editor, click inside of **Step 1** to place the cursor, and then select **Workflow ➤ Insert ➤ Action ➤ Core Actions ➤ Add Time to Date**.

9. Click **0** in the sentence for the workflow action and type **7** in the text box that appears.

10. Click **minutes** in the sentence for the workflow action and select **days** from the drop-down list box that appears.

11. Click **date** in the sentence for the workflow action, and then click the formula button (second button) behind the text box that appears.

12. On the **Lookup for Date/Time** dialog box, select **Workflow Context** from the **Data source** drop-down list box, select **Date and Time Started** from the **Field from source** drop-down list box, and click **OK**.

13. Click **Variable: date** in the sentence for the workflow action and select **Variable: expirationDate** from the drop-down list box that appears. You have now set the value of the **expirationDate** variable to a date that lies 7 days in the future from the date the workflow was started. The completed sentence for the workflow action should now say:

    ```
    Add 7 days to Workflow Context:Date and Time Started (Output to Variable: expirationDate)
    ```

14. For a manager to be able to approve or reject the leave request, a task must be assigned to the manager. And before you can assign a task to the manager, you must know who the manager of the employee is, so you must perform a lookup. So click below the previous workflow action to place the cursor, and then select **Workflow ➤ Insert ➤ Action ➤ Relational Actions ➤ Lookup Manager of a User**.

15. Click **this user** in the sentence for the second workflow action.

16. On the **Select Users** dialog box, select **Workflow Lookup for a User** in the existing users and groups list, and click **Add**.

17. On the **Lookup for Person or Group** dialog box, leave **Current Item** selected in the **Data source** drop-down list box, select **Employee** from the **Field from source** drop-down list box, and click **OK**.

18. On the **Select Users** dialog box, click **OK**. The account ID of the manager of the employee should automatically be stored in a variable that is listed after **output to Variable** in the sentence for the workflow action. By default, this should be a variable named **manager**. The completed sentence for the workflow should now say:

    ```
    Add 7 days to Workflow Context:Date and Time Started (Output to Variable: expirationDate)

    then Find Manager of Current Item:Employee (output to Variable: manager)
    ```

19. Tasks are stored in a **Task** SharePoint list for the workflow. You could either use the **Task** list that is added to a site by default or you could create a new **Task** list for the workflow. Here you will create a new **Task** list to see how you would go about doing this. So click **Workflow ➤ Manage ➤ Workflow Settings**.

Chapter 5: Use SharePoint Designer Workflows with InfoPath Forms

20. On the workflow settings page under the **Settings** section, select **New Task List** from the **Task List** drop-down list box, and when prompted, confirm you want to create a new task list. A new **Task** list that has the name of the workflow as part of its own name should be created. You could perform a similar step to create a new **History List** for the workflow if you wanted to.

21. On the workflow settings page under the **Customization** section, click **Edit workflow** to go back to the workflow editor.

22. Under the action that retrieves the manager, you can assign a task to that manager. So click below the last workflow action to place the cursor, and then select **Workflow ➤ Insert ➤ Action ➤ Task Actions ➤ Start Custom Task Process**.

23. Click **these users** in the sentence for the third workflow action.

24. On the **Select Task Process Participants** dialog box, click the address book button behind the **Participants** text box.

25. On the **Select Users** dialog box, select **Workflow Lookup for a User** in the existing users and groups list, and click **Add**.

26. On the **Lookup for Person or Group** dialog box, select **Workflow Variables and Parameters** from the **Data source** drop-down list box, select **Variable: manager** from the **Field from source** drop-down list box, select **Email Address** from the **Return field as** drop-down list box, and click **OK**.

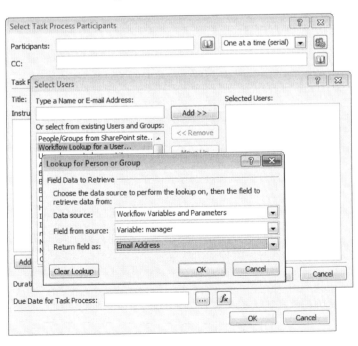

Figure 277. Selecting the manager as a workflow participant in an approval workflow.

27. On the **Select Users** dialog box, click **OK**.

28. On the **Select Task Process Participants** dialog box, enter a **Title** (for example **Leave request approval required**), enter a few **Instructions**, select a **Duration per Task** of **1 Day(s)**, and click the formula button (second button) behind the **Due Date for Task Process** text box.

29. On the **Lookup for Date/Time** dialog box, select **Workflow Variables and Parameters** from the **Data source** drop-down list box, select **Variable: expirationDate** from the **Field from source** drop-down list box, and click **OK**. With this you have set the task to be due within 7 days from the day the workflow is started.

30. On the **Select Task Process Participants** dialog box, click **OK**. With this you have assigned a task to the manager who should approve the leave request.

Figure 278. The completed Select Task Process Participants dialog box.

31. Now you must configure the task so that it contains a field in which the value of the **StartupRequest** initiation parameter can be stored and subsequently displayed on the task form. So click **Task ([number])** in the sentence for the third workflow action.

32. On the task process summary page under the **Task Form Fields** section, click **New** to add a new task form field. If you are prompted with a message, read the warning, and then click **OK**.

33. On the **Add Field** dialog box, enter **StartupRequest** in the **Field name** text box, select **Multiple lines of text** from the **Information type** drop-down list box, click

Chapter 5: Use SharePoint Designer Workflows with InfoPath Forms

Next, and then click **Finish**. This step should also automatically add a column named **StartupRequest** to the **Task** list.

Figure 279. The newly added StartupRequest task form field in SharePoint Designer 2010.

34. Once you publish the workflow, the initiation and task forms will be created, and then you can edit them. For now, continue configuring the task by clicking **Change the behavior of a single task** under the **Customization** section on the task process summary page.

35. You must set the value of the **StartupRequest** field in the task list to be equal to the value of the **StartupRequest** initiation parameter before the task is assigned, so click to place the cursor inside of the **Before a Task is Assigned** task behavior, and then select **Workflow ► Insert ► Actions ► Task Behavior Actions ► Set Task Field**.

36. Click **field** in the sentence for the workflow action you just added and select **StartupRequest** from the drop-down list box that appears.

37. Click **value** in the sentence for the workflow action, and then click the formula button (second button) behind the text box that appears.

38. On the **Lookup for Multiple lines of text** dialog box, select **Workflow Variables and Parameters** from the **Data source** drop-down list box, select **Parameter: StartupRequest** from the **Field from source** drop-down list box, leave **As String** selected in the **Return field as** drop-down list box, and click **OK**.

Figure 280. The completed Before a Task is Assigned task behavior.

39. Currently, the task is set to expire after 7 days. When the task expires, you could let the workflow take an appropriate action such as escalate the task to the manager of the manager. To do this, click to place the cursor inside of the **When a Task**

Expires task behavior, and then select **Workflow ▶ Insert ▶ Action ▶ Task Behavior Actions ▶ Escalate Task**.

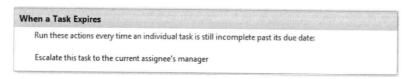

Figure 281. The completed When a Task Expires task behavior.

40. Click **Task ([number])** in the breadcrumbs to return to the task process summary page.

41. On the task process summary page under the **Customization** section, click **Change the completion conditions for this task process**.

42. On the **Completion Conditions** page, click to place the cursor inside of the completion condition, and then select **Workflow ▶ Insert ▶ Condition ▶ Other Conditions ▶ If task outcome equals value**.

43. Click the first **value** in the sentence for the workflow condition and select **Number of Approved** from the drop-down list box that appears.

44. Click the second **value** in the sentence for the workflow condition and type **1** in the text box that appears.

45. Click to place the cursor within the **If** condition, and then select **Workflow ▶ Insert ▶ Action ▶ Core Actions ▶ Log to History List**.

46. Click **message** in the sentence for the workflow action you just added and type **approved** in the text box that appears.

47. Click to select the first **If** condition, and then select **Workflow ▶ Insert ▶ Condition ▶ Other Conditions ▶ If task outcome equals value** to add a second **If** condition. Note that the second **If** condition should automatically become an **Else if** condition.

48. Click the first **value** in the sentence for the workflow condition, and select **Number of Approved** from the drop-down list box that appears.

49. Click **equals** in the sentence for the workflow condition and select **not equals** from the drop-down list box that appears.

50. Click the second **value** in the sentence for the workflow condition and type **1** in the text box that appears.

51. Click to place the cursor within the second **If** condition (the **Else if** condition), and then select **Workflow ▶ Insert ▶ Action ▶ Core Actions ▶ Log to History List**.

52. Click **message** in the sentence for the workflow action you just added and type **rejected** in the text box that appears.

Chapter 5: Use SharePoint Designer Workflows with InfoPath Forms

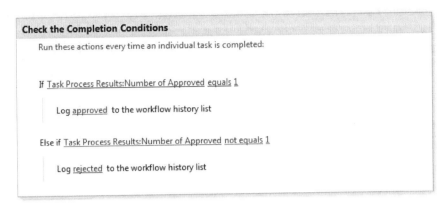

Figure 282. The completed workflow completion conditions in SharePoint Designer 2010.

53. Click **Workflow ➤ Save ➤ Publish** to publish the workflow and create the InfoPath form templates for the workflow.

Figure 283. The workflow forms created by SharePoint Designer 2010.

54. Click **Workflow ➤ Manage ➤ Workflow Settings**.

55. On the workflow settings page under the **Forms** section, click the task form (XSN file of type **Task**) to open it in InfoPath Designer 2010.

56. In InfoPath, a text box that is bound to the **StartupRequest** field should have already been added to the view of the form template. Click the text box for the **StartupRequest** field, select **Control Tools ➤ Properties ➤ Modify ➤ Read-Only** on the Ribbon to make the text box read-only, and then give the text box a different background color through the **Properties ➤ Color ➤ Shading** option on the Ribbon to make it distinguishable from the other fields on the form.

343

InfoPath 2010 Cookbook 2

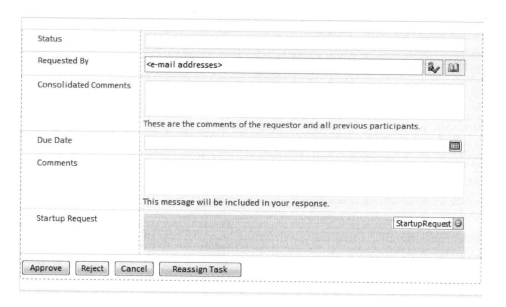

Figure 284. The workflow task form template in InfoPath Designer 2010.

57. Click **File ➤ Publish ➤ Workflow**, click **File ➤ Info ➤ Quick Publish**, or click the **Quick Publish** button on the **Quick Access Toolbar** to publish the form template to SharePoint. Note that you may have to save the form template first before you publish it.

In SharePoint, navigate to the **LeaveRequestFormsLib** form library and add a new form. Manually start the **GetManagerApprovalWF** workflow on the form you just added (also see recipe *73 Manually start a workflow to run on a form*) and enter a textual request in the **Startup Request** text box before clicking **Start**. Click the text **In Progress** behind the form, and then on the workflow status page under **Tasks**, click the **GetmanagerApprovalWF Tasks** link.

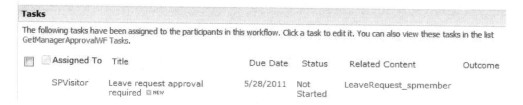

Figure 285. Tasks section on the workflow status page in SharePoint 2010.

Click on the **Title** of the task to edit the task in the task list. When the **Workflow Task** page opens, you should see the startup request text you entered earlier.

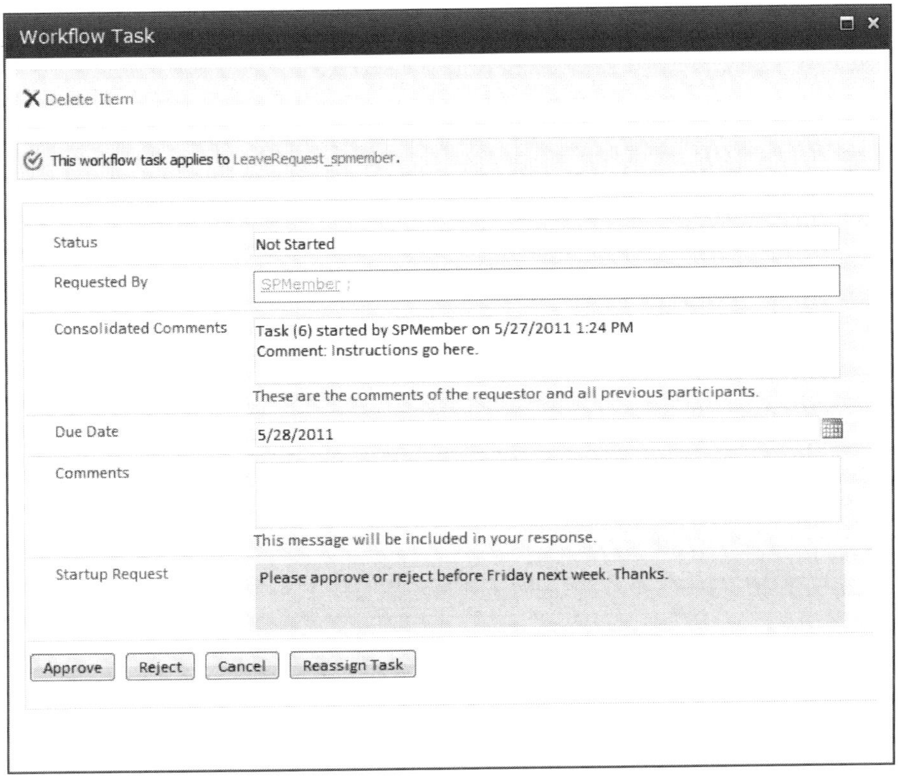

Chapter 5: Use SharePoint Designer Workflows with InfoPath Forms

Figure 286. Workflow task form in SharePoint 2010.

Click **Approve** or **Reject**, and then navigate to the **LeaveRequestFormsLib** form library and verify that the workflow has **Completed**. Click on the text **Completed** and verify that the correct value ("approved" or "rejected") was written to the workflow history list.

Note that you did not have to sign in as the actual manager of the person specified in the person/group picker control on the InfoPath form to be able to approve or reject the task, because the task list for the workflow does not restrict user access. If you want managers to only see the tasks that are assigned to them and which only they should be able to approve or reject, you could for example create a new SharePoint view that filters the items in the task list on the **Assigned To** field being equal to **[Me]** and make that view the default view of the task list.

Discussion

When you create a workflow that allows an approval process that contains tasks to be assigned, you can use workflow task forms to pass data to the workflow for completing or further progressing the task. In recipe *77 Pass data to a workflow at startup* you saw how to modify a workflow initiation form. In the solution described above you not only learned how to modify a workflow task form, but also how to pass a value that was specified at startup via an initiation parameter to that workflow task form through the use of task form fields and the **Set Task Field** task behavior action.

The workflow created above was kept simple in order not to clutter the demonstration of the concepts. Therefore you logged the results of the workflow to the history list instead of performing more complex actions. In addition, you added actions to only 2 of the 5 task behaviors that are available on an approval workflow, but you could have extended the workflow by adding actions to the rest of the task behaviors; for example, used a **Send an Email** action to send an email to the employee when the task completes or used a combination of the **Copy List Item** and **Delete Item** actions to move the leave request form to another form library (also see recipe *87 Move a form from one form library to another using a workflow* for how to move an InfoPath form using a workflow) when the task completes. The possibilities with approval workflows are endless and this recipe only served as a practical introduction to them. For a thorough explanation of approval workflows, consult the SharePoint Designer 2010 documentation on the Microsoft Office Online web site.

83 Add an event to a SharePoint calendar with a check for overlapping events

Problem

You have an InfoPath form which you want to use to fill out details for an event or meeting and then when you submit this form, a new event should be added to a calendar on a SharePoint site. In addition, you also want the form to check for and prevent times to be selected that would overlap with existing events in the SharePoint calendar.

Solution

You can use a SharePoint Designer workflow to add a new item to a calendar on a SharePoint site. And to detect whether there are any overlapping events, you can use SharePoint's REST interface to retrieve all of the events between a start date and an end date, and then narrow down the search results further by using filters in the InfoPath form.

This solution consists of two parts: 1. Design a form template that can check for overlapping events, and 2. Create a SharePoint Designer workflow that adds a new event to the SharePoint calendar whenever a new form is submitted.

To create an InfoPath form that can check for overlapping events in a SharePoint calendar:

1. In InfoPath, create a new SharePoint form library form template or use an existing one.
2. Add a **Text Box** control to the view of the form template and name it **eventTitle**.

Chapter 5: Use SharePoint Designer Workflows with InfoPath Forms

3. Add two **Date and Time Picker** controls to the view of the form template and name them **startDateTime** and **endDateTime**, respectively.

4. Add **Validation** rules to both **startDateTime** and **endDateTime** that ensure that **startDateTime** falls before **endDateTime**, and **endDateTime** falls after **startDateTime**.

5. Add a **Button** control to the view of the form template and label it **Check Overlapping Events**.

6. Add a second **Button** control to the view of the form template and label it **Add Event**.

7. Add a **Section** control to the view of the form template and type the text "One or more events already exist for the time slot you selected" on the section. Change the color of the text to red.

8. Whenever a user selects a start or end date and time, a check must be performed on the SharePoint calendar to see whether the dates and times for the new event would overlap with those of existing events. For this, you must first retrieve all of the events that fall on and between the start and end dates entered on the form. You can use SharePoint's REST interface to do this, so select **Data ▶ Get External Data ▶ From Web Service ▶ From REST Web Service**.

9. On the **Data Connection Wizard**, enter the REST Web Service URL for the SharePoint calendar:

   ```
   http://servername/sitename/_vti_bin/ListData.svc/Calendar?$select=Title,StartTime,EndTime&$inlinecount=allpages
   ```

   where **servername** is the name of the SharePoint server where a site named **sitename** and a SharePoint calendar named **Calendar** are located. Click **Next**. Important: Ensure the SharePoint calendar contains at least one event; otherwise the **entry** group node will be missing from the resulting data source.

10. On the **Data Connection Wizard**, name the data connection **GetCalendarEvents**, deselect the **Automatically retrieve data when form is opened** check box, and click **Finish**.

11. The REST web service data connection should retrieve all of the events on the days on and between the days specified in the **startDateTime** and **endDateTime** fields, so you still have to filter the results to find only those events where not only the dates but also the times specified in the **startDateTime** and **endDateTime** fields would overlap with other events. For this you can use a comparison filter on the **GetCalendarEvents** secondary data source. On the **Fields** task pane, add a hidden **Field (element)** with the data type **Text (string)** to the Main data source and name the field **amountOfOverlappingEvents**. You will use this field to store the results of the filtering.

12. Add a **Formatting** rule to the section control you added in step 7 with a **Condition** that says:

    ```
    amountOfOverlappingEvents is blank
    or
    amountOfOverlappingEvents = "0"
    ```

    and that has a formatting of **Hide this control**. This formatting rule hides the section if the **amountOfOverlappingEvents** field is blank or has a value equal to **0**.

13. Add an **Action** rule to the **Check Overlapping Events** button with a **Condition** that says:

    ```
    startDateTime is not blank
    and
    endDateTime is not blank
    ```

    and with a first action that says:

    ```
    Change REST URL: REST Web Service
    ```

    that changes the **REST Web Service URL** using the following formula:

    ```
    concat("http://servername/sitename/_vti_bin/ListData.svc/Calendar?$select=T
    itle,StartTime,EndTime&$inlinecount=allpages&$filter=(StartTime le
    datetime'", startDateTime, "' or StartTime le datetime'", endDateTime, "')
    and (EndTime ge datetime'", startDateTime, "' or EndTime ge datetime'",
    endDateTime, "')")
    ```

    This action adds parameters to the REST web service URL to retrieve only those events that fall between the selected start date and end date.

    Add a second action that says:

    ```
    Query using a data connection: GetCalendarEvents
    ```

    This action queries the data connection to retrieve the results.

    Add a third action that says:

    ```
    Set a field's value: amountOfOverlappingEvents = count(entry[(msxsl:string-
    compare(StartTime, startDateTime) < 0 or msxsl:string-compare(StartTime,
    endDateTime) < 0) and (msxsl:string-compare(EndTime, startDateTime) > 0 or
    msxsl:string-compare(EndTime, endDateTime) > 0)])
    ```

    or

    ```
    count(xdXDocument:GetDOM("GetCalendarEvents")/ns1:feed/ns1:entry[(msxsl:str
    ing-compare(ns1:content/m:properties/d:StartTime, xdXDocument:get-
    DOM()/my:myFields/my:startDateTime) < 0 or msxsl:string-
    compare(ns1:content/m:properties/d:StartTime, xdXDocument:get-
    DOM()/my:myFields/my:endDateTime) < 0) and (msxsl:string-
    compare(ns1:content/m:properties/d:EndTime, xdXDocument:get-
    DOM()/my:myFields/my:startDateTime) > 0 or msxsl:string-
    compare(ns1:content/m:properties/d:EndTime, xdXDocument:get-
    ```

Chapter 5: Use SharePoint Designer Workflows with InfoPath Forms

```
DOM()/my:myFields/my:endDateTime) > 0)])
```

if you have the **Edit XPath (advanced)** check box selected on the **Insert Formula** dialog box when constructing the formula. What this formula does is filter the **entry** group node in the **GetCalendarEvents** secondary data source on the following:

```
(StartTime < startDateTime or StartTime < endDateTime)
and
(EndTime > startDateTime or EndTime > endDateTime)
```

where **StartTime** and **EndTime** are located under the **m:properties** group node of the **GetCalendarEvents** secondary data source and **startDateTime** and **endDateTime** are located in the Main data source of the form.

The third action sets the value of the **amountOfOverlappingEvents** field to a formula that counts the amount of events that overlap with the specified start and end times.

Note: If the **entry** group node is missing from the schema of the **GetCalendarEvents** secondary data source, ensure the calendar already contains at least one event. If it does not, add a dummy event to the calendar, refresh the schema of **GetCalendarEvents** secondary data source by clicking **Data** ➤ **Get External Data** ➤ **Data Connections** and modifying the data connection by just going through the steps of the **Data Connection Wizard** again without changing any existing settings, and then try again.

14. In SharePoint, create a form library named **SubmittedCalendarEvents** (also see the first part of recipe *16 Create a form library and edit its form template*).

15. In InfoPath, configure a **Submit** data connection to submit the form to the **SubmittedCalendarEvents** form library (also see recipe *18 Submit a form to a form library and then close it*) and name the data connection **SharePoint Library Submit**.

16. Add an **Action** rule to the **Add Event** button with a **Condition** that says:

```
startDateTime is not blank
and
endDateTime is not blank
```

and two actions that say:

```
Submit using a data connection: SharePoint Library Submit
Close this form: No Prompt
```

where **SharePoint Library Submit** is the submit data connection that submits the form to the **SubmittedCalendarEvents** form library.

17. Remove all of the toolbars from the browser form's interface as described in recipe *17 Hide or show toolbar buttons for a form*.

InfoPath 2010 Cookbook 2

18. Publish the form template as a site content type named **AddCalendarEventCT** (see recipe *26 Publish a form template as a site content type*), and promote the **eventTitle**, **startDateTime**, and **endDateTime** fields during the publishing process (also see recipe *23 Promote form fields to columns of a form library* and *24 Promote form fields to existing site columns*). Note that you could also publish the form template directly to a SharePoint form library instead of a site content type. A site content type is used here to be able to create a reusable workflow that runs only on forms that are based on the **AddCalendarEventCT** content type.

To create a SharePoint Designer workflow that runs and adds a new event to the SharePoint calendar whenever a new form is submitted to the form library:

1. In SharePoint Designer 2010, create a new reusable workflow that is based on the **AddCalendarEventCT** content type, and name the workflow **AddCalendarEventWF** (also see recipe *75 Create a workflow that runs on a specific type of form*).

2. On the workflow editor, click to place the cursor inside of **Step 1**, and then select **Workflow ➤ Insert ➤ Action ➤ List Actions ➤ Create List Item**.

3. Click **this list** in the sentence for the workflow action.

4. On the **Create New List Item** dialog box, select **Calendar** from the **List** drop-down list box, and then set the **Title** field to get its value from the **eventTitle** field in the **Current Item**, the **Start Time** field to get its value from the **startDateTime** field in the **Current Item**, and the **End Time** field to get its value from the **endDateTime** field in the **Current Item**.

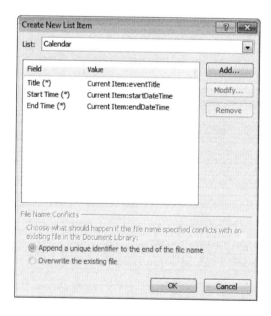

Figure 287. The completed Create New List Item dialog box in SharePoint Designer 2010.

Chapter 5: Use SharePoint Designer Workflows with InfoPath Forms

Click **OK** when you are done.

Figure 288. The completed workflow step in SharePoint Designer 2010.

5. Publish the workflow.
6. In SharePoint, add the **AddCalendarEventCT** content type to the **SubmittedCalendarEvents** form library (also see recipe *27 Enable different types of forms to be created in one form library*) and then add the workflow to the **AddCalendarEventCT** content type (also see recipe *76 Add a workflow to a specific type of form in a form library*) and select the option to **Start this workflow when a new item is created** when you add the workflow to the content type.

In SharePoint, navigate to the **SubmittedCalendarEvents** form library and add a new form that is based on the **AddCalendarEventCT** content type to the form library. When the form opens, enter event details and then click the **Check Overlapping Events** button to verify that it is working properly and to find overlapping events. Click the **Add Event** button to submit the form to the form library and start the workflow. Once the workflow has run and completed, navigate to the SharePoint calendar and verify that a new event was created for the form you submitted.

Discussion

In the solution described above you used a combination of the filtering of SharePoint list data on the server and data filtering in the InfoPath form itself to be able to find overlapping events in a SharePoint calendar. You performed filtering on the server through SharePoint's REST interface and you performed filtering in the InfoPath form through filters on the secondary data source of the REST web service data connection.

Because standard SharePoint list data connections only allow exact queries to be sent to SharePoint, you are not able to use them to check for overlapping events in a period of time. For example, suppose there is an event booked in a SharePoint calendar on April 13. If you wanted to know whether there were any events that fell between April 7 and April 20, you could set the **StartTime** and **EndTime** query fields of a data connection for the SharePoint calendar list to the respective dates, but that query would return zero results, because when you pass a start date of April 7 and an end date of April 20 to query the data connection, an event with that exact start date and end date would try to be retrieved. And while there may be one or more events that lie within that period of time, you would not be able to find them. Here is where using SharePoint's REST interface proves to be a bit more useful.

84 Start a SharePoint workflow by clicking on a button on an InfoPath form

Problem

You want to click a button on an InfoPath form to start and run a workflow in SharePoint.

Solution

You can use the **UpdateListItems** operation of SharePoint's **Lists** web service and a 'helper list' in SharePoint to start a workflow when an item is added to that list.

To start and run a SharePoint workflow by clicking on a button on an InfoPath form:

1. In SharePoint, create a custom list via **Site Actions** ➤ **More Options** or **Site Actions** ➤ **View All Site Content** ➤ **Create** with a **Title** column, and name the list **StartWorkflow**.

2. Click **List Tools** ➤ **List** ➤ **Settings** ➤ **List Settings** to navigate to the **List Settings** page of the **StartWorkflow** list and then copy the GUID from the browser's address bar. It should look something like the following:

   `%7BADFA2558%2DB237%2D491B%2D8E86%2D1F8A7ADFF3E0%7D`

3. Convert the **%7B** characters to **{**, **%2D** to **-**, and **%7D** to **}**. The resulting list GUID should now resemble the following:

   `{ADFA2558-B237-491B-8E86-1F8A7ADFF3E0}`

   Copy it to the Windows clipboard.

4. In Notepad, create a file with the following contents:

   ```
   <Batch>
     <Method ID="1" Cmd="New">
       <Field Name="Title">Start Workflow</Field>
     </Method>
   </Batch>
   ```

   Save the file to disk with the name **StartWorkflowBatch.xml**. The **StartWorkflowBatch.xml** file is also available for download from www.bizsupportonline.com.

5. In InfoPath, create a new SharePoint form library form template or use an existing one.

6. On the **Fields** task pane, add a hidden field named **listName** to the Main data source and set its **Default Value** to be equal to the list GUID from step 3.

Chapter 5: Use SharePoint Designer Workflows with InfoPath Forms

7. Select **Data** ▶ **Get External Data** ▶ **From Other Sources** ▶ **From XML File** to add an XML data connection for the **StartWorkflowBatch.xml** file, and leave the **Automatically retrieve data when form is opened** check box on the **Data Connection Wizard** selected when you add the data connection.

8. The contents of the XML file should be submitted to the **Lists** web service in SharePoint to add a new item to the **StartWorkflow** list. So select **Data** ▶ **Submit Form** ▶ **To Other Locations** ▶ **To Web Service**.

9. On the **Data Connection Wizard**, enter the URL of the **Lists** web service, for example:

    ```
    http://servername/sitename/_vti_bin/Lists.asmx
    ```

    and click **Next**. Here, **servername** is the name of the SharePoint server and **sitename** is the site where the **StartWorkflow** SharePoint list is located.

10. Select the **UpdateListItems** operation from the list of operations, and click **Next**.

11. Select **tns:listName** in the **Parameters** list and click the button behind the **Field or group** text box.

12. On the **Select a Field or Group** dialog box, select **listName**, and click **OK**. With this you have set the **listName** parameter of the web service to be equal to the value of the **listName** field in the Main data source of the form that contains the GUID of the **StartWorkflow** SharePoint list.

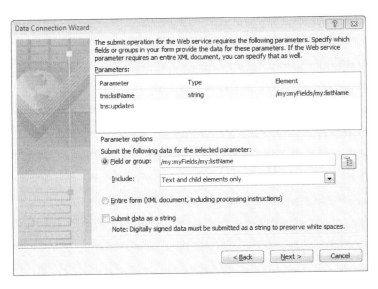

Figure 289. The Data Connection Wizard after setting the value of the first parameter.

13. On the **Data Connection Wizard**, select **tns:updates** in the **Parameters** list, and click the button behind the **Field or group** text box.

353

InfoPath 2010 Cookbook 2

14. On the **Select a Field or Group** dialog box, select **StartWorkflowBatch (Secondary)** from the **Fields** drop-down list box, select the **Batch** group node, and click **OK**. With this you have set the **updates** parameter of the web service to be equal to the contents of the entire **Batch** node in the secondary data source for the XML file you added earlier.

15. On the **Data Connection Wizard**, select **XML subtree, including selected element** from the **Include** drop-down list box, and click **Next**.

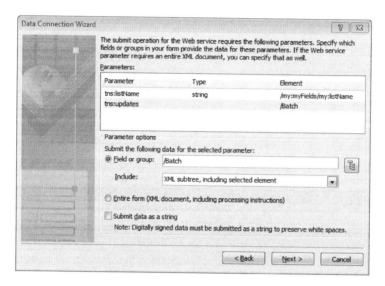

Figure 290. The Data Connection Wizard after setting the second parameter.

This setting will submit the entire XML contents of the **Batch** node including its child nodes and values to the web service.

16. Name the data connection **UpdateListItems**, deselect the **Set as the default submit connection** check box, and click **Finish**.

Note that while you have created a submit connection to call the **Lists** web service, you should add another submit connection to the form template that does the actual submitting of the form, for example to a SharePoint form library (also see recipe *18 Submit a form to a form library and then close it*). The submit connection for the web service is not meant to submit the form; it is only meant to call the web service to add a new item to the **StartWorkflow** SharePoint list.

17. Add a **Button** control to the view of the form template and label it **Start Workflow**.

18. Add an **Action** rule to the button that says:

    Submit using a data connection: UpdateListItems

This action rule calls the **UpdateListItems** operation of the **Lists** web service to add a new list item to the **StartWorkflow** SharePoint list.

354

Chapter 5: Use SharePoint Designer Workflows with InfoPath Forms

19. Publish the form template to a SharePoint form library.

20. In SharePoint Designer 2010, create a new **List Workflow** that runs on the **StartWorkflow** SharePoint list (also see recipe *72 Create a workflow that runs on new forms in a specific form library*) and that performs actions of your choice, for example creates a list item in another list, logs a message to the workflow history list, or sends an email. Ensure you set the start options for the workflow to **Start workflow automatically when an item is created** before you publish the workflow.

In SharePoint, navigate to the form library where you published the form template and add a new form. When the form opens, click the **Start Workflow** button. Close the form. Navigate to the **StartWorkflow** SharePoint list and check whether a new item was created and that the workflow was started. Once the workflow has completed, verify that the workflow performed the actions you wanted it to perform.

If no new item was added to the **StartWorkflow** SharePoint list after you clicked the **Start Workflow** button, you should get an administrator to check for any error messages that could be related to the form (such as "Form submission failed.") in the SharePoint log files, which in a default SharePoint installation are located under

```
C:\Program Files\Common Files\Microsoft Shared\Web Server Extensions\14\LOGS
```

For example, if you made a mistake while copying and converting the GUID of the **StartWorkflow** SharePoint list (steps 2 and 3 of the solution), you could wind up with an error message such as the following in the SharePoint log files:

List does not exist. The page you selected contains a list that does not exist. It may have been deleted by another user.

If you get this error, double-check the GUID of the SharePoint list, correct it if necessary, republish the form template, and try again.

Discussion

The solution described above is based on two principles:

1. You can add a new item to a SharePoint list from within an InfoPath form by calling the **UpdateListItems** operation of the **Lists** web service through a web service submit data connection.

2. You can automatically start and run a workflow in SharePoint whenever a new item is added to a SharePoint list.

Because there is no direct way to start a workflow from within an InfoPath form without writing code, the solution described above can be seen as a workaround, so should be used sparingly.

85 Create a new InfoPath form through a workflow

Problem

You want to use a SharePoint Designer 2010 workflow to create a new InfoPath form in a particular form library and also have the workflow fill out the values of fields in the form it creates.

Solution

You can add a site content type that inherits from the **Form** content type to a SharePoint site and then set a copy of the XML file for the form you want to create a new instance of as the document template of the content type. Once you have added the content type to the SharePoint site, you can use this content type and a SharePoint Designer workflow to create a new InfoPath form.

There are two parts to this solution: First you must add a site content type to a SharePoint site, and then you must create a SharePoint Designer workflow.

To add a new site content type for creating InfoPath documents:

1. In InfoPath, create a new SharePoint form library form template or use an existing one, ensure it contains a text field named **lastName**, and publish the form template as a site content type named **CreateFormsCT** (also see recipe *26 Publish a form template as a site content type*). When you publish the form template to SharePoint, ensure you promote the **lastName** field as an existing site column named **Last Name** (also see recipe *24 Promote form fields to existing site columns*) and that you select the **Allow users to edit data in this field by using a datasheet or properties page** check box for the promoted field.

2. In SharePoint, create a form library named **CreateFormsLib** or use an existing form library, and then add the **CreateFormsCT** content type to this form library (also see recipe *27 Enable different types of forms to be created in one form library*). When you add the site content type to the form library, the **Last Name** site column should automatically appear on the form library as a column.

Columns

A column stores information about each document in the document library. Because this document library allows multiple content types, some column settings, such as whether information is required or optional for a column, are now specified by the content type of the document. The following columns are currently available in this document library:

Column (click to edit)	Type	Used in
Last Name	Single line of text	CreateFormsCT
Title	Single line of text	
Created By	Person or Group	
Modified By	Person or Group	
Checked Out To	Person or Group	

Figure 291. The Last Name column has become available in the form library.

Chapter 5: Use SharePoint Designer Workflows with InfoPath Forms

3. Navigate to the **CreateFormsLib** form library and add a new form that is based on the **CreateFormsCT** content type to the form library. You can prefill this form with data or leave all fields empty; whichever fits your scenario. Save the form to the form library and name it **template** or anything else you wish; the name you give the form is irrelevant for making the solution work.

4. Hover over the new form you just added to the form library, click the drop-down arrow that appears on the right-hand side of the form's name, and select **Send To ➤ Download a Copy** from the drop-down menu.

5. On the **File Download** dialog box, click **Save**, and save the file somewhere locally on disk as **template.xml**.

6. In SharePoint, delete the **template** form from the **CreateFormsLib** form library, since you do not need it anymore.

7. Now you must create a second site content type that uses the InfoPath form you just downloaded. So click **Site Actions ➤ Site Settings**.

8. On the **Site Settings** page under **Galleries**, click **Site content types**.

9. On the **Site Content Types** page, click **Create**.

10. On the **New Site Content Type** page, enter a **Name** for the content type (for example **CreateFormDocCT**), select **Document Content Types** from the **Select parent content type from** drop-down list box, select **Form** from the **Parent Content Type** drop-down list box, leave **Custom Content Types** selected in the **Existing group** drop-down list box, and click **OK**.

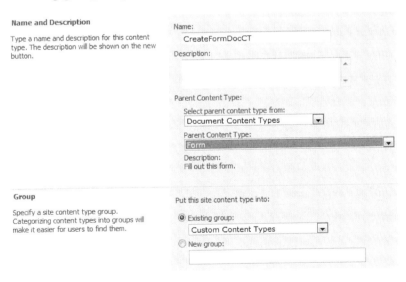

Figure 292. Creating a new Form content type in SharePoint 2010.

Because InfoPath forms are generally created from content types that have the **Form** content type as their parent, it is logical to base the **CreateFormDocCT** content type on the **Form** parent content type, so that the **CreateFormDocCT** inherits the same metadata from the **Form** parent content type as a normal content type for an InfoPath form would. However, you could have also based the new site content type on the **Document** parent content type, which is the parent content type of the **Form** parent content type; or even on the site content type of the form template you published in step 1.

11. On the details page of the new content type under **Settings**, click **Advanced settings**.

12. On the **Advanced Settings** page, select **Upload a new document template**, and click **Browse**.

13. On the **Choose a File to Upload** dialog box, select the **template.xml** file you saved earlier, and click **Open**.

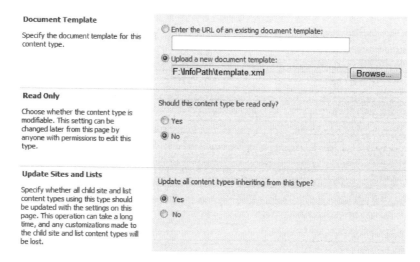

Figure 293. Setting the InfoPath form as the document template for the content type.

14. On the **Advanced Settings** page, click **OK**. With this you have set the new site content type to use an XML file (InfoPath form) instead of an XSN file (InfoPath form template) as its document template.

15. On the details page of the new site content type under **Columns**, click **Add from existing site columns**.

16. On the **Add Columns to Content Type** page, search for the site columns you used in step 1 in the list of **Available columns**, and click **Add** to add them to the list of **Columns to add**. Click **OK** when you are done.

17. Navigate to the **CreateFormsLib** form library, and add the **CreateFormDocCT** content type to the form library (also see recipe *27 Enable different types of forms to*

Chapter 5: Use SharePoint Designer Workflows with InfoPath Forms

be created in one form library). Use the **Change new button order and default content type** link to deselect the **Visible** check boxes for the **Form** and **CreateFormDocCT** content types, so that users cannot use them to add forms to the form library. This should automatically make the **CreateFormsCT** the **Default Content Type** of the form library (also see recipe *28 Change the default form template of a form library*). Note that the **CreateFormDocCT** content type should only be used by the SharePoint Designer 2010 workflow (and not by users) to create InfoPath forms.

Content Types

This document library is configured to allow multiple content types. Use content types to specify the information you want to display about an item, in addition to its policies, workflows, or other behavior. The following content types are currently available in this library:

Content Type	Visible on New Button	Default Content Type
CreateFormsCT	✔	✔
Form		
CreateFormDocCT		

Figure 294. Content types associated with the form library in SharePoint 2010.

After adding the **CreateFormDocCT** content type to the form library, you should notice that the **Last Name** column is now shared by the **CreateFormsCT**, the **CreateFormDocCT**, and the form library.

Columns

A column stores information about each document in the document library. Because this document library allows multiple content types, some column settings, such as whether information is required or optional for a column, are now specified by the content type of the document. The following columns are currently available in this document library:

Column (click to edit)	Type	Used in
Last Name	Single line of text	CreateFormsCT, CreateFormDocCT
Title	Single line of text	
Created By	Person or Group	
Modified By	Person or Group	
Checked Out To	Person or Group	

Figure 295. Columns on the form library in SharePoint 2010.

With this you have added a site content type that can be used by a workflow to create new InfoPath forms based on the form template you published earlier to the form library. Note that if you change and republish the form template in the future, you will have to go through all of the steps (except for creating a new site content type) again to replace the old **template.xml** file of the **CreateFormDocCT** content type with a new form that is based on the modified form template.

For simplicity's sake, let us say you have a SharePoint list named **Contacts**, which contains last names stored in its **Title** column. Whenever a new item is added to this list, you want to have a SharePoint Designer workflow create a new InfoPath form in the **CreateFormsLib** form library with the same name you entered into the **Title** column and also write this name to the **lastName** text field in the form and which you promoted as a site column named **Last Name**.

InfoPath 2010 Cookbook 2

To create a SharePoint Designer 2010 workflow that creates an InfoPath form:

1. In SharePoint Designer 2010, open a connection to the SharePoint site where the **Contacts** list and **CreateFormsLib** form library are located.

2. Add a **List Workflow** and associate it with the **Contacts** list (also see recipe *72 Create a workflow that runs on new forms in a specific form library*). Name the workflow **CreateFormWF**. Note that you could also create a reusable workflow instead of a list workflow if you wanted to.

3. On the workflow editor, click to place the cursor inside of **Step 1**, and then select **Workflow ▶ Insert ▶ Action ▶ List Actions ▶ Create List Item** to add a **Create List Item** workflow action to **Step 1**.

4. Click **this list** in the sentence for the workflow action.

5. On the **Create New List Item** dialog box, select the **CreateFormsLib** form library from the **List** drop-down list box, select **Content Type ID** in the fields list, and click **Modify**.

6. On the **Value Assignment** dialog box, select **CreateFormDocCT** from the **To this value** drop-down list box, and click **OK**.

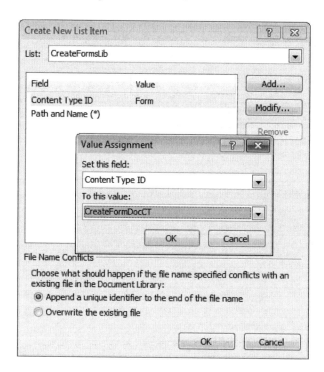

Figure 296. Selecting the content type to use to create a list item in SharePoint Designer 2010.

Chapter 5: Use SharePoint Designer Workflows with InfoPath Forms

With this you have set the content type of the new list item that should be created to be equal to the **CreateFormDocCT** content type, which makes use of an InfoPath form (XML file) as its document template.

7. On the **Create New List Item** dialog box, select **Path and Name (*)** in the fields list, and click **Modify**.

8. On the **Value Assignment** dialog box, click the formula button (second button) behind the **To this value** text box.

9. On the **Lookup for String** dialog box, leave **Current Item** selected in the **Data source** drop-down list box (this is the **Contacts** list item the workflow is running on), select **Title** from the **Field from source** drop-down list box, and click **OK**.

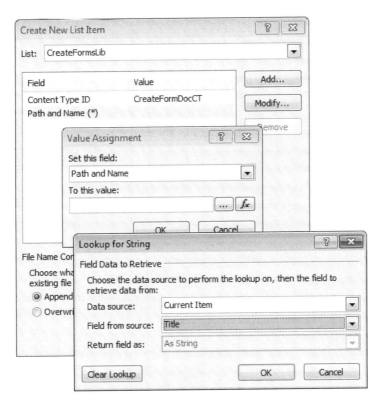

Figure 297. Setting the path and name of the new item in SharePoint Designer 2010.

Note that the path and name field should not contain any periods, since this would interfere with the newly created InfoPath form being recognized as a valid file type. And since it is difficult to prevent users from adding periods to any text they enter unless you customize the SharePoint list form and add data validation to the InfoPath form for the SharePoint list to prevent faulty data entry, you may want to use something other than the value of the **Title** field of the list item as the path and

InfoPath 2010 Cookbook 2

name for the newly created InfoPath form (see for example steps 26 through 31 of recipe *86 Create a new form and link it to an existing form through a workflow*).

10. On the **Value Assignment** dialog box, click **OK**.

11. On the **Create New List Item** dialog box, click **Add**.

12. On the **Value Assignment** dialog box, select **Last Name** from the **Set this field** drop-down list box, and click the formula button (second button) behind the **To this value** text box.

13. On the **Lookup for Single line of text** dialog box, leave **Current Item** selected in the **Data source** drop-down list box (this is the **Contacts** list item the workflow is running on), select **Title** from the **Field from source** drop-down list box, and click **OK**.

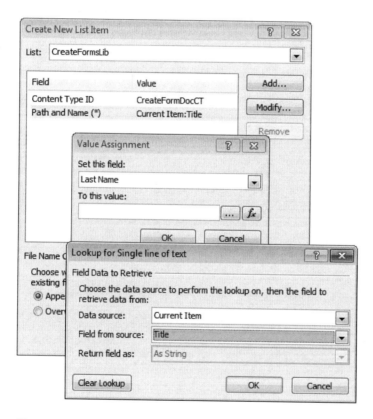

Figure 298. Setting the value of the last name field in SharePoint Designer 2010.

14. On the **Value Assignment** dialog box, click **OK**. With this you have set the value of the **Last Name** column of the content type (**lastName** field on the InfoPath form) to be equal the value of the **Title** field in the **Contacts** list.

Chapter 5: Use SharePoint Designer Workflows with InfoPath Forms

15. On the **Create New List Item** dialog box, click **OK**.

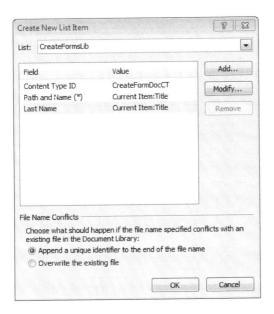

Figure 299. The final Create New List Item dialog box in SharePoint Designer 2010.

Figure 300. The completed workflow step in SharePoint Designer 2010.

16. Click **Workflow** ➤ **Manage** ➤ **Workflow Settings**.

17. On the workflow settings page under the **Start Options** section, select the **Start workflow automatically when an item is created** check box.

18. Click **Workflow Settings** ➤ **Save** ➤ **Publish** to publish the workflow.

In SharePoint, navigate to the **Contacts** list and add a new list item. The workflow should automatically start. After the workflow has run and completed, navigate to the **CreateFormsLib** form library to see whether a new InfoPath form with the name you entered as the **Title** for the item in the **Contacts** list has been created. Click to open the InfoPath form and check whether the **lastName** field was populated with the value from the workflow.

Discussion

In the solution described above you made use of two different content types to create InfoPath forms: One content type (**CreateFormsCT**) was used by users to manually create InfoPath forms within SharePoint, while the other content type

InfoPath 2010 Cookbook 2

(**CreateFormDocCT**) was used by a SharePoint Designer 2010 workflow to automatically create InfoPath forms in a form library.

The main difference between the two content types used in the solution described above is that the content type that is used by users in SharePoint to create InfoPath forms (**CreateFormsCT**) has an InfoPath form template (XSN file) defined as its document template, while the content type that is used by SharePoint Designer 2010 to create InfoPath forms (**CreateFormDocCT**) has an XML file defined as its document template. The XML file of the second content type is an InfoPath form that is linked to the same InfoPath form template that is defined as the document template of the first content type.

Using the XML file as the document template for the content type used by the workflow is required, because if you use the **Create List Item** workflow action to create an item based on a content type that has an InfoPath form template (XSN file) as its document template, a new XSN file (InfoPath form template) will be created in the form library instead of a new XML file (InfoPath form). This also means that if you ever update and republish the InfoPath form template linked to the first content type, you must recreate the XML file and update the document template of the second content type to keep them in sync with each other.

While you published the form template as a site content type, you could have also published the form template directly to the form library, promoted the **lastName** field as a list column on the form library, and then added that list column to the content type that should automatically create forms. You will learn how to do the latter in recipe *86 Create a new form and link it to an existing form through a workflow*. In addition to promoting the form field, you also enabled the field to be editable by selecting the **Allow users to edit data in this field by using a datasheet or properties page** check box when promoting the field through the **Publishing Wizard** during the publishing process, so that the workflow could update the value of that field.

The figure below summarizes the construction of this solution and also shows the relationship between the form library, site columns, content types, and document templates.

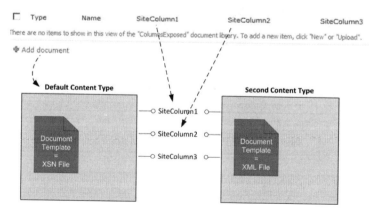

Figure 301. Relationship between the form library, site columns, and content types.

Chapter 5: Use SharePoint Designer Workflows with InfoPath Forms

In the previous figure:

- The **Default Content Type** is used whenever a user clicks **Add document** to create a new form in the form library in SharePoint, while the **Second Content Type** is used by a SharePoint Designer 2010 workflow to create new InfoPath forms. In the solution described above, **CreateFormsCT** was the default content type, but you could add more form templates as content types to the form library as described in recipe *27 Enable different types of forms to be created in one form library* and the solution should still work.

- Both content types are linked to the same site columns, which are also defined on the form library, so all share the same type of columns.

- Because you enabled the form fields to be editable when you promoted them from within InfoPath Designer 2010 when you published the form template, users are able to update the values of the fields through the properties page of a list item and have these changes appear in forms created using either content type. In addition, this also enables a SharePoint Designer workflow to update the values of fields in forms derived from the **Second Content Type**.

Note that the sole purpose of the SharePoint Designer workflow in the solution described above is to create and fill out a new form with data. The SharePoint Designer workflow cannot run rules and other business logic that are contained within an InfoPath form

86 Create a new form and link it to an existing form through a workflow

Problem

You have a form in which project information is entered, and you want to be able to submit this form to a form library and have a related form in which project approval information is entered to be automatically created in another form library.

Solution

You can use a combination of property promotion in forms and a SharePoint Designer workflow to create related forms in two separate form libraries.

It is recommended that you go through recipe *85 Create a new InfoPath form through a workflow* first before going through this recipe, since recipe 85 explains the basics of creating InfoPath forms through a SharePoint Designer workflow and this recipe expands on the concepts learned in recipe 85.

To create a new form and link it to an existing form through a SharePoint Designer workflow:

1. In InfoPath, create a new SharePoint form library form template and save it as **ProjectInfo.xsn**.

2. Add two **Text Box** controls to the view of the form template and name them **projectName** and **projectDescription**, respectively.

3. Publish the form template to a form library named **ProjectInfoLib** (also see recipe *21 Publish a form template to a form library*), and promote the **projectName** field as a readable but not editable field to the form library during the publishing process (also see recipe *23 Promote form fields to columns of a form library*).

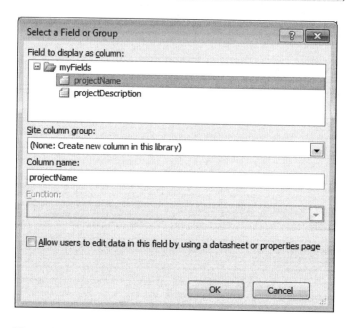

Figure 302. Promoting the projectName field to a new column of the form library.

4. Create a second SharePoint form library form template and save it as **ProjectApproval.xsn**.

5. Add a **Receive** data connection to the **ProjectInfoLib** form library to the form template (also see recipe *57 Retrieve a list of forms from a form library*). Ensure you select **ID** and **project Name** as fields to include in the data source, and that you deselect the **Automatically retrieve data when form is opened** check box.

6. On the **Fields** task pane, add a hidden **Field (element)** of type **Text (string)** and which has the name **projectID** to the Main data source. You are going to use this field to store the **ID** of the **ProjectInfo** form that should be linked to the **ProjectApproval** form.

7. On the **Fields** task pane, select **ProjectInfoLib (Secondary)** from the **Fields** drop-down list box, and then drag-and-drop the **projectName** field from under the **d:SharePointListItem_RW** repeating group node under the **dataFields** group node onto the view and bind it to a **Repeating Section with Controls**.

Chapter 5: Use SharePoint Designer Workflows with InfoPath Forms

8. Click **Data** ➤ **Rules** ➤ **Form Load** and add an **Action** rule that has two actions that say:

   ```
   Set a field's value: ID = projectID
   Query using a data connection: ProjectInfoLib
   ```

   where **ID** is the **ID** field that is located under the **q:SharePointListItem_RW** group node under the **queryFields** group node of the **ProjectInfoLib (Secondary)** data source, and **projectID** is the hidden field located in the Main data source. What this action rule does is query the secondary data source to retrieve the project that corresponds to the ID stored in the **projectID** field. The **projectID** field serves as the link between the two forms.

9. Add any other controls that you would like to place on the project approval form.

10. Publish the form template to a form library named **ProjectApprovalLib**, and promote the **projectID** field as an editable field to the form library (select the **Allow users to edit data in this field by using a datasheet or properties page** check box) during the publishing process.

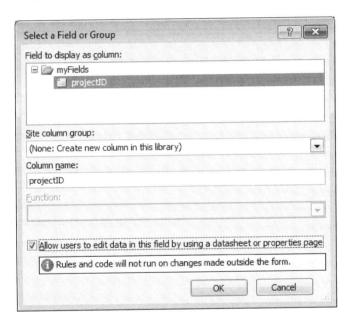

Figure 303. Promoting the project ID field to a new column of the form library.

11. In SharePoint, navigate to the **ProjectApprovalLib** form library and add a new blank form to it. Name the form **template** or anything you like.

12. Download a copy of the newly created form, save it locally on disk, and then delete it from the **ProjectApprovalLib** form library.

13. Manually create a new site content type named **ApprovalFormDocCT** (also see *Create a new site content type* in the Appendix) that inherits from the **Form** parent

367

content type. Do not set its document template or add any columns to the new site content type.

14. Add the **ApprovalFormDocCT** content type to the **ProjectApprovalLib** form library (also see recipe *27 Enable different types of forms to be created in one form library*).

15. On the **Form Library Settings** page of the **ProjectApprovalLib** form library, click **ApprovalFormDocCT** under **Content Types** to navigate to the details page of the **ApprovalFormDocCT** list content type.

16. On the details page of the **ApprovalFormDocCT** list content type, under **Columns**, click **Add from existing site or list columns**.

17. On the **Add Columns to Content Type** page, leave **List Columns** selected in the **Select columns from** drop-down list box, select **projectID** from the **Available columns** list, click **Add**, and then click **OK**. This action copies the **projectID** column of the form library, which is also the column the **projectID** field was promoted to, onto the content type.

Figure 304. Adding the projectID column of the form library to the list content type.

18. On the details page of the **ApprovalFormDocCT** list content type, under **Settings**, click **Advanced settings**.

19. On the **Advanced Settings** page, select **Upload a new document template**, click **Browse**, and then browse to and open the InfoPath form you downloaded earlier as the document template for the content type. Click **OK** when you are done.

20. Navigate back to the **Form Library Settings** page and then under **Content Types**, click the **Change new button order and default content type** link, and then make the **ApprovalFormDocCT** content type invisible.

Chapter 5: Use SharePoint Designer Workflows with InfoPath Forms

Content Types

This document library is configured to allow multiple content types. Use content types to specify the information you want to display about an item, in addition to its policies, workflows, or other behavior. The following content types are currently available in this library:

Content Type	Visible on New Button	Default Content Type
Form	✔	✔
ApprovalFormDocCT		

Figure 305. Content types defined on the SharePoint form library.

Columns

A column stores information about each document in the document library. Because this document library allows multiple content types, some column settings, such as whether information is required or optional for a column, are now specified by the content type of the document. The following columns are currently available in this document library:

Column (click to edit)	Type	Used in
projectID	Single line of text	Form, ApprovalFormDocCT
Title	Single line of text	
Created By	Person or Group	
Modified By	Person or Group	
Checked Out To	Person or Group	

Figure 306. Columns defined on the SharePoint form library.

As shown in the figure above, the default content type (**Form**) of the form library, the invisible **ApprovalFormDocCT** list content type associated with the form library, and the form library share the same **projectID** column.

21. In SharePoint Designer 2010, create a new **List Workflow** and associate it with the **ProjectInfoLib** form library (also see recipe *72 Create a workflow that runs on new forms in a specific form library*). Name the workflow **CreateApprovalFormWF**.

22. On the workflow editor, click inside of **Step 1** to place the cursor, and then select **Workflow ➤ Insert ➤ Action ➤ List Actions ➤ Create List Item** to add a **Create List Item** workflow action to **Step 1**.

23. Click **this list** in the sentence for the workflow action.

24. On the **Create New List Item** dialog box, select **ProjectApprovalLib** from the **List** drop-down list box, select the **Content Type ID** in the list of fields, and click **Modify**.

25. On the **Value Assignment** dialog box, leave **Content Type ID** selected in the **Set this field** drop-down list box, select **ApprovalFormDocCT** from the **To this value** drop-down list box, and click **OK**. With this you have set the new item to be based on the **ApprovalFormDocCT** content type.

26. On the **Create New List Item** dialog box, select the **Path and Name (*)** in the list of fields, and click **Modify**.

InfoPath 2010 Cookbook 2

27. On the **Value Assignment** dialog box, leave **Path and Name** selected in the **Set this field** drop-down list box, and click the ellipsis button (first button) behind the **To this value** text box.

28. On the **String Builder** dialog box, type **ApprovalForm_** and then click **Add or Change Lookup**.

29. On the **Lookup for String** dialog box, leave **Current Item** selected in the **Data source** drop-down list box, select **ID** from the **Field from source** drop-down list box, and click **OK**.

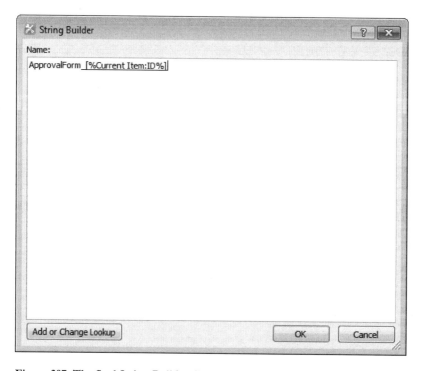

Figure 307. The final String Builder dialog box in SharePoint Designer 2010.

30. On the **String Builder** dialog box, click **OK**.

31. On the **Value Assignment** dialog box, click **OK**. With this you have set the name of the new item to be equal to the text "ApprovalForm_" plus the **ID** of the **ProjectInfoLib** InfoPath form the workflow is running on.

32. On the **Create New List Item** dialog box, click **Add**.

33. On the **Value Assignment** dialog box, select **projectID** from the **Set this field** drop-down list box, and click the formula button (second button) behind the **To this value** text box.

Chapter 5: Use SharePoint Designer Workflows with InfoPath Forms

34. On the **Lookup for Single line of text** dialog box, leave **Current Item** selected in the **Data source** drop-down list box, select **ID** from the **Field from source** drop-down list box, and click **OK**.

35. On the **Value Assignment** dialog box, click **OK**. With this you have set the **projectID** field of the new item (**ProjectApprovalLib** InfoPath form) to be equal to the **ID** of the **ProjectInfoLib** InfoPath form the workflow is running on.

36. On the **Create New List Item** dialog box, leave the **Append a unique identifier to the end of the file name** option selected, and click **OK**.

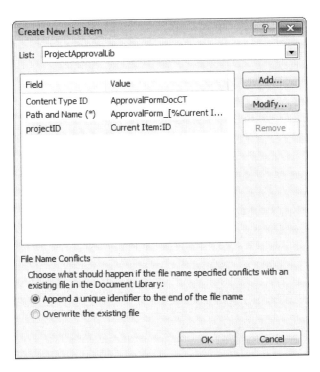

Figure 308. The final Create New List Item dialog box in SharePoint Designer 2010.

37. Click **Workflow ▶ Manage ▶ Workflow Settings**.

38. On the workflow settings page under the **Start Options** section, select the **Start workflow automatically when an item is created** check box.

39. Click **Workflow Settings ▶ Save ▶ Publish** to publish the workflow.

In SharePoint, navigate to the **ProjectInfoLib** form library and add a new form to the form library. Wait until the **CreateApprovalFormWF** workflow has run and completed, and then navigate to the **ProjectApprovalLib** to verify that a new form has been created. Open the form and verify that the project name you entered in the project information form has been loaded in the project name text box on the approval form.

Discussion

In the solution described above you saw how you can use a SharePoint Designer 2010 workflow to set the value of a field in a newly created InfoPath form so that it is linked to an existing form in a different form library. You also used a similar technique as the one described in recipe *85 Create a new InfoPath form through a workflow* to be able to automatically create new InfoPath forms in the **ProjectApprovalLib** form library whenever a new **ProjectInfo** InfoPath form is added to the **ProjectInfoLib** form library. But in this recipe you made use of a list column instead of a site column on the form library to promote a form field to and which was copied onto a list content type (**ApprovalFormDocCT**) used by the workflow to create new InfoPath forms. You also published the form templates directly to form libraries instead of as site content types. The solution for creating InfoPath forms through a SharePoint Designer 2010 workflow does not depend on the way you publish an InfoPath form template or whether you promote form fields as list columns or site columns.

87 Move a form from one form library to another using a workflow

Problem

You want to be able to select an item on the drop-down menu of a form and then have that form automatically moved to another form library on the same site.

Solution

You can publish a form template as a site content type, so that the form template can be associated with the two form libraries between which you want to move forms, create a SharePoint Designer workflow that can copy and delete a form, and then add a custom action to the source form library to be able to start the workflow.

To move a form from one library to another using a SharePoint Designer 2010 workflow:

1. In InfoPath, create a new SharePoint form library form template or use an existing one, and publish the form template as a site content type (also see recipe *26 Publish a form template as a site content type*) on the site where the form libraries are located. Name the content type **FormToMoveCT**.

2. In SharePoint, create two form libraries (also see the first part of recipe *16 Create a form library and edit its form template*): One named **FormsSourceLib** and another one named **FormsDestinationLib**.

3. Add the **FormToMoveCT** content type to the **FormsSourceLib** form library (also see recipe *27 Enable different types of forms to be created in one form library*).

Chapter 5: Use SharePoint Designer Workflows with InfoPath Forms

4. In SharePoint Designer 2010, create a new **List Workflow** named **MoveFormWF** and associate it with the **FormsSourceLib** form library (also see recipe *72 Create a workflow that runs on new forms in a specific form library*).

5. Moving an InfoPath form from one form library to another entails copying the form to the destination form library and then deleting it from the source form library. So on the workflow editor, click to place the cursor inside of **Step 1**, and then select **Workflow ▶ Insert ▶ Action ▶ List Actions ▶ Copy List Item** to add a **Copy List Item** workflow action to **Step 1**.

6. Click the first **this list** in the sentence for the workflow action.

7. On the **Choose List Item** dialog box, leave **Current Item** (which represents the current InfoPath form the workflow is running on) selected in the **List** drop-down list box, and click **OK**.

8. Click the second **this list** in the sentence for the workflow action, and select **FormsDestinationLib** from the drop-down list box that appears. With this you have set the workflow to copy the InfoPath form it is currently running on to the **FormsDestinationLib** form library. The workflow action should now say:

```
Copy item in Current Item to FormsDestinationLib
```

9. Click to place the cursor below the previous workflow action, and then select **Workflow ▶ Insert ▶ Action ▶ List Actions ▶ Delete Item** to add a **Delete Item** workflow action to **Step 1**.

10. Click **this list** in the sentence for the second workflow action.

11. On the **Choose List Item** dialog box, leave **Current Item** selected in the **List** drop-down list box, and click **OK**. With this you have set the workflow to delete the InfoPath form it is currently running on from the **FormsSourceLib** form library.

Figure 309. The completed workflow step in SharePoint Designer 2010.

12. Click **Workflow ▶ Manage ▶ Workflow Settings**.

13. On the workflow settings page under **Start Options**, leave the **Allow this workflow to be manually started** check box selected as the only selected option, to allow users to manually move forms from one form library to the next.

14. Click **Workflow Settings ▶ Save ▶ Publish** to publish the workflow.

InfoPath 2010 Cookbook 2

15. In the left **Navigation** pane, click **List and Libraries** to bring up all of the lists and libraries on the site.

16. On the **List and Libraries** page under **Document Libraries**, click **FormsSourceLib**, and follow the instructions in recipe *74 Start a workflow from a custom action in a library* to add a custom action named **Move to FormsDestinationLib** and that initiates the **MoveFormWF** workflow to move forms from the **FormsSourceLib** to the **FormsDestinationLib**.

In SharePoint, navigate to the **FormsSourceLib** form library, and add a new form that is based on the **FormToMoveCT** content type. Hover with the mouse pointer over the newly added form, click the drop-down arrow that appears on the right-hand side of the form's name, and select **Move to FormDestinationLib** from the drop-down menu that appears.

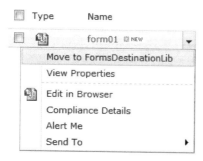

Figure 310. Selecting to start a workflow from a custom action on a form's drop-down menu.

Click **Start** on the workflow start page to start the workflow. Once the workflow has run and completed, the form should have disappeared from the **FormsSourceLib** and appeared in the **FormsDestinationLib**. Navigate to the **FormsDestinationLib** to check whether this is the case.

Discussion

In recipe *40 Move a form to another form library on the same site*, you learned how to manually move forms between form libraries on a SharePoint site. Moving forms with a workflow is similar to manually moving forms, which means that links to form templates can be broken when forms are moved. By publishing a form template as a site content type, and then adding that site content type to the source form library that is involved in moving the forms, you minimize the likelihood of form template links being broken when forms are moved. In any case, if links are broken, you can relink forms as described in recipe *42 Relink InfoPath forms in a form library*.

In the solution described above you also saw how you can add a custom action to InfoPath forms in a form library to make it easier for users to start a workflow. By adding a custom action you remove a couple of extra steps a user would have to perform to manually start the workflow as described in recipe *73 Manually start a workflow to run on a form*.

374

88 Make a specific type of form read-only to a user when added to a form library

Problem

You want to be able to move a form to a form library and if the form is of a certain type, allow a particular user to only view (and not edit or delete) that form.

Solution

You can configure a form library to have item-level permission and then use a SharePoint Designer 2010 workflow to change permissions on any forms that are added to that form library and that are of the type of form you want to make read-only to a specific user.

Before you create the workflow, you must have a form library from which forms will be copied or moved, and another form library to which forms will be copied or moved and that does not inherit permissions from the site on which it resides.

To create a form library from which forms will be copied or moved:

1. In InfoPath, create a new SharePoint form library form template or use an existing one.

2. Publish the form template to a form library (also see recipe *21 Publish a form template to a form library*) named **FormsSourceLib**.

To create a form library that does not inherit permissions and which a user does not have access to:

1. In SharePoint, create a new form library as described in the first part of recipe *16 Create a form library and edit its form template* and name it **ViewOnlyFormsLib**.

2. Click **Library Tools ➤ Library ➤ Settings ➤ Library Permissions**.

3. Click **Permission Tools ➤ Edit ➤ Inheritance ➤ Stop Inheriting Permissions** to stop the form library from inheriting permissions from the site.

4. Select the check box in front of the user who should have read-only access to forms in the form library, and click **Permission Tools ➤ Edit ➤ Modify ➤ Remove User Permissions**. Also ensure that the user is not a member of any of the groups that have been assigned permissions to the form library.

Once you have a form library that is not inheriting permissions and which the user does not have rights to access, you must create a custom permission level that the workflow can use to assign permissions to the user. You can follow the steps outlined in *Add a custom permission level* in the Appendix to create a custom permission level. Name the custom permission level **ViewOnlyForms** and select **View Items** under **List Permissions** when you create the permission level. Selecting **View Items** should automatically also select **View Pages** and **Open** under **Site Permissions**. Now you are ready to create the SharePoint Designer workflow that assigns this permission level to the user.

To create a workflow that assigns view permissions to a particular user for forms of a particular type in a form library:

1. In SharePoint Designer 2010, create a new **List Workflow** and associate it with the **ViewOnlyFormsLib** form library to which forms will be copied or moved (also see recipe *72 Create a workflow that runs on new forms in a specific form library*).

2. On the workflow editor page, click anywhere below **Step 1**, and then click **Workflow ➤ Insert ➤ Impersonation Step**. You are going to use this impersonation step to assign permissions to the user.

3. Click **Step 1** to select it, and then press **Delete** on your keyboard to delete it. This should leave only the impersonation step on the workflow editor.

4. The workflow must first check whether the form that is being copied or moved is linked to a particular form template, so must check whether the **Template Link** property of the **Current Item** data source has a particular value. You can lookup that value by going to the form library (**FormsSourceLib**) from which you will be copying or moving forms in SharePoint, selecting **Library Tools ➤ Library ➤ Manage Views ➤ Current View ➤ Relink Documents**, and then copying the URL that is listed under the **Template Link** column for one of the types of forms you will be copying or moving. Note that forms must be present in the form library before you can copy a **Template Link** URL.

5. Back in SharePoint Designer 2010, click anywhere inside of the **Impersonation Step** to place the cursor, and then select **Workflow ➤ Insert ➤ Condition ➤ Common Conditions ➤ If any value equals value**.

6. Click on the first **value** in the sentence for the workflow condition, and then click on the formula button behind the text box.

7. On the **Define Workflow Lookup** dialog box, leave **Current Item** selected in the **Data source** drop-down list box, select **Template Link** from the **Field from source** drop-down list box, and click **OK**.

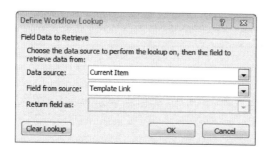

Figure 311. The Define Workflow Lookup dialog box in SharePoint Designer 2010.

Chapter 5: Use SharePoint Designer Workflows with InfoPath Forms

8. Click on the second **value** in the sentence for the workflow condition and paste the URL you copied earlier in step 4 into the text box.

9. Click to place the cursor inside of the **If** condition, and then select **Workflow ➤ Insert ➤ Action ➤ List Actions ➤ Add List Item Permission**.

10. Click **these permissions** in the sentence for the workflow action.

11. On the **Add List Item Permissions** dialog box, click **Add**.

12. On the **Add Permissions** dialog box, click **Choose**.

13. On the **Select Users** dialog box, select the user to whom you want to assign permissions, click **Add**, and then click **OK**.

14. On the **Add Permissions** dialog box, select the check box in front of the **ViewOnlyForms** custom permission level you created earlier, and click **OK**.

Figure 312. Assigning a permission level to a specific user in a SharePoint Designer workflow.

15. On the **Add List Item Permissions** dialog box, click **OK**.

16. Click **this list** in the sentence for the workflow action.

17. On the **Choose List Item** dialog box, leave **Current Item** selected in the **List** drop-down list box, and click **OK**.

377

InfoPath 2010 Cookbook 2

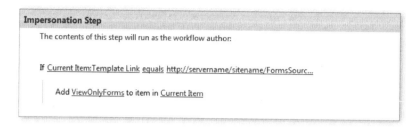

Figure 313. The completed workflow step in SharePoint Designer 2010.

18. Click **Workflow** ▶ **Manage** ▶ **Workflow Settings**.

19. On the workflow settings page under the **Start Options** section, select the **Start workflow automatically when an item is created** check box.

20. Click **Workflow Settings** ▶ **Save** ▶ **Publish** to publish the workflow. Read the warning on the message box that appears, and then click **OK**.

In SharePoint, navigate to the **FormsSourceLib** form library from which you want to copy or move forms, and copy or move a couple of forms to the **ViewOnlyFormsLib** form library you created earlier. Ensure that at least one of the forms is the type of form on which the workflow should run. Log onto the SharePoint site as the user who should only have read-only permissions on forms in the **ViewOnlyFormsLib** form library. Navigate to the **ViewOnlyFormsLib** form library and verify that the user can only view forms of the type you specified, but that she cannot edit or delete any forms.

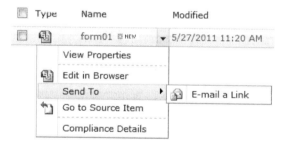

Figure 314. A user who has permissions to only view forms of a particular type in a form library.

Note that to view an InfoPath form, the user also needs to have access to the form template that is linked to the InfoPath form.

Discussion

When you copy a form to a different form library, that form is automatically changed to be based on the default content type that is defined on the form library. This default content type may or may not be linked to the same form template that the form you are copying is linked to. So when you are trying to identify forms, it is best to use the

Chapter 5: Use SharePoint Designer Workflows with InfoPath Forms

Template Link property instead of the **Content Type** property of the form to identify a certain type of form in a workflow.

The workflow in the solution described above used an **Impersonation Step** to change the permissions of a form added to a form library. You can use an **Impersonation Step** in a SharePoint Designer 2010 workflow if you want to perform actions that require elevated privileges as is the case when assigning permissions to a user. While a workflow runs by default with the permissions of the user who starts the workflow, an **Impersonation Step** on the other hand runs with the permissions of the user who creates and publishes the workflow. SharePoint Designer makes you aware of the latter by prompting you with a warning message as you saw in the last step of the solution. This also means that whoever creates and publishes the workflow template must have the necessary permissions to perform all of the actions contained in the **Impersonation Step** of the workflow.

Also note that before you could add the **Impersonation Step** to the workflow editor, you had to click outside of the existing **Step 1** workflow step that was present on the workflow editor, because you cannot add an **Impersonation Step** inside of another step.

There are several other list permission actions you can use within an **Impersonation Step** such as:

- Inherit List Item Parent Permissions
- Remove List Item Permissions
- Replace List Item Permissions

In addition, you can use the following permission-specific conditions if you have a situation where you want to check whether a user has a certain permission or permission level before executing an action:

- Check list item permission levels
- Check list item permissions

Chapter 6: Use Word, Excel, and Access with InfoPath via SharePoint

Use a document information panel in Word

Users are sometimes required to enter additional information when saving their documents for the purpose of managing documents across an organization. An example of this would be a Word document template that is used to create release notes for a software product. A document containing release notes generally has common fields such as project name, project manager, author, release date, release version, review date, reviewed by, etc. that are required to be filled out whenever a new version of software is released. These fields can be added to a Word document template as document properties that have to be filled out.

A document information panel is an InfoPath form that can be displayed in Word, Excel, or PowerPoint to enable users to easily fill out document properties. While a document information panel is not required for users to be able to fill out document properties, because there are several other ways to fill out document properties, a document information panel that has been customized in InfoPath Designer 2010 can provide additional InfoPath functionality such as data validation, data retrieval, and business logic to users when filling out document property fields.

In the recipes in this section, you will go through the process of creating a document information panel for a release notes document from beginning to end, so that you get a feel for where the document information panel fits in the broader picture of what you can do with InfoPath in SharePoint.

89 Use a Word document as a template for documents in a document library

Problem

You have a standard Word document template that your company uses to streamline the creation of release notes for the deployment of software products. You want to use this document template as the base template from which all documents are created and stored in a document library.

Solution

You can set a Word document to be the document template of the default **Document** content type that is associated with the document library, so that the Word document can be used as a starter template for all documents that are created in the document library.

To use a Word document as the template for documents in a document library:

1. In Word 2010, create a document that can be used as a starter template for other documents and save it as **ReleaseNotes.docx**. You can download the **ReleaseNotes.docx** sample Word document shown below from www.bizsupportonline.com.

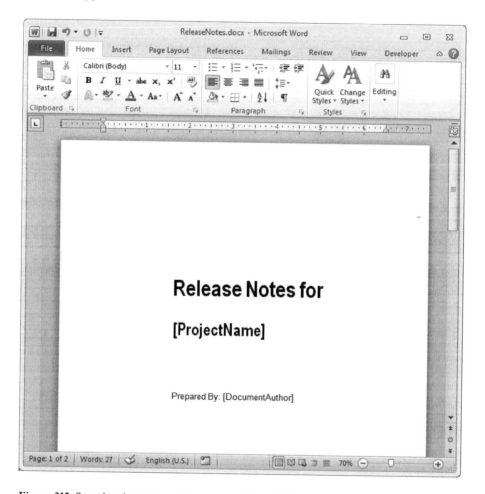

Figure 315. Sample release notes document in Word 2010.

2. In SharePoint, create a new **Document Library** and name it **ReleaseNotes**. By default, when you create a document library, the default content type it is associated with is linked to a blank Word document.

3. Navigate to the **Document Library Settings** page, and enable management of content types as described in steps 3 and 4 of recipe *27 Enable different types of forms to be created in one form library*.

Chapter 6: Use Word, Excel, and Access with InfoPath via SharePoint

4. On the **Document Library Settings** page under **Content Types**, click **Document**. The **Document** list content type is the default content type that is added to a document library when you create a new document library. Note that you could also add a custom content type that is based on the **Document** parent content type to the document library if you wanted to and use that content type instead of the default **Document** list content type.

5. On the details page of the **Document** list content type under the **Settings** section, click **Advanced settings**.

6. On the **Advanced Settings** page, select **Upload a new document template**, and click **Browse**.

7. On the **Choose File to Upload** dialog box, browse to and select the Word document you created in step 1, and click **Open**.

Figure 316. Setting a Word document as a template for a content type in SharePoint 2010.

8. On the **Advanced Settings** page, click **OK**. With this you have set the default content type of the document library to use the **ReleaseNotes.docx** Word document as the base template for creating new documents.

In SharePoint, navigate to the **ReleaseNotes** document library, and click **Documents ➤ New Document ➤ Document**. If the **Open Document** dialog box appears, click **OK**. The release notes document should open in Word.

Discussion

In the solution described above you learned how to set a Word document to be the document template of the default content type of a document library. While you first created a document library and then modified the default content type of the document library, you could have also started by adding a new site content type (also see *Create a new site content type* in the Appendix), adding site columns to the content type (also see *Create a new site column* and *Add a site column to a site content type* in the Appendix), associating that content type with a document library, and then adding the Word document as a document template to that custom content type. Both methods should work equally well, and just like you can add multiple types of InfoPath forms to a form library (also see recipe *27 Enable different types of forms to be created in one form library*), you can add multiple content types with different document templates (Word, Excel, etc.) to a document library.

383

InfoPath 2010 Cookbook 2

As mentioned in the introduction of this section, there are several ways to view and enter values for document properties. First you can use the standard document **Properties** dialog box to fill out document properties.

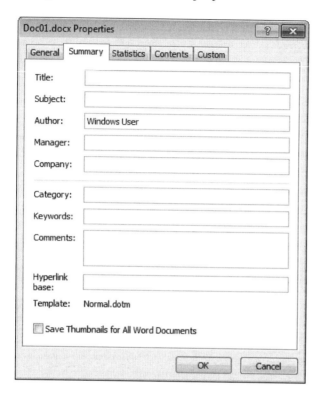

Figure 317. The Properties dialog box of a Word document.

Then there is the **Properties** section on the right-hand side of the **File ➤ Info** tab in Word 2010, which you can use to fill out document properties.

Properties ▼

Size	33.3KB
Pages	2
Words	27
Total Editing Time	4 Minutes
Title	Add a title
Comments	Add comments

Related Dates

Last Modified	Today, 11:27 a.m.
Created	Today, 11:27 a.m.
Last Printed	Never
ReviewDate	Add a date

Figure 318. Properties section on the Info tab in Word 2010.

Chapter 6: Use Word, Excel, and Access with InfoPath via SharePoint

And finally, you can open the document information panel via **File ➤ Info ➤ Properties ➤ Show Document Panel** to fill out document properties.

Figure 319. Opening the document information panel in Word 2010.

When the document information panel opens at the top of the Word document, you will see that there is currently only one field named **Title** being shown. That **Title** field comes from the one column that is currently defined on the **Document** content type associated with the document library. If you go back to the details page of the **Document** list content type and look at its list of **Columns**, you will see **Title** listed there. With this you now also know that if you want fields to appear on the document information panel, you must add columns to the content type from which the document is created.

The release notes document has a few fields that you may want to be able to easily fill out through the document information panel, such as for example: project name, project manager, document author, release date, release version, review date, and reviewed by. Therefore, you must define these document properties as columns on the content type. And the easiest way to define these fields on the content type is to add them as columns to the document library; these columns will then automatically be added to the default content type of the document library (because the **Add to all content types** check box on the **Create Column** page is selected by default), which in this case is the content type you are using to create the Word documents.

Create the following columns on the **ReleaseNotes** document library:

- **ProjectName** (Single line of text)
- **ProjectManager** (Person or Group)
- **DocumentAuthor** (Person or Group)
- **ReleaseDate** (Date and Time)
- **ReleaseVersion** (Number with 1 decimal place)
- **ReviewDate** (Date and Time)
- **ReviewedBy** (Person or Group)

Once you have created these columns, open a Word document again via the document library, and when you are in Word, click **File ➤ Info**. You should see the new document properties listed on the right-hand side in the list of properties. Theoretically speaking, you could fill them out here without ever having to open the document information panel

InfoPath 2010 Cookbook 2

to do so. But if you open the document information panel, you should also see the newly added fields there on the InfoPath form that SharePoint automatically generated.

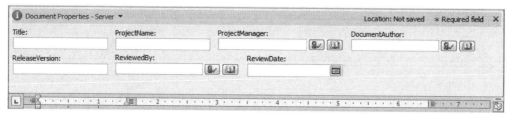

Figure 320. The document information panel with the newly added fields in Word 2010.

90 Link Word document fields to document panel fields

Problem

You have a standard Word document template that your company uses to streamline the creation of release notes for the deployment of software products. The release notes document has common fields such as project name, project manager, document author, release date, release version, review date, reviewed by, etc. that are required to be filled out whenever a new version of software is released. You want to make the process of filling out these document properties easier by linking them to the fields on the document information panel, so that whenever the document information panel fields are filled out the data automatically appears in fields throughout the Word document.

Solution

Before you begin, ensure you have gone through recipe *89 Use a Word document as a template for documents in a document library*.

After you have added columns to a content type that is used to create Word documents, you can use **Quick Parts** in Word to link document properties to columns of the content type (document information panel fields).

To link Word document fields to document information panel fields, or more precisely, to the columns of a content type:

1. In SharePoint, add the columns listed in the discussion section of recipe *89 Use a Word document as a template for documents in a document library* either as site columns or as list columns to the content type of the document template.

2. Navigate to the details page of the content type for the document. This content type could be the default **Document** content type that is used when you create a document library or it could be a custom content type that you manually added to the document library.

3. On the content type details page under the **Settings** section, click **Advanced settings**.

Chapter 6: Use Word, Excel, and Access with InfoPath via SharePoint

4. On the **Advanced Settings** page under the **Document Template** section, click **Edit Template**. This should open the document template in Word.

5. In Word, on a location where you want to add a document property field, select the piece of text you want to replace with a document property field (for example **[ProjectName]**), click **Insert ▶ Text ▶ Quick Parts**, select **Document Property**, and then select the name of the field you want to add as a document property from the menu that appears.

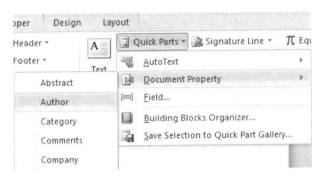

Figure 321. Inserting a document property Quick Part in Word 2010.

Note that the **Quick Parts** command places a content control on the document that should automatically make use of the formatting of the text you replaced.

Document Information			
Document Author	[DocumentAuthor]	Release Date	[ReleaseDate]
Project Manager	[ProjectManager]	Release Version	[ReleaseVersion]
Reviewed By	[ReviewedBy]	Review Date	[ReviewDate]

Figure 322. Text replaced by a content control on the Word document.

Ensure you format the text first before you replace it with a content control for any textual formatting to be used by the content control. Repeat this step for each document property you want to add.

6. Save and close the document template. The changes should automatically be updated in SharePoint.

7. In SharePoint, on the **Advanced Settings** page, click **OK**.

In SharePoint, navigate to the document library and add a new document. When the document opens in Word, open the document information panel (**File ▶ Info ▶ Properties ▶ Show Document Panel**) if it does not automatically open, fill out the fields on the document information panel, and verify that the values you entered into the fields on the document information panel automatically updated the corresponding fields (content controls) on the document. Save the document and close Word. Back in

InfoPath 2010 Cookbook 2

SharePoint, verify that the values you entered in the fields in the Word document also appear in the columns of the document library.

Discussion

In the solution described above, the columns you added to the content type automatically became the fields for the default document information panel that is created by SharePoint. This document information panel is an InfoPath form template that also functions as a starter template when you modify the template in InfoPath Designer 2010 as described in recipe *91 Create a document information panel from within SharePoint* or recipe *92 Create a document information panel from within InfoPath*.

The usefulness of document information panels becomes apparent when you notice how easy it is to fill out all of the document properties by just filling out one form at the top of a Word document and then have the fields (content controls) on the Word document automatically populate with the information you entered.

However, you do not have to use a document information panel if you do not want to. For example, if you wanted to fill out the document properties in Word on the standard way, you could go to the **Info** tab (**File ➤ Info**) and then on the right-hand side of the screen, fill out the properties listed there. You could also enter values directly in the fields (content controls) that are located throughout the document.

If you want to prevent users from entering data directly into the content controls and force them to use the controls on the document information panel instead to enter data, you can lock content controls as follows:

1. In SharePoint, start the editing process for the document template as you did in steps 2 through 4 of the solution described above.

2. In Word, select the content control you want to lock by clicking on it, and then click **Developer ➤ Controls ➤ Properties**. If the **Developer** tab is not present on the Ribbon, you can open it as follows:

    a. Click **File ➤ Options**.

    b. On the **Word Options** dialog box, click **Customize Ribbon**.

    c. On the **Word Options** dialog box under the **Customize the Ribbon** drop-down list box, ensure that the **Developer** check box is selected, and then click **OK**.

3. On the **Content Control Properties** dialog box under **Locking**, select the **Content control cannot be deleted** and **Contents cannot be edited** check boxes, and then click **OK**.

Chapter 6: Use Word, Excel, and Access with InfoPath via SharePoint

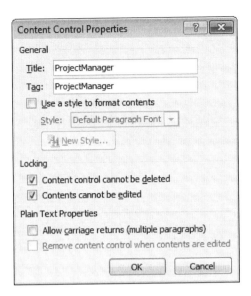

Figure 323. Locking a content control in Word 2010.

Because the document property fields are also accessible through columns of the document library, you could also fill them out by selecting **Edit Properties** on the context menu of a document (or select the check box in front of the document, click **Library Tools** ➤ **Documents** ➤ **Manage** ➤ **Edit Properties** on the Ribbon, and then enter the data through the document's **Properties** page.

Tip:

> Once you have linked document properties to content controls in a Word document, you can use a similar technique as the one described in recipe *85 Create a new InfoPath form through a workflow* to create a workflow that automatically generates and fills out a Word document (see recipe *94 Automatically generate simple Word documents from InfoPath forms*).

91 Create a document information panel from within SharePoint

Problem

You have a standard Word document template that your organization uses to streamline the creation of release notes for the deployment of software products. This release notes

InfoPath 2010 Cookbook 2

document contains document properties, which you want users to be able to easily fill out through the document information panel in Word.

Solution

Before you begin, ensure you have gone through recipe *89 Use a Word document as a template for documents in a document library*.

You can use the **Create a new custom template** link on the **Document Information Panel Settings** page in SharePoint to start the process of creating a document information panel from within SharePoint.

To create a new document information panel form template from within SharePoint:

1. In SharePoint, navigate to the details page of the content type associated with the document library for which you want to create a document information panel and then under the **Settings** section, click **Document Information Panel settings**. Note that the content type you select can be either a site content type that you access via **Site Actions** ➤ **Site Settings** ➤ **Galleries** ➤ **Site content types**, or a list content type associated with a document library and which you access via the **Content Types** section on the **Document Library Settings** page.

2. On the **Document Information Panel Settings** page under the **Document Information Panel Template** section, click **Create a new custom template**.

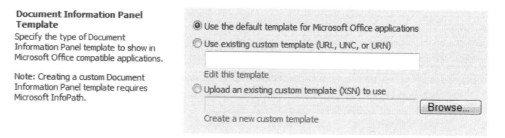

Figure 324. The document information panel template settings in SharePoint 2010.

This should open the **Data Source Wizard** in InfoPath Designer 2010.

3. In InfoPath, on the **Data Source Wizard**, click **Finish**. The InfoPath form template for the document information panel should appear. You can customize this form template as you would do with any other type of form template in InfoPath.

4. When you are done customizing the form template, click the **Quick Publish** button on the **Quick Access Toolbar**, click **File** ➤ **Info** ➤ **Quick Publish**, or click **File** ➤ **Publish** ➤ **Document Information Panel** to publish the form template back to SharePoint. The **Quick Publish** button is enabled, because the document library to which the document information panel belongs, is already known and was already set when you created the form template from within SharePoint. Note that you cannot change the publish location of a document information panel form template.

Chapter 6: Use Word, Excel, and Access with InfoPath via SharePoint

5. Close InfoPath Designer 2010.

In SharePoint, click the link that says **Go back to the Document Information Panel settings page**. The **Use existing custom template (URL, UNC, or URN)** option should now be selected and you should see the URL of the form template you customized and published listed under **Document Information Panel Template** as an indication that the document information panel template has been customized. Click **OK**.

Figure 325. Settings for a customized document information panel in SharePoint 2010.

SharePoint automatically assigns a name to the customized form template and stores it in a folder that has the same name as the content type (**Document** in the case above) which is located under the **Forms** folder of the document library.

Discussion

Once you have created a custom template as you have done in the solution described above, you can go back to the **Document Information Panel Settings** page and click the **Edit this template** link to edit the existing form template in InfoPath Designer 2010.

Note that you could also open the document library in SharePoint Designer 2010 (**Navigation ➤ All Files ➤ ReleaseNotes**), navigate to the **Document** folder (or a folder that has the same name as the content type for which you created a document information panel in SharePoint) under the **Forms** folder, and then click on the XSN file located in the content type's folder to open and modify the form template in InfoPath Designer 2010.

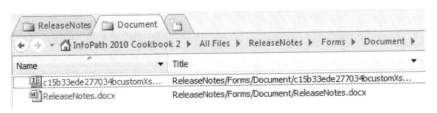

Figure 326. The document information panel template in SharePoint Designer 2010.

In the next recipe you will learn how to create a document information panel form template from within InfoPath Designer 2010.

92 Create a document information panel from within InfoPath

Problem

You have a standard Word document template that your organization uses to streamline the creation of release notes for the deployment of software products. This release notes document contains document properties, which you want users to be able to easily fill out through the document information panel in Word.

Solution

Before you begin, ensure you have gone through recipe *89 Use a Word document as a template for documents in a document library*.

You can use the **Document Information Panel** advanced form template in InfoPath Designer 2010 to create a new document information panel form template from within InfoPath.

To create a document information panel from within InfoPath:

1. In InfoPath, on the **New** tab under **Advanced Form Templates**, click **Document Information Panel**, and then click **Design Form**.

2. On the **Data Source Wizard**, enter the URL of the document library for which you want to create a document information panel for a content type associated with the document library, and click **Next**. The URL should have a format such as

   ```
   http://servername/sitename/libraryname
   ```

   where **servername** is the name of the SharePoint server and **sitename** is the name of the site where a document library named **libraryname** is located.

3. On the **Data Source Wizard**, select a content type from the list of content types that are associated with the document library, and click **Next**. If a custom form template has already been defined for the content type you selected, InfoPath will display a message telling you that this is the case, but that you can still go ahead and create a new form template. When you publish the new form template, it will replace the existing form template. Click **OK** if this message appears. Note that this action creates a new form template and does not modify the existing form template. If you want to edit the existing form template, you must use the **Edit this template** link that was mentioned in the discussion section of the previous recipe.

4. On the **Data Source Wizard**, click **Finish**.

You should now be able to customize the form template by adding business logic, formatting, data validation, etc. to the form template. When you are done customizing the form template, click **File ➤ Info ➤ Quick Publish**, click **File ➤ Publish ➤ Document Information Panel**, or click **Quick Publish** on the **Quick Access Toolbar** to publish

Chapter 6: Use Word, Excel, and Access with InfoPath via SharePoint

the form template to SharePoint. Because you specified the form library location when you first created the form template, the publish location has already been defined and cannot be changed once you have created the form template.

Discussion

In recipe *91 Create a document information panel from within SharePoint* you learned how to create a document information panel from within SharePoint and then customize it in InfoPath Designer 2010. In the solution described above you learned how to create a new document information panel starting from within InfoPath Designer 2010.

In step 3 of the solution described above, you also had to select a content type for which you wanted to create the document information panel, since document information panels are created on a per content type basis, and not on a per document library basis. And because a document information panel form template is based on the schema of a content type, you could also create a document information panel form template by using the **XML or Schema** form template as follows:

1. In InfoPath, on the **New** tab under **Advanced Form Templates**, click **XML or Schema**, and then click **Design Form**.
2. On the **Data Source Wizard**, enter the URL of the document library for which you want to create a document information panel for a content type associated with the document library, and click **Next**. The URL should have a format such as

   `http://servername/sitename/libraryname`

   where **servername** is the name of the SharePoint server and **sitename** is the name of the site where a document library named **libraryname** is located.

3. On the **Data Source Wizard**, select a content type from the list of content types that are associated with the document library, and click **Next**. If a custom form template has already been defined for the content type you selected, InfoPath will display a message telling you that this is the case, but that you can still go ahead and create a new form template. When you publish the new form template, it will replace the existing form template. Click **OK** if this message appears. Note that this action creates a new form template and does not modify the existing form template. If you want to edit the existing form template, you must use the **Edit this template** link that was mentioned in the discussion section of the previous recipe.
4. On the **Data Source Wizard**, click **Finish**.

One thing to note about document information panel form templates is that the **Compatibility** is set to **Document Information Panel**, which is a form type that does not appear when you create any of the other types of form templates in InfoPath.

InfoPath 2010 Cookbook 2

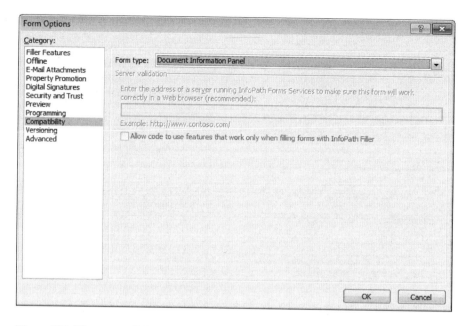

Figure 327. The compatibility setting for a document information panel form template in InfoPath.

In addition, you cannot change a document information panel form template to be a Web Browser Form or InfoPath Filler Form.

93 Change settings for a document information panel

Set a document panel to automatically open in Word

Problem

You opened a Word document that is based on a content type for which a document information panel form has been created, but the document information panel does not open as soon as you open the document in Word. You do not want to have to manually open the document information panel in Word every time you open a document.

Solution

Before you begin, ensure you have gone through recipe *91 Create a document information panel from within SharePoint* or recipe *92 Create a document information panel from within InfoPath*.

You can change a setting on the document information panel of the content type so that the document information panel automatically opens when a document that is based on that content type opens in the client application (Word in this case).

Chapter 6: Use Word, Excel, and Access with InfoPath via SharePoint

To set a document information panel to automatically open when you open a Word document:

1. In SharePoint, navigate to the details page of the content type associated with the document information panel and then under the **Settings** section, click **Document Information Panel settings**.

2. On the **Document Information Panel Settings** page under **Show Always**, select the **Always show Document Information Panel on document open and initial save for this content type** check box, and click **OK**.

Show Always

Require that the Document Information Panel is displayed automatically for the user under specific conditions.

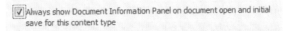

Figure 328. Setting to always open the document information panel.

In SharePoint, navigate to the document library that is associated with the content type you updated, and open an existing or add a new document that is based on the content type. In Word, verify that the document information panel automatically opens at the top of the document as soon as the document opens.

Discussion

In the solution described above you set the document information panel to automatically open when you open a document that is based on the content type that the document information panel is linked to. You can also open the document information panel from within Word as you have already seen in the discussion section of recipe *89 Use a Word document as a template for documents in a document library*.

Restore the default document information panel for a document library

Problem

You have previously customized the form template that is used as the document information panel form template for a content type associated with a document library, but now you want to change the form template back to the default document information panel template that is generated by SharePoint.

Solution

Before you begin, ensure you have gone through recipe *91 Create a document information panel from within SharePoint* or recipe *92 Create a document information panel from within InfoPath*.

You can change the form template that is used by a content type on the **Document Information Panel Settings** page.

To restore the default document information panel template for a content type associated with a document library:

1. In SharePoint, navigate to the details page of the content type associated with the document information panel you want to restore, and then under the **Settings** section, click **Document Information Panel settings**.

2. On the **Document Information Panel Settings** page under the **Document Information Panel Template** section, select the **Use the default template for Microsoft Office applications** option, and click **OK**.

In SharePoint, navigate to the document library that is associated with the content type you updated, and open an existing or add a new document that is based on the content type. In Word, open the document information panel if it did not automatically open, and verify that the document information panel is the default template for Microsoft Office applications that SharePoint generates.

Discussion

In the solution described above, you changed the form template for the document information panel back to the default document information panel template. Note that this action does not delete the existing template and that if you wanted to, you could switch back to using the custom form template at a later stage by selecting the **Use existing custom template (URL, UNC, or URN)** on the **Document Information Panel Settings** page.

Use InfoPath data in Word through SharePoint

An often requested functionality regarding InfoPath and Word is the conversion of InfoPath forms into Word documents. Because InfoPath does not offer an easy way to generate Word documents that use InfoPath form data, you would have to write code to implement such functionality.

The recipe described in this section shows you how you can take an InfoPath form that contains a limited amount of text fields that should be used to create a Word document, and combine this with SharePoint and SharePoint Designer to create a codeless solution that converts InfoPath forms into Word documents. While this solution has its limitations, it provides non-programmers with a method to automatically create Word documents from simple InfoPath forms.

Chapter 6: Use Word, Excel, and Access with InfoPath via SharePoint

94 Automatically generate simple Word documents from InfoPath forms

Problem

You have a standard Word document template that your organization uses to streamline the creation of release notes for the deployment of software products. You want to be able to automatically create and fill out documents that are based on this Word template whenever a new InfoPath form is saved or submitted to a form library.

Solution

You can use a SharePoint Designer 2010 workflow that runs whenever a new form is submitted or saved to a form library to create a Word document that is based on the values of fields on the form.

To automatically generate a Word document that is based on data from an InfoPath form:

1. Follow the instructions in recipe *89 Use a Word document as a template for documents in a document library* and recipe *90 Link Word document fields to document panel fields* to create a document library that has a content type that is linked to a Word document template on which you have placed content controls that are linked to columns of the content type.

2. In InfoPath, create a new SharePoint form library form template or use an existing one.

3. Add a **Text Box** control to the view of the form template and name it **projectName**.

4. Add a **Person/Group Picker** control to the view of the form template and name its main group node **projectManager**.

5. Add a **Person/Group Picker** control to the view of the form template and name its main group node **documentAuthor**.

6. Add a **Date and Time Picker** control to the view of the form template and name it **releaseDate**.

7. Add a **Text Box** control to the view of the form template and name it **releaseVersion**. Change the data type of the **releaseVersion** field to **Decimal (double)**.

8. Add a **Date and Time Picker** control to the view of the form template and name it **reviewDate**.

9. Add a **Person/Group Picker** control to the view of the form template and name its main group node **reviewedBy**.

397

10. Promote all of the fields to columns as described in recipe *23 Promote form fields to columns of a form library*. Ensure you promote the first **AccountId** field of all of the person/group picker controls and name them as their respective main group nodes.

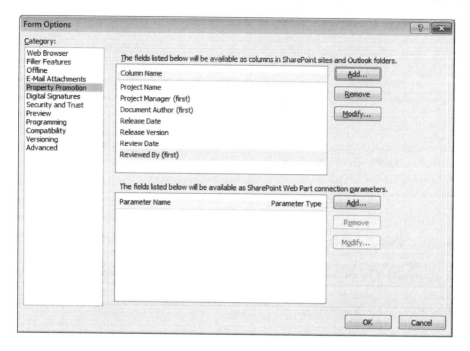

Figure 329. Promoted fields on the Form Options dialog box in InfoPath Designer 2010.

11. Publish the form template to a SharePoint form library named **ReleaseNotesFormLib**.

12. In SharePoint Designer 2010, create a new **List Workflow** named **CreateWordDocWF** and associate it with the **ReleaseNotesFormLib** form library (also see recipe *72 Create a workflow that runs on new forms in a specific form library*).

13. Creating a Word document using a workflow entails creating an item that is based on the content type that is linked to a Word document template. This process is similar to creating InfoPath forms using a workflow as described in recipe *85 Create a new InfoPath form through a workflow*. So select **Workflow ➤ Insert ➤ Action ➤ List Actions ➤ Create List Item** to add a **Create List Item** workflow action to **Step 1**.

14. Click the first **this list** in the sentence for the workflow action.

15. On the **Create New List Item** dialog box, select **ReleaseNotes** from the **List** drop-down list box, select **Path and Name (*)**, and then click **Modify**. Note that when you select **ReleaseNotes** from the **List** drop-down list box, the default **Document** content type is automatically assigned to the **Content Type ID** field. Note that if you used a custom content type on the **ReleaseNotes** document library,

Chapter 6: Use Word, Excel, and Access with InfoPath via SharePoint

you must modify the **Content Type ID** field to use that content type instead of the default content type.

16. On the **Value Assignment** dialog box, click the formula button behind the **To this value** text box.

17. On the **Lookup for String** dialog box, leave **Current Item** selected in the **Data source** drop-down list box, select **Name** from the **Field from source** drop-down list box, and then click **OK**.

18. On the **Value Assignment** dialog box, click **OK**. With this you have set the name of the newly created Word document to be the same as the name of the InfoPath form.

19. On the **Create New List Item** dialog box, click **Add**.

20. On the **Value Assignment** dialog box, select **ProjectManager** from the **Set this field** drop-down list box, and then click the formula button behind the **To this value** text box.

21. On the **Lookup for Person or Group** dialog box, leave **Current Item** selected in the **Data source** drop-down list box, select **Project Manager** from the **Field from source** drop-down list box, and then click **OK**.

22. On the **Value Assignment** dialog box, click **OK**. With this you have set the value of the **ProjectManager** field (content control) on the Word document to be equal to the value of the promoted **Project Manager** field on the InfoPath form.

23. Repeat steps 19 through 22 for each one of the form fields you promoted and which you would like to use to fill out the Word document.

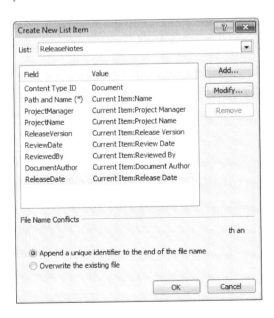

Figure 330. The final Create New List Item dialog box in SharePoint Designer 2010.

24. On the **Create New List Item** dialog box, click **OK**.

25. Click **Workflow** ➤ **Manage** ➤ **Workflow Settings**.

26. On the workflow settings page under **Start Options**, select the **Start workflow automatically when an item is created** check box. This will allow the workflow to run whenever a new InfoPath form is saved or submitted to the form library. Leave the **Allow this workflow to be manually started** check box selected so that users can manually start the workflow on an InfoPath form in case the workflow failed to create the Word document.

27. Publish the workflow.

In SharePoint, navigate to the **ReleaseNotesFormLib** form library and add a new form. Fill out the form and save or submit it. Once you have saved the form in the form library, the workflow should automatically start to run. Once the workflow has completed, navigate to the **ReleaseNotes** document library and check whether a Word document that has the same name as the InfoPath form was created in the document library. Open the Word document and verify that the fields (content controls) have been filled out with the information you entered on the InfoPath form.

Discussion

If you have an InfoPath form that contains simple data such as text and date fields, you can use the technique described in the solution above to automatically generate Word documents that are based on InfoPath form data through a SharePoint Designer 2010 workflow. If on the other hand, you have an InfoPath form that contains complex data such as repeating tables, bulleted lists, pictures, file attachments, etc., you will most likely have to write code to be able to convert the InfoPath form into a Word document.

Use Excel data in InfoPath through SharePoint

SharePoint 2010 offers several ways to integrate InfoPath 2010 with Excel 2010, a couple of which include:

- Exporting Excel data to a SharePoint list and then creating a data connection to that SharePoint list in InfoPath.
- Connecting InfoPath to an Excel workbook through the SOAP or REST web services offered by Excel Services.
- Connect an InfoPath Form Web Part to an Excel Web Access web part to send data from an InfoPath form to an Excel workbook.

The recipes in this section are meant to provide you with ideas for solutions that combine InfoPath forms with Excel workbooks through SharePoint.

Chapter 6: Use Word, Excel, and Access with InfoPath via SharePoint

95 Display Excel data in a browser form – method 1

Export Excel data to a SharePoint list

Problem

You have tabular data in an Excel 2010 spreadsheet which you want to display in a repeating table on an InfoPath form.

Solution

You can export the Excel spreadsheet to a SharePoint list and then add a data connection for that SharePoint list in InfoPath.

Suppose you have an Excel workbook named **Fruits.xlsx** that has the following contents:

FruitName	FruitColor
Apple	Red
Banana	Yellow
Kiwi	Brown
Plum	Purple
Orange	Orange

Note:

> The **Fruits.xlsx** file, which you can download from www.bizsupportonline.com, contains the data listed in the table above.

To display data from an Excel spreadsheet in an InfoPath browser form:

1. In Excel 2010, create an Excel spreadsheet with tabular data or use an existing one.
2. Select all of the tabular data including headers by clicking in the top-left cell, holding the mouse button pressed down, dragging the cursor to the bottom-right cell, and then releasing the mouse button.
3. Click **Home** ➤ **Styles** ➤ **Format as Table** and select a table format from the drop-down list of table formats.

4. On the **Format As Table** dialog box, the **Where is the data for your table?** field should already contain a correct reference to the cells on the spreadsheet. Select the **My table has headers** check box and click **OK**.

5. Click on any cell in the table, and then click **Table Tools ▶ Design ▶ External Table Data ▶ Export ▶ Export Table to SharePoint List**.

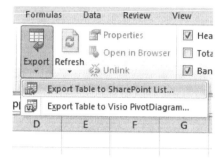

Figure 331. Export Table to SharePoint List command in Excel 2010.

6. On the **Export Table to SharePoint List** dialog box, enter the URL of the SharePoint site (where you want to publish the table) in the **Address** combo box, enter a **Name** and **Description** for the SharePoint list, and click **Next**.

Figure 332. Selecting the SharePoint site to which to export the Excel data.

7. On the **Export Table to SharePoint List** dialog box, read the information displayed, and then click **Finish**. A confirmation message box should appear once the tabular data has been exported to SharePoint.

Chapter 6: Use Word, Excel, and Access with InfoPath via SharePoint

Figure 333. Confirmation message box that table was successfully published.

You can verify whether the data was successfully exported to SharePoint by clicking on the link that Excel provides on the confirmation message box or by going to the SharePoint site, clicking on **Site Actions** ➤ **View All Site Content**, and searching for the SharePoint list on the **All Site Content** page.

8. In InfoPath, create a new SharePoint form library form template or use an existing one.

9. Add a **Receive** data connection to the SharePoint list (also see *Use a SharePoint list data connection* in recipe *43 3 Ways to retrieve data from a SharePoint list*) you just created for the tabular data in Excel to the form template.

10. Bind the secondary data source for the SharePoint list to a repeating table as described in recipe *44 Display SharePoint list data in a repeating table*.

11. Publish the form template to a SharePoint form library.

In SharePoint, navigate to the form library where you published the form template and add a new form. When the form opens, the data from the Excel spreadsheet should appear in the repeating table.

Discussion

In the solution described above, you exported data from a table on an Excel spreadsheet to SharePoint. If you wanted to make changes to the Excel spreadsheet after you have already exported it to SharePoint and then synchronize your changes with the SharePoint list, you could make use of SharePoint Workspace together with the **Sync to SharePoint Workspace** command of the SharePoint list to maintain the data in the SharePoint list. And then if you wanted to recreate the Excel file from the SharePoint list, you could use the **List Tools** ➤ **List** ➤ **Connect & Export** ➤ **Export to Excel** command of the SharePoint list to export the data in the SharePoint list to an **.iqy** file, which you could then open in Excel 2010.

Another feature worth mentioning is that once you have exported Excel data to a SharePoint 2010 list, you can create a SharePoint list form with which you can add and edit items in the SharePoint list (also see recipe *1 Customize a SharePoint list form from within SharePoint* or recipe *2 Customize a SharePoint list form from within InfoPath*). This customized form for the SharePoint list would then also become available in SharePoint Workspace and any data validation contained in the SharePoint list form would be enforced through SharePoint Workspace.

InfoPath 2010 Cookbook 2

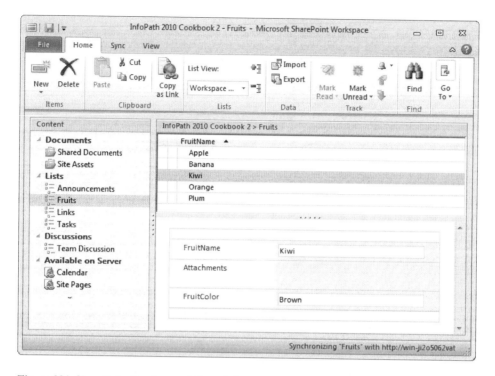

Figure 334. SharePoint list data and SharePoint list form in SharePoint Workspace.

The discussion of SharePoint Workspace is beyond the scope of this book, but you are encouraged to explore its features and capabilities.

96 Display Excel data in a browser form – method 2

Use the Excel Services REST web service interface

Problem

You have tabular data in an Excel 2010 spreadsheet which you want to be able to display in a repeating table on an InfoPath form.

Solution

You can upload an Excel workbook to a SharePoint document library that serves as a trusted file location for Excel Services and then use the Excel Services Application REST API to access data stored within that Excel workbook from within an InfoPath form.

To display Excel data in a browser form using Excel Services and REST:

Chapter 6: Use Word, Excel, and Access with InfoPath via SharePoint

1. Save the Excel workbook you created in recipe *95 Display Excel data in a browser form – method 1* including the table formatting to disk and name it **Fruits.xlsx** or use the **Fruits.xlsx** file, which you can download from www.bizsupportonline.com.

2. In Excel, click **File ➤ Save & Send ➤ Save to SharePoint ➤ Publish Options**.

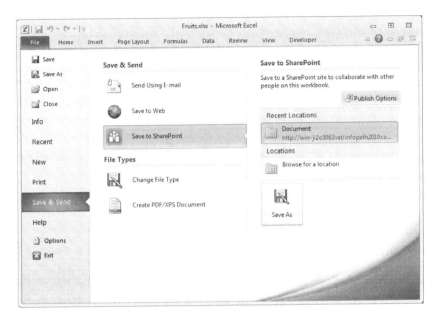

Figure 335. The Save to SharePoint command in Excel 2010.

3. On the **Publish Options** dialog box on the **Show** tab, select **Sheets** from the drop-down list box, deselect all of the check boxes except for the **Sheet 1** check box (the table is located on **Sheet 1**), and click **OK**.

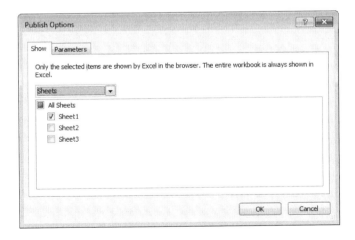

Figure 336. The Publish Options dialog box in Excel 2010.

405

InfoPath 2010 Cookbook 2

4. Click **File** ➤ **Save & Send** ➤ **Save to SharePoint** ➤ **Browse for a location** ➤ **Save As**.

5. On the **Save As** dialog box, enter the URL of the SharePoint site where you want to publish the Excel workbook in the address bar at the top of the dialog box, and press **Enter**.

6. On the **Save As** dialog box, select a document library in which to store the Excel workbook (for example the **Shared Documents** library), ensure **Fruits.xlsx** is listed in the **File name** combo box, deselect the **Open with Excel in the browser** check box, and click **Save**.

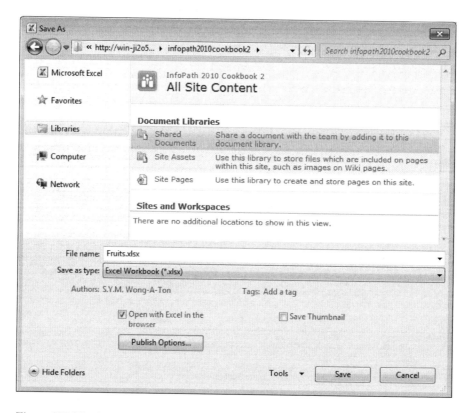

Figure 337. The Save As dialog box to save the Excel workbook to SharePoint 2010.

Note that you can also access the **Publish Options** dialog box by clicking the **Publish Options** button on the **Save As** dialog box instead of clicking the **Publish Options** button on the **Save & Send** tab in Excel. In addition, you could have also uploaded the Excel workbook to the document library from within SharePoint via the **Library Tools** ➤ **Documents** ➤ **Upload Document** functionality of the document library in SharePoint instead of saving the file in the document library via Excel 2010.

Chapter 6: Use Word, Excel, and Access with InfoPath via SharePoint

7. Once the Excel file has been uploaded, you can go ahead and create an Excel Services REST web service data connection to it in InfoPath. So in InfoPath, create a new SharePoint form library form template or use an existing one.

8. Select **Data ➤ Get External Data ➤ From Web Service ➤ From REST Web Service**.

9. On the **Data Connection Wizard**, enter the URL of the Excel Services REST web service and the Excel workbook, for example:

    ```
    http://servername/sitename/_vti_bin/ExcelREST.aspx/Shared%20Documents/Fruit
    s.xlsx/model/Ranges('Sheet1!A2%7CB6')?$format=atom
    ```

    and click **Next**. Here, **servername** is the name of the SharePoint server, **sitename** is the name of the site where the Excel workbook is located, **Fruits.xlsx** is the name of the Excel workbook, and **Sheet1!A2|B6** (the pipe symbol has been encoded as **%7C** in the URL, so the range then becomes **Sheet1!A2%7CB6** in the URL) is the range of cells on **Sheet1** in the workbook. The latter retrieves the data contained in all cells that are located between cells **A2** and **B6**; note that the range of cells does not contain the table header cells. The

    ```
    ?$format=atom
    ```

    in the URL listed above specifies that the data should be returned as an Atom XML feed.

10. On the **Data Connection Wizard**, name the data connection **GetFruits**, leave the **Automatically retrieve data when form is opened** check box selected, and click **Finish**.

11. On the **Fields** task pane, select **GetFruits (Secondary)** from the **Fields** drop-down list box, expand the entire **content** group node under the **entry** group node, drag-and-drop the **row** repeating group node onto the view and bind it to a repeating table.

12. Publish the form template to a SharePoint form library.

In SharePoint, navigate to the form library where you published the form template and add a new form. When the form opens, all of the data from the selected range of cells from the Excel spreadsheet should be displayed in the repeating table.

Fruit
Apple
Red

Fruit
Banana
Yellow

Fruit
Kiwi
Brown

Fruit
Plum
Purple

Fruit
Orange
Orange

Figure 338. The InfoPath form displaying data from the Excel spreadsheet through Excel Services.

Discussion

In the solution described above, you used Excel Services with a REST web service data connection to retrieve data from an Excel workbook and use this data in an InfoPath form. For this you had to publish the Excel workbook to a trusted file location in SharePoint.

All SharePoint sites are configured by default as trusted file locations when SharePoint is first installed, so you need not explicitly define the document library to which you publish the Excel workbook as a trusted file location. But if the solution is not working for you, you may want to have your administrator check whether the document library in which you saved the Excel file is indeed a trusted file location.

Your administrator can verify the existence of trusted file locations as follows:

1. In SharePoint 2010 Central Administration under **Application Management**, click **Manage service applications**.
2. On the **Manage Service Applications** page ensure that the **Excel Services Application** has a status of **Started**, and then click **Excel Services Application**.
3. On the **Manage Excel Services Application** page, click **Trusted File Locations**.
4. On the **Trusted File Locations** page, ensure that **http://** has been added as a trusted file location or click **Add Trusted File Location** and follow the instructions to add a trusted file location.

Chapter 6: Use Word, Excel, and Access with InfoPath via SharePoint

When you access Excel Services through its REST interface, you can access resources like charts, pivot tables, tables, and named ranges in a workbook directly through the REST URL.

The REST URL for Excel Services consists of four parts:

1. A REST ASPX page URI – This is the entry point to the **ExcelREST.aspx** page. For example:

   ```
   http://serverName/siteName/_vti_bin/ExcelRest.aspx
   ```

2. A workbook location – This is the path to the workbook. For example:

   ```
   /DocumentLibraryName/WorkbookName.xlsx
   ```

3. A resource location – This is the path to the requested resource inside the workbook. For example:

   ```
   /model/Tables('TableName')
   ```

   or

   ```
   /model/Ranges('Sheet1!A1|G5')
   ```

   or

   ```
   /model/Ranges('NameOfTheNamedRange')
   ```

   or

   ```
   /model/Charts('ChartName')
   ```

4. The format in which to return the data. For example:

   ```
   $format=atom
   ```

   or

   ```
   $format=html
   ```

For more information about Excel Services and its REST interface, consult the MSDN documentation.

Tip:

> Always test a REST web service URL in a browser to verify that it is working properly before you use it in InfoPath. If it does not work in a browser, it is likely not to work in InfoPath either.

97 Calculate work days between two dates using Excel Services – method 1

Use the Excel Services SOAP web service

Problem

You have two date picker controls on a form and want to calculate the difference in business days between these two dates excluding holidays and weekends.

Solution

You can create an Excel workbook that contains the calculation for the amount of work days between two dates and a list of dates for holidays, publish this Excel workbook to a trusted file location for Excel Services, and then call the Excel Services SOAP web service from within the InfoPath form to perform the calculation.

To calculate the amount of work days between two dates excluding holidays:

1. In Excel 2010, create an Excel workbook that contains a list of dates for holidays (or download the **WorkdaysCalculator.xlsx** sample file from www.bizsupportonline.com) and the following formula in cell **A3** on **Sheet1**:

   ```
   =NETWORKDAYS(DATE(MID(A1,1,4),MID(A1,6,2),MID(A1,9,2)),DATE(MID(A2,1,4),MID(A2,6,2),MID(A2,9,2)),Sheet2!A1:A16)
   ```

   where cell **A1** on **Sheet1** contains a start date that has a format of **yyyy-MM-dd** and a default value of **2011-01-01**, cell **A2** on **Sheet1** contains an end date that has a format of **yyyy-MM-dd** and a default value of **2012-01-01**, and cells **A1** to **A16** on **Sheet2** contain a range of dates that represent holidays. The dates for the holidays have the **Date** data type in Excel. Note that you can make the start and end dates text by selecting **Text** from the drop-down list box on the **Home** tab under the **Number** group. You can convert the dates for the holidays to have the **Date** data type by selecting **Date** from the same drop-down list box. Also note that you will be changing the default values of cells **A1** and **A2** on **Sheet1** later through InfoPath. The Excel formula uses the **NETWORKDAYS**, **DATE**, and **MID** functions to calculate the amount of work days minus holidays.

2. Save the Excel workbook to disk and name it **WorkdaysCalculator.xlsx**.

3. Click **File ▶ Save & Send ▶ Save to SharePoint ▶ Save As** and save the entire workbook (including all of its sheets) to a document library (for example the **Shared Documents** library) on the SharePoint site where you will be publishing the form template (also see steps 2 through 6 of recipe *96 Display Excel data in a browser form – method 2*).

Chapter 6: Use Word, Excel, and Access with InfoPath via SharePoint

4. In InfoPath, create a new SharePoint form library form template or use an existing one.

5. Add two **Date Picker** controls to the view of the form template and name them **startDate** and **endDate**, respectively.

6. Add a **Text Box** control to the view of the form template and name it **workdaysDiff**. Make the text box read-only or change it into a calculated value control, since the user should not be able to change the value of this field.

7. Add a **Button** control to the view of the form template and label it **Calculate**.

8. In Notepad, create an XML file that has the following contents:

   ```
   <ExcelServicesInput>
     <sheetName/>
     <rangeName/>
     <cellValue/>
   </ExcelServicesInput>
   ```

   and name the XML file **ExcelServicesInput.xml** or download the **ExcelServicesInput.xml** file from www.bizsupportonline.com. You will use the fields in this XML file as helper fields to set the values of parameters for making the Excel Services SOAP web service calls. By using a separate secondary data source and not including these fields in the Main data source of the form, you will keep the InfoPath form free from irrelevant data.

9. In InfoPath, add a **Receive** XML data connection to the **ExcelServicesInput.xml** file, accept the data connection name of **ExcelServicesInput**, and leave the **Automatically retrieve data when form is opened** check box selected.

10. Select **Data** ▶ **Get External Data** ▶ **From Web Service** ▶ **From SOAP Web Service**.

11. On the **Data Connection Wizard**, enter the URL of the Excel Services SOAP web service on the site where the workbook is located, for example:

    ```
    http://servername/sitename/_vti_bin/ExcelService.asmx
    ```

    where **servername** is the name of the SharePoint server, **sitename** is the name of the site where the workbook is located, and **ExcelService.asmx** is the Excel Services SOAP web service ASMX page. Click **Next**.

12. On the **Data Connection Wizard**, select **OpenWorkbook** from the list of operations, and click **Next**.

13. On the **Data Connection Wizard**, leave **tns:workbookPath** selected, and click **Set Value**.

14. On the **Parameter Details** dialog box, enter the full URL of the workbook location, for example:

    ```
    http://servername/sitename/libraryname/WorkdaysCalculator.xlsx
    ```

where **servername** is the name of the SharePoint server, **sitename** is the name of the site, and **libraryname** is the name of the document library and Excel Services trusted file location where the **WorkdaysCalculator.xlsx** Excel file is located. Click **OK** when you are done.

15. On the **Data Connection Wizard**, leave the other two parameters as is, and click **Next**.

16. On the **Data Connection Wizard**, leave the **Store a copy of the data in the form template** check box deselected, and click **Next**.

17. On the **Data Connection Wizard**, accept the default name for the data connection (**OpenWorkbook**), deselect the **Automatically retrieve data when form is opened** check box, and click **Finish**. You will use this data connection to open the Excel workbook and get a session ID that you can use in all subsequent calls you make to Excel Services.

18. Select **Data** ▶ **Submit Form** ▶ **To Other Locations** ▶ **To Web Service**.

19. On the **Data Connection Wizard**, enter the URL of the Excel Services SOAP web service on the site where the workbook is located, for example:

    ```
    http://servername/sitename/_vti_bin/ExcelService.asmx
    ```

    where **servername** is the name of the SharePoint server, **sitename** is the name of the site where the workbook is located, and **ExcelService.asmx** is the Excel Services SOAP web service ASMX page. Click **Next**.

20. On the **Data Connection Wizard**, select **SetCellA1** from the list of operations, and click **Next**.

21. On the **Data Connection Wizard**, leave **tns:sessionId** selected, and click the button behind the **Field or group** text box.

22. On the **Select a Field or Group** dialog box, select **OpenWorkbook (Secondary)** from the **Fields** drop-down list box, expand the **dataFields** group node, select the **OpenWorkbookResult** field under the **tns:OpenWorkbookResponse** group node, and click **OK**. With this you have set the value of the **sessionId** parameter to be equal to the value of the session ID returned by the call to the **OpenWorkbook** operation.

23. On the **Data Connection Wizard**, leave **Text and child elements only** selected in the **Include** drop-down list box, select **tns:sheetName** from the **Parameters** list box, and click the button behind the **Field or group** text box.

24. On the **Select a Field or Group** dialog box, select **ExcelServicesInput (Secondary)** from the **Fields** drop-down list box, select the **sheetName** field, and click **OK**.

Chapter 6: Use Word, Excel, and Access with InfoPath via SharePoint

25. On the **Data Connection Wizard**, leave **Text and child elements only** selected in the **Include** drop-down list box, select **tns:rangeName** from the **Parameters** list box, and click the button behind the **Field or group** text box.

26. On the **Select a Field or Group** dialog box, select **ExcelServicesInput (Secondary)** from the **Fields** drop-down list box, select the **rangeName** field, and click **OK**.

27. On the **Data Connection Wizard**, leave **Text and child elements only** selected in the **Include** drop-down list box, select **tns:cellValue** from the **Parameters** list box, and click the button behind the **Field or group** text box.

28. On the **Select a Field or Group** dialog box, select **ExcelServicesInput (Secondary)** from the **Fields** drop-down list box, select the **cellValue** field, and click **OK**.

29. On the **Data Connection Wizard**, leave **Text and child elements only** selected in the **Include** drop-down list box, and click **Next**.

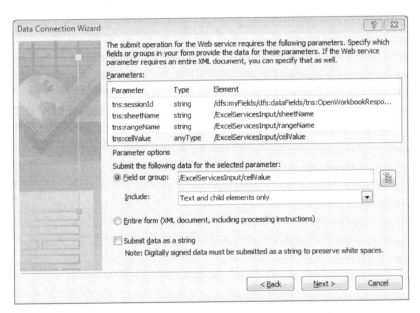

Figure 339. The completed settings for the web service parameters in InfoPath 2010.

30. On the **Data Connection Wizard**, name the data connection **SetCellValue**, deselect the **Set as the default submit connection** check box, and click **Finish**. You will use this data connection to set the values of the cells for the start date and the end date in the Excel workbook. At this point, the fields in the **ExcelServicesInput** secondary data source are still empty; you will use rules later to set their values before making the web service call.

413

31. Select **Data ▶ Get External Data ▶ From Web Service ▶ From SOAP Web Service**.

32. On the **Data Connection Wizard**, enter the URL of the Excel Services SOAP web service on the site where the workbook is located, for example:

    `http://servername/sitename/_vti_bin/ExcelService.asmx`

    where **servername** is the name of the SharePoint server, **sitename** is the name of the site where the workbook is located, and **ExcelService.asmx** is the Excel Services SOAP web service ASMX page. Click **Next**.

33. On the **Data Connection Wizard**, select **GetCellA1** from the list of operations, and click **Next**.

34. On the **Data Connection Wizard**, do not set any values for the parameters, and click **Next**.

35. On the **Data Connection Wizard**, leave the **Store a copy of the data in the form template** check box deselected, and click **Next**.

36. On the **Data Connection Wizard**, name the data connection **GetCellValue**, deselect the **Automatically retrieve data when form is opened** check box, and click **Finish**. You will use this data connection to retrieve the result of the calculation.

37. Select **Data ▶ Submit Form ▶ To Other Locations ▶ To Web Service**.

38. On the **Data Connection Wizard**, enter the URL of the Excel Services SOAP web service on the site where the workbook is located, for example:

    `http://servername/sitename/_vti_bin/ExcelService.asmx`

    where **servername** is the name of the SharePoint server, **sitename** is the name of the site where the workbook is located, and **ExcelService.asmx** is the Excel Services SOAP web service ASMX page. Click **Next**.

39. On the **Data Connection Wizard**, select **CloseWorkbook** from the list of operations, and click **Next**.

40. On the **Data Connection Wizard**, leave **tns:sessionId** selected, and click the button behind the **Field or group** text box.

41. On the **Select a Field or Group** dialog box, select **OpenWorkbook (Secondary)** from the **Fields** drop-down list box, expand the **dataFields** group node, select the **OpenWorkbookResult** field under the **tns:OpenWorkbookResponse** group node, and click **OK**.

42. On the **Data Connection Wizard**, leave **Text and child elements only** selected in the **Include** drop-down list box, and click **Next**.

Chapter 6: Use Word, Excel, and Access with InfoPath via SharePoint

43. On the **Data Connection Wizard**, name the data connection **CloseWorkbook**, deselect the **Set as the default submit connection** check box, and click **Finish**. You will use this data connection to close the workbook and the Excel Services session.

44. Add an **Action** rule to the **Calculate** button control with a **Condition** that says:

    ```
    startDate is not blank
    and
    endDate is not blank
    ```

    and that has the following action:

    ```
    Query using a data connection: OpenWorkbook
    ```

    Name the action rule **OpenWorkbook**. This action rule opens the workbook and returns a session ID that can be used for subsequent calls to Excel Services.

45. Add a second **Action** rule to the **Calculate** button control with a **Condition** that says:

    ```
    startDate is not blank
    and
    endDate is not blank
    ```

    and that has the following 4 actions:

    ```
    Set a field's value: sheetName = "Sheet1"
    ```

    where **sheetName** is located in the **ExcelServicesInput** secondary data source.

    ```
    Set a field's value: rangeName = "A1"
    ```

    where **rangeName** is located in the **ExcelServicesInput** secondary data source and **A1** is the cell in the Excel workbook that takes a start date.

    ```
    Set a field's value: cellValue = startDate
    ```

    where **cellValue** is located in the **ExcelServicesInput** secondary data source and **startDate** is the date field in the Main data source.

    ```
    Submit using a data connection: SetCellValue
    ```

    Name the action rule **SetStartDate**. This action rule calls the **SetCellA1** operation of the web service to set the value of the start date in cell **A1** on **Sheet1** in the Excel workbook to the value of the **startDate** date picker on the InfoPath form.

46. Add a third **Action** rule to the **Calculate** button control with a **Condition** that says:

    ```
    startDate is not blank
    and
    endDate is not blank
    ```

    and that has the following 3 actions:

415

InfoPath 2010 Cookbook 2

```
Set a field's value: rangeName = "A2"
```

where **rangeName** is located in the **ExcelServicesInput** secondary data source and **A2** is the cell in the Excel workbook that takes an end date.

```
Set a field's value: cellValue = endDate
```

where **cellValue** is located in the **ExcelServicesInput** secondary data source and **endDate** is the date field in the Main data source. Note that the value of the **sheetName** field in the **ExcelServicesInput** secondary data source does not have to be set, because you already set it to **Sheet1** in the **SetStartDate** action rule.

```
Submit using a data connection: SetCellValue
```

Name the action rule **SetEndDate**. This action rule calls the **SetCellA1** operation of the web service to set the value of the end date in cell **A2** on **Sheet1** in the Excel workbook to the value of the **endDate** date picker on the InfoPath form.

47. Add a fourth **Action** rule to the **Calculate** button control with a **Condition** that says:

```
startDate is not blank
and
endDate is not blank
```

and that has the following 4 actions:

```
Set a field's value: sessionId = OpenWorkbookResult
```

where **sessionId** is located under the **tns:GetCellA1** group node under the **queryFields** group node in the **GetCellValue** secondary data source and **OpenWorkbookResult** is located under the **tns:OpenWorkbookResponse** group node under the **dataFields** group node in the **OpenWorkbook** secondary data source. This action sets the session ID in preparation to call the web service operation.

```
Set a field's value: sheetName = sheetName
```

where the first **sheetName** is located under the **tns:GetCellA1** group node under the **queryFields** group node in the **GetCellValue** secondary data source and the second **sheetName** is located in the **ExcelServicesInput** secondary data source. The second **sheetName** field should still have a value of **Sheet1**.

```
Set a field's value: rangeName = "A3"
```

where **rangeName** is located under the **tns:GetCellA1** group node under the **queryFields** group node in the **GetCellValue** secondary data source and **A3** is the cell in the Excel workbook that contains the result of the formula that performs the calculation.

```
Query using a data connection: GetCellValue
```

Chapter 6: Use Word, Excel, and Access with InfoPath via SharePoint

Name the action rule **GetWorkdaysDiff**. This action rule sets the values of the required parameters and calls the **GetCellA1** operation of the web service to be able to retrieve the value of cell **A3** on **Sheet1** in the Excel workbook, which contains the result of the work days difference calculation.

48. Add a fifth **Action** rule to the **Calculate** button control with a **Condition** that says:

```
startDate is not blank
and
endDate is not blank
```

and that has the following action:

```
Submit using a data connection: CloseWorkbook
```

Name the action rule **CloseWorkbook**. This action rule closes the workbook and the Excel Services session.

The following figure displays the list of action rules that you should now have on the **Calculate** button and the details for the **GetWorkdaysDiff** rule.

Figure 340. The action rules on the Calculate button on the InfoPath form.

49. Set the **Default Value** of the **workdaysDiff** field to be equal to the value of the **GetCellA1Result** field that is located under the **tns:GetCellA1Response** group node under the **dataFields** group node in the **GetCellValue** secondary data source.

50. Publish the form template to a SharePoint form library.

In SharePoint, navigate to the form library where you published the form template and add a new form. When the form opens, select a start date, select an end date, and then click the **Calculate** button. Check whether the result for the date difference calculation took the holidays that were specified in the Excel workbook into account.

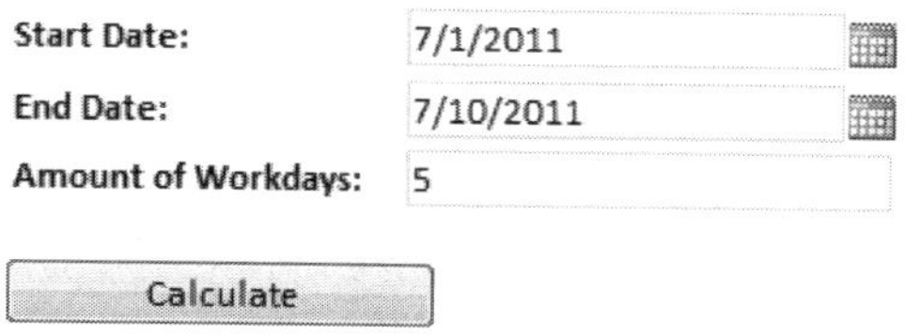

Figure 341. The InfoPath form displaying the amount of work days with July 4 being a holiday.

Discussion

In the solution described above you used operations of the Excel Services SOAP web service in SharePoint 2010 to:

1. Open an Excel workbook.
2. Set the value of a cell that contains the start date.
3. Set the value of a cell that contains the end date.
4. Perform a calculation and retrieve the results.
5. Close the Excel workbook.

Each one of these steps was executed by an action rule on the **Calculate** button on the form. Note that you could have also placed all of the actions under one rule, but by grouping the actions in 5 rules as you have done in the solution, you can easily disable any of the rules should you have to debug the calls made to the web service in order to resolve any errors.

You also used Excel's **NETWORKDAYS** function to calculate the amount of work days between two days and take holidays into account. From the Excel formula in step 1 you can see that the dates are passed to Excel in the ISO date format (**yyyy-MM-dd**) that is also used by default in InfoPath. The date is then parsed in Excel by using the **MID** function and the individual day, month, and year values are used in Excel's **DATE** function to construct dates that can be used by the **NETWORKDAYS** function.

The list of dates for holidays specified in the Excel formula does not affect the web service calls made by the InfoPath form, so if you want to update the list of holidays in the Excel workbook afterwards by adding more dates to it or by removing dates from it, you can freely do so. Just remember to also update the range (third argument) specified in

Chapter 6: Use Word, Excel, and Access with InfoPath via SharePoint

the **NETWORKDAYS** function to include more or less cells depending on the updates you make. Note that in the solution above, the list of holidays is located on **Sheet2** instead of **Sheet1**, but you could have also placed the dates on **Sheet1** if you wanted to; just remember to update the Excel formula accordingly if you do make such a change. If you want to update the list of holidays in the Excel workbook, you can do so by manually updating the file stored in the SharePoint document library, or update and then republish the file from within Excel as described in step 3.

Web service calls from within InfoPath are very error-prone and can be difficult to debug. So if you get any errors while trying to design a form template that makes use of web service data connections, for example

An error occurred querying a data source

or

There has been an error while processing the form.

with a detailed error message of

There was a form postback error. ..., Type: KeyNotFoundException, Exception Message: The given key was not present in the dictionary.)

The first step would be to check the SharePoint log files, which in a default SharePoint installation are located under

```
C:\Program Files\Common Files\Microsoft Shared\Web Server Extensions\14\LOGS
```

to see what the exact error message is. If you are not an administrator, so cannot access the log files, the next step would be to disable all of the action rules in InfoPath, enable them one-by-one, check the values that are returned, and try to narrow down which rule (or action) is causing the error. You can disable a rule by clicking on the drop-down arrow on the right-hand side of the rule on the **Rules** task pane and then selecting **Disable** from the drop-down menu that appears.

If you happen to get the error message mentioned above (*The given key was not present in the dictionary*), you can try adding an **arrayOfAnyType** node to the Main data source of the form and see whether it helps. Note that you need not do anything else with the node but just add it to the Main data source of the form.

To add an **arrayOfAnyType** node to the Main data source:

1. In Notepad, create an XML file that has the following contents:

    ```
    <tns:ArrayOfAnyType xmlns:xsd="http://www.w3.org/2001/XMLSchema"
    xmlns:xsi="http://www.w3.org/2001/XMLSchema"
    xmlns:tns="http://schemas.microsoft.com/office/excel/server/webservices"
    >
        <tns:anyType type="xsd:string"></tns:anyType>
        <tns:anyType type="xsd:string"></tns:anyType>
    </tns:ArrayOfAnyType>
    ```

    and name the XML file **ArrayOfAnyType.xml** or download the **ArrayOfAnyType.xml** file from www.bizsupportonline.com.

2. In InfoPath, on the **Fields** task pane, right-click the **myFields** group node, and select **Add** from the drop-down menu that appears.
3. On the **Add Field or Group** dialog box, select **Complete XML Schema or XML document** from the **Type** drop-down list box.
4. On the **Data Source Wizard**, click **Browse**, and browse to, select, and open the **ArrayOfAnyType.xml** file.
5. On the **Data Source Wizard**, click **Next**.
6. On the **Data Source Wizard**, leave the **No** option selected, and click **Finish**.

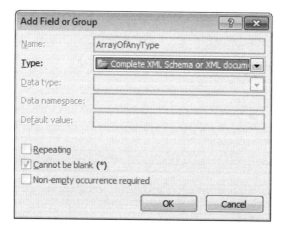

Figure 342. The dialog box after adding the ArrayOfAnyType XML file.

7. On the **Add Field or Group** dialog box, click **OK**.
8. Republish the form template to SharePoint and test it.

Designing a form template that makes web service calls can require quite a few steps to complete and/or action rules that could cause time-outs. So in the next recipe you will learn how you can reduce the amount of steps to set up a similar solution as the one described above by using the REST web service of Excel Services instead of its SOAP web service.

98 Calculate work days between two dates using Excel Services – method 2

Use the Excel Services REST web service

Problem

You have two date picker controls on a form and want to calculate the difference in business days between these two dates excluding holidays and weekends.

Chapter 6: Use Word, Excel, and Access with InfoPath via SharePoint

Solution

You can create an Excel workbook that contains the calculation for the amount of work days between two dates and a list of dates for holidays, publish this Excel workbook to a trusted file location for Excel Services, and then call the Excel Services REST web service from within the InfoPath form to perform the calculation.

To calculate the amount of work days between two dates excluding holidays:

1. In Excel 2010, create an Excel workbook that contains a list of dates for holidays (or download the **WorkdaysCalculator.xlsx** sample file from www.bizsupportonline.com) and the following formula in cell **A3** on **Sheet1**:

   ```
   =NETWORKDAYS(DATE(MID(A1,1,4),MID(A1,6,2),MID(A1,9,2)),DATE(MID(A2,1,4),MID(A2,6,2),MID(A2,9,2)),Sheet2!A1:A16)
   ```

   where cell **A1** on **Sheet1** contains a start date that has a format of **yyyy-MM-dd** and a default value of **2011-01-01**, cell **A2** on **Sheet1** contains an end date that has a format of **yyyy-MM-dd** and a default value of **2012-01-01**, and cells **A1** to **A16** on **Sheet2** contain a range of dates that represent holidays. The dates for the holidays have the **Date** data type in Excel. Note that you can make the start and end dates text by selecting **Text** from the drop-down list box on the **Home** tab under the **Number** group. You can convert the dates for the holidays to have the **Date** data type by selecting **Date** from the same drop-down list box. Also note that you will be changing the default values of cells **A1** and **A2** on **Sheet1** later through InfoPath. The Excel formula uses the **NETWORKDAYS**, **DATE**, and **MID** functions to calculate the amount of work days minus holidays.

2. Save the Excel workbook to disk and name it **WorkdaysCalculator.xlsx**.

3. Click **File** ➤ **Save & Send** ➤ **Save to SharePoint** ➤ **Save As** and save the entire workbook (including all of its sheets) to a document library (for example the **Shared Documents** library) on the SharePoint site where you will be publishing the form template (also see steps 2 through 6 of recipe *96 Display Excel data in a browser form – method 2*).

4. In InfoPath, create a new SharePoint form library form template or use an existing one.

5. Select **Data** ➤ **Get External Data** ➤ **From Web Service** ➤ **From REST Web Service**.

6. On the **Data Connection Wizard**, enter the URL of the Excel Services REST web service and the Excel workbook, for example:

   ```
   http://servername/sitename/_vti_bin/ExcelREST.aspx/Shared%20Documents/WorkDaysCalculator.xlsx/model/Ranges('A3')?$format=atom
   ```

   and click **Next**. Here, **servername** is the name of the SharePoint server and **sitename** is the name of the site where the **WorkDaysCalculator.xlsx** workbook has been stored in the **Shared Documents** document library. **A3** is the cell on

InfoPath 2010 Cookbook 2

Sheet1 of the Excel workbook that contains the formula to calculate the amount of work days. See the discussion section of recipe *96 Display Excel data in a browser form – method 2* for the meaning of the different parts that the REST web service URL is composed of.

7. On the **Data Connection Wizard**, name the data connection **GetWorkdaysDifference**, deselect the **Automatically retrieve data when form is opened** check box, and click **Finish**.

8. Add two **Date Picker** controls to the view of the form template and name them **startDate** and **endDate**, respectively.

9. Add a **Text Box** control to the view of the form template and name it **workdaysDiff**. Make the text box control read-only or change it into a calculated value control, since the user should not be able to change the value of this field.

10. Add an **Action** rule to the **startDate** date picker with a **Condition** that says:

    ```
    startDate is not blank
    and
    endDate is not blank
    ```

    and that has a first action that says:

    ```
    Change REST URL: REST Web Service
    ```

    that changes the **REST Web Service URL** to the following formula:

    ```
    concat("http://servername/sitename/_vti_bin/ExcelREST.aspx/Shared%20Documen
    ts/WorkDaysCalculator.xlsx/model/Ranges('A3')?Ranges('A1')=", .,
    "&Ranges('A2')=", endDate, "&$format=atom")
    ```

    Add a second action that says:

    ```
    Query using a data connection: GetWorkdaysDifference
    ```

    The first action sets the values of the parameters for the start date and the end date in the REST web service URL.

    ```
    Ranges('A1')=.
    ```

    sets the value of the **A1** cell in the Excel workbook to be equal to the value of the **startDate** date picker and

    ```
    Ranges('A2')=endDate
    ```

    sets the value of the **A2** cell in the Excel workbook to be equal to the value of the **endDate** date picker. The second action queries the data connection and returns the result from the **A3** cell, which is specified through

    ```
    Ranges('A3')
    ```

    in the REST web service URL.

Chapter 6: Use Word, Excel, and Access with InfoPath via SharePoint

11. Add an **Action** rule to the **endDate** date picker with a **Condition** that says:

    ```
    startDate is not blank
    and
    endDate is not blank
    ```

    and that has a first action that says:

    ```
    Change REST URL: REST Web Service
    ```

    that changes the **REST Web Service URL** to the following formula:

    ```
    concat("http://servername/sitename/_vti_bin/ExcelREST.aspx/Shared%20Documen
    ts/WorkDaysCalculator.xlsx/model/Ranges('A3')?Ranges('A1')=", startDate,
    "&Ranges('A2')=", ., "&$format=atom")
    ```

    Add a second action that says:

    ```
    Query using a data connection: GetWorkdaysDifference
    ```

    The first action sets the values of the parameters for the start date and the end date in the REST web service URL.

    ```
    Ranges('A1')=startDate
    ```

    sets the value of the **A1** cell in the Excel workbook to be equal to the value of the **startDate** date picker and

    ```
    Ranges('A2')=.
    ```

    sets the value of the **A2** cell in the Excel workbook to be equal to the value of the **endDate** date picker. The second action queries the data connection and returns the result from the **A3** cell, which is specified through

    ```
    Ranges('A3')
    ```

    in the REST web service URL.

12. Set the **Default Value** of the **workdaysDiff** field to be equal to:

    ```
    v
    ```

    or

    ```
    xdXDocument:GetDOM("GetWorkdaysDifference")/ns1:entry/ns1:content/ns2:range
    /ns2:row/ns2:c/ns2:v
    ```

    if you have the **Edit XPath (advanced)** check box selected on the **Insert Formula** dialog box. **v** is a field that is located in the **GetWorkdaysDifference** secondary data source.

13. Publish the form template to a SharePoint form library.

InfoPath 2010 Cookbook 2

In SharePoint, navigate to the form library where you published the form template and add a new form. When the form opens, select a start date and an end date and verify that the calculated amount of work days is correct.

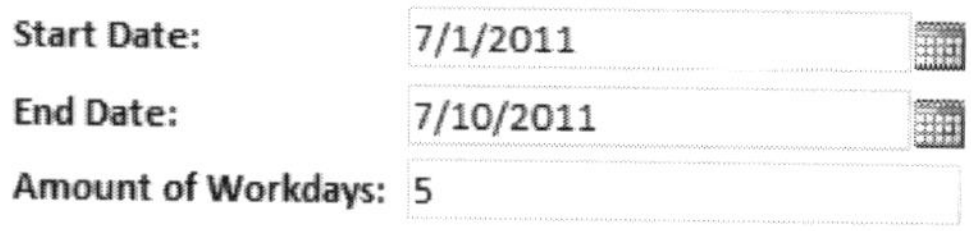

Start Date:	7/1/2011
End Date:	7/10/2011
Amount of Workdays:	5

Figure 343. The InfoPath form displaying the amount of work days with July 4 being a holiday.

Discussion

The solution described above uses the Excel Services REST web service to set values in an Excel workbook, perform a calculation, and return the results. The Excel formula used in the workbook was explained in the discussion section of recipe *97 Calculate work days between two dates using Excel Services – method 1*.

If you look at the following REST web service URL

```
http://servername/sitename/_vti_bin/ExcelREST.aspx/Shared%20Documents/WorkDaysCa
lculator.xlsx/model/Ranges('A3')?Ranges('A1')=2011-07-01&Ranges('A2')=2011-07-
10&$format=atom
```

you can see that

```
/model/Ranges('A3')
```

returns the result for the work days calculation, while all of the parameters that come after the question mark in the REST web service URL, define the values for the parameters that you want to set in the formula to perform the calculation.

To make the formula a little bit more user-friendly, you may want to define meaningful names for the cells. For example, you could name cell A3 **workdaysDifference** in Excel as follows:

1. Click cell **A3** to select it.
2. Click **Formulas** ➤ **Defined Names** ➤ **Define name**.
3. On the **New Name** dialog box, type **workdaysDifference** in the **Name** text box, leave the **Scope** of **Workbook** selected, and click **OK**.

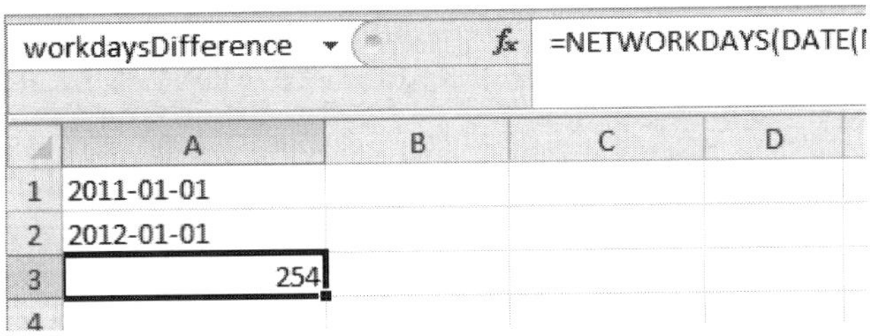

Chapter 6: Use Word, Excel, and Access with InfoPath via SharePoint

![workdaysDifference cell showing =NETWORKDAYS formula with value 254 in cell A3]

Figure 344. Work days difference cell with a defined name in Excel 2010.

Note that if you change the names of cells, you must also change the range names in the REST web service URL. The REST web service URL would then become

```
http://servername/sitename/_vti_bin/ExcelREST.aspx/Shared%20Documents/WorkDaysCa
lculator.xlsx/model/Ranges('workdaysDifference')?Ranges('A1')=2011-07-
01&Ranges('A2')=2011-07-10&$format=atom
```

If you want to revert back to the default names for cells in Excel:

1. Click **Formulas** ➤ **Defined Names** ➤ **Name Manager**.
2. On the **Name Manager** dialog box, select the previously defined name you want to delete, and then click **Delete**.

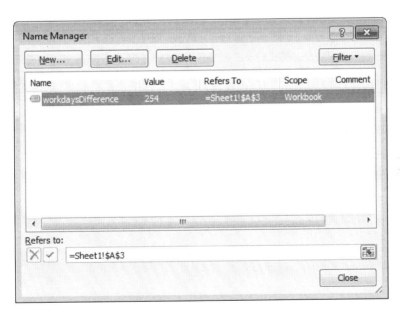

Figure 345. The Name Manager dialog box in Excel 2010.

3. Click **Close** when you are done.

425

InfoPath 2010 Cookbook 2

Excel is a great application to perform calculations that would otherwise require code in InfoPath. So if you are creating browser forms and have Excel Services running on SharePoint, you can leverage the power of Excel to perform calculations in InfoPath. This technique works for any formula in Excel.

If you do not want to use or are unable to make REST web service calls on your SharePoint server, you can still make use of Excel Services calculations by going through its SOAP web service interface as described in recipe *97 Calculate work days between two dates using Excel Services – method 1*. Please note that the amount of steps you will have to perform when designing a form template that makes use of the SOAP web service far exceeds the amount of steps to design a form template that makes use of the REST web service.

99 Send InfoPath form data to an Excel workbook

Problem

You have an InfoPath form and an Excel workbook, and you want to enter data in a field on the InfoPath form, click a button to send the data to the Excel workbook, and then use the data passed to Excel in a formula in the Excel workbook to perform a calculation.

Solution

You can embed both the InfoPath form and the Excel workbook in web parts on a SharePoint page and then set up web part connections to pass data from the InfoPath form to the Excel workbook. The example used in this solution will be kept simple to make the basic concepts clear.

Suppose you want to create an Excel workbook named **SimpleCalculation.xlsx** (you can download the sample **SimpleCalculation.xlsx** file from www.bizsupportonline.com), which contains a formula that adds 10 to a specific number in a cell, and you want to set the value of that cell from within an InfoPath form. Before you can set the value of an Excel cell from within an InfoPath form, you must set up the Excel workbook to accept parameters being sent to it.

To set up the Excel workbook to receive parameters:

1. In Excel 2010, create a new workbook.
2. Place the cursor in cell **A1** on **Sheet1**, and then click **Formulas ▶ Defined Names ▶ Define name**.
3. On the **New Name** dialog box, type **valueFromInfoPath** in the **Name** text box, leave the **Scope** of **Workbook** selected, and click **OK**. With this you have assigned the name **valueFromInfoPath** to cell **A1**. You will use this name later as a parameter.
4. Place the cursor in cell **B1** on **Sheet1**, and enter the following formula:

Chapter 6: Use Word, Excel, and Access with InfoPath via SharePoint

```
=valueFromInfoPath+10
```

This formula adds **10** to the value of the **valueFromInfoPath** cell.

5. Save the workbook locally on disk and name it **SimpleCalculation.xlsx** or download the sample **SimpleCalculation.xlsx** file from www.bizsupportonline.com and store that file on disk.

6. Click **File** ➤ **Save & Send** ➤ **Save to SharePoint** ➤ **Publish Options**.

7. On the **Publish Options** dialog box on the **Show** tab, select **Sheets** from the drop-down list box, deselect all of the check boxes except for the **Sheet 1** check box, and click **OK**.

8. On the **Publish Options** dialog box, click the **Parameters** tab, and then click **Add**.

9. On the **Add Parameters** dialog box, select the check box in front of **valueFromInfoPath**, and click **OK**.

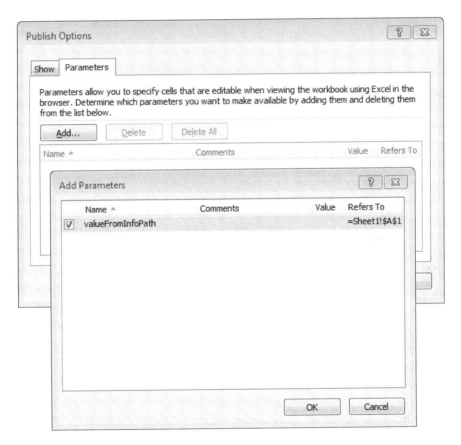

Figure 346. Adding a parameter in Excel 2010.

10. On the **Publish Options** dialog box, click **OK**.

11. Click **File** ▶ **Save & Send** ▶ **Save to SharePoint** ▶ **Browse for a location** ▶ **Save As**.

12. On the **Save As** dialog box, enter the URL of the SharePoint site where you want to publish the Excel workbook in the address bar at the top of the dialog box, and press **Enter**.

13. On the **Save As** dialog box, select a document library in which to store the Excel workbook (for example the **Shared Documents** library), ensure **SimpleCalculation.xlsx** is listed in the **File name** combo box, deselect the **Open with Excel in the browser** check box, and click **Save**.

Once you have set up parameters in the Excel workbook, you can design an InfoPath form template that sends data to that Excel workbook.

To create the InfoPath form template:

1. In InfoPath, create a new SharePoint form library form template or use an existing one.

2. Add a **Text Box** control and a **Button** control to the view of the form template. Name the text box control **numberToAdd**, change its data type to **Whole Number (integer)**, and label the button control **Send Data to Excel**.

3. Add an **Action** rule to the **Send Data to Excel** button that has the following action:

   ```
   Send data to Web Part
   ```

   and then on the **Rule Details** dialog box, click **Property Promotion**.

4. On the **Form Options** dialog box, click **Add** in the section for managing SharePoint Web Part connection parameters (the bottom section).

5. On the **Select a field** dialog box, select **numberToAdd** in the tree view, enter **NumberToAdd** as the **Parameter name**, select the **Output** option, and click **OK**. With this you have created an output web part connection parameter for the **numberToAdd** field.

6. On the **Form Options** dialog box, click **OK**.

7. On the **Rule Details** dialog box, click **OK**.

8. Publish the form template to a SharePoint form library.

Once you have created and published both the Excel workbook and the InfoPath form template to SharePoint, you can embed them in web parts on a SharePoint page.

To send data from the InfoPath form to the Excel workbook:

1. In SharePoint, navigate to a wiki page or a web part page on which you want to place the InfoPath form and Excel workbook, and edit the page. If you are unsure how to edit a wiki or a web part page, see recipe *33 Embed an InfoPath form on a SharePoint*

Chapter 6: Use Word, Excel, and Access with InfoPath via SharePoint

page for instructions on editing a wiki page and recipe *34 Master/detail across two forms linked through one field* for instructions on creating and editing a web part page.

2. Add an **InfoPath Form Web Part** (located under the **Forms** category of web parts) to the page.

3. Add an **Excel Web Access** web part (located under the **Business Data** category of web parts) to the page.

4. On the **InfoPath Form Web Part**, click the **Click here to open the tool pane** link.

5. On the web part tool pane, select the form library where you published the InfoPath form template from the **List or Library** drop-down list box, and click **OK**.

6. On the **Excel Web Access** web part, click the **Click here to open the tool pane** link.

7. On the web part tool pane, click the ellipsis (...) button behind the **Workbook** text box.

8. On the **Select an Asset** webpage dialog, navigate to the location where you published the Excel workbook, select the **SimpleCalculation** Excel workbook, and click **OK**.

9. On the web part tool pane under **Interactivity**, deselect the **Display Parameters Task Pane** check box, and then click **OK**.

10. Click the drop-down arrow in the upper right-hand corner of the **InfoPath Form Web Part**, and then select **Connections ▶ Send Data To ▶ Excel Web Access – SimpleCalculation** from the drop-down menu that appears.

11. On the **Configure Connection** webpage dialog, select **valueFromInfoPath** from the **Consumer Field Name** drop-down list box, and click **Finish**. With this you have configured the **InfoPath Form Web Part** to send data to the **Excel Web Access** web part.

12. Save or stop editing the page.

In SharePoint, navigate to the page on which you placed the two web parts. Enter a number into the text box on the InfoPath form and click the button. The number you entered should appear in the Excel workbook and cell B1 should contain a value that is the sum of the number you entered plus 10.

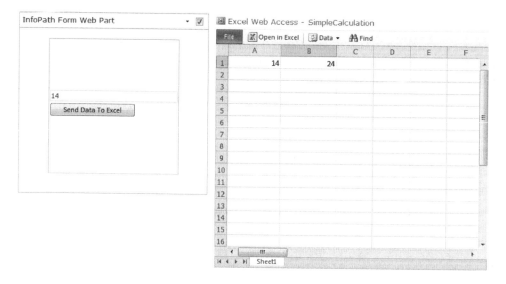

Figure 347. The InfoPath form and Excel workbook embedded on a SharePoint page.

Discussion

In the solution described above you made use of Excel Services and the Excel Web Access web part to embed an Excel workbook on a SharePoint page to be able to send data from an InfoPath form embedded in an InfoPath Form Web Part to that Excel workbook through web part connection parameters. You thereby used the **Send data to Web Part** action in InfoPath to send the value of one InfoPath form field to the Excel workbook. If your scenario calls for passing multiple parameters to an Excel workbook, you could set up multiple web part connection parameters in InfoPath, define multiple parameters in the Excel workbook, and then use SharePoint Designer 2010 as described in recipe *35 Pass data from a selected row in a repeating table to another form* to set up the web part connections between the InfoPath Form Web Part and Excel Web Access web parts in SharePoint.

The power of Excel lies in its ability to perform complex calculations. The formula used in the solution described above was kept simple for demonstration purposes, but you could make it as complex as you like.

Use Access data in InfoPath through SharePoint

SharePoint 2010 offers several ways to integrate InfoPath 2010 with Access 2010, a couple of which include:

- Moving Access data to a SharePoint list and then creating a data connection to that SharePoint list in InfoPath.
- Using a SharePoint list form to maintain data in an Access database table.

- Using a SharePoint list form to maintain data and then exporting the SharePoint list data to Access for reporting purposes.

The recipes in this section are meant to provide you with ideas for solutions that combine InfoPath forms with Access database tables through SharePoint.

100 Display Access data in a browser form

Problem

You have an Access database table which you want to be able to use in an InfoPath browser form to display data in a drop-down list box, but InfoPath does not allow you to directly connect to an Access database table from a browser form. You get the error message

The selected database is not supported in Web browser forms. Select a Microsoft SQL Server database.

when you try to connect to an Access database from an InfoPath browser-compatible form template.

Solution

You can publish the Access database table to a SharePoint list and then use a SharePoint list data connection in InfoPath to be able to read data from the Access table bound to the SharePoint list.

To display data from an Access database table in a browser form:

1. In Access 2010, create a new database that contains a table with data that has the same structure and values as the Excel spreadsheet from recipe *95 Display Excel data in a browser form – method 1* or download the **Fruits.accdb** file from www.bizsupportonline.com. When you create the table, leave the **ID** column intact as an **AutoNumber** column.

2. Click **Database Tools** ➤ **Move Data** ➤ **SharePoint**.

   Figure 348. The Move Data group on the Database Tools tab in Access 2010.

3. On the **Export Tables to SharePoint Wizard**, enter the URL of the SharePoint site to which you want to export the table (or select the URL from the list if you have already previously connected to the site), and click **Next**.

InfoPath 2010 Cookbook 2

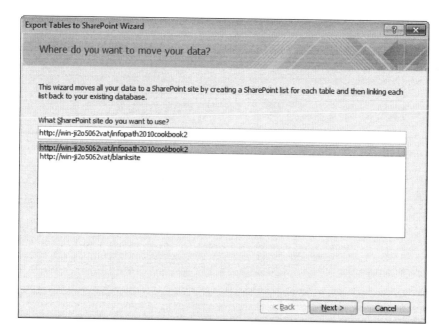

Figure 349. The **Export Tables to SharePoint Wizard** in Access 2010.

After this, Access should back up the database by creating a copy of the original database, connect to SharePoint to create the SharePoint list, and convert the existing table into a linked table in the database.

4. On the **Export Tables to SharePoint Wizard**, click **Finish**.

5. In SharePoint, navigate to the site to which you exported the Access database table, click **Site Actions** ➤ **View All Site Content**, and then under **Lists**, verify that the SharePoint list was created for the Access database table.

6. In InfoPath, create a new SharePoint form library form template or use an existing one.

7. Click **Data** ➤ **Get External Data** ➤ **From SharePoint List** to add a data connection to the SharePoint list that you created for the Access database table (also see *Use a SharePoint list data connection* in recipe *43 3 Ways to retrieve data from a SharePoint list*).

8. Bind the secondary data source for the SharePoint list to a repeating table on the view as described in recipe *44 Display SharePoint list data in a repeating table*.

9. Add a **Button** control to the view of the form template and change its **Action** property to **Refresh**.

10. Publish the form template to a SharePoint form library.

432

In SharePoint, navigate to the form library where you published the form template and add a new form. When the form opens, the repeating table should contain the same rows that are present in the Access database table. Open the database in Access and add a new row to the table. Then go to the form again, and click the **Refresh** button. The row you just added in Access should now also appear in the repeating table.

Discussion

In the solution described above, you connected an InfoPath browser form to an Access database table through SharePoint. You also used the **Refresh** button action to refresh the data in the secondary data source for the SharePoint list.

The **Export Tables to SharePoint Wizard** in Access 2010 allows you to move data to SharePoint lists and maintain a "live link" with this data. The latter means that you can update the data locally in the Access database and have those changes automatically reflected in the SharePoint list. You can use this method to centralize and make data from an Access database available over the network using SharePoint as the solution above demonstrates.

Because direct connections to Access databases from within an InfoPath browser-compatible form template are not supported, whether you want to have read-only access or read/write access, you can only connect to SQL Server databases from within an InfoPath browser-compatible form template. Therefore, the solution described above is a workaround for connecting InfoPath browser forms to Access databases by going through SharePoint.

101 Edit and update Access data through a browser form

Problem

You have an Access database table which you want to connect to from an InfoPath browser form to add, edit, or delete records in it, but InfoPath does not allow you to connect to an Access database when you are designing a browser form. You get the error message

The selected database is not supported in Web browser forms. Select a Microsoft SQL Server database.

when you try to connect to an Access database from an InfoPath browser-compatible form template.

Solution

You can create a SharePoint list form that has been enabled for editing multiple items to be able to add, edit, and delete records from an Access database table from within an InfoPath browser form.

To perform create, update, and delete (CRUD) operations on an Access table using an InfoPath form:

InfoPath 2010 Cookbook 2

1. In Access 2010, export a table to a SharePoint list as described in steps 2 through 4 of recipe *100 Display Access data in a browser form*.

2. In InfoPath, create a new SharePoint list form for the SharePoint list to which you exported the Access database table and enable it to manage multiple items as described in recipe *3 Create a SharePoint list form to manage multiple list items with one form*.

3. On the view of the form template, right-click the **Repeating Section** that InfoPath automatically added, and select **Repeating Section Properties** from the context menu that appears.

4. On the **Repeating Section Properties** dialog box on the **Data** tab, select the **Allow users to insert and delete the sections** check box, select the **Show insert button and hint text** check box, and then click **OK**.

Figure 350. Setting the repeating table to allow insertion and deletion of sections.

5. Delete the **Title** and **_OldID** rows from the table within the repeating section control. **_OldID** contains the value of the **ID** field (which is automatically generated) from the Access database table, while **Title** is a SharePoint field that you are not required to fill out.

6. Add a **Button** control to the view of the form template, and change its **Action** property to **Run Query**.

7. Click the **Quick Publish** button on the **Quick Access Toolbar**, click **File ▶ Info ▶ Quick Publish**, or click **File ▶ Publish ▶ SharePoint List** to publish the form template to SharePoint.

Chapter 6: Use Word, Excel, and Access with InfoPath via SharePoint

In SharePoint, navigate to the SharePoint list that is connected to the Access database table. Add a new item or modify data for an existing item. Click the **Run Query** button to retrieve all of the items from the SharePoint list. Click **Insert item** to insert a new section. Enter some values, and click **Save**. Note that you can delete items from the SharePoint list by deleting the sections for those items and then saving your changes. Verify that the new item was added to the SharePoint list. Open the Access database table and verify that the changes you made were written back to the database.

Discussion

In the solution described above you learned how to create an InfoPath browser form with which you can manage all of the records in an Access database table through a SharePoint list.

Because a SharePoint list form displays only one section to enter or modify a list item when you add or edit a list item, you must either add a **Run Query** button to the form or add a **Query for data** action rule that runs for example during the **Form Load** event to query the **Main data connection**, so that all of the list items are retrieved whenever the form is opened.

While this and the previous recipe showed you how to export only one Access database table to SharePoint, you could export multiple tables including the relationships between those tables in order to create linked lists in SharePoint, and then customize the SharePoint list forms of those lists to simulate master/detail functionality across SharePoint lists.

You could also go in the opposite direction (from SharePoint to Access) and use an InfoPath form to maintain data in a SharePoint list and then export that SharePoint list to Access by using the **Open with Access** command that is available on the SharePoint list in order to use Access to create reports based on the SharePoint list data.

When you create a SharePoint form library form and publish it to a SharePoint form library, it becomes a bit more difficult to export data from InfoPath forms to create a report in Access, since the **Open with Access** command is not available on SharePoint form libraries. One workaround would be to use the **Export to Excel** command instead and then import the Excel data in Access to create a report. However, you must promote fields from the InfoPath form to the SharePoint form library as columns to be able to export the values of the InfoPath form fields to the Excel file and then use that data for reporting purposes in Access.

InfoPath 2010 Cookbook 2

Appendix

Content types and site columns

A content type as the name suggests is a certain type of content. Content in the context of SharePoint refers to a list item, document, or folder. So a content type defines the properties of a list item, document, or folder.

There are two types of content types in SharePoint: Site content types and list content types. A site content type is created in the context of a site and can be added to multiple lists or libraries. A list content type is an instance of a site content type that has been associated with a list or library and is private to that list or library; you cannot use it on any other list or library. When you associate a site content type with a list or library, you enable users to create list items, folders, or documents that are based on that content type, and store them in that list or library.

The use of content types in SharePoint is important to understand, not only because content types are a core element of lists and libraries, but also because they are pivotal for creating and using InfoPath forms in SharePoint. As far as InfoPath goes, it is good to know a bit about content types, because:

- When you create a SharePoint list form template, you base it on a content type that is associated with a SharePoint list.
- When you publish an InfoPath form template to a form library or as a site content type, the form template becomes the document template of a content type.
- Content types allow form libraries to contain different types of InfoPath forms.
- Content types allow you to run SharePoint workflows on specific types of InfoPath forms.
- The fields in document information panel form templates are derived from the columns associated with a content type.
- The logic behind several recipes in this book is based on the use of content types.

Since a thorough explanation of content types is beyond the scope of this book, this book instead focuses on providing you with the basic knowledge you need to be able to work with content types as they relate to InfoPath forms in SharePoint.

Add existing content types to a SharePoint list

Problem

You want a custom SharePoint list to be able to contain tasks, contacts, and custom items, so you want the SharePoint list to contain three different types of list items.

Solution

You can enable management of content types on a SharePoint list and then add a **Task** and **Contact** content type to the list, so that users can create items that are based on those content types to add tasks, contacts, and custom list items to the SharePoint list.

To add existing content types to a SharePoint list:

1. In SharePoint, create a custom SharePoint list via **Site Actions ➤ More Options** or **Site Actions ➤ View All Site Content ➤ Create**.

2. Once you have created the custom SharePoint list, navigate to its settings page by clicking on **List Tools ➤ List ➤ Settings ➤ List Settings**.

3. When you create a custom SharePoint list, an **Item** content type is added to it by default. But you will not be able to see that this is the case, unless you enable management of content types, which is disabled by default. So on the **List Settings** page under **General Settings**, click **Advanced settings**.

4. On the **Advanced Settings** page, select the **Yes** option for **Allow management of content types**, and click **OK**.

5. Back on the **List Settings** page, you should now see a section called **Content Types** appear, and under that the **Item** content type should be listed. This is the default content type on the list. Now you can add more content types to the list by clicking on the **Add from existing site content types** link under the **Content Types** section.

6. Content types are ordered in groups in SharePoint. You can find those groups listed in the **Select site content types from** drop-down list box on the **Add Content Types** page. Because you want to add **Task** and **Contact** content types to the SharePoint list and these content types are generally added to SharePoint lists, you must select **List Content Types** from the **Select site content types from** drop-down list box, hold the **Ctrl** key on your keyboard pressed down and click **Task** and then **Contact** to select both content types from the **Available Site Content Types** list box, click **Add** to add the content types to the **Content types to add** list box, and then click **OK**. Back on the **List Settings** page, you should now see three content types listed: **Item**, **Task**, and **Contact**, of which **Item** is marked as the **Default Content Type**.

In SharePoint, navigate to the SharePoint list. Click **Add new item** to add a new item that is based on the **Item** content type to the list. Select **List Tools ➤ Items ➤ New Item ➤**

Appendix

Task to add a new task item that is based on the **Task** content type to the list. Select **List Tools ▶ Items ▶ New Item ▶ Contact** to add a new contact item that is based on the **Contact** content type to the list.

Discussion

SharePoint comes with an entire range of content types right out of the box, so you need not always have to create content types yourself, but can make use of the ones that already exist in SharePoint.

In the solution described above, you added a **Task** content type to a custom SharePoint list that already had an **Item** content type associated with it. Before you can add additional content types to a SharePoint list or library, you must enable management of content types on that list or library. And once enabled, you can choose to add content types from different groups of content types that are available in SharePoint. You can navigate to the **Site Content Types** page (**Site Actions ▶ Site Settings ▶ Site Galleries ▶ Site Content Types**) to see the list of content types that are available on a SharePoint site.

The method described in this recipe applies to both SharePoint lists and libraries. In the next recipe you will learn how to create a custom content type and learn more about the relationship between content types.

Create a new site content type

Problem

You want to add a site content type to a SharePoint site so that you can associate it later with a SharePoint list or library.

Solution

You can create a new site content type via the settings page of a SharePoint site.

To create a new site content type:

1. Decide on which site you should create the site content type based on the scope of a site content type as described in the discussion section of this recipe.

2. In SharePoint, navigate to the SharePoint site where you want to create the site content type, and click **Site Actions ▶ Site Settings**.

3. On the **Site Settings** page under **Galleries**, click **Site content types**.

4. On the **Site Content Types** page, click **Create**.

5. On the **New Site Content Type** page, enter a **Name** for the content type, select the **Parent Content Type** that the content type should inherit from (for example the **Document** parent content type from the **Document Content Types** category),

select the **Group** to place the new content type in (you can accept the default group of **Custom Content Types** for most cases), and click **OK**.

Once SharePoint has created the new site content type, you should be redirected to the details page of the new site content type. There you can do things such as add site columns to the content type under the **Columns** section, set the document template for the content type via the **Advanced settings** link under the **Settings** section, add a workflow to the content type via the **Workflow settings** link under the **Settings** section, or even delete the content type. And once you have configured the new content type, you can add it to a document or form library.

Discussion

Let us take the abstract concept of a content type in SharePoint and try to relate it to something you might be more familiar with in real life such as for example a résumé. A résumé is typically a Word document that describes the work history of a person. A résumé belongs to one person who has a first name, last name, address, telephone number, etc. A résumé typically also contains common sections such as contact details, a list of skills, a list of past employers, a list of referees, etc. You could use a Word template that defines the layout and structure of a résumé to create a résumé Word document for any person. So a résumé is a specific type of content.

If you wanted to take a résumé and bring it into the world of SharePoint, you would have to create a **Document** content type that has the first name, last name, etc. of a person as its columns. This content type could then be used to create and store data for a person. This data would not only define who that person is, but it could also be used to find and retrieve the résumé of that person within SharePoint. In addition, every time you create a résumé for a new person, you would want to use a generic Word template for a résumé as a starting document to create a specific résumé Word document for that person. To make this possible in SharePoint, you would have to set the Word template as the document template of the content type. And finally, if résumés should go through for example an approval process, you could associate the content type for the résumé with an approval workflow, so that this workflow could be started on all résumés that are created from that specific résumé content type.

Content types in SharePoint follow a hierarchy, that is, a content type always inherits from a parent content type, so when you create a custom content type, you will always be basing it on another content type, most likely the **Document** or **Form** content type in the case of InfoPath forms. When you base a content type on another content type, the new content type inherits the fields and behavior from its parent content type.

Content types in SharePoint have scopes, which are important to understand especially if you are planning to publish InfoPath form templates that should be used across sites in a site collection. The scope of a content type determines the locations in the site collection where the content type would become available for use.

The scope of a content type is defined as follows:

Appendix

1. A content type that has been defined in the top-level site of a site collection is available to all sites and child sites in that site collection, but not available to sites and child sites in a different site collection.
2. A content type that has been defined in a site is available to all child sites below that site.
3. A content type that has been defined in a child site is not available in the parent site of that child site or in any sites above the child site.
4. A content type that has been defined in a site is not available in a site that is located in the same site collection, but that is not a child site of that site.

In summary: The scope of a content type works down the site hierarchy, but not upwards or sideways. This has been visualized in the following figure.

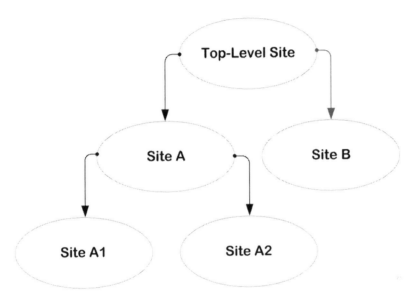

Figure 351. The flow of content type availability in sites within a SharePoint site hierarchy.

In the figure above:

- A content type defined in the Top-Level Site is available in all of the sites.
- A content type defined in Site A is only available in Site A, Site A1, and Site A2, but not in the Top-Level Site.
- A content type defined in Site A is not available in Site B.
- A content type defined in Site A1 is only available in Site A1, because Site A1 does not have any child sites.

441

In addition, a site content type that is defined in a site can only be modified in the site where it was defined. For example, if you define a content type in Site A, you can only modify it by going to Site A, and not by going to Site A1 or Site A2. If you go to the **Site Content Types** page of Site A1 or Site A2, you will see that the name of the content type has been dimmed (disabled) as an indication that you cannot edit it from within that site, and a link to the site on which the content type was defined should be clickable under the **Source** column on the **Site Content Types** page. So you can click on the link in the **Source** column to navigate to the **Site Content Types** page of Site A where you can modify the content type.

The primary benefit of content types is that they can be reused across several SharePoint lists or libraries. A secondary benefit is that you can associate more than one content type with the same list or library. Where InfoPath form templates are concerned, content types enable you to:

1. Publish a form template once and then reuse it across multiple form libraries, which may be located on different sites.
2. Associate more than one form template with one form library, so that users can create and store different types of forms in the same form library.

But before you publish a form template as a site content type, you must know to which site you should publish the content type so that the form template is accessible on all of the sites and in all of the form libraries in which you intend to create forms. And therefore you must understand its scope.

Content types are a core element from which InfoPath forms are created in SharePoint, so understanding them will give you an edge for working with InfoPath forms in SharePoint.

Let us now go through the steps for creating a site column and see how you can add one to an existing content type.

Create a new site column

Problem

You want to add a site column to a SharePoint site so that you can use it later as a column on a form library or content type.

Solution

You can create a new site column via the settings page of a SharePoint site.

To create a new site column:

1. Decide on which site you should create the site column based on the scope of a site column, which is similar to the scope of a content type.

2. In SharePoint, navigate to the site on which you want to create the new site column, and click **Site Actions ➤ Site Settings**.

3. On the **Site Settings** page under **Galleries**, click **Site columns**.

4. On the **Site Columns** page, click **Create**.

5. On the **New Site Column** page, enter a name for the column, select a data type, configure the rest of the data on the page as you require for the column, and click **OK**.

The new site column should now be listed under the **Custom Columns** group (if you accepted the default group setting) on the **Site Columns** page.

Discussion

Site columns are reusable columns that can be added to one or more lists, libraries, or content types, and that follow the same 'rules' for scope as content types (see the discussion section of *Create a new site content type*). Site columns differ from list columns in that list columns are created within the scope of a list or library, so are private to that list or library, while site columns are created within the scope of a site, so are available to all lists or libraries on a site or its child sites.

Add a site column to a site content type

Problem

You want to add an existing site column to an existing site content type in SharePoint.

Solution

You can use the details page of a content type to add a new or an existing site column to the content type.

To add an existing site column to an existing site content type:

1. In SharePoint, navigate to the site where the site content type is located, and click **Site Actions ➤ Site Settings**.

2. On the **Site Settings** page under **Galleries**, click **Site content types**.

3. On the **Site Content Types** page, locate the content type you want to add a site column to, and then click it to open its details page.

4. On the details page of the content type under **Columns**, click **Add from existing site columns**. Note: If you wanted to add a new site column to the content type, you would have to click the **Add from new site column** link instead, which would open the **New Site Column** page to add a new column to the site as described in *Create a new site column*.

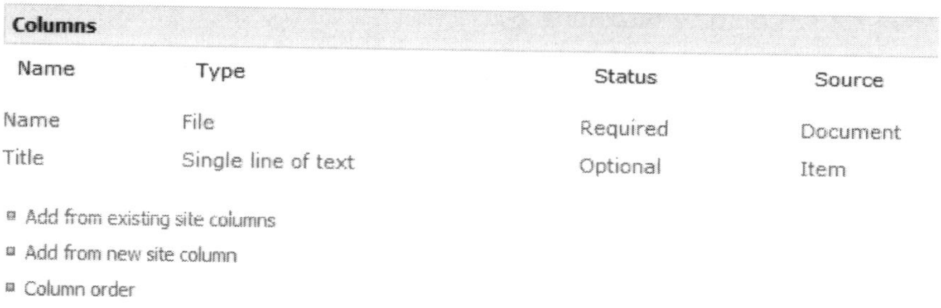

Columns			
Name	Type	Status	Source
Name	File	Required	Document
Title	Single line of text	Optional	Item

- Add from existing site columns
- Add from new site column
- Column order

Figure 352. Links to add an existing or new site column to a content type in SharePoint 2010.

5. On the **Add Columns to Content Type** page, select the site column you want to add from the list of **Available columns**, and click **Add** to add it to the list of **Columns to add**. Note: You must hold the **Ctrl** key pressed down if you want to select and add multiple site columns at once.

6. On the **Add Columns to Content Type** page, click **OK**.

The site column should now appear under the **Columns** section on the details page of the content type.

Discussion

In the solution described above, you learned how to add an existing or new site column to a site content type. While you can add columns to a content type, a content type may already have columns defined on it. Such columns have most likely been inherited from the parent content type when you created the content type based on a parent content type. If a column was inherited from a parent content type, the name of that parent content type should be listed under the **Source** column in the **Columns** section on the details page of the content type.

SharePoint permissions

Add a custom permission level

Problem

You want to grant custom permissions to a user or group.

Solution

You can add a custom permission level to the top-level site of a site collection and then grant this permission level to users on sites and objects in the site collection.

Appendix

To add a custom permission level:

1. In SharePoint, navigate to the top-level site of the site collection.
2. Click **Site Actions** ➤ **Site Permissions**.
3. Click **Permission Tools** ➤ **Edit** ➤ **Manage** ➤ **Permission Levels**.
4. On the **Permission Levels** page, click **Add a Permission Level**.
5. On the **Add a Permission Level** page, enter a **Name** for the new permission level, select the required **List Permissions** and **Site Permissions**, and then click **Create**.

Once you have created the custom permission level, you can grant permissions on a form library (or any other object) to either a user or a group a user belongs to as follows:

1. In SharePoint, navigate to the form library, and click **Library Tools** ➤ **Library** ➤ **Settings** ➤ **Library Permissions**.
2. On the permissions page, click **Permission Tools** ➤ **Edit** ➤ **Inheritance** ➤ **Stop Inheriting Permissions**. This should stop the form library from automatically getting the same permissions as the site on which it is located.
3. Click **Permission Tools** ➤ **Edit** ➤ **Grant** ➤ **Grant Permissions**.
4. On the **Grant Permissions** page, enter or select the users or groups you want to assign permissions to, select the **Grant users permissions directly** option, select the check box for the custom permission level you created earlier, enter a **Personal Message** to be sent in an e-mail to the users, and click **OK**.

If the user or group you want to grant permission to was already listed on the page, you must either edit the permissions of the user or group, or delete the user or group and then reassign permissions. You can edit or delete an existing user or group by selecting the check box in front of the user or group, and then clicking **Permission Tools** ➤ **Edit** ➤ **Modify** ➤ **Edit User Permissions** or **Remove User Permissions** on the Ribbon.

Tip:

> If a user is in a particular group, that user automatically inherits the permissions assigned to that group, which may grant the user additional permissions you are unaware of and that are not included in your custom permission level. So always double-check the memberships of the user you are granting permissions to.

List Templates

Upload a list template to a List Template Gallery

Problem

You exported a SharePoint list or library as a list template and now want to upload the list template to the List Template Gallery of a site collection.

Solution

You can use the **Upload Document** functionality of a List Template Gallery to upload an exported list template to the gallery.

To upload a list template to a List Template Gallery:

1. In SharePoint, navigate to the top-level site of the site collection where you want to upload the list template.
2. Click **Site Actions** ➤ **Site Settings**.
3. On the **Site Settings** page under **Galleries**, click **List templates**.
4. On the **All Templates** page, click **Library Tools** ➤ **Documents** ➤ **New** ➤ **Upload Document**.
5. On the **Upload Template** page, click **Browse**.
6. On the **Choose File to Upload** dialog box, browse to and select the list template (.stp) file you want to upload, and then click **Open**.
7. On the **Upload Template** page, click **OK**.
8. On the **List Template Gallery** page for the newly uploaded list template, change the **Name**, **Title**, and **Description** if you wish, and then click **Save**.

The new list template should now be listed in the gallery and you should be able to use it to create new lists or libraries by selecting it via the **Create** page.

Index

A

A form template (.xsn) file cannot be accessed, 93
A value in the form may be used to specify the file name, 60
Access
    centralize data through SharePoint, 433
    CRUD operations through InfoPath, 433
    Export Tables to SharePoint Wizard, 432, 433
    Move Data, 431
    reports, 435
Access and InfoPath, 430–35
Access the data from the specified location, 163, 181, 255
action
    Change REST URL, 189, 192, 204
    Close the form, 49
    Close this form, 70, 349
    Query for data, 34, 170, 188, 210, 239, 243, 267, 273, 435
    Send data to Web Part, 115, 118, 119, 430
    Submit data, 62, 69, 72, 249, 349, 354, 415
    Switch views, 72
activate site collection feature, 126, 260
add a workflow to a content type, 310
add a workflow to a form library, 308, 323
add custom action, 300
Add document, 57, 97
    opens Open With Form Template dialog box, 58
add document to SharePoint form library, 57, 58, 96, 97
add event to SharePoint calendar, 346
add field to SharePoint list form, 16
Add from existing site columns, 57, 358
Add from existing site content types, 95, 103, 438
Add from existing site or list columns, 368
add heading to Quick Launch, 109
add InfoPath form to Document Set content type, 127
add link to Quick Launch, 109
Add List Item Permission workflow action, 377
Add List Item Permissions dialog box, 377
add new folder to SharePoint form library, 67
add parameter in Excel, 427
Add Permissions dialog box, 377
add record to Access table through InfoPath form, 433
add SharePoint calendar event through SharePoint Designer workflow, 346–51
add SharePoint list form to page, 35–38
add site column to content type, 443
add submit data connection, 63
add summary view to survey form, 136–38
add task form field to SharePoint Designer workflow, 340
Add Time to Date workflow action, 337
add web part connection in SharePoint Designer 2010, 122–24
add web part connection parameter, 115, 120
Administrator-approved form template (advanced) publishing option, 79
advanced settings for content type, 98
advanced settings for SharePoint form library, 56
advanced view, 13
aggregate functions for promoting fields, 86
Allow management of content types, 94, 438
Allow overwrite if file exists, 64, 68, 71
allow user to specify file name on submit, 64
Allow users to browser-enable form templates, 78
Allow users to edit data in this field by using a datasheet or properties page, 83, 87, 88, 325, 327, 328, 332, 356, 364, 367
Allow users to insert and delete the sections, 131
Allow users to submit this form, 63, 71
Always postback setting, 51
An error occurred querying a data source, 419
approval SharePoint Designer workflow, 336–46
archive InfoPath forms, 148
arrayOfAnyType, 419
ascending, 178, 180, 185
assign InfoPath form field value through a workflow, 327
assign unique file name to form, 59
assign user permissions through SharePoint Designer workflow, 375–80
associate Document Set content type with document library, 127
Associate view, 320, 323
associate workflow with list, 296
Association and Initiation Form Parameters dialog box, 314, 322

447

association form, 321, 324
automatically
    close form after submit, 60
    create InfoPath form through SharePoint Designer workflow, 356–72
    generate Word document when form is submitted, 397–400
    open document information panel, 395
Automatically determine security level (recommended), 69
Automatically retrieve data when form is opened, 158
auto-populate fields on drop-down selection, 168–70
average function, 86
avg function, 132, 137

B

basic view, 11
Before a Task is Assigned task behavior, 341
benefit of
    Refresh button action, 188
    REST web service, 159, 185
    URL protocol, 165, 182, 211
BETWEEN filter on SharePoint list, 188–90, 348
Blank Form (InfoPath Filler) form template, 47
Blank Form form template, 17, 47, 55, 77
browse through InfoPath forms in form library, 211–32
Browser forms tab, 51
browser-compatible form template, 47, 49, 77, 78, 433
    limitations of, 49
browserEnable attribute, 77
browser-enable InfoPath form template, 77, 78
    Allow users to browser-enable form templates, 78
    configure in InfoPath Designer 2010, 73, 78
    configure in SharePoint 2010, 78
    Render form templates that are browser-enabled by users, 79
build a string in SharePoint Designer, 370
button action
    New Record, 23, 31
    Refresh, 23, 33, 186–88, 432
    Rules, 23
    Run Query, 23, 26, 434
    Submit, 23
    Update Form, 23, 52, 280, 285
button control, 22, 26, 31, 32, 70, 114, 119, 137, 171, 186, 189, 191, 201, 203, 212, 216, 251, 256, 262, 269, 280, 285, 347, 354, 411, 428, 432, 434

C

calculate date difference, 410
calculated value control, 136
cannot
    be promoted, 85
    browser-enable form template, 78
    change publish location, 82
    enable management of multiple list items, 14
    open forms in browser, 77–79
cascading drop-down list boxes, 233–44
change
    content type name, 100
    permissions through SharePoint Designer workflow, 379
    publish location, 4, 81, 390, 393
Change new button order and default content type, 97, 99, 359, 368
Change REST URL action, 189, 192, 204
Change the behavior of a single task, 341
Change the completion conditions for this task process, 342
check box control, 67
Check for Errors in SharePoint Designer 2010, 293
Choice (allow multiple selections), 276, 279
Choice (menu to choose from), 279
Choice column, 278
Choice with Fill-in (allow multiple selections), 279
Choice with Fill-in (menu to choose from or text), 279
close the form, 37
Close the form action, 49
Close this form action, 70, 349
CloseWorkbook, 414
column
    add list column to content type, 368
    Choice, 278
combo box control, 244–50, 282
    Show only entries with unique display names, 250
compatibility
    Document Information Panel, 394
    InfoPath Filler Form, 394
    Web Browser Form, 47, 49, 55, 394
    Web Browser Form (InfoPath 2007), 49
    Workflow Form, 320

Index

Complete XML Schema or XML document data type, 420
concat function, 64, 184, 192, 201, 204, 209, 216, 218, 226, 254, 257, 267, 271, 281
Condition dialog box, 138, 204, 213, 248
   Use a formula, 204, 213, 248
conditional formatting, 27, 30, 137, 194, 198, 203, 212, 218, 226, 348
configure
   InfoPath Forms Services, 52, 78
   submit data connection, 63
   web part, 121
   web part connection, 41, 117
Configure Connection webpage dialog, 41
connect
   InfoPath form to Access table, 430
   InfoPath Form Web Part to SharePoint list form, 45
   to InfoPath Form Web Part, 41, 117, 122–24
contains function, 29, 30, 194
content control, 387, 388
   Content control cannot be deleted, 388
   Contents cannot be edited, 388
content type, 437–44
   add a workflow, 310
   add columns, 368
   Add from existing site columns, 358
   Add from existing site or list columns, 368
   add site column, 443
   add to SharePoint form library, 95
   Advanced settings, 98
   allowed in Document Set content type, 127
   change order on SharePoint form library, 99
   correct document template, 148
   create, 439
   default, 99
   Default Content Type, 97, 359, 438
   delete, 102
   difference between list and site content types, 437
   Document, 358, 383, 398, 440
   Document Content Types, 103, 357, 439
   Document Set, 126
   document template, 77, 80, 358, 364, 381, 437, 440
   for InfoPath form, 80
   Form, 54, 77, 97, 101, 103, 112, 356, 357, 440
   forms, 6
   list content type, 437
   management of, 3, 56, 94, 98, 101, 438
   Microsoft InfoPath group, 95
   name and description, 101
   New Document button menu, 96
   publish form template as, 79, 90–94, 91
   relink InfoPath forms, 149–52
   SharePoint list form, 3
   site content type, 437
   Upload a new document template, 358, 368, 383
   Visible on New Button, 97
Content Type Forms, 6
Content Type is still in use, 103
control
   Browser forms tab, 51
   button, 22, 26, 31, 32, 70, 114, 119, 137, 171, 186, 189, 191, 201, 203, 212, 216, 251, 256, 262, 269, 280, 285, 347, 354, 411, 428, 432, 434
   calculated value, 136
   check box, 67
   combo box, 244–50, 282
   date and time picker, 347, 397
   date picker, 411, 422
   drop-down list box, 24–28, 114, 168, 173, 183, 195, 200, 233–44, 251, 318
   file attachment, 85
   hyperlink, 212, 217, 332
   merge settings, 131
   multiple-selection list box, 132, 275–88
   option button, 132
   person/group picker, 263–75, 279, 284, 318, 328, 333, 337, 397
   picture, 85, 250–63
   repeating section, 131, 184, 189, 191, 203, 256, 434
   repeating section with controls, 366
   repeating table, 15, 114, 119, 164, 167, 173, 175, 211, 259
   section, 347
   text box, 82, 88, 120, 132, 169, 171, 191, 193, 196, 201, 216, 251, 269, 281, 328, 346, 366, 397, 411, 422, 428
convert InfoPath form to Word document, 397–400
copy
   InfoPath form through SharePoint Designer workflow, 373
   multiple InfoPath forms, 143
   one InfoPath form, 142
copy data
   from row in repeating table, 170–72
   from secondary data source to main, 168–77
   to row of repeating table, 168–77
Copy List Item workflow action, 373

449

count function, 86, 136, 176, 214, 248, 262, 281, 283, 348
create
   document information panel, 390, 392
   InfoPath survey form, 131–38
   list workflow in SharePoint Designer, 289–94, 325–26, 329–31, 333–36, 337–44, 360–63, 369–71, 373–74, 376–78, 398–400
   new file name when form is submitted, 59, 63
   new task list for SharePoint Designer workflow, 339
   reusable workflow in SharePoint Designer, 304–8, 312–19, 350–51
   SharePoint calendar event, 346
   SharePoint form library, 53–54
   SharePoint form library form, 48
   SharePoint list form, 1–15
   SharePoint search scope, 225
   SharePoint view, 44, 161, 179
   site column, 442
   site content type, 439
   table in Excel, 401
   Word document from InfoPath form, 397–400
   workflow form, 320
Create a new form library, 74
Create Custom Action dialog box, 302
create InfoPath form
   in document set, 128
   through SharePoint Designer workflow, 356–72
Create List Item workflow action, 325, 350, 360, 369, 398
Create List Workflow dialog box, 291
Create New List Item dialog box, 325, 350, 360, 369, 398
Create Reusable Workflow dialog box, 304
create workflow
   list workflow, 289–94, 325–26, 329–31, 333–36, 337–44, 360–63, 369–71, 373–74, 376–78, 398–400
   reusable workflow, 304
created by current user, 161–65, 209
CreatedBy, 208, 210
Current Item, 292, 321, 325
   Encoded Absolute URL, 321
Current Item URL, 316, 321
Current Site URL, 321
Current View drop-down menu
   Merge Documents, 138
   on InfoPath form toolbar, 62
   on SharePoint form library Ribbon, 138
   Relink Documents, 144, 149, 376
current(), 176, 214
custom action in SharePoint Designer 2010, 302
customize
   SharePoint list form, 1–15
   workflow form, 320
Customize Form, 2
   disable on Ribbon, 5

D

Data
   Submit Form, 63, 67, 68, 70, 71, 245, 353, 412
data connection
   configure submit, 63
   copy data from, 168–77
   dataFields, 167
   From REST Web Service, 158, 183, 189, 191, 200, 203, 212, 251, 347, 407, 421
   From SOAP Web Service, 217, 269, 411
   From XML File, 25, 29, 162, 181, 245, 254, 353
   Include data for the active form only, 208
   InfoPath to SharePoint, 153–232
   InfoPath to SharePoint Lists web service, 244–50
   InfoPath to SharePoint Search Service, 216–32
   InfoPath to SharePoint User Profile Service, 268–75
   queryFields, 167
   queryFields and dataFields, 158
   to retrieve data from SharePoint list, 153
   To Web Service, 412
Data Connection Wizard
   Access the data from the specified location, 163, 181, 255
   Allow overwrite if file exists, 64, 68, 71
   Create a new SharePoint list, 8
   Customize an existing SharePoint list, 10, 14
   Include data for the active form only, 208
   Manage multiple items with this form, 14
   Set as the default submit connection, 68, 71, 247, 354, 413
   Sort by, 178
   Sort order, 178
   Store a copy of the data for offline use, 163, 181, 255
Data Connections dialog box, 157
data source

Index

Current Item, 292, 321, 325
dataFields, 13
delete field, 19
Filter Data, 136, 169, 233, 239, 248, 267, 283, 286
queryFields, 13, 239
refresh fields, 19
SharePoint list form, 3
Workflow Context, 292
Workflow Variables and Parameters, 292, 315, 321, 330, 334, 339
Data Source Wizard dialog box, 390, 392, 420
data type
    Choice (allow multiple selections), 276, 279
    Choice (menu to choose from), 279
    Choice with Fill-in (allow multiple selections), 279
    Choice with Fill-in (menu to choose from or text), 279
    Complete XML Schema or XML document, 420
data type matching for property promotion, 86
databases InfoPath supports, 431
dataFields, 13, 157, 167, 273
date and time picker control, 347, 397
date difference calculation, 410
DATE Excel function, 410, 418, 421
date picker control, 411, 422
debug workflow, 295
Default Content Type, 97, 359, 438
Default Value
    Refresh value when formula is recalculated, 174, 176, 214, 220, 228, 267
Default Values, 173, 176, 211, 281, 285
DefaultItemOpen query string parameter, 106
Define E-mail Message dialog box, 316, 334
define name in Excel, 424, 426
Define Workflow Lookup dialog box, 334, 376
delete
    content type, 102
    custom action, 303
    field from SharePoint list form, 19
    form template, 102
    InfoPath form from SharePoint form library, 143
    InfoPath form through SharePoint Designer workflow, 373
    link or heading on Quick Launch, 110
    promoted field, 89
    record from Access table through InfoPath form, 433
    reusable workflow, 311
    workflow, 297
    workflow template, 298
Delete Item workflow action, 373
Delete this form library, 56
department of user who opened the InfoPath form, 198
deploy InfoPath form template, 72–82, 90–94
descending, 178, 180, 185
Design Checker, 50
design SharePoint list form, 1–15, 8, 10, 13
Developer tab in Word, 388
dialog box
    Add List Item Permissions, 377
    Add Permissions, 377
    Association and Initiation Form Parameters, 314, 322
    Condition, 138, 204, 213, 248
    Content Control Properties, 388
    Create Custom Action, 302
    Create List Workflow, 291
    Create New List Item, 325, 350, 360, 369, 398
    Create Reusable Workflow, 304
    Data Connections, 157
    Data Source Wizard, 390, 392, 420
    Define E-mail Message, 316, 334
    Define Workflow Lookup, 334, 376
    Edit Default Values, 173, 281, 285
    Export Table to SharePoint List, 402
    Form Options, 49, 55, 61, 85, 89, 115, 120, 141, 320, 398, 428
    Lookup for Date/Time, 338
    Lookup for Person or Group, 315, 329, 333, 338, 399
    Lookup for Single line of text, 325, 330, 362, 371
    Lookup for String, 292, 305, 316, 361, 370, 399
    Merge Settings, 131
    Open With Form Template, 57
    Person/Group Picker Properties, 264
    Publish Options, 405
    Select Task Process Participants, 340
    Select Users, 315, 329, 333, 338, 377
    Specify Filter Conditions, 235, 248
    String Builder, 370
    Submit Options, 63
    Update List Item, 330
    Value Assignment, 325, 330, 360, 369, 399
difference between
    InfoPath form template types, 48
    list and site content types, 437
    saving and submitting InfoPath forms, 58–60

SharePoint Form Library and Blank Form templates, 47
SharePoint list forms and SharePoint form library forms, 49
disable
   a rule, 419
   customize form on Ribbon, 5
Disable automatic start on item change option, 306, 318
Disable automatic start on item creation option, 318
display SharePoint list data in InfoPath, 166–67
display SharePoint list items created by current user, 161–65
Document content type, 358, 383, 398, 440
Document Content Types, 103, 357, 439
Document ID Service, 260
document information panel, vi, 381
   create, 390, 392
   Create a new custom template, 390
   Edit this template, 391
   open from SharePoint Designer 2010, 391
   settings, 390, 394–96
   Show Document Panel, 385, 387
   Use existing custom template (URL, UNC, or URN), 391, 396
   Use the default template for Microsoft Office applications, 396
Document Information Panel form template, 392
Document Information Panel form type, 394
document management in SharePoint, 130
document properties, 381
Document Property, 387
Document Set content type, 126
   add default content, 129
   add InfoPath form template and default form, 127
   associate with document library, 127
   content types allowed in, 127
   create new, 126
   settings, 127
Document Sets feature, 125
document template, 54, 57, 77, 80, 93, 98, 103, 144, 149–50, 307, 358, 364, 381, 437, 440
   correct the InfoPath form template for, 147
   Edit Template, 54, 55, 96, 387
   Upload a new document template, 358, 368, 383
Domain security level, 69
Download a Copy, 59, 128, 150, 357
download a form, 59, 128, 150, 357

drop-down list box control, 24–28, 114, 168, 173, 183, 195, 200, 233–44, 251, 318
   automatically populate InfoPath form fields, 168–70
   cascading, 233–44
   Show only entries with unique display names, 235

E

edit
   document information panel, 391
   link on Quick Launch, 110
   record in Access table through InfoPath form, 433
   SharePoint wiki page, 105
Edit Default Values dialog box, 173, 281, 285
Edit item (default) view, 13
Edit Template, 54, 55, 96, 387
email address from person/group picker control, 265–68
Email Addresses, Semicolon Delimited, 315
embed
   an image, 251
   InfoPath form on SharePoint page, 110–25
   SharePoint list form on page, 35–38
enable
   form merging, 133, 141
   management of content types, 94
   Submit button, 62
Enable this form to be filled out by using a browser, 73, 78
Encoded Absolute URL, 321
endswith filter method, 192
enter document properties, 384
entry group node missing, 347, 349
error message
   A form template (.xsn) file cannot be accessed, 93
   An error occurred querying a data source, 419
   Form submission failed, 355
   List does not exist, 355
   The given key was not present in the dictionary, 419
   The page you selected contains a list that does not exist, 355
   The selected database is not supported in Web browser forms, 431
   The session has exceeded the amount of allowable resources, 52
   There has been an error while loading the form, 93

There has been an error while processing the form, 419
You may not have the required permission to open the file, 93
Escalate Task workflow action, 342
eval function, 267, 282
event
    Form Load, 29, 31, 198, 209, 367, 435
    Form Submit, 69, 72
exact filter on SharePoint list, 185–88
Excel, 400–430
    DATE function, 410, 418, 421
    Define name, 424, 426
    delete defined name, 425
    Export Table to SharePoint List, 402
    Format as Table, 401
    get data from InfoPath form, 426
    MID function, 410, 418, 421
    Name Manager, 425
    NETWORKDAYS function, 410, 418, 421
    Parameters, 427
    Publish Options, 405, 427
    save file to SharePoint, 405
    Save to SharePoint, 405, 410, 421, 427
Excel and InfoPath, 400–430
Excel Services, 404–26
    Add Trusted File Location, 408
    CloseWorkbook, 414
    GetCellA1, 414
    OpenWorkbook, 411
    REST URL, 409
    REST web service, 407, 421
    SetCellA1, 412
    SOAP web service, 411, 412
Excel Web Access web part, 429
export Excel data to SharePoint, 402
Export Table to SharePoint List dialog box, 402
Export to Excel, 403, 435

F

feature
    Document ID Service, 260
    Document Sets, 125
field type
    Choice (allow multiple selections), 276, 279
    Choice (menu to choose from), 279
    Choice with Fill-in (allow multiple selections), 279
    Choice with Fill-in (menu to choose from or text), 279

Fields inside repeating groups are not supported as Web Part connection parameters, 118
Fields task pane
    dataFields, 13
    queryFields, 13
    Show advanced view, 12
fields that cannot be promoted as editable, 332
file attachment control, 85
fill out
    document properties, 384
    forms without InfoPath, 48
    InfoPath form through SharePoint Designer workflow, 356–72
Filter Data, 136, 169, 233, 239, 248, 267, 283, 286
filter method
    endswith, 192
    startswith, 192
    substringof, 192, 252
filter query option, 190, 192
filter SharePoint list data, 22–30, 185–94, 243
    BETWEEN, 188–90, 348
    exact, 185–88
    LIKE, 191–94
filter SharePoint list on top x items, 200–202
find department of user who opened the InfoPath form, 198
first function, 86
force InfoPath forms to open in browser, 77–79
Form content type, 54, 77, 97, 101, 103, 112, 356, 357, 440
Form Library publishing option, 73, 79
Form Library Settings, 56–57
    Add from existing site columns, 57
    Delete this form library, 56
    Relink documents to this library, 57, 150
    Save form library as template, 57, 146
Form Load event, 29, 31, 198, 209, 367, 435
form merging, 130–41
Form Options dialog box, 49, 55, 61, 85, 89, 115, 120, 141, 320, 398
    Enable form merging, 133, 141
    Form type, 320
    Full Trust, 69
    Property Promotion, 85, 120, 398
    Security and Trust, 69
    web part connection parameters, 115, 428
form publishing methods, 79
form security level, 69
Form Settings, 2
    Delete the InfoPath Form from the server, 21

Use the default SharePoint form, 21
Form submission failed, 355
Form Submit event, 69, 72
form template
    Blank Form, 17, 47, 49, 55, 77
    Blank Form (InfoPath Filler), 47
    Document Information Panel, 392
    SharePoint Form Library, 17, 47, 49, 77
    XML or Schema, 393
form template cannot be found, 57
form toolbar
    Close button, 59
    commands, 62
    Current View drop-down, 62
    effect of permissions on, 66
    Save As button, 62, 66
    Save button, 62, 66
    Submit button, 62
    Update button, 62
form type
    Association/Initiation, 319
    Document Information Panel, 394
    Web Browser Form, 47, 49, 55, 394
    Web Browser Form (InfoPath 2007), 49
    Workflow Form, 320
formatting rule, 27, 30, 137, 194, 198, 203, 212, 218, 226, 348
Forms folder, 55, 63, 391
FormServer.aspx, 104-10, 216, 316, 321
Full Trust security level, 69, 72, 79
function
    average, 86
    avg, 132, 137
    concat, 64, 184, 192, 201, 204, 209, 216, 218, 226, 254, 257, 267, 271, 281
    contains, 29, 30, 194
    count, 86, 136, 176, 214, 248, 262, 281, 283, 348
    eval, 267, 282
    first, 86
    last, 86
    max, 86
    merge, 86
    min, 86
    normalize-space, 271
    not, 30
    now, 63, 67, 71
    SharePointListUrl, 215
    SharePointServerRootUrl, 215, 254, 257
    SharePointSiteCollectionUrl, 216
    SharePointSiteUrl, 216
    string, 201, 218, 226
    substring-after, 220, 224, 228
    substring-before, 220, 224, 228
    sum, 86, 132
    translate, 29, 30, 194, 199, 209
    userName, 63, 71, 198, 209

G

generate
    InfoPath form through SharePoint Designer workflow, 356–72
    new file name when form is submitted, 59, 63
get
    data from SharePoint, 154–65
    email address from person/group picker control, 265–68
    filter values from web part, 41
    form from web part, 45
    InfoPath form field value in a workflow, 325
    InfoPath form template from SharePoint form library, 55
    manager of user, 268–75
Get External Data, 153
    Data Connections, 157, 349
    From REST Web Service, 158, 183, 189, 191, 200, 203, 212, 251, 347, 407, 421
    From SharePoint List, 154, 178
    From SOAP Web Service, 217, 269, 411
    From XML File, 162, 181, 254, 353
GetCellA1, 414
GetUserProfileByName, 270
GetUserPropertyByAccountName, 269
give user permissions through SharePoint Designer workflow, 375–80
GUID
    SharePoint list, 162, 180, 245, 352
    SharePoint picture library, 255
    SharePoint view, 162, 180

H

hide toolbar buttons for InfoPath form, 60
Hyperlink (anyURI), 85
hyperlink control, 212, 217, 332

I

If any value equals value workflow condition, 334, 376
If task outcome equals value workflow condition, 342
If you know what that value is, modify it and try submitting the form again, 60

image
    embed, 251
    link to, 251, 262
Impersonation Step, 376, 379
Include data for the active form only, 208
InfoPath and
    Access, 430–35
    Excel, 400–430
    Word, 381
InfoPath Filler 2010, 47, 52, 57, 69, 77, 106, 139, 216, 254, 263
InfoPath Filler Form form type, 394
InfoPath form opens in InfoPath Filler instead of browser, 77–79
InfoPath form template not found, 57
InfoPath Form Web Part, 6, 36, 40, 45, 46, 111, 116, 121, 429
    add to SharePoint web part page, 116, 121
    add to SharePoint wiki page, 111
    Appearance, 38
    Click here to open the tool pane, 36, 111, 116, 121, 429
    Content Type, 37
    Display a read-only form (lists only), 37, 46
    embed on SharePoint page, 110–25
    Get Filter Values From, 41
    Get Form From, 45
    List or Library, 36
    SharePoint list form, 35–38
    Submit Behavior, 38
InfoPath forms in SharePoint, v
InfoPath Forms Services, 47, 50
    Allow users to browser-enable form templates, 78
    force InfoPath forms to open in browser, 77–79
    postbacks, 52
    Render form templates that are browser-enabled by users, 79
    Thresholds, 52
    User Browser-enabled Form Templates, 78
InfoPath limitations, 177
InfoPath required to fill out forms, 48
InfoPath survey in SharePoint, 131–38
InfoPath to SharePoint data connection, 153–232
InfoPath to SharePoint data type matching for property promotion, 86
initiation form, 312, 320
initiation form parameters, 313, 322, 324, 337
inlinecount query option, 206
input web part connection parameter, 120
insert hyperlink on SharePoint wiki page, 105

insert workflow action, 291, 295

K

keyword query syntax, 223

L

last function, 86
leave the form open, 37
LIKE filter on SharePoint list, 191–94
limitations of
    browser-compatible form template, 49
    InfoPath, 177
    SharePoint list form, 49
link to an image, 251, 262
linked SharePoint lists, 239, 435
list content type, 437
List does not exist, 355
List Template Gallery, 146, 446
list workflow, 289–94, 290, 296, 325–26, 329–31, 333–36, 337–44, 360–63, 369–71, 373–74, 376–78, 398–400
    Allow this workflow to be manually started, 293, 297, 326, 331, 373, 400
    delete, 297
    disadvantage, 307
    Encoded Absolute URL, 321
    start options, 293
    Start workflow automatically when an item is created, 293
    vs. reusable workflow, 307
ListData REST web service, 158, 183, 189, 191, 200, 203, 212, 251, 347
local variables in workflow, 337
lock content control, 388
Log to History List workflow action, 291, 295, 305, 342
lookup column, 241
Lookup for Date/Time dialog box, 338
Lookup for Person or Group dialog box, 315, 329, 333, 338, 399
Lookup for Single line of text dialog box, 325, 330, 362, 371
Lookup for String dialog box, 292, 305, 316, 361, 370, 399
Lookup Manager of a User workflow action, 329, 333, 338

M

Main data source
    dataFields, 13

delete field, 19
of SharePoint list form, 3
queryFields, 13
refresh fields, 19
make InfoPath forms browser-enabled, 73, 78
Manage multiple list items with this form, 14
manager of user, 268–75
manually close form, 59
master detail functionality, 38–43, 112–18, 195–96
max function, 86
Merge Documents, 138
merge function, 86
merge InfoPath forms, 130–41
controls to use, 134
create summary view, 136–38
enable form merging, 133, 141
in SharePoint, 138–41
in SharePoint form library, 139
merge cannot be started message, 140
merge settings of control, 131
Remove blank groups (recommended), 131
role of InfoPath Filler 2010, 140
ways to design, 134
merge InfoPath survey responses, 138–41
Merge Settings dialog box, 131
Remove blank groups (recommended), 131
merge settings of control, 131
merge-ready InfoPath survey form, 131–38
message
A value in the form may be used to specify the file name, 60
Content Type is still in use, 103
Fields inside repeating groups are not supported as Web Part connection parameters, 118
If you know what that value is, modify it and try submitting the form again, 60
The data type of the selected site column does not match the data type of the field to promote, 88
The document library already contains a file with the same name, 60
The form cannot be submitted to the specified SharePoint document library, 60
The form has been closed, 106
The merge cannot be started, because the merge feature is disabled for the selected form template, 140
This action will delete all information in the current form, 24

This form template is browser-compatible, but it cannot be browser-enabled on the selected site, 78
Microsoft Access, 430–35
Microsoft Excel, 400–430
Microsoft Word, 381
Microsoft.Search.Query, 223
MID Excel function, 410, 418, 421
min function, 86
missing entry group node, 347, 349
Modify Form Web Parts, 5, 21, 42
modify SharePoint view, 162, 180
move InfoPath forms, 141–52
between form libraries, 141, 372–74
between site collections, 151
move entire form library, 146
multiple forms at the same time, 143
one form at a time, 141
things to consider before the move, 144–45
to a site in another site collection, 148
with SharePoint Designer workflow, 372–74
multiple submit data connections in one form, 67
multiple web part connections, 119
multiple-selection list box control, 132, 275–88
Allow users to enter custom values, 279
get email addresses, 279–88

N

NETWORKDAYS Excel function, 410, 418, 421
Never postback setting, 51
New Document button menu, 58, 96
change order of menu items, 99
rename menu item, 100
New Record button action, 23, 31
New Task List, 339
non-browser-compatible form template, 47
non-exact filtering of SharePoint list data, 188–94
NoRedirect query string parameter, 107
normalize-space function, 271
not function, 30
now function, 63, 67, 71

O

Only when necessary for correct rendering of the form (recommended), 51
open
a new form, 37
document information panel, 385, 387, 395
Open in the browser, 79

open InfoPath form
    from hyperlink on SharePoint wiki page, 104
    from Quick Launch, 108
    in browser, 77–79, 211–16
Open Site in SharePoint Designer 2010, 290
Open with Access, 435
Open With Form Template dialog box, 57
OpenIn query string parameter, 106, 107, 214, 216, 316, 321
    Browser, 107, 216, 316
    Client, 107
    PreferClient, 107
OpenWorkbook, 411
option button control, 132
order of content types, 99
orderby query option, 185, 190
output web part connection parameter, 115, 120, 428
ows_NameOrTitle, 257
ows_RequiredField, 257

P

paginate
    InfoPath forms in form library, 211–32
    SharePoint list items, 202–6, 262
Parallel Block in SharePoint Designer 2010, 295
parallel workflow actions, 295
partially match SharePoint list items, 192
pass data
    between two form library forms, 119
    from a form library form to a list form, 112
pass data to workflow, 312–24, 336–46
    association form, 321
    initiation form, 312
    task form, 336
Perform custom action using Rules submit option, 69, 72
perform non-exact search on SharePoint list, 188–94
permissions
    SharePoint form library form, 65, 80
    SharePoint list form, 4
permissions required for
    publishing form template, 80
    saving form, 65–66
    submitting form, 65–66
person/group picker control, 263–75, 279, 284, 318, 328, 333, 337, 397
    Allow multiple selections, 265, 280, 285
    Cannot be blank, 265
    get email address, 265–68
    get manager of user, 268–75

People Only, 280, 285
Person/Group Picker Properties dialog box, 264
picture control, 85, 250–63
    As a link, 250, 262
    Included in the form, 250
populate form fields on drop-down selection, 168–70
Postback settings, 51
preceding-sibling, 176, 214, 262
preconfigure property promotion, 89
previous next navigation, 202–6, 211–32, 262
process of relinking InfoPath forms, 151
promote a field, 82–89, 328, 365
    Allow users to edit data in this field by using a datasheet or properties page, 83, 87, 88, 325, 327, 328, 332, 356, 364, 367
    cannot be promoted, 85
    cannot be promoted as editable, 332
    data type matching between InfoPath and SharePoint, 86
    delete column, 89
    Form Options dialog box, 85
    Hyperlink (anyURI), 85
    repeating fields, 86
    Select a Field or Group dialog box, 83
    The data type of the selected site column does not match the data type of the field to promote, 88
    to a new form library column, 83
    to an existing form library column, 83
    update data type, 87
    when to use Publishing Wizard, 85
property promotion, 82–89, 82, 328, 365
    cannot be promoted, 85
    cannot be promoted as editable fields, 332
    repeating fields, 86
PropertyData, 274
Publish
    Quick Publish, 2, 55, 81, 390
    SharePoint List, 2
    SharePoint Server, 73, 91
publish Excel spreadsheet to SharePoint, 405
Publish in SharePoint Designer 2010, 293
publish InfoPath form template, 72–82, 90–94
    as site content type, 79, 91
    cannot change publish location, 82
    create new content type, 91
    methods, 79
    permissions required, 80
    republish, 81
    to SharePoint form library, 73, 79
    troubleshooting, 77–79
    update existing site content type, 91

Publish Options dialog box, 405
publish options in Excel, 405
Publishing Wizard, 73
   Administrator-approved form template (advanced), 79
   browser-enable InfoPath form template, 78
   Create a new content type, 91
   Create a new form library, 74
   Enable this form to be filled out using a browser, 73
   force InfoPath forms to open in browser, 77–79
   Form Library, 73, 79
   missing browser-enable check box, 78
   promote fields, 76, 85
   publishing options, 79
   Site Content Type (advanced), 79, 91
   Update an existing site content type, 91
   Update the form template in an existing form library, 75
pull data into rows of repeating table, 175–77

Q

Query and QueryEx, 223, 230
Query for data action, 34, 170, 188, 210, 239, 243, 267, 273, 435
query option
   filter, 190, 192
   inlinecount, 206
   orderby, 185, 190
   select, 206
   skip, 206
   top, 202, 206
query SharePoint list data, 22–30, 185–94
query string parameter
   DefaultItemOpen, 106
   NoRedirect, 107
   OpenIn, 106, 214, 216, 316, 321
   SaveLocation, 106
   Source, 105, 106
   XmlLocation, 106, 214, 321
   XsnLocation, 106
query syntax
   keyword, 223
   SQL, 230
query to open SharePoint list form based on linked ID, 114
Query web service operation, 218
queryFields, 13, 158, 167, 177, 186, 195, 199, 239, 273
Quick Launch, 56, 108–10
   add heading, 109
   add link, 109
   delete link or heading, 110
   edit link, 110
Quick Parts, 387
Quick Publish, 2, 55, 81, 390

R

read from an InfoPath form field from within a workflow, 325
read-only data, 167
recover lost InfoPath form template, 55
Refresh button action, 23, 33, 186–88, 432
   benefit of, 188
refresh data
   in one secondary data source, 187
   in SharePoint list form, 34
Refresh Fields, 19
Refresh value when formula is recalculated, 174, 176, 214, 220, 228, 267
Refresh vs. Query for data action, 188
Relink Documents, 144, 149, 376
   Content Type, 144
   Template Link, 144, 149
Relink documents to this library, 57, 150
relink InfoPath forms, 149–52
   diagram explaining the process, 151
remove
   form toolbar commands through permissions, 66
   InfoPath web browser form toolbar buttons, 60
Render form templates that are browser-enabled by users, 79
repeating section control, 131, 184, 189, 191, 203, 256, 434
   Allow users to insert and delete the sections, 131, 434
   Merge Settings, 131
   Remove blank groups (recommended), 131
   Show insert button and hint text, 434
repeating section with controls, 366
repeating table control, 15, 114, 119, 164, 167, 173, 175, 211, 259
   copy data from row, 170–72
   copy data to row, 168–77
   current(), 176, 214
   map data one-on-one to SharePoint list, 175–77
reports, 435
republish form template, 4, 81, 390, 393
REST web service, 158, 183, 189, 191, 200, 203, 212, 251, 347, 407, 421

benefit of, 159, 185
missing entry in RSS feed, 347, 349
secondary data source, 160
retrieve
data from SharePoint, 154–65
InfoPath form field value in a workflow, 325
InfoPath forms, 207–32
manager of user, 268–75
name of user who created InfoPath form, 208
return top x SharePoint list items, 200–202
reusable workflow, 296, 304–8, 312–19, 350–51
add to content type, 310
add to content type via form library, 308
advantage of, 307
All content type, 307
association form, 321
content type, 307
Current Item URL, 321
delete from content type, 311
Disable automatic start on item change option, 306, 318
Disable automatic start on item creation option, 318
start options, 306
Update List and Site Content Types, 310
root folder of SharePoint form library, 67
Rules button action, 23
Run Query button action, 23, 26, 434
runtimeCompatibility attribute, 77

S

save and close SharePoint wiki page, 105
Save and Save As commands missing from form toolbar, 66
save Excel file to SharePoint, 405
Save form library as template, 57, 146
save form locally on disk, 59, 128, 150, 357
save InfoPath form, 59
close form after submit, 60
difference between save and submit, 58–60
permissions required, 65–66
SaveLocation query string parameter, 106
search scope, 230
search SharePoint list through InfoPath form, 22–30, 185–94
secondary data source, 157
copy data from, 168–77
dataFields, 167
display data, 166–67
modify values of fields, 208

queryFields, 167
queryFields and dataFields, 158
refresh one or all in InfoPath form, 187
REST web service, 160
section control, 347
Security and Trust, 69
security level, 69
select data from row in repeating table, 170–72
select query option, 206
Select Task Process Participants dialog box, 340
Select the form template to open this XML file, 57
select top x items of SharePoint list, 200–202
Select Users dialog box, 315, 329, 333, 338, 377
Send an Email workflow action, 315, 334
send data
from InfoPath to Excel, 426
from SharePoint form library form to SharePoint list form, 112
Send data to Web Part action, 115, 118, 119, 430
Send Data To web part connection, 116, 122, 429
send email on form submit, 333
Send form data to a single destination submit option, 63
send form to other location, 142
serial workflow actions, 295
Set as the default submit connection, 68, 71, 247, 354, 413
set default content type, 99
set InfoPath form field value through a workflow, 327
Set Task Field workflow action, 341
set up web part connection
multiple, 119–25
single, 112–18
set web service parameters, 246, 353–54, 413
SetCellA1, 412
SharePoint calendar, 3, 346
SharePoint Designer 2010
about workflows and InfoPath, 289
Add or Change Lookup, 316, 335, 370
add web part connection, 122–24
associate workflow with list, 296
Check for Errors, 293
create list workflow, 289, 325–26, 329–31, 333–36, 337–44, 360–63, 369–71, 373–74, 376–78, 398–400
create reusable workflow, 304–8, 312–19, 350–51
create Word document from InfoPath form, 397–400

Current Item, 292
Custom Actions, 302
debug workflow, 295
delete custom action, 303
delete workflow, 297
delete workflow template, 298
Design Forms in InfoPath, 7
Disable automatic start on item change option, 306, 318
Disable automatic start on item creation option, 318
document information panel, 391
Editor, 291
Initiation Form Parameters, 313, 322, 324, 337
insert workflow action, 291, 295
list workflow, 290, 296
Lists and Libraries, 301
Local Variables, 337
Open Site, 290
Parallel Block, 295
Publish, 293
Refresh command, 305
reusable workflow, 296
site workflow, 296
Start Options, 293
Start workflow automatically when an item is created, 293
start workflow manually, 298
String Builder, 370
types of workflows, 296
workflow action, 294
workflow condition, 294
Workflow Context, 292
workflow forms, 319
workflow history, 294
Workflow Settings, 293
workflow step, 294
workflow template, 294
Workflow Variables and Parameters, 292, 315, 321, 330, 334, 339
SharePoint Designer workflow, 289–380
Add List Item Permission, 377
add SharePoint calendar event, 346–51
Add Time to Date, 337
approval workflow, 336–46
automatically create InfoPath forms, 356–72
Change the behavior of a single task, 341
Change the completion conditions for this task process, 342
Completion Conditions, 342
Copy List Item, 373
Create List Item, 325, 350, 360, 369, 398

create list workflow, 289–94, 325–26, 329–31, 333–36, 337–44, 360–63, 369–71, 373–74, 376–78, 398–400
create reusable workflow, 304–8, 312–19, 350–51
Delete Item, 373
Escalate Task, 342
give user permissions, 375–80
If any value equals value, 376
Impersonation Step, 376, 379
list permission actions, 379
Log to History List, 291, 295, 305, 342
Lookup Manager of a User, 329, 333, 338
move InfoPath forms, 372–74
New Task List, 339
Send an Email, 315, 334
Set Task Field, 341
Start Custom Task Process, 339
start running workflow from InfoPath form, 352–55
Task Form Fields, 340
Template Link, 376
Update List Item, 330
user selects who to send email to, 312–24
SharePoint document library Forms folder, 391
SharePoint document management, 130
SharePoint form library, 54–58
add a workflow, 308
Add document, 57, 97
Add from existing site columns, 57
Add from existing site content types, 95, 103, 438
add new folder, 67
Advanced settings, 56
Change new button order and default content type, 97, 99, 359, 368
content type management, 56, 94, 98, 101, 438
Content Types, 95
copy multiple InfoPath forms, 143
copy one InfoPath form, 142
create InfoPath form through SharePoint Designer workflow, 356–72
create manually, 53–54
Current View drop-down menu, 138
Default Content Type, 97, 359
delete, 56
delete form template, 102
delete InfoPath form, 143
difference between save and submit, 58–60
Document Template, 54
Edit Template, 54
Export to Excel, 435

Index

force InfoPath forms to open in browser, 77–79
Form content type, 77, 97, 101, 103, 112, 356, 440
Forms folder, 55, 63
get InfoPath form template, 55
merge documents, 138
move forms between, 141–52
move to another site, 146
New Document, 58, 96
Open in the browser, 79
Open with Explorer, 143
paginate InfoPath forms, 211–32
publish form template to, 72–82, 73, 79
Relink and Relink All, 150
relink documents, 57, 150
relink InfoPath forms, 149–52
rename form template on New Document button menu, 100
republish form template, 81
root folder, 67
Save form library as template, 57, 146
save form to, 59
Send To, 141
set default form template, 99
settings, 56–57
submit form to, 59, 62–72
Template URL, 54, 96
Use the server default (Open in the browser), 79
Visible on New Button, 97
Workflow Settings, 308
SharePoint form library form, v, 17, 47–152, 77
create, 48
permissions, 65, 80
publish, 73, 91
SharePoint Foundation, 47, 319
SharePoint list
BETWEEN filter, 188–90, 348
content type management, 3
copy data from, 168–77
Customize Form, 2
Default Content Type, 438
Design Form, 8, 10, 13
disable Customize Form, 5
display data in InfoPath form, 166–67
Export to Excel, 403
filter on exact data, 185–88
filter on non-exact data, 188–94
get data from, 154, 178
GUID, 162, 180, 245, 352
LIKE filter, 191–94
linked, 239, 435
Open with Access, 435
paginate, 202–6
partially match items, 192
select top x items, 200–202
sort ascending or descending, 178, 180, 185
sort dynamically on multiple fields, 183–85
sort statically on multiple fields, 179
sort statically on one field, 178
Sync to SharePoint Workspace, 403
User Information List, 197, 199, 209, 266, 274, 282, 285
web part, 40, 44
SharePoint list form, v, 1–46, 49, 82, 275, 403, 433
add to page, 35–38
cannot change publish location, 82
cannot enable management of multiple list items, 14
content type, 3
Content Type Forms, 6
controls, 17
customize, 1–15
customize form for default content type, 2
customize form for non-default content type, 2
customize from SharePoint Designer 2010, 6
delete field, 19
delete from server, 21
Design Form, 8, 10, 13
filter, 22–30
Form Settings, 2
ignore data changes, 24
InfoPath Form Web Part, 35–38
limitation, 49
Main data source, 3, 13
manage multiple items, 13–15
manage one item, 1
Modify Form Web Parts, 5, 21, 42
permissions, 4
publish, 2
query, 22–30, 113
refresh data, 34
refresh fields, 19
repeating table instead of repeating section, 15
SharePointListItem_RW, 16, 20, 22, 26, 30
web part connection, 118
working with fields, 16
SharePoint list web part, 40, 44
SharePoint ListData REST web service, 158, 183, 189, 191, 200, 203, 212, 251, 347
SharePoint Lists web service, 244–50, 244, 352
SharePoint page

461

web part, 35, 40, 44, 116, 121
wiki, 35, 104, 111
SharePoint permissions, 4, 65, 80, 375, 379, 444
   to publish InfoPath form templates, 80
   to save or submit InfoPath forms, 65–66
SharePoint picture library, 251–63
   GUID, 255, 257
SharePoint Search Service, 216–32, 217
   keyword query syntax, 223
   Query, 218
   SQL query syntax, 230
SharePoint survey form in InfoPath, 131–38
SharePoint to InfoPath data type matching for property promotion, 86
SharePoint view, 44, 161, 179
   GUID, 162, 180
   modify, 162, 180
SharePoint web part page, 35, 40, 44, 116, 121
   create, 116, 121
SharePoint web service
   Lists, 244–50
   Search Service, 216–32
   User Profile Service, 268–75
SharePoint wiki page, 35, 104, 111
   delete hyperlink, 108
   edit, 105
   edit hyperlink, 108
   insert hyperlink, 105
   insert web part, 111
   save and close, 105
SharePoint Workspace, 403
SharePointListItem_RW, 15, 16, 20, 22, 26, 30
   add field, 16
   conditional formatting, 30
   delete field, 20
   query, 22, 26
SharePointListUrl function, 215
SharePointServerRootUrl function, 215, 254, 257
SharePointSiteCollectionUrl function, 216
SharePointSiteUrl function, 216
show
   document information panel, 385, 387
   SharePoint list items created by current user, 161–65
   Submit button, 62
   toolbar buttons for InfoPath form, 60
Show advanced view, 12
Show on the View menu when filling out this form, 70, 136
Show only entries with unique display names, 235, 250

single web part connection, 112
Site collection features
   Document ID Service, 260
   Document Sets, 126
site column
   add to content type, 358
   add to SharePoint form library, 57
   create, 442
site content type, 437
Site Content Type (advanced) publishing option, 79, 91
site workflow, 296
skip query option, 206
SOAP web service, 217, 269, 411
sort SharePoint list
   dynamically on multiple fields, 183–85
   statically on multiple fields, 179
   statically on one field, 178
sort SharePoint list data, 178–85
   ascending or descending, 178, 180, 185
Source query string parameter, 105, 106
Specify Filter Conditions dialog box, 235, 248
SQL query syntax, 230
Start (default) view, 320
start a new workflow, 299
Start Custom Task Process workflow action, 339
Start Options
   Disable automatic start on item change option, 306, 318
   Disable automatic start on item creation option, 318
   in SharePoint Designer 2010, 293
start running workflow from InfoPath form, 352–55
Start workflow automatically when an item is created, 293
start workflow manually, 298
startswith filter method, 192
storage location of InfoPath forms in SharePoint, 4
Store a copy of the data for offline use, 163, 181, 255
Store a copy of the data in the form template, 155
String Builder dialog box, 370
string function, 201, 218, 226
submit and close form, 62
Submit button
   show or hide, 62
Submit button action, 23
Submit data action, 62, 69, 72, 249, 349, 354, 415

Index

Submit Form, 63, 67, 68, 70, 71, 245, 353, 412
    Submit Options, 63, 68, 71
    To SharePoint Library, 67, 70
    To Web Service, 245, 353, 412
submit InfoPath form, 59, 62–72
    After submit options, 64, 71
    Allow overwrite if file exists, 64, 68, 71
    allow user to specify file name, 64
    Allow users to submit this form, 63, 71
    close form after submit, 60, 64
    difference between save and submit, 58–60
    generate or specify file name on submit, 65
    leave form open after submit, 71
    permissions required, 65–66
    Set as the default submit connection, 68, 71, 247, 354, 413
    switch views, 72
    The form cannot be submitted to the specified SharePoint document library, 60
    to multiple destinations, 69
    to SharePoint form library, 62–72
    two submit data connections in one form, 67
    using rules, 69, 72
Submit Options, 63, 68, 71
Submit Options dialog box, 63
    add data connection for submit, 63
    After submit, 64, 71
    Allow users to submit this form, 63, 71
    Close the form, 64
    Leave the form open, 71
    Perform custom action using Rules, 69, 72
    Send form data to a single destination, 63
submit part of InfoPath form to web service, 246, 354
substring-after function, 220, 224, 228
substring-before function, 220, 224, 228
substringof filter method, 192, 252
sum function, 86, 132
survey, 131–38
    summary view, 136–38
switch to a 'Thank You' view, 70
Switch views action, 72

T

table in Excel, 401
task behavior
    Before a Task is Assigned, 341
    When a Task Expires, 342
task behavior action
    Escalate Task, 342

Set Task Field, 341
task form fields, 340
task process customization
    Change the behavior of a single task, 341
    Change the completion conditions for this task process, 342
Template Link, 144, 149, 376
Template URL, 54, 96
    disabled, 96
template.xml, 55
template.xsn, 7
text box control, 82, 88, 120, 132, 169, 171, 191, 193, 196, 201, 216, 251, 269, 281, 328, 346, 366, 397, 411, 422, 428
The data type of the selected site column does not match the data type of the field to promote, 88
The document library already contains a file with the same name, 60
The expression, 138, 249
The form cannot be submitted to the specified SharePoint document library, 60
The form has been closed, 106
The given key was not present in the dictionary, 419
The merge cannot be started, because the merge feature is disabled for the selected form template, 140
The page you selected contains a list that does not exist, 355
The selected database is not supported in Web browser forms, 431
There has been an error while loading the form, 93
There has been an error while processing the form, 419
This action will delete all information in the current form, 24
This form template is browser-compatible, but it cannot be browser-enabled on the selected site, 78
This session has exceeded the amount of allowable resources, 52
To SharePoint Library, 67, 70
To Web Service, 245, 353, 412
top query option, 202, 206
translate function, 29, 30, 194, 199, 209
troubleshoot publishing browser forms, 77–79

U

unable to change publish location, 82
unique file name for form, 59

463

update data type of promoted field, 87
Update Form
    button action, 23, 52, 280, 285
    toolbar button, 52, 62
Update List and Site Content Types, 310
Update List Item dialog box, 330
Update List Item workflow action, 330
Update the form template in an existing form library, 75
Update toolbar button, 52, 62
UpdateListItems, 246, 353
Upload a new document template, 358, 368, 383
URL protocol, 161, 164, 182, 254
    benefit of, 165, 182, 211
    SortField and SortDir, 181
    View, 182
Use a formula, 204, 213, 248
Use existing custom template (URL, UNC, or URN), 391, 396
Use the default SharePoint form, 21
Use the default template for Microsoft Office applications, 396
Use the server default (Open in the browser), 79
use Windows Explorer to move forms, 143
user filling out the InfoPath form, 198
user form templates, 72
User Information List, 197, 199, 209, 266, 274, 282, 285
User Profile Service, 50, 269
    get manager of user, 268–75
    GetUserProfileByName, 270
    GetUserPropertyByAccountName, 269
    PropertyData, 274
user roles, 50
userName function, 63, 71, 198, 209
users who do not have InfoPath, 47

V

Value Assignment dialog box, 325, 330, 360, 369, 399
Verify on server, 50
view
    Associate, 320, 323
    create in SharePoint, 44, 161, 179
    create summary view for survey form, 136–38
    Edit item (default), 13
    Merge Documents, 140
    Show on the View menu when filling out this form, 70, 136

    Start (default), 320
view document properties, 384
Visible on New Button, 97

W

ways to design forms for merging, 134
Web Browser Form type, 47, 49, 55, 394
web part
    add connection in SharePoint Designer 2010, 122–24
    configure, 112, 116
    connections, 118
    Excel Web Access, 429
    Get Filter Values From, 41
    Get Form From, 45
    InfoPath Form Web Part, 6, 36, 40, 45, 46, 111, 116, 121, 429
    insert on SharePoint wiki page, 111
    Send data to Web Part, 115, 118, 119, 430
    SharePoint list, 40, 44
    SharePoint list form, 35–38
    tool pane, 37, 112, 116, 121
web part connection
    add in SharePoint Designer 2010, 122–24
    configure, 117
    Configure Connection webpage dialog, 41
    Get Filter Values From, 41
    Get Form From, 45
    Input, 118, 120
    Input and Output, 118
    multiple, 119–25
    on a SharePoint list form, 118
    Output, 115, 118, 120, 428
    parameters, 118, 428
    Send Data To, 116, 122, 429
    SharePoint Designer 2010, 119
    single, 112–18
web part page, 35, 40, 44, 116, 121
web service
    arrayOfAnyType, 419
    CloseWorkbook, 414
    dataFields, 273
    Excel Services, 404–26
    Excel Services REST web service, 407, 421
    Excel Services SOAP web service, 411
    GetCellA1, 414
    GetUserProfileByName, 270
    GetUserPropertyByAccountName, 269
    OpenWorkbook, 411
    parameters, 246, 353–54, 413
    Query and QueryEx, 223, 230
    queryFields, 273

Index

SetCellA1, 412
SharePoint ListData REST web service, 158, 183, 189, 191, 200, 203, 212, 251, 347
SharePoint Lists, 244, 352
SharePoint Search Service, 216–32
submit part of InfoPath form, 246, 354
UpdateListItems, 246, 353
User Profile Service, 269
When a Task Expires task behavior, 342
where are InfoPath forms stored in SharePoint, 4
wiki page, 35, 104, 111
Word
   automatically create document from InfoPath form, 397–400
   automatically open document information panel, 395
   content control, 387, 388
   Developer tab, 388
   Document Property, 387
   Quick Parts, 387
   Show Document Panel, 385, 387
Word and InfoPath, 381
work days calculation, 410
workflow, 289–380
   action, 294
   add a workflow, 308
   add SharePoint calendar event, 346–51
   assign user permissions, 375–80
   associate workflow with list, 296
   association form, 324
   Association/Initiation form type, 319
   Change the behavior of a single task, 341
   Change the completion conditions for this task process, 342
   check for errors, 292
   Completed, 294
   Completion Conditions, 342
   condition, 294
   content type, 307
   context, 292
   create list workflow, 289–94, 325–26, 329–31, 333–36, 337–44, 360–63, 369–71, 373–74, 376–78, 398–400
   create reusable workflow, 304
   create Word document from InfoPath form, 397–400
   Current Item, 325
   Current Item URL, 316, 321
   Current Site URL, 321
   custom action, 302
   Date and Time Started, 292, 338
   debug, 295
   delete, 297
   delete workflow template, 298
   Disable automatic start on item change option, 306, 318
   Disable automatic start on item creation option, 318
   Email Addresses, Semicolon Delimited, 315
   Encoded Absolute URL, 321
   Error Occurred, 294
   forms, v, 318, 319
   history, 294
   In Progress, 293
   initiation form, 299, 312, 320
   Initiation Form Parameters, 313, 322, 324, 337
   insert condition, 334
   Item Name, 305
   list workflow, 296
   Local Variables, 337
   move InfoPath forms, 372–74
   Parallel Block, 295
   pass data, 312–24, 336
   person/group picker control, 318
   publish, 293
   reusable workflow, 296
   send email, 333
   site workflow, 296
   start automatically when item is created, 293
   start manually, 293, 297, 298, 326, 331, 373, 400
   start options, 293, 299, 306
   start running from InfoPath form, 352–55
   status, 294
   step, 294
   Task Form Fields, 340
   template, 294
   types, 296
   Update List and Site Content Types, 310
   user selects who to send email to, 312–24
   Workflow Variables and Parameters, 315, 321, 330, 334, 339
workflow action
   Add List Item Permission, 377
   Add Time to Date, 337
   Copy List Item, 373
   Create List Item, 325, 350, 360, 369, 398
   Delete Item, 373
   Escalate Task, 342
   Log to History List, 291, 295, 305, 342
   Lookup Manager of a User, 329, 333, 338
   Send an Email, 315, 334
   Set Task Field, 341

Start Custom Task Process, 339
Update List Item, 330
workflow condition, 334
If any value equals value, 334, 376
If task outcome equals value, 342
Workflow Context, 292
Current Item URL, 316, 321
Current Site URL, 321
Date and Time Started, 292, 338
Item Name, 305
workflow editor in SharePoint Designer 2010, 291
workflow form
cannot change publish location, 82
Workflow Form type, 320
workflow settings
remove a workflow, 297
start options, 293
Workflow Settings in SharePoint Designer 2010, 293
workflow variables
Initiation Form Parameters, 313, 322, 324, 337
local, 337

Workflow Variables and Parameters, 292, 315, 321, 330, 334, 339
working with fields of SharePoint list form, 16
write to an InfoPath form field from within a workflow, 327

X

xdXDocument, 30, 174, 176, 214, 236, 248, 262, 267, 271, 281, 287, 348, 423
xml data connection, 25, 29, 162, 181, 245, 254, 353
XML or Schema form template, 393
XML subtree including selected element, 246, 354
XmlLocation query string parameter, 106, 214, 321
XsnLocation query string parameter, 106

Y

You may not have the required permission to open the file, 93

Made in the USA
Middletown, DE
06 April 2016